Dubai

timeout.com/dubai

PENGUIN BOOKS

Published by the Penguin Group
Penguin Books Ltd, 80 Strand, London WC2R ORL, England
Penguin Books USA Inc., 375 Hudson Street, New York, New York 10014, USA
Penguin Books Australia Ltd, 250 Camberwell Road, Camberwell, Victoria 3124, Australia
Penguin Books Canada Ltd, 10 Alcorn Avenue, Toronto, Ontario, Canada M4V 3B2
Penguin Books (NZ) Ltd, cnr Rosedale and Airborne Roads, Albany, Auckland, New Zealand

Penguin Books Ltd, Registered Offices: 80 Strand, London WC2R ORL, England

First edition 2004
10 9 8 7 6 5 4 3 2 1

Copyright © Time Out Guides Ltd 2004
All rights reserved

Colour reprographics by Icon, Crowne House, 56-58 Southwark Street, London SE1 1UN
Printed and bound by Cayfosa-Quebecor, Ctra. de Caldes, Km 3 08 130 Sta, Perpètua de Mogoda, Barcelona, Spain

Edited & designed by
The Information & Technology
Publishing Co Ltd
PO Box 500024
Dubai
United Arab Emirates
Tel +971 4 210 8000
Fax +971 4 210 8080
www.itp.com

For
Time Out Guides Limited
Universal House
251 Tottenham Court Road
London W1T 7AB
Tel + 44 (0)20 7813 3000
Fax + 44 (0)20 7813 6001
Email guides@timeout.com
www.timeout.com

Editorial

Editor Justin Etheridge
Deputy Editors Rob Orchard, Marcus Webb
Proofreader Marion Moisy
Indexer Jonathan Cox

Editorial/Managing Director Peter Fiennes
Series Editor Ruth Jarvis
Deputy Series Editor Lesley McCave
Guides Co-ordinator Anna Norman
Accountant Sarah Bostock

Design

Art Director Wakeel Khan
Acting Art Director Scott Moore

Advertising

Advertisement Manager Steve Lee
Deputy Advertisement Manager Andy Baker
Sales Director Mark Phillips
International Sales Manager Ross Canadé
International Sales Executive James Tuson
Advertising Assistant Lucy Butler

Marketing

Marketing Manager Mandy Martinez

Production

Production Manager James Rawlins
Guides Production Director Mark Lamond
Production Controller Samantha Furniss

Time Out Group

Chairman Tony Elliott
Managing Director Mike Hardwick
Group Financial Director Richard Waterlow
Group Commercial Director Lesley Gill
Group Marketing Director Christine Cort
Group General Manager Nichola Coulthard
Group Art Director John Oakey
Online Managing Director David Pepper
Group Production Director Steve Proctor
Group IT Director Simon Chappell

Contributors

Contributing Editors Dan Ford, Camilla Gee, Jason Leavy, Charlotte McDonald.

Introduction Justin Etheridge, Dan Ford. **History** Antonia Carver. **Dubai Today** Antonia Carver. **Architecture** Antonia Carver. **Culture & Customs** Antonia Carver. **Where to Stay** Dan Ford, Marcus Webb. **Sightseeing** Lucy Monro (*Hatta, Pool position, Big Red* Shelley Frost). **Restaurants** Rob Orchard. **Cafés & Bars** Rob Orchard. **Shops & Services** Kate MacWhannell. **Festivals & Events** Antonia Carver. **Children** Antonia Carver. **Film & Theatre** Antonia Carver. **Galleries** Antonia Carver. **Nightlife** Marcus Webb. **Spectator Sports** Steve Hill. **Participations Sports** Steve Hill. **Health & Fitness** Steve Hill. **Abu Dhabi** Mike Shakespeare. **Northern Emirates** Brian Scudder, Shelley Frost. **East Coast** Brian Scudder. **Directory** Alice Urquhart.

Maps JS Graphics (john@jsgraphics.co.uk). Maps based on material supplied by Net Maps.

Photography Sevag Davidian, except: page 9 courtesy of Dubai Municipality; page 13 US Navy/Getty Images; pages 15, 64 Rabih Moghrabi/Getty Images; page 19 courtesy of Nakheel; pages 21, 29 Chris Hondros/Getty Images; pages 26, 175, 205 courtesy of TheOne&Only Royal Mirage; page 38 courtesy of the Shangri-La Dubai; page 47 courtesy of the Dusit Dubai; page 48 courtesy of the Al Bustan Rotana Dubai; page 49 courtesy of the Sheraton Creek Dubai; page 69 courtesy of Hatta Fort Hotel; pages 73, 181 Julian Herbet/Getty Images; page 75 courtesy of Arabian Adventures; page 83 Victoria Calaguian; page 92 courtesy of JW Marriott; page 97 courtesy of the Hilton Dubai; page 139 Hywell Waters; page 150 courtesy of Jumeirah International; pages 162, 164, 167 Wadih El-Najjar; page 182 courtesy of the Victory Team; pages 184, 185 Ross Kinnaird/Getty Images; page 190 David Cannon/Getty Images; pages 198, 199 leonardo.com; page 206 courtesy of the Ritz-Carlton Dubai; page 219 courtesy of the Millennium Hotel Abu Dhabi; page 221 courtesy of Voyagers Xtreme; page 239 courtesy of Le Meridien Al Aqah; page 284 Jorge Ferrari/AFP/Getty Images.

The Editor would like to thank Sarah Cooper, Rob Corder, Christine Cort, Will Fulford-Jones, Craig Hawes, David Ingham, John Irish, Kathy Johnston, Lesley McCave, Marion Moisy, Zoe Moleshead, Andrew Picken, Carolyn Robb, Stuart Robertson, Ros Sales, John Thatcher.

Contents

Introduction

For all its extraordinary wealth, outrageous rate of development and luxury living, the most striking thing about the UAE is its youth. Before 1971 there was nothing: no official flag or country; no roads to speak of; very few buildings and certainly no tourists, just the occasional expat oil prospector living on a huge hardship supplement. In no more than 30 years, the vast revenues generated from the UAE's enormous reserves of black gold have turned this piece of desert on the Arabian Gulf into one of the world's richest and fastest-growing economies.

Where one or two generations ago Bedouin families eked out a hand-to-mouth existence in the sand, they now live in luxury villas, drive 4x4s and cruise the Gulf in private yachts. Their city is speeding forward at an incredible pace, with new hotels, shopping malls, residential properties, offshore islands, industrial zones and office space transforming the skyline on a monthly basis. But while the wealth is still based in part on oil, there's a new force filling the coffers of the Dubaian economy: this is the age of trade and tourism.

The city's unique location at a crossroads between Asia, Europe and Africa makes it a perfect trading post as well as a travel hub. The coast is peppered with hotels and more are being built all the time, while its miles of beach and almost perpetually blue skies make it an ideal leisure destination. What the city lacks in terms of art galleries, theatres and historical sights (though look closely and you'll see it has those too), it more than makes up for in shoreline and shopping – if mornings on the beach, afternoons in the malls and evenings in excellent restaurants are what you're after, then Dubai is your place.

But away from the bright lights of the big city you'll find a wealth of day-trip (and overnight) locations to lend a traditional edge to your trip. Travel to Fujairah on the east coast, surrounded on one side by the Hajjar mountains and on the other by the Gulf of Oman, and you could be a million miles away from Dubai's high-rise, gleaming glass-and-steel lifestyle. Traditional fishing villages stretch along the shoreline, natural wadis snake through the mountains and waterfalls, palm tree oases and spectacular flora abound, and desert adventures on camels or in 4WDs are practically obligatory.

So while beaches, shopping and restaurants may be high on the agenda, there's another side to this seductive and appealing holiday destination. Hire a car and head a little out of town, where the charm of old Arabia awaits.

ABOUT THE TIME OUT CITY GUIDES

Time Out Dubai is one of an expanding series of Time Out City Guides, now numbering 45, produced by the people behind London and New York's successful listings magazines. Our guides are written and updated by resident experts, in this case the same team that produces the monthly listings magazine *Time Out Dubai*. We have striven to provide you with all the most up-to-date information you'll need to explore the city, whether you're a local or first-time visitor.

THE LOWDOWN ON THE LISTINGS

Above all, we've tried to make this book as useful as possible. Addresses, phone numbers, transport information, opening times, admission prices, websites and credit card details are all included in our listings. And, as far as possible, we've given details of facilities, services and events, all checked and correct at the time we went to press. However, since owners and managers can change their arrangements at any time, we always advise readers to phone and check opening times and other particulars. While every effort has been made to ensure the accuracy of the information contained in this guide, the publishers cannot accept responsibility for any errors it may contain.

PRICES AND PAYMENT

We have noted whether venues such as shops, hotels and restaurants accept credit cards or not but have only listed the major cards – American Express (**AmEx**), Diners Club (**DC**), MasterCard (**MC**) and Visa (**V**). Many businesses will also accept other cards and travellers' cheques.

The prices we've supplied should be treated simply as guidelines. Fluctuating exchange rates and inflation can cause charges, in shops and restaurants particularly, to change rapidly. If prices vary wildly from those we've quoted, please write and let us know. We aim to give the best and most up-to-date advice, so we always want to know if you've been badly treated or overcharged.

THE LIE OF THE LAND

The city of Dubai is roughly divided in two halves by the Creek, forming the basic areas of Deira, to the north, and Bur Dubai, to the south. Many Dubaians refer to locations as being Deira-side or Bur Dubai-side respectively. Beyond Bur Dubai lies Jumeirah, the stretch of golden shoreline now home to opulent hotels and wealthy expats. Each of these areas has its own chapter within the Sightseeing section, and each is further subdivided into loosely defined areas such as Karama. In this guide, in chapters not already divided by area, these districts are included within the addresses. Wherever possible, a map reference is provided for places listed.

TELEPHONE NUMBERS

The international code for Dubai is 9714; the first three digits designate the country of the UAE, while the remaining '4' indicates the emirate of Dubai (each of the emirates – and other significant areas – have a corresponding number). International calls to Abu Dhabi, for example, should begin with 9712. Add '0' before this emirate-specific digit to create an area code (eg 04), but this is necessary only when dialling from one emirate to another. All phone numbers are seven digits. For more on telephones, *see p256.*

ESSENTIAL INFORMATION

For all the practical information you might need for visiting the city – including visa and customs information, emergency phone numbers, useful websites and the local transport network – turn to the **Directory** chapter at the back of this guide. It starts on p242.

MAPS

The maps section at the back of this book, which starts on p269, includes overview maps of Dubai and the UAE, as well as street maps of the city. There is a map of Abu Dhabi on pp210-11. Bookshops such as Book Corner (*see p119*) and Magrudy's (*see p120*) also sell fairly useful maps of the UAE, covering major roads and highways.

LET US KNOW WHAT YOU THINK

We hope you enjoy *Time Out Dubai*, and we'd like to know what you think of it. We welcome tips for places that you consider we should include in future editions and take notice of your criticism of our choices. There's a reader's reply card at the back of this book – or you can email us on guides@timeout.com.

There is an online version of this book, along with guides to 45 other international cities, at **www.timeout.com**.

A most enchanting hideaway.

The Ritz-Carlton, Dubai

© 2004 The Ritz-Carlton Hotel Company LLC

The impeccable pedigree of this romantic retreat is coupled with superb cuisine and attentive service, reflecting the traditions of excellence for which Ritz-Carlton is renowned. An intimate beach hotel of elegant design and considerable character, The Ritz-Carlton, Dubai is a delightful Mediterranean-style property hidden in lush, tropical gardens that lead to beautiful siver-white sands on the beachfront.

THE RITZ-CARLTON®
DUBAI

P. O. Box 26525, Dubai, United Arab Emirates
Telephone: (971) 4 399 4000, Fax: (971) 4 399 4001, Website: www.ritzcarlton.com

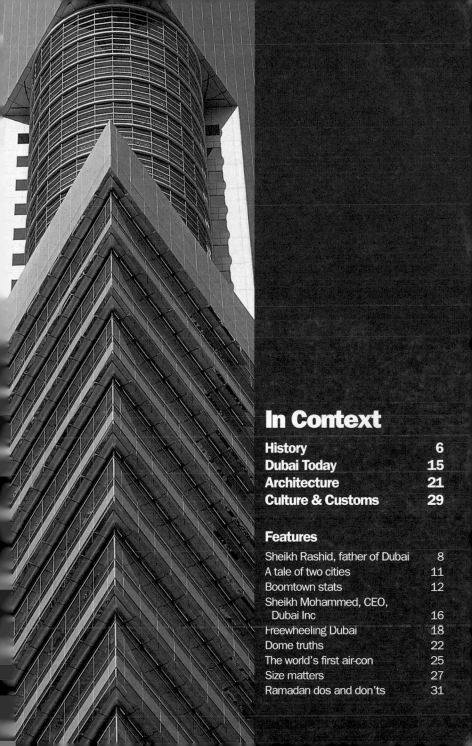

In Context

History

Dubai's development from a small fishing village to a cutting-edge commercial hub has been swift.

The first written reference to Dubai was made by Venetian jeweller Gasparo Balbi, who visited 'Dibei' in 1580 to evaluate the small fishing village's potential as a source for pearls. Archaeological digs have since unearthed human remains from as far back as 4000 BC, with evidence of a well-developed Bronze Age settlement in the suburb of Al Qusais in around 2000-1000 BC. A more lasting settlement dating from the 5th and 6th centuries AD has been found in what is now Jumeirah – an indication that with the advent of Islam, the Ummayad and then Abbasid Islamic dynasties, Dubai was already established in its core business of trade, acting as a stop-off point for the caravans that served the Islamic epicentre of the day, Iraq.

THE GENESIS OF MODERN DUBAI

Dubai, strategically located on a ten-kilometre (six-mile) creek, started its remarkable evolution from a small, sleepy fishing village some time during the 18th century. The town was wedged between the two powerful clans

who held sway over the lower Gulf, the Bani Yas of Liwa Oasis, who had gone on to settle in Abu Dhabi, the modern capital of the UAE, and the Qawasim, based in the northern emirates and parts of modern-day Oman.

The Qawasim's powerful navy had already triggered the ire of the British empire's ruling classes, which led to the area becoming known as the 'Pirate Coast' owing to the agile, armed Arab dhows that plundered ships from the British East India Company. The disruption to British commercial interests prompted a show of superior British naval power that brought the ruling families of this part of the Arabian coastline to their knees. Britain, fearing attempts from Russia and France to challenge its dominance of the region, then signed exclusivity treaties with the leaders of the 'Trucial States', offering protection and non-interference in local politics on the condition that leaders didn't even correspond with other global powers. Dubai and the rest of the Trucial coast were now firmly within the sphere of British influence.

THE MAKTOUMS TAKE CONTROL

In 1833, the era of Maktoum family rule began, probably as a result of an internal quarrel among the Bani Yas of Abu Dhabi, when 'violent conduct' on the part of its leader Sheikh Khalifa prompted the emigration of around 800 members of the Al Bu Falasah branch of the tribe. There was little resistance in Dubai to Obaid bin Said and Maktoum bin Butti, who took over the then village-sized settlement along the Creek. With Obaid's death a few years later, Maktoum took the reigns of power, ushering in the bloodline that continues to rule Dubai today.

The Maktoums based themselves in Shindagah, which provided easy access to the sources of Dubai's wealth: the Gulf for pearling and fishing and the Creek for trade. In 1820 Mohammed bin Hazza, then ruler of Dubai, signed the trading village's first preliminary truce with London, all too aware of the superior manpower of neighbouring Abu Dhabi and the Qawasim, who controlled much of the northern emirates and modern-day Oman.

Under the protection of the British navy, which helped to stamp out the constant disruptions to trade caused by raids among the various tribes along the Trucial coast, Dubai concentrated on making money. Like the other city-ports that went on to form the United Arab Emirates, Dubai evolved around its creek, an inlet from the Persian Gulf (known on this side of the water – make no mistake – as the Arabian Gulf). Like the other creeks along the northern coast, Dubai's creek suffered from sandbars formed at its entrance by strong tides – but at least it was much longer than those of its neighbours. With the seas pacified, the pearling industry thrived and its wares were exported both to India and to Europe. Trade with India and Persia encouraged more foreign traders to open up shop in the city-port, which was already developing its reputation as a town not only open for business, but one that warmly welcomed non-Arabs to take their share.

In the mid 19th century, Shindagah may have been the preserve of around 250 Arab homes, but neighbouring community Bur Dubai was the base for almost 100 houses belonging to Indian traders. Across the Creek, Deira boasted 1,600 compounds, housing Arabs, Persians and Baluchis from modern-day Pakistan. Deira souq was also thriving, with around 350 shops.

THE ARRIVAL OF PERSIAN TRADERS

It was the liberal, open-minded Maktoum bin Hashar, whose rule began in 1894, who capitalised most fully on Dubai's emergence as a business and commercial centre. Fore-shadowing Dubai's modern-day obsession with

the free trade zone and tax-free environment, Dubai in the late 19th century exempted almost half of the men who worked in the pearling industry from taxes levied by the ruler. Although more divers worked the pearl banks than in any other Trucial state, the ruler ended up receiving only half the revenue of neighbouring Abu Dhabi.

No matter: Dubai's population exploded. As the pearling industry continued to bring more wealth to the town, Sheikh Maktoum deftly implemented business-oriented policies that attracted traders from Lingah, the Persian port on the other side of the Gulf. Run by the Qawasim family, Lingah had, through the 1800s, acted as the main entry point for goods coming into the entire Persian Gulf region. The Persians, desperate for tax revenue, wrested control of the port from the Arabs at the turn of the century, replacing Arab port officials with Persians and then Belgians, whose rigid bureaucracy and high tariffs persuaded merchants to head off in search of cheaper trade environments on the Arab side of the Gulf.

As the 20th century began, Sheikh Maktoum made Dubai a free zone by abolishing commercial taxes. The leader also courted the big players in the Persian warehousing trade, offering important Indian and Persian traders cheap land. As he attracted these trade giants, others followed in their wake. In the first two decades of the 20th century, Dubai's population doubled to around 20,000, rapidly catching up with Sharjah, its larger neighbour and sometime trade rival.

Traders who had reckoned on a temporary sojourn in Dubai settled in the city once it became clear that taxes and regulations in Persia were there to stay. The pearling industry was now booming. Many people emigrated from the Persian district of Bastak, part of the Arab-dominated province of Lars, naming their new-found home on the Creek after their homeland; Bastakia soon became another thriving commercial area.

Sheikh Maktoum's power rose with the fortunes of his city-state. He began the process of building bridges between the rival sheikhdoms of the coast, calling a meeting of the Trucial leaders in 1905 that foreshadowed the creation of the federation agreed just under 70 years later.

RECESSION HITS THE GULF

After experiencing years of growing prosperity, Dubai and the rest of the Gulf fell prey to the worldwide recession of the 1930s – a warning to its leaders as to how the trade-based city's fortunes would ebb and flow with the tide of global economic prosperity. The

Sheikh Rashid, father of Dubai

This city has a lot of time for Sheikh Rashid (*pictured*), the ruler who put it on the international map. Port Rashid, Sheikh Rashid Terminal, Sheikh Rashid Hall, Sheikh Rashid Road – visitors are endlessly reminded of his influence. His official photo still adorns residences, cars and businesses, along with images of his sons Sheikhs Maktoum, Mohammed and Hamdan.

Born in 1912, Sheikh Rashid learned the business of trade and statecraft from his father, Sheikh Saeed. Sitting in his father's majlis, or ruler's court – where local and foreign businessmen shared their knowledge with the ruler of the day – Sheikh Rashid quickly understood the value of business. Developing the liberal policies of his predecessors, Rashid took hold of most levers of power from his father in the late 1930s.

As a child Sheikh Rashid would run up and down the Creek, collecting the landing fees that were taking over from pearl revenues as the main revenue of the city-port. It was then that he realised Dubai had to create economies of scale if the city was to survive in the cut-throat world of international trade. He went on to dream up Port Rashid and then Jebel Ali Port, positioning Dubai as the pre-eminent re-export hub in a region whose demand for imports surged on the back of the oil boom.

Hagiographies laud Sheikh Rashid's business acumen as second to none. Time after time, his ambitious grand schemes were scoffed at, only for them to be proved remarkably prescient. But he didn't develop Dubai alone: the ruler surrounded himself with visionary and efficient advisers. His majlis served as a forum for ideas and debate about industrial development, as well as the vast amount of civic development work that he carried out – from creating a police force and bringing water and power to the entire city, to building affordable housing in the new neighbourhoods of Karama and Satwa during the early 1960s.

British colonial hangers-on continued to advise the Sheikh from the moment Dubai and the other six emirates achieved their independence in 1971. Some of them, notably Bill Duff (economic affairs) and Brigadier Berkeley (oil), continue to advise the government. Others, such as Bahraini customs official Mahdi al-Tajer, were headhunted by Sheikh Rashid himself.

Tajer advised the ruling family on potential developments and saw his fortunes grow along with those of the city, as the bustling port on the Creek speedily turned into the international trading hub it is today. Tajer, who also spent time as UAE ambassador to the UK, is said to have introduced Sheikh Rashid to Harrods owner Mohammed Al Fayed, who claims to have made a lasting contribution to the growth of Dubai.

Fayed, who brokered many building contracts for UK firm Costain, eventually fell out of favour with the ruling family in the mid 1980s, losing the management contract for Dubai's World Trade Centre complex, which he helped to build. But the millions he earned in the emirate's 'Wild East' early days helped him to expand his European business empire. The

pearling industry first became a victim of the weak international demand for luxury goods, then the Japanese discovery of cultured pearls finished off the fragile trade, throwing thousands of pearl fishermen out of work. In the final years of the trade, financiers were taking up to 36 per cent annual interest on the loans that captains needed to fit out boats and hire staff. As the pearling industry declined, traders redoubled their efforts in black market trade with Persia, where tariffs continued to soar higher than in those ports on the Arabian Peninsula.

As the pearling industry fell into terminal decline, Dubaians with Persian connections built up their illicit cargo trade, making up for the city's lost revenue. But the increasing financial inequities between the traders and the recently unemployed Arab pearl divers amplified societal pressures. Further north in Kuwait, yearnings for political reform influenced the setting up of a parliament, giving that emirate the most developed political system in the Gulf. Mirroring growing unease within Dubai's society, splits within the royal family also emerged. The ruler's cousin, Mani bin Rashid, led the reform movement that challenged the ruling family's autocratic rule. Domestic slaves pressed for their freedom, not because the British decided to enforce its ban on trading slaves, but because owners could no longer afford them. It wasn't until after World War II that the UK government started to enforce general manumission after having

controversial Egyptian still owns beach-front land on the Sufouh tourist strip near the Burj Al Arab hotel.

Sheikh Rashid's hands-on approach to governance influenced the style of his son, the current de facto ruler, Sheikh Mohammed. Twice-daily trips to the city's various industrial and business projects kept him informed of rapid developments. The ruler oversaw the creation of the Gulf's first modern hospital and the Maktoum bridge across the Creek, funded by a loan from regional neighbour Qatar. As one

observer put it, he created the world's smallest bureaucracy, in which businessmen could just get on with the business of making money.

Sheikh Rashid, who sent his sons to be educated at the British officers' college at Sandhurst, seems to have reserved special affection for the UK. He was the only ruler to express disquiet at the British withdrawal from the Trucial States. Over the years he developed a close friendship with Queen Elizabeth II, even accompanying her to church – although not attending the service – on her state visit to the UAE in 1979.

While his role in international affairs was always subsidiary to that of the rulers in Abu Dhabi, Sheikh Rashid would often speak out in favour of the Palestinian people, many of whom ended up taking residence in Dubai. He also funded many projects, particularly schools, in the Palestinian territories. Pakistan, visited by the Sheikh on hunting trips, also benefited from his largesse. As did the mid 1980s campaign against famine in Africa: Sheikh Rashid reportedly made one of the largest donations to Bob Geldof's Live Aid concert for famine relief in Africa.

By the mid 1980s, health problems and the death of his wife Sheikha Latifa had taken most of the old man's energy. He took more holidays, but still found the time to intervene in a border dispute between Ras al-Khaimah and the neighbouring Sultanate of Oman. But, having divested most of his powers to his sons over the decade, he died in 1990, plunging the city into shock. After over half a century in power, he left Dubai poised to become a global as well as regional commercial player.

called on a halt to the trading of slaves in the Gulf states a century earlier.

Against this background of social flux, events turned violent in October 1938. Sheikh Saeed and his followers set up their base in Dubai, while his cousins lined up against the ruler from across the Creek in Deira. After mediation from neighbouring sheikhs and the British political agent, or colonial ambassador, in Bahrain, Sheikh Saeed agreed to the setting up of a consultative council or majlis ('place of sitting'), heading up a cohort of 15 members, all of whom were proposed by leading members of the community and theoretically had the power to veto his decisions.

Sheikh Saeed was a reluctant leader and only attended the first few sessions, smarting at a

system in which his office was allocated an eighth of the national budget, the remaining earmarked for the majlis' projects. He still controlled the treasury and was reluctant to open up the state coffers for the council's projects – such as building state-run schools for the general populace, regulating the customs service and its payroll, adjusting tariffs and setting up a council of merchants to oversee the city-state's expanding commerce.

Six months after the council's foundation, Sheikh Saeed ordered some loyal Bedouin to storm and dissolve it. A strong believer in benign autocratic rule, he suspected that some of his royal rivals were exploiting the majlis for their own benefit. Though short-lived, Dubai's six-month flirtation with democracy nonetheless had lasting implications at the highest levels. It sounded the political death-knell for Sheikh Saeed: he devolved most of his authority to his son, Sheikh Rashid, who in time initiated many of the ideas of civic development proposed by the council's members.

POST-WAR DEVELOPMENT

Although spared the horrors that Europe and Asia endured during World War II, Dubai still struggled during those six tough years. The flourishing business of trade was brought to a near standstill and short supplies of rice and sugar caused hunger to grip parts of the city. The British government – which was landing seaplanes in the Creek throughout the conflict – imported food supplies that were to be rationed among the population. Never ones to miss a money-spinning trick, Dubai's traders began buying up some of these supplies and smuggled them to Iran's black market, where shortages were even more pressing.

'Gold smuggling, which peaked in 1970, contributed to the new surge in business.'

Malnutrition was an even more urgent issue in the internal desert countryside, still ruled by autonomous nomadic tribes. Here there was almost constant warfare as the tribes fought for rations, and the leaders of Abu Dhabi and Dubai argued over the boundary between their territories. Open warfare between the two distant relatives, as well as among their allied and rival tribes of the hinterland, continued after World War II until the high level of casualties from Bedouin raids and counter-raids prompted the townsfolk and tribesmen to demand peace in 1948. The British authorities took it upon themselves to research the boundary dispute and draw the new frontier – London's first direct intervention in the internal politics of the Trucial states.

DISCOVERY OF OIL

While trade remained at the core of Dubai's development, a revolutionary new prospect came the Trucial States' way in the early 1950s: oil. For a couple of decades, most petroleum engineers had concluded that large deposits would be found somewhere along the Trucial coast. After all, massive reserves had been found across the Middle East and particularly in the Arabian peninsula and Persian Gulf. Oil had first been discovered in Iran in 1908; Bahrain had started significant exports in 1936; and on the eve of World War II, neighbouring

Saudi Arabia had found the first of its huge reservoirs. Companies began to explore across the region, frantically searching for more deposits of this black gold. Petroleum Development (Trucial Coast), a British-owned company, won the concession to explore for oil across the Trucial States and Oman.

But the war put a stop to the exploration, condemning the emirates to endure more years of poverty, and encouraging thousands of locals to emigrate to neighbouring Kuwait and Saudi Arabia to work on the massive post-war oil development projects there.

While a consortium formed by British Petroleum and France's Total found commercially viable oil deposits offshore Abu Dhabi in 1958, progress was limited in Dubai's onshore and offshore exploration blocks.

DREDGING THE CREEK

Nevertheless, Dubai sought to capitalise on the massive trade opportunities brought by oil companies with huge equipment and manpower needs. Mortgaging Dubai with a huge loan from oil-rich Saudi Arabia and Kuwait of $850,000 – an amount that far outstripped the city's yearly income – Sheikh Rashid had the Creek dredged by an Australian firm. The ambitious project, which allowed vessels of up to 500 tons to anchor there, greatly increased shipping capacity. The emirate's trade levels jumped by 20 per cent, outpacing the growth in neighbouring Sharjah, which had been snapping at Dubai's heels. Gold smuggling, which peaked in 1970, contributed to the new surge in business. The 3.5 per cent import levies imposed on dhows and steamers docking along its wharfage became the emirate's biggest revenue earner after the war, rising to 4.6 per cent in 1955, still lower than its regional rivals.

After seeing off Sharjah's maritime trade competition, Sheikh Rashid also took on his neighbour's airport. Sheikh Sultan of Sharjah had started levying taxes on gold arriving at Sharjah airport, which grew commercially on the back of the UK Royal Air Force base there. In 1960, Sheikh Rashid opened an airport, little more than an airstrip made from the hard sand found in Dubai's salt flats, which he expanded a few years later as demand for weekly flights to the UK grew. An open-skies policy allowed any airline to use the airport at a cheaper cost than other airports in the region, triggering its eventual rise as an international passenger and freight hub.

Before then, however, Dubai too struck black gold. In 1966, oil was discovered in the offshore Fatah field; exports began three years later. The prospect of imminent oil exports, along with severe overcrowding of the Creek

A tale of two cities

It's a classic image that says so much, and yet so little. You'll see it on posters or emblazoned on the back windscreens of Toyota Landcruisers: Sheikh Rashid Al Maktoum, the father of modern Dubai, and Sheikh Zayed Al Nahayan, leader of Abu Dhabi and the UAE's President, sharing an intimate joke, heads clocked together. In the UAE, this classic image of brotherly respect is everywhere; to question the unity of purpose between each of the country's seven emirates is taboo.

Yet, privately, historians recount stories of arguments between the leaders of all the emirates, especially the two powerhouses, oil-rich Abu Dhabi and commerce-friendly Dubai. Go back 50 years, and the two emirates were locked in all-out war, with the two leaders' Bedouin allies carrying out raids on the other's territory over three bloody years. Rivalries have cooled since the leaders of the seven Trucial States yoked themselves under one flag in the early 1970s. But even in those early days of unity, Dubai's Sheikh Rashid – while committed to the union – fought for as much autonomy as possible for his emirate.

Abu Dhabi's superior size and population translated into greater political power. The discovery of huge oil reserves in Abu Dhabi gave Sheikh Zayed's emirate even more financial clout, as well as military muscle. When the UAE was formed, Abu Dhabi earned ten times more money from its oil revenues than Dubai, whose oil production has fallen to an estimated 150,000 barrels a day. Meanwhile, Abu Dhabi is the world's fourth largest oil exporter – while also earning more than $20 billion a year interest on its huge investments in Western financial markets. The capital controls perhaps 90 per cent of the UAE's national capital wealth.

The federal government developed around Abu Dhabi's financial largesse. This helped the union's development, but sparked fears in Dubai and other poorer emirates, who were concerned that Abu Dhabi's bureaucrats, keen to control the disbursement of their funds, would whittle away at the emirates' close-knit tribal roots. In 1979, the UAE was in crisis, as Abu Dhabi pushed for more centralised authority than the other emirates would accept. The crisis abated as Sheikh Rashid accepted the post of UAE Prime Minister, while securing the rights of individual rulers to continue developing their fiefdoms along their own lines.

The air of international turmoil in the 1980s, as the Iran-Iraq War loomed large over the region, glued the emirates together. With Islamic Revolution boiling in Iran and civil shipping under attack in their own backyard, the seven emirates' petty squabbles paled into insignificance. Abu Dhabi, as generous as ever, continued to fund welfare systems for the entire country, especially the resource-starved northern emirates. Dubai got on with being Dubai: attracting businesses and allowing its anything-goes attitude to flourish.

Today, Abu Dhabi and Dubai are brothers with their different characters. Many Abu Dhabians, more restrained and conservative than go-getting Dubaians, are frustrated at the international attention their precocious neighbour receives – but they are also aware that the UAE is all the better for it. Dubai's go-getting attitude (*see p18* **Freewheeling Dubai**) has not always met with unanimous approval from traditionalists in the capital, but nobody is denying that the city's dynamic economy has also brought regional recognition and offers a blueprint for what Abu Dhabi might achieve as its oil resources dwindle.

Dubai, too, has benefited greatly from Abu Dhabi's generosity. The meeting of minds between Sheikhs Zayed and Rashid has been extended to the latter's son, Mohammed, who now runs Dubai very much like his father did. Abu Dhabi only very recently stopped giving Dubai around 100,000 barrels of oil a day – almost doubling the smaller emirate's production. When Dubai overextends itself, it can fall back on its rich cousin: when in 1997 its autonomous armed forces became too much of a financial burden, Sheikh Mohammed just turned them over to the federal government.

Cynics say the Dubai/Abu Dhabi relationship could be tested once Sheikh Zayed, the ageing president, dies. The trust inherent in the relationship between the president and Sheikh Mohammed (*see p16* **Sheikh Mohammed, CEO, Dubai Inc**) might be tested by the succession of Abu Dhabi's Crown Prince, Sheikh Khalifa. But why would the UAE want to ruin such a successful system, in which Abu Dhabi plays Washington to Dubai's New York?

and the commercial centres around it, persuaded the government in 1967 to start building a $40 million seaport, Port Rashid, which eventually opened in 1972 and was expanded again in 1978.

Trade and oil combined to give economic growth a massive injection. The petrodollar boom had finally arrived in Dubai, even though its oil reserves and revenues were minnow-like compared with its oil-rich neighbour Abu Dhabi. The population skyrocketed in response, as migrant labour poured into the city to extract the oil and build and maintain the public services that Sheikh Rashid – remembering the demands of the reform movement when he was being groomed for power – made sure became a high priority for his government. In 1967, as the government planned Sheikh Rashid port, the population stood at 59,000. Five years later, in 1973, the city had doubled in size. By the end of the booming 1970s, 250,000 people lived in Dubai.

CREATION OF THE UAE

In 1967, Britain decided that its moment in the Middle East was over. London announced its intention to withdraw from its colonial outposts east of Suez, giving the Trucial States a departure date of 1971. Unlike in Aden, in southern Yemen, where years of insurgency showed a stark desire to see off the imperialists, the leaders of Dubai and the other Trucial States felt almost abandoned by the hasty nature of the British retreat. The Conservative opposition of the day also criticised the Labour government's decision to withdraw, arguing that British business exposure across the Gulf amounted to much more than the £16 million annual cost of keeping British forces in the area, and that withdrawal would merely encourage new imperialists, such as the Soviet Union, to extend their influence over a strategic region of vital importance owing to its oil deposits.

Some Trucial leaders hoped the Conservative government, once it gained power, would reverse the decision to withdraw. But it wasn't to be. Sheikh Zayed of Abu Dhabi and Sheikh Rashid of Dubai met at the frontier between their two sheikhdoms and agreed to form a federation that would jointly decide foreign, defence and social policy. On the encouragement of the British, the rulers of the Trucial States – Abu Dhabi, Dubai, Sharjah, Ajman, Umm al-Quwain, Ras al-Khaimah and Fujairah – met in Dubai with the leaders of Bahrain and Qatar in February 1968 to discuss forming a joint federation. The leaders came up with an agreement expressing their intention to form a nine-strong federation, which met with broad regional approval, except from Iran, the Shi'a-led state that had a territorial claim on the majority Shi'a island of Bahrain.

The nine leaders of these islands, city-states and desert regions met on several occasions in the run-up to independence in 1971, discussing models of federation. Differences plagued the meetings, with Bahrain's larger, better-educated population suspicious of a federation in which political power would be spread evenly across the nine emirates, rather than being based on the population of each emirate. Bahrain, having ended border disputes with Iran, told the other prospective federation members that it would retain its independence, yoking its interests to its rich neighbour, Saudi Arabia. Qatar chose the same path.

In July 1971, with the British withdrawal approaching, the seven Trucial leaders met and hammered out a federal document. Six of them, excluding Ras al-Khaimah, signed the provisional constitution, which was used to proclaim a federation in November 1971. Ras al-Khaimah had felt undervalued in the negotiations and wanted to focus on three Gulf islands that Iran had occupied once the British forces left the area. But once the other emirates agreed to take on the issue of Abu Musa and the Greater and Lesser Tunb islands, it too acceded to the federation in February 1972. The

Boomtown stats

The numbers behind the city...

18 million passengers passed through Dubai Airport in 2003.

40 million passengers are expected to pass through in 2010.

400 metres (1,300 feet) is the length of the world's largest indoor ski run, set to open in Dubai in 2005.

30,000kg (66,140lb) of fresh snow will be manufactured in the desert and dumped on the slopes every night.

$12,174 per night is the price of the most expensive suite at the Burj Al Arab.

50 fils will buy you a ticket across the Creek on an abra.

1 in 5,000 are the odds on winning US$1million if you enter Dubai Duty Free's Millennium Millionaire draw.

690,000 was Dubai's population in 1995.

1.1 million was the population in 2002.

1.61 million people are predicted to be living in Dubai in 2008.

33 per cent of the UAE's local population is clinically obese.

17 per cent of them have diabetes.

Far trek: USS *Enterprise* docks at **Jebel Ali**.

federation was born, led by Abu Dhabi owing to its disproportionate financial contribution to the federal budget, but with significant autonomy for all emirates in local affairs. Sheikh Zayed Al Nahayan became the country's first president; Sheikh Rashid – who through the 1970s pressed for more autonomy for his freewheeling emirate – acted as Zayed's vice president and prime minister (*see p11* **A tale of two cities**).

THE 1970S: PETRODOLLAR BOOM

The 1970s were a decade of excess across the Gulf. Petrodollars flowed into the area as the world's seemingly unquenchable appetite for oil lapped up the region's exports. Oil revenues spiralled ever higher during the price shock of 1973 and 1974, triggered by the Arab producing states' boycott of nations supporting Israel in the third Arab-Israeli conflict. Dubai has never had the oil revenues that its rich cousin Abu Dhabi enjoys (by 1980, Dubai's annual oil income stood at $3 billion compared with Abu Dhabi's $15 billion), but these revenues went a long way towards helping Dubai to develop the infrastructure it needed to realise fully the potential of its core economic activity – trade and commerce.

DEVELOPING TRADE

Sticking to Dubai's maritime heritage, the first major expansion beyond the Creek came with the completion of Port Rashid, near downtown Dubai, in 1973. On completion, the port had 16 berths for ocean-going vessels, rising to 35 after initial success allowed for expansion. Port Rashid itself had been regarded as overly ambitious, so when Sheikh Rashid announced the construction of a new port in Jebel Ali,

40 kilometres (25 miles) along the coast towards Abu Dhabi from the centre of Dubai, the sceptics questioned the ruler's judgement. Not only was the port a speedy success, but the soaring oil prices after the Arab boycott also eased the ruler's repayment schedule.

> **'Dubai Dry Dock benefited from the maritime war between Iran and Iraq, serving the steady stream of tanker war victims.'**

By 1976, flush with petrodollars, Dubai ploughed $2.5 billion into building the 66-berth Jebel Ali Port, the world's largest man-made harbour. Completed in 1983, Jebel Ali Port remained empty, seemingly Dubai's first white elephant and its ambition worrying even some of Sheikh Rashid's closest advisers. The massive port, along with the Jebel Ali Hotel, stood alone in the vast expanses of desert. But by 1985, spurred on by the construction of Jebel Ali Free Zone, business at the port boomed. The free zone was an idea borrowed from Sheikh Rashid's grandfather Sheikh Hasher, who'd lured Persian traders to Dubai at the beginning of the century with similar incentives. The port's fortunes were also helped by the bloody, extended war between Saddam Hussein's Iraq and the Islamic republic of Iran, which disrupted shipping as both sides started to attack tankers and oil facilities. With insurance rates sky-high in the northern Gulf, shippers looked for an alternative in the lower Gulf, turning to Jebel Ali.

OIL FUNDS INFRASTRUCTURE

Dubai, founded as a trade hub, quickly used growing oil revenues to diversify its economic base to include heavy industry. With abundant oil and gas resources, the emirates had a competitive advantage in large-scale industrial projects that require vast amounts of energy. Dubai's first great industrial project took the form of Dubai Dry Dock, constructed in 1973 as a ship repair yard, which Sheikh Rashid passed on to his third son and current de facto ruler, Sheikh Mohammed. This venture, too, benefited from the outbreak of maritime war between Iran and Iraq, serving the steady stream of tanker war victims. Two years later, Dubai set up Dubai Aluminium Co, or Dubal, with an initial investment of $1.4 billion, which took advantage of cheap oil and gas supplies to create one of the world's most profitable smelters. As well as industrial projects, the oil wealth of the 1970s brought modern infrastructure to Dubai. By the end of the decade, a further bridge and a tunnel complemented the original Maktoum Bridge linking Bur Dubai with Deira. The population rose to 207,000 in 1977, compared with 20,000 in the 1940s.

Massive infrastructure investment was needed to meet the huge population increases of the day. As Dubai grew from the 1950s on, so did the number of roads, hospitals and schools. The police force, set up in 1956 under the command of British officers, came under local control in 1975. Immigrants started their own schools, complementing the state-run schools that catered for locals and expatriate Arabs.

If the 1970s spelled industrial development, the 1980s saw the arrival of big-time commerce. While strong global demand for oil underpinned the soaring revenues enjoyed by oil-producing countries, Dubai continued to diversify. The World Trade Centre, opened in 1979, attracted some of the world's biggest companies to set up local or regional headquarters in Dubai. Once again, cynics whispered that the centre, today dwarfed by the high-rises of Sheikh Zayed Road, was too far from the central commercial district in Deira. But little did it matter, as foreign companies set up shop in a land free of bureaucracy, boasting political stability and liberal social mores; the economy further diversified, and the city kept booming – through the 1980s, Dubai's population doubled to over half a million people.

GROWTH OF TOURISM

In the 1970s, businessmen travelling to Dubai were hard-pushed to find a single decent hotel. Sheikh Rashid even built a personal guesthouse for the trailblazing corporates who visited in the early days. By 1975, the InterContinental had opened on the Deira side of the Creek, but never satisfied the growing hordes of travellers touching down at the new airport – executives even used to bunk up together in the rooms.

How times change. By the 1990s, after the death of Sheikh Rashid, Dubai was busy reinventing itself as a tourist destination. There were 42 hotels in 1985, jumping to 272 by 2002. The establishment in 1985 of Emirates, the Dubai-based international airline, helped the tourism sector flourish as the airline encouraged its passengers to stop over in the emirate en route to Asia, Africa or Europe. With initial start-up capital of $10 million, the airline – managed by British expatriates – rapidly expanded, even staying profitable through the global travel slump following 9/11.

With its oil reserves running out, Dubai has turned increasingly to tourism. International events such as the Dubai World Cup horse race, desert rally, golf, tennis and rugby tournaments helped to fuel the boom. But Dubai's love affair with shopping has underpinned the industry. Launched in 1996, the Dubai Shopping Festival attracted a million or so visitors that year, rising to 2.6 million last year, spending a cool $2.5 billion during their visit. A second shopping festival, Dubai Summer Surprises, was launched in 1998, attracting Gulf visitors who are used to the soaring summer temperatures that put off many western tourists. Combined with sea, sun and liberal attitudes to entertainment, annual tourist numbers have now reached around five million, five times the city's resident population.

SERVICE REVOLUTION

Having done trade, commerce and industry, Dubai – punchdrunk on the MBA jargon of its foreign-educated apparatchik hordes – adopted the cluster concept. By zoning similar service-related industries together, say the business gurus, services are sourced from one's neighbours, improving networking potential and reducing costs. Dubai Internet City (DIC), announced in 1999, was the first such attempt to attract more professionals to the emirate. The venture was tailor-made to attract high-tech firms, offering tax-free 100 per cent ownership (outside free zones businesses need a local partner). DIC has since grown rapidly, attracting over 500 companies by 2003 – although some critics say it's little more than a sales park as few products are actually created on the site. With the opening of Dubai Media City in 2000, a high-tech cluster catering to news agencies and publishing start-ups, the city's new industries now have the infrastructure and support they need for success. The age of pearling and black gold is set to give way to an era of international media ventures and Dubaian dotcoms.

Dubai Today

An oasis of roaring capitalism in a sea of struggling states, Dubai is an Arab version of Las Vegas mixed with Legoland.

Dubai is a mirage, where nothing is as it seems. It is a country where the local Emirati population is dwarfed by the numbers of expatriates from India, Pakistan and other Arab states. Its people are conservative Muslims, but the city has adopted a live-and-let-live attitude to all religions and social groups. While lacking deep-rooted public culture or heritage and suffering overpowering heat and humidity for one-third of the year, the city has still managed to turn itself into a popular tourist destination. And even though the United Arab Emirates (through Abu Dhabi) is one of the world's most oil-rich states, Dubai – 'blessed' with a lack of natural resources – is hailed as a model of economic development in the Middle East, which, apart from Africa, ranks bottom in the world in terms of wealth and human development.

SIZE ISN'T EVERYTHING

Dubai is no more than a small city-state, but its reputation has grown beyond those of the six, more parochial neighbouring emirates that make up the United Arab Emirates, thanks largely to its merciless self-promotion. Be it Bill Clinton, the English football team or C-list celebrities from the British entertainment circuit, Dubai has an eye for enticing those who can attract the media's attention to what began life as a sleepy little trading port perched on the edge of a desert backwater.

True, it's got a lot to be proud of. While its neighbours face rising levels of unemployment and economic uncertainty, Dubai continues to grow, attracting foreign workers from all over the world. Throughout the expat explosion, the government has looked after its own local population by tilting the business world in its citizens' favour, offering them perks such as free land and cheap loans. Underpinning its relentless self-promotion is the city's 'can-do' culture, where projects are realised on time, no matter how ambitious.

Government heads are never subjected to the trials of re-election by the entire population. Not that it matters, as there are few rulers in the Middle East that enjoy such widespread support among their own people. Here, the autocratic nature of government – which in the West is regarded as detrimental to economic development – has been central to the UAE's success. Sheikh Zayed, leader of Abu Dhabi and the federation of seven emirates, is idolised by almost every Emirati national. Controlling huge oil and investment incomes, his family bankrolls the entire UAE and is renowned for its charitable generosity.

> **'Dubai has grabbed the position of regional trade, commercial and financial hub.'**

Dubai residents have also anointed Sheikh Rashid (*see p8* **Sheikh Rashid, father of Dubai**), who over more than 50 years of rule strengthened the foundations on which the city's affluence was built. Today, similar reverence is reserved for his third son and de facto leader of Dubai, Sheikh Mohammed

(*see below*), who over the past decade has accelerated Dubai's development and built on its international standing.

Dubai, as it has been for just over a century, is a celebration of moneymaking. Like a Middle Eastern version of Hong Kong, it has grabbed the position of regional trade, commercial and financial hub. On the outskirts of the troubled Middle East – it boasts Iran and Saudi Arabia as neighbours – Dubai has emerged as an oasis of stability. Free of political torment, it's a place where individuals and businesses feel comfortable to come and profit, either through hard graft in the city's thriving services sector, or by exploiting opportunities in this oil- and cash-rich region. Some of Dubai's biggest names in business, such as the Al Futtaim family, were originally Iranian, arriving in the 19th century to set up commercial enterprises. Other families, such as the Jashanmals from India, have become part of local society after creating huge retail empires here. Below the Royal Family, these captains of industry lie second in Dubai's social hierarchy.

Sheikh Mohammed, CEO, Dubai Inc

Equestrian, fighter pilot, poet and, above all, businessman, Sheikh Mohammed (*pictured*) is the leading force behind the emirate's lightning modern-day development. Acting as chief executive of the huge holding company that is the Dubai government, the crown prince is behind the strategic and day-to-day running of the emirate. His elder brother Sheikh Maktoum retains the title of ruler but this shy, self-effacing man has, since their father's death in 1990, been happier leading a private life. Conversely, Sheikh Mohammed's boundless energy and unmistakable charisma have propelled him into this definitive role, formalised in 1995 when he was named crown prince – or heir apparent – by his brother. Sheikh Mohammed learned the trade of statecraft first under the watchful eyes of his grandfather, Sheikh Saeed, and then his father, Sheikh Rashid (*see p8* **Sheikh Rashid, father of Dubai**), who as early as the 1960s was grooming his third son for power.

As UAE defence minister, he had to deal with international crises such as the Arab-Israeli war of 1973 and terrorist hijackings at Dubai airport. Then, as his father's health faltered in the 1980s, Sheikh Mohammed took a greater role in fostering Dubai's

businesses and pro-business image. Most notably this included the oil industry, already in terminal decline, and the setting up of Dubai's airline, Emirates.

Today, 'Sheikh Mo', as he's affectionately nicknamed by most expats, continues to develop and update the liberal policies of his Maktoum forefathers. Almost every month he announces a new scheme aimed at raising the emirate's business profile: 'Dubai doesn't need investors, investors need Dubai,' he proclaimed recently. To achieve this goal, he has surrounded himself with the emirate's sharpest minds, drawing on the legions of nationals who have returned with Western educations and business experience.

Yet while they advise, it is Dubai's clear lines of executive power, all of which end with Sheikh Mohammed, that have fostered the emirate's legendary clear-cut decision-making. A military man, trained in the arts of war by the British Army, Sheikh Mohammed knows the benefits of clear lines of command, which allow Dubai to follow through its plans with enviable efficiency. Senior employees across the spectrum of government say that just one phone call to 'His Highness' can put a plan into action.

CITY OF OPPORTUNITIES

Tens of thousands of workers stream into the city every year, fuelling an ongoing construction boom that keeps Dubai's skyline in constant flux. Many are Western (especially British) professionals who have escaped the prying eyes and greedy hands of the European taxman. Arabs from Lebanon, Syria and Palestine also fill many professional and clerical positions; they come to Dubai seeking work and fleeing the inefficient and corrupt bureaucracies of their homelands. Increasingly, Arabs living in the West are coming to work in Dubai, where they find the professional standards of the West combined with the home comforts of the Arab world. Indian and Pakistani labourers and taxi drivers, although paid peanuts compared to everyone else in Dubai, will often return to their home villages with enough money to set up a business. Filipinas are maids, shopkeepers and the best karaoke and band singers in Dubai. Chinese women are also taking up more and more positions in the hospitality industry, be it in five-star opulence or two-star seediness.

Asian migrant workers make up the vast majority of residents and form the city's backbone. Indian and Pakistani labourers toil day and night, throughout the searing heat of the summer, building, maintaining and cleaning the city. Without their labour, or that of the tens of thousands of east Asians employed in the services and hospitality industries, Dubai wouldn't be what it is today. Workers descend on Dubai and the rest of the Gulf region every year, eking out a poor wage that goes far in their homelands. The unshrinking stream of labour is used to justify the poor conditions in which they work and live, not to mention their indentured status, with their sponsors or employers often holding their passports and dictating when the worker can spend some time back home. International human rights organisations criticise the government about these conditions, but the only charge Dubai has reacted to so far is the use of children as camel jockeys – the practice is now banned.

Still, tree-hugging liberals are rare in Dubai. Generations of subcontinental and Arab expats are more than content to bring up their families

With so much power vested in a single pair of hands, the cult of personality runs deep. The sheikh's daily schedule receives in-depth, adoring coverage from a fawning press; his presence at public gatherings commands reverential respect. But Sheikh Mohammed has a common touch too: he drives himself around in a white Mercedes 4x4 (licence plate #1, of course). The Noodle House in the Emirates Towers is one of the crown prince's frequent lunch spots thanks to its no-nonsense attitude and speedy service. And when Palestinian expats gathered to

protest (illegally) against Israeli abuses in their homeland, the Sheikh arrived to show his support.

Equestrianism is both a hobby and a business for Sheikh Mohammed, who says his love of horses runs through his veins. Raised on a diet of falconry and horse riding, his personal sporting forte lies in the equestrian world's version of the marathon, the punishing discipline of endurance riding, in which he has led UAE teams to many victories in international competitions. His fascination with horseracing, sparked as a young student in the UK, almost inevitably mutated into business. Set up in the mid 1990s, the royal family's stable, Godolphin, has quickly emerged as one of the world's top three equine operations, rivalled only by the Aga Khan and Ireland's Coolmore. The company's Dubai stables train their horses through the Gulf's pleasant winter months, before dispersing the steeds across the world for the spring racing season.

The sycophancy surrounding Sheikh Mohammed may seem excessive to Western visitors, brought up to regard politicians with deep cynicism, but in a region of under-achieving leaders, the never-ending adulation of Dubai's 'Big Man' is for once well placed.

here. Many of these long-term residents are taking advantage of the newly offered opportunity to buy property in designated areas, such as the planned Palm Islands (*see p27* **Size matters**) or the real estate developments by local firm Emaar, which is building Burj Dubai, the world's tallest building (*see p27* **Size matters**). Furnished with a permanent residency visa, the property buyer cuts out rent, an expat's main living cost. The legalities of non-residential purchases aren't sorted out yet, but most expats believe in the Dubai system and shrug off issues such as the lack of federal laws and land title. Not only is it proving popular with expats, but non-resident foreigners are also taking interest in the potential for holiday homes, especially on top-notch developments such as the Palm. The blue-rinse communities of the Costa del Sol would be welcomed by Dubai, which needs consumers like these to fuel its ever-growing retail sector.

A LOCAL TOWN FOR LOCAL PEOPLE

Dubai has arrived on the global map by creating opportunities for foreigners, but it also looks after its own. The government has developed a successful social pact with its people that keeps the emirate safe and stable.

Those born in Dubai to Arabs who've lived here for more than a few generations – known as the Locals, or Nationals – still own this town. Everyone else is a resident. Emirati family businesses still form a major part of the economy, having won lucrative agency agreements with importers, such as car and electronics manufacturers. Locals, who until very recently were the only residents who could own property, make oodles of cash by renting it out. Others, for a fee, will 'sponsor' foreigners to stay and work in the emirate; most act as silent business partners, allowing a foreign company to set up shop in a town where, by law, locals have to hold the majority stake in a company. The opening up of land ownership to foreigners is one of the few moves that has prompted local grumbles in recent years. Taking away one source of the privileges that have served them so well during Dubai's boom years, locals fear, will further erode their status. Landlords – with reason – fear rents will tumble as more and more expats buy property.

These grumbles, the government hopes, will be warded off by political reforms planned over the next few years. In the old days, locals' concerns could be aired at the ruler's *majlis*.

Freewheeling Dubai

Dubai has grown through a relentless pursuit of two theories: reduce tax and bureaucracy, and then open your arms to all those who want to exploit this business haven. With no spare fat in this parched land, Dubai has exploited trade and commerce. Since the late 19th century, when taxes on commerce were dropped to attract traders from Iran to Dubai, the government has pursued similar *laissez-faire* policies to keep the emirate growing. As long-term residents will tell you, the tactic has worked: the emirate's skyline is constantly changing as new skyscrapers and apartment blocks rise out of the desert sand. But dig slightly deeper beneath this shiny veneer, and the flip side of this open-mindedness becomes clear. The lax regulation that made Dubai rich has also resulted in financial malpractices, including a history of international money laundering by criminal and terrorist organisations.

Re-exporting goods from the outside world to various spots around the Persian Gulf became the backbone of Dubai's economy. Re-exporting, of course, is often a euphemism for smuggling. Particularly strong demand

could be found in Iran, where the Shah banned American cigarettes to protect his indigenous industry. Iran's Islamic regime, sanctioned by the US in the early 1980s, provided further fertile ground for the smuggler. From the 1960s, when Indian gold taxes made smuggling bullion from Dubai to Bombay extremely profitable, most major traders in the town were entering into syndicates to ship vast quantities of the treasure across the Arabian Sea. The illicit trade with India left its mark, forging ties between Dubai and organised crime groups in India and Pakistan. Despite governmental efforts, subcontinental gangsters continue to live in Dubai. Only on very rare occasions, however, will a gangland killing upset the peace of daily life in the city, which prides itself on having some of the safest streets in the world – if one discounts traffic accidents.

With re-export firmly woven into the fabric of Dubai's trading community, banks and other financiers worked on the sidelines, themselves building up huge operations in Dubai and the UAE. Today, Dubai boasts many international banks, but the emirate's

After the 2003 war in Iraq, the government decided to form community councils with elected members. While details are sketchy at the time of writing, the move seems similar to reforms across the largely autocratic Gulf region amid rising domestic and international calls for broadening the decision-making process. The top-down nature of politics and business in Dubai won't change too quickly, but the significant move – echoing the clamour for political reform around 70 years ago – forms another strand of Dubai's bid to become a world city, playing by global rules.

DUBAI'S BID FOR GLOBAL STATUS

Tourism continues to play a major role in Dubai's bid for global domination. In all its hot, sweaty modernity, the emirate may seem a curious tourist destination, but it's even nipping at the heels of established regional attractions like Egypt. The rapid growth of Dubai-based carrier Emirates Airline has certainly helped the town to attract tourists. The award-winning airline has put Dubai on the holiday map by encouraging passengers en route to Asia or Europe to stop over in the emirate. So too has the establishment of iconic hotels, such as the 'seven-star' Burj Al Arab, a huge sail-like

structure that rises out of the sea next to Jumeirah Beach, Emirates Towers, the world's ninth tallest building, or the Royal Mirage, a tasteful but stunning hotel based on a Moroccan palace. Water parks, beach life and desert safaris combine with the ubiquitous shopping and entertainment experience, encouraging more and more Europeans to make the six-plus hour trip to Dubai.

As Dubai expands its airport, airline and hotel infrastructure, more tourists are expected to descend on the go-getting emirate, clutching their stuffed camels and designer apparel on their return journey. At the time of going to press, the emirate had just announced a huge $4 billion investment project, Dubailand, the region's largest tourism and leisure destination. Built in the desert outskirts of the city, the massive development will house 45 separate 'worlds', from a covered eco-tourism zone to indoor ski slopes, the world's largest mall, space-age hotels and dinosaur parks (*see p27* **Size matters**). The scale of its vision is matched only by its ambition to attract more visitors to Dubai: the government wants its current crop of five million tourists to grow to 15 million by the end of this decade.

reputation for financial probity isn't that good. Money laundering emerged as a by-product of the smuggling that contributed to the nation's economy. Only in 2002 did the UAE central bank introduce anti-money laundering legislation requiring all banks to report suspicious transactions. But Dubai's small size – compared with global financial centres such as New York and London – meant that the impact of dirty money flows never really attracted international scrutiny. Abu Dhabi's central involvement in the massive scandal of the BCCI banking collapse in 1990 certainly drew attention to the workings of the UAE's financial sector. However, poor regulation in Dubai often appeared merely comical, as in the time when an African fraudster hypnotised the management of a prominent Islamic bank, walking off with millions of dollars.

That all changed after the terrorist attacks of 11 September, 2001. It emerged that many of the fund transfers to the 19 hijackers who flew planes into US landmarks came via formal exchange houses in Dubai, as well as via *hawala*, an informal money transfer

system used by subcontinental workers to remit their wages. Of course, as Dubai officials will tell you, terrorist financiers ended up using the Western financial system too, and Western officials are now pleased with the co-operation taken by the UAE to freeze suspect bank accounts and arrest suspected terrorists and their financiers. And most local bankers and diplomats remain convinced that the UAE is determined to recover its besmirched reputation by co-operating with international authorities in clamping down on illicit financial flows.

Yet of all Dubai's underworld activities, the only one that is likely to reveal itself to the tourist is that of the oldest profession in the world. Despite several attempts by police to purge the city of prostitutes, a steady influx of new women from Asia and the former Soviet Union means that seedier parts of Dubai continue to suffer from the problem. Actions by the police have resulted in largely driving the problem off the streets, but there are several notorious bars that act as little more than brothels, and all the city's taxi drivers know exactly where they are.

KNOWLEDGE ECONOMY

But tourism can only go so far in securing Dubai's future. Sheikh Mohammed, who wants to double the emirate's population by the end of the decade, sees expanding knowledge-based industries as the means of attracting more residents and providing desirable jobs for the local population. The rapid rise of media and internet clusters have only encouraged the young breed of city planners, who help along Sheikh Mohammed's ambitious, futuristic vision of the city. The curiously named Knowledge Village is the latest part of Dubai's strategy of attracting more service-based companies into the rapidly evolving southern end of Dubai, between Umm Suqeim and Jebel Ali port.

> ## 'Theft and crime against the person are rare; indeed, driving is the only dangerous activity in the emirate.'

Breaking into the world of international finance is also on Dubai's radar screen. The Arab Gulf region has billions of dollars invested in Western and Asian financial markets – and Dubai International Financial Centre, scheduled to start up in 2004, will attempt to lure back that capital and keep more from flowing out of the region. By offering asset management to the rich and a stock market in which anyone can invest, DIFC hopes to become the region's answer to New York, London and Hong Kong.

Battling against Dubai's less-than-perfect reputation in terms of regulating money flows, DIFC has hired senior regulators from around the world to ease investors' concerns about the town's chequered history of financial probity (*see p18* **Freewheeling Dubai**).

Dubai can plan all it wants, but it's the combination of location and attitude that will probably secure its ongoing success. The city has made a mint from the troubles that plague the Middle East, and the Persian (or, in Dubai, the Arabian) Gulf region – from Persian taxation in the 19th century, via the eight-year Iran-Iraq war in the 1980s, through the invasion of Kuwait by Iraq in 1990 and, now, to the reconstruction of Iraq following the ousting of Saddam Hussein by the US-led 'coalition'. Dubai has always been an R&R stop for Western military forces patrolling the Gulf, and local companies are set to profit from the massive reconstruction effort in Iraq: within months of the war's end, dhows from Dubai were dropping off consumer goods at the southern Iraqi port of Umm Qasr.

Amid this regional turbulence, Dubai offers politically stable and, perhaps more importantly, hassle-free living. The phones are connected quickly and bills are easy to pay. Theft and crime against the person are rare; indeed, driving is the only dangerous activity in the emirate. And Dubaians' toleration of drinks and parties is more than enough to make expats forget that they are living in the cradle of Islam.

Reclaiming land for the **Palm**. See *p18*.

Architecture

From wind towers to the world's tallest building.

There can be few cities in the world that have undergone such rapid urbanisation as Dubai: photographs of the city a mere 50 years ago show a town of sand-coloured one- and two-storey buildings hugging the Creek, surrounded by desert, as if from another age. A comparison of Dubai, the sleepy pearl-diving town, with today's sprawling city of towers – let alone the titanic plans for its development over the next ten years – is enough to bring the architecturally conservative out in a rash.

But anyone overtaken by nostalgia needs to bear in mind that Dubai's architectural history is extraordinarily compressed: wind tower houses started replacing palm-frond shelters in the early 20th century; following the oil boom, these were torn down to make way for cheap, concrete apartment blocks, which in turn were replaced by postmodernist skyscrapers. Now, in the noughties, a penchant for Arabian chic sees architects re-incorporating wind towers into their designs for 'grand boutique' hotels.

With the first exports of oil from the UAE in the early 1960s, Dubai set about dragging itself into the 20th century with an almost religious zeal. The mantra of 'out with the old, in with the new' – and the urgent need for mass housing –

resulted in the razing of most of its old town and the rapid rise of towers and cheap apartment blocks. It wasn't until the 1990s that the government turned its attention to preserving and restoring what was left of the old town – and by then, for many historians, it was too little, too late. Critics maintain that only Oman offers true examples of traditional Gulf architecture, but there are atmospheric pockets of authenticity left in early 21st-century Dubai.

However, speak of architecture, and most Dubaians will think of the contemporary. The audacious Burj Al Arab hotel became an instant icon on its completion in 2000 and started Dubai's passion for breaking height records; the sleek lines of Emirates Towers are widely admired, as are Carlos Ott's National Bank of Dubai and Hilton Dubai Creek. Meanwhile, international architects' drawing boards are stacked with plans for future Dubai cities-within-cities; the world's tallest tower and first underwater hotel are scheduled for completion by 2007. Not surprisingly, a debate is currently rageing among local architects as to how to develop a local architectural language that references the past as well as Dubai's high-rise, gleaming future.

BACK IN THE DAY: TRIBAL LIVING

It was the Bani Yas tribe – ancestors of the Bedouin – who first set up camp in the deserts and mountains of Abu Dhabi and Dubai, splitting their time between animal hair and skin tents, ideal for winter wanderings, and *arish* or *barasti* (palm-frond shelters) for the summer months spent on date plantations. *Barasti* were also popular among fishermen, pearlers and traders.

Coastal areas featured blocky homes built from bricks of fossilised coral, bonded with *sarooj* (a blend of Iranian red clay and manure, dried and baked in a kiln), or a lime mixture derived from seashells and plastered with chalk and water paste. Large courtyard houses built of *farush* (beach rock) and covered with lime plaster have been excavated in Jumeirah and dated back to the second century of the Islamic era (ninth century AD). When a branch of the Bani Yas – the Maktoums – settled by the Creek in the early 19th century, more permanent homes were built of *guss* (mud blocks) and roofed with palm fronds. In sharp contrast to today's widespread use of steel and glass, the materials were known for keeping their cool.

Besides ventilation and what is known today as 'intelligent building', the houses prioritised family privacy, as is typical in traditional compounds throughout the Arab world. Most rooms opened on to an airy central courtyard restricted to family use, and male guests were entertained in a separate *majlis* (meeting room). While in many new villas the *majlis* is in the main house, this layout will be familiar to those living in 'old' villas built in the 1970s and '80s.

Public buildings were mostly limited to stone forts, which doubled up as seats of government, and **mosques** (*see below* **Dome truths**) – check out Bastakia's Grand Mosque (although non-Muslims are not permitted to enter inside). Dubai's oldest building is the **Al Fahidi fort**, now home to Dubai Museum, built in 1799 to guard landward approaches to the town. Parts

Dome truths

Mosque building in the UAE reached a peak in the 1970s and '80s, as the population and, more importantly, the wealth of the emirate grew, but it does have a few examples of older structures. The UAE's oldest mosque – the '**Ottoman Mosque**' – is in Badiyah village, Fujairah, along the road between Khor Fakkan and Dibba. A recent study dates the simple, pleasing structure to around the end of the 15th century; some say that it was built by a fisherman grateful for the discovery of an outsized pearl. Other notable mosques include the modestly designed **Grand Mosque** in Bastakia (the oldest in the city), the more elaborate **Ali Ibn Ali Taleb Mosque** (also in Bastakia), the intricately tiled **Iranian Mosque** in Satwa, and – for modern aesthetics – **Bin Madiya Mosque** near Al Nasser Square, Deira, built in the 1970s by Greek architects. If taking a trip to **Abu Dhabi**, you can't miss its Grand Mosque, just outside the city. Currently under construction, when finished it'll be one of the grandest in the world and possibly the largest built in modern times. At the other end of the scale are tiny, prefab, roadside mosques that closely resemble the kitschy alarm clock versions you can snap up for Dhs10 in Karama.

Most mosques in the UAE feature a simple, open space for praying, generally roofed over, that includes a *mihrab*, from where the *imam* leads prayer, and a *minbar*, a kind of pulpit that often features a minaret off it. The floor is covered in mats, and worshippers leave their shoes at the door. There is sometimes a separate area for women to pray.

The UAE does not allow non-Muslims to enter mosques – with the exception of the **Jumeirah Mosque** on Jumeirah Beach Road (*pictured*). While nothing like the spectacular examples to be found in Syria or Iran, the Jumeirah Mosque is grand, reflecting Egyptian fatimid design and modelled – as are most mosques in the UAE – on an Anatolian structure, with a massive central dome. The **Sheikh Mohammed Centre for Cultural Understanding** conducts interesting and informative tours of the mosque on Thursdays and Sundays at 10am.

Young guides from the non-profit-making centre, set up to bridge the gap between the different cultures in the UAE, are on hand to explain the mosque's layout, describe the five pillars of Islam, and take questions. Visitors should dress conservatively (no shorts) and women bring a headscarf; children under five are not usually admitted. There are extra tours during Ramadan, the ninth month in the lunar Muslim calendar, when the usually frenetic Dubai takes time out for fasting and spiritual reflection (*see p31* **Ramadan dos and don'ts**).

of the old **Dubai wall**, built in 1800, can also be seen in Bastakia.

As Dubai's pearling industry took off in the late 1800s, Bedouin and mountain communities began to gravitate towards the coastal trading villages. The simple, outwardly minimalist homes they built were decorated inside with intricate rugs and wooden latticework on windows, and outside by elaborately carved doors – again, this tradition has continued in the brightly painted metal doors and gates on old villas by the beach, and there are some great antique wooden examples in Bastakia. Historians disagree on whether these decorations were traditionally Arab, based on Islamic designs, or inspired by Indian decorative principles. Homes were built close to each other, with shady *sikkas* (narrow alleys) running down towards the water.

By the late 19th century, spurred on in part by a devastating fire in 1894, Deira's wealthy began to build their homes from coral stone and gypsum, although the poor still lived in *barasti*.

Today, *barasti* are constructed to shade farm workers in the desert, picnickers in villa gardens, and cocktail drinkers at hotel beach bars.

Sheikh Saeed Al Maktoum House was built in 1896 on the southern bank of the Creek in Shindagha as a residence for the ruling family, remaining their home until Sheikh Saeed's death in 1958. Probably one of the first houses in the area to sport Iranian-inspired wind towers (*see p25* **The world's first air-con**), it is a traditional coral-block structure built around a large central courtyard. Emirati historian and architect Rashad Bukash, formerly head of the Historical Buildings Section of Dubai Municipality, describes it as 'the best example of traditional architecture, with all the wooden, decorative elements – such as carved lattice work, teak doors – that were typical of the times'. The restored house now acts as a museum, displaying old photographs and documents.

By the mid 20th century, a village of around 50 compounds, each with a wind tower or two, had built up in Bastakia along the Bur Dubai side of the Creek. It remained more or less intact until the 1970s and '80s. A collection of wind tower shops still exists by the abra station; other fine examples open to the public are the **Majlis Gallery** and **XVA**, a newly restored café, gallery and guesthouse. Former residents of Bastakia today look back with fondness to less hurried times. Hafsa Al Ulama, now a senior adviser to Sheikh Mohammed, recalls growing up in Bastakia in the 1960s and '70s: 'The doors were always open and we used to run between the houses as if they all belonged to us. We never had air-conditioning so used to sit under the wind towers to cool off. All the women used to sit on the floor with the children, eat food, take tea, talk and decorate garments with beads. We were self-sufficient: livestock was kept and slaughtered at home in the courtyard and my aunt would make *labneh* from the goats' milk. To go shopping meant a trip on a rowed abra to Deira-side near the gold souk.'

OIL-BOOM BUILDING

Dubai's pace of urbanisation – like every other facet of then-Trucial States life – was dramatically fast-tracked by the discovery of oil in the early 1960s, first in Abu Dhabi and then in Dubai. The city's skyline was transformed by sweeping changes that followed the formation of the UAE in 1971, notably the explosion in Dubai's population.

The first house built from concrete blocks was constructed in Dubai in 1956, but much of the population continued to live in *barasti* until well into the 1960s. Typically, extended families grouped together into compounds separated by thin alleyways; transport was by donkey, camel or abra until the 1960s, when the first roads opened up.

Even before the oil days, Dubai's ambition was evident. Sheikh Rashid, who succeeded his father in 1958, spent his first few years in power setting up a Municipal Council, building and widening roads, constructing the first airport and bridging the Creek. The arrival of the car created the need for the establishment of a system of land management and ownership – after all, those losing half their compound to a widened road required compensation – and the concept of town planning was introduced. Working out who owned what in the tribal quarters of the city proved tricky but became essential as land value rose. Territory outside built-up areas and any reclaimed land (following the dredging of the Creek), belonged to the ruler – a decree that continues to this day.

> **'The thoroughly 1980s Deira Tower features a distinctive white "cap" like that worn by Emirati men under their *ghutra*.'**

International commentators were sceptical of Sheikh Rashid's grand plans, but there was no shortage of believers; Dubai's population doubled to 120,000 between the late 1960s and early '70s, and by 1981 had reached well over a quarter of a million. The few apartment blocks that sprung out of the desert around Deira's clock tower roundabout (1963) in the '60s weren't lonely for long and by the mid '70s, the Creek was lined with low and high-rise structures. Already soaring fortunes, built on increased trade, went stratospheric during the oil crisis of 1973, and the government began construction in earnest. Developing infrastructure took precedence – the **Shindagha tunnel** and **Al Maktoum Bridge** (1969), the dry docks, **Port Rashid**, mosques, hospitals, schools and power stations all date from around this time. Sadly, however, the need for build-'em-quick residential and office accommodation led to some entirely uncharismatic blocks being erected.

One exception is **Dubai Municipality** (1979), on the Deira side of the Creek, a building that's still widely admired for its abstract sensitivity – although the inner glass courtyard and water pools, which create a cool microclimate, weren't added until the '80s. The **World Trade Centre**, also built in 1979 and at the time the signature Dubai landmark and its highest building at 39 storeys, hasn't withstood history quite as well. Unmistakably '70s, it is now dwarfed in size and stature by Emirates Towers and in function by

the efficient Ibis and Novotel hotels, built to accommodate delegates to 2003's World Bank and IMF meetings.

Dubai's ritual building up and tearing down saw many of the smaller structures of the '60s and '70s cleared to make way for skyscrapers. But tradition sat cheek by jowl with the shiny and new: timber for interiors and furniture was still imported to the Creek on wooden dhows and, even in the early 1980s, Bur Dubai was still a wind-tower village compared to Deira's burgeoning metropolis across the water.

By the end of the decade, Dubai's passion for the shock of the new began to soften slightly, perhaps owing in part to the emergence of the first wave of local architecture graduates. Rumour has it that Prince Charles, the UK's ambassador for architectural conservatism, expressed great enthusiasm for wind towers on a tour of Bastakia, encouraging Dubaians to start conservation projects. Meanwhile, the launch of Emirates Airline in 1985 brought increasing numbers of tourists hungry for a taste of Arabia. The first restoration project – Sheikh Saeed's House – was completed in 1986, and through the '90s another 70 buildings were saved. Architects began incorporating traditional or Islamic references in their designs. The thoroughly 1980s **Deira Tower** (1984) in Baniyas Square, for example, features a distinctive circular white 'cap', like that worn by Emirati men under their *ghutra* (headdress).

THE 1990S

On Sheikh Rashid's death in 1990, his sons, notably Sheikh Mohammed (*see p16* **Sheikh Mohammed, CEO, Dubai Inc**) set about furthering their father's plans to create the Hong Kong of the Middle East, with the most notable new buildings dedicated to commerce and tourism. Dubai's macho love affair with the tower became ever more fervent, while foreign architects' efforts to relate their buildings to the local environment ranged from the ultra-literal to the ultra-kitsch. Some managed to be both: visitors heading in to the city from the airport can't miss the mock airplane hull of **Emirates Training Centre**. **Jumeirah Beach Hotel** (1997) represents a surfer's dream wave, and the unusually low-rise **Dubai Creek Golf & Yacht Club** (1993), the billowing sails of a dhow. Other architects' favourites include Carlos 'Opera de la Bastille, Paris' Ott's **National Bank of Dubai** building (1998), known locally as the Pregnant Lady. Supported by two giant columns, the gold, glass and granite sculptural tower references the curved hulls and taut sails of abras and dhows, but in a subtly contextual manner. It's best viewed from an abra on a sunny day, when its curvaceous belly reflects all the nuances of the Creek. Ott is also responsible for the nearby **Hilton Dubai Creek** (2001), a minimalist's dream.

Emirates Towers, currently the place to do business in Dubai, are equally sleek. The Australian design is frowned upon by some as 'anywhere architecture', but remain the city's most spectacular corporate buildings. The office tower rises up 355 metres (1,165 feet) – take a ride in the swooping glass lifts up to Vu's bar on the 51st floor. **Children's City** in Creek Park has a Duplo-style series of exhibition rooms, and is equally unashamedly modern and unusual in that it provides a spatial as well as a formal experience – as does the ultra-chic **One&Only Royal Mirage** hotel, which uses elements of traditional Islamic architecture. **Madinat Jumeirah**, a massive hotel and souk complex due for completion in late 2004, also harks back to the days of wind towers and coral block hues.

But it was with Madinat's neighbour, the **Burj Al Arab** hotel (2000), that Dubai really earned its reputation as a record-breaking architect's playground. Architect Tom Wright of WS Atkins aimed to build a 'state-of-the-art, almost futuristic building' that was 'Arabic, extravagant and super-luxurious'. The Burj became an instant icon and upon its completion, the most recognised landmark in the city. Built 300 metres (985 feet) off shore, it's the world's tallest hotel at 321 metres (1,053 feet), and is supported by 250 columns descending 45 metres (148 feet) into the seabed. Rumour has it that sand from around the base has to be hoovered out each night to prevent subsidence, and that the tower sways up to 30 centimetres (12 inches) at the top. Even if you can't afford a night's stay in the hotel, you can check out its 60 floors of pure opulence by paying a Dhs200 entrance fee (this is

The world's first air-con

Dubai's early architecture, like its modern-day equivalent, reflected the town's strategic position at a crossroads for caravans following trade routes from Iraq to Oman, and for dhows travelling between India, East Africa and the northern Gulf. Bastakia, now known as Dubai's traditional quarter, was settled by Iranians who brought with them early air-conditioning know-how. By the early 20th century *barjeels* (wind towers) adorned most of the compounds in the area and wealthy families in Deira, Shindagha and Bur Dubai also adopted the technology. They've since become the most feted element of UAE architecture.

Blocky structures, wind towers rose around seven metres (23 feet) above the roofs of the houses – which at that time were constructed from African chandel timber, palm-frond matting, mud and straw. The towers are open on all sides, capturing the breeze and driving it down into the dwelling via triangular chimneys; water thrown on to the floor beneath the tower cools as it evaporates. Even by today's standards, wind tower houses are notably cooler places to hang out when the torpor begins to descend in May each year.

With the trade and oil boom and, gradually, the high-rise, came modern air-conditioning technology. Nowadays, there's still a wide disparity between the whirring, dripping units that serve older villas and apartments and the silent, centralised systems of new homes

and hotels, but anyone who's been hit by a sub-zero blast on entering a hotel room or shivered through a film can testify to Dubai's love-affair with the big chill.

Still, we pampered people really shouldn't whinge. Most Dubaians have at some time or other suffered the sweaty horror of air-conditioning in cars, homes and offices suddenly failing them mid summer, and it's not a pleasant experience. The relief in the words of one old desert-bound Bedouin lady, taped by her film student granddaughter, says it all: 'I thank Allah and Sheikh Zayed every day for the air-conditioning!'

redeemable in the bars and restaurants) and taking in the thrilling views from the Al Muntaha bar located in the oval pod that sits at the top of the 'mast'. But go easy on the cocktails – in delicate natures, the ostentatious gold decorative features and swirly carpets can induce a little seasickness!

By the late '90s, local architects were beginning to mutter about an identity crisis among Dubai's buildings. For some, the attempts by the likes of the Royal Mirage and intimate eco-resort **Al Maha** to reference local or regional history were key to creating a contextual and distinctive Dubai 'look'. For those who question the notion of 'Islamic architecture', these attempts amounted to mere pastiche: they say that Dubai's age-old position on the trading crossroads and its new-found identity as a global city necessitate universal buildings.

Dubaians often wryly joke that they go to sleep at night only to wake up next to a skyscraper the next day. Reflecting the transient and impatient nature of the new Dubai, many of the structures are impressive, but few of them are truly innovative, especially when it comes to environmental concerns. Old-timers question why today's architects have yet to master the integrated use of cool air, shade and natural light perfected in the wind-tower house. While European, American and Asian capitals patronise the new breed of superstar architects, Dubai tends to rely on faceless foreign corporations for its construction needs, and the public's imagination has yet to be grabbed by any cultural or public buildings.

But the city has no problem grabbing the headlines with its commercial plans, and the ambition that saw Sheikh Rashid dredging the Creek and reclaiming land back in the 1960s is more than evident today. A raft of proposals have emerged in the early 2000s, many of which make the construction of the Burj Al Arab seem like a walk in the park.

Dubai's new role as one massive real estate project has been facilitated by the launch of freehold property ownership for foreigners, enabling non-Emiratis to buy homes for the first time. Despite concerns over a lack of land and mortgage legislation, and the rapid scale of development, local and international investors have, so far, proved to be more than willing to partake in the Emirates Dream. And Dubai has displayed its usual marketing acumen, persuading most of the England national football team to snap up luxury villas on the Palm Jumeirah, thus securing a series of headline-grabbing announcements.

The next decade should see construction of the world's tallest tower, first underwater hotel and longest indoor ski slope, plus accommodation for over a million new people in futuristic cities-within-cities. Exciting? Definitely. Risky? Maybe. Environmentally devastating? Only time will tell.

Step back in time at the Arabian Court at the **One&Only Royal Mirage**. *See p25.*

Size matters

A number of vast new cities-within-cities are set to transform Dubai over the next few years. These include **Dubai Festival City**, a 1,600-acre (648-hectare), 20,000-home development with an 18-hole championship golf course that runs up the Creek from Garhoud Bridge, and **Dubai Marina**, at the other end of town next to the Al Sufouh strip of beach hotels. With six residential towers up, and another 200 to go (scheduled for completion between 2008 and 2013), the marina – and neighbouring **Jumeirah Beach Residences** (36 towers and four hotels) – is likely to move the epicentre of Dubai away from its traditional heart, the Creek. Besides these and other new cities, Dubai plans a series of world-record-beating, punchline projects set to redefine global architectural and engineering standards...

Mall of the Emirates (due 2005)

Scheduled to be the largest mall outside North America when it opens, Mall of the Emirates will have a multiplex cinema and the usual range of hypermarkets and stores, but its calling card is the Middle East's first indoor ski slope. An 'authentic snow mountain', complete with 6,000 tons of fine powder, will offer a choice of five ski and snowboard runs, the longest measuring a world-record-beating 400 metres (1,300 feet), complete with a 62-metre (203-feet) vertical drop. Massive snow blowers will replenish the slopes with fresh snow every night. Builders are currently working away on a site located just after interchange four on Sheikh Zayed Road.

Hydropolis (2006)

Trains will take aquatic tourists from a land station opposite Dubai Marina to the submarine complex of the world's first underwater hotel. Unusually, Hydropolis boasts a philosophy as well as plans for underwater art installations and operas on its 'stage on sea'. Gimmicky? Yes, but the project certainly has a passionate champion in architect-inventor Joachim Hauser. What cynic can deny the appeal of a deep-sea poetry seminar?

Palm Islands (2006 and 2007)

The world's largest man-made islands, the Palm Jumeirah and Palm Jebel Ali have commandeered newspaper headlines, due in part to the canny sale of some of the Palm Jumeirah's 5,000 homes to members of the England football team. This, the first island, will also include 50 hotels and artificial reefs, complete with – believe it or not – hidden gold ingots to tempt divers. The five-kilometre (three-mile) wide Palm Jumeirah, visible from space, is located opposite Dubai Media City. Its younger, larger sibling, the Palm Jebel Ali, is also in the form of a palm tree, with 17 fronds protected by a crescent-shaped breakwater. In between lies a 12-kilometre (7.5-mile) chain of elevated 'water homes' built in a pattern that forms a verse of poetry by Sheikh Mohammed.

Dubailand (2006)

Billed as the Middle East's premier tourism, leisure and family entertainment attraction, the imaginatively titled Dubailand is a jumble of ideas collated in one vast, American-style theme park. Located off the Emirates Road, it will incorporate six 'worlds of wonder', from extreme sports zones and car-racing tracks to life-size dinosaur parks and medieval castles, via 'eco-tourism' hotels and, inevitably, the biggest mall in the world, the Mall of Arabia.

Burj Dubai (2007)

The tallest proposed tower in the world, the Burj Dubai, will dwarf Sheikh Zayed Road's current flock of skyscrapers. Designed by Chicago-based tower specialists Skidmore, Owings and Merrill, the complex boasts residential, commercial, hotel and leisure outlets, plus parks, a lake and – naturally – a huge shopping mall.

The World (2008)

Just when the world had absorbed the concept of the Palm Islands, Dubai announced The World, a collection of 250 islands to be constructed, you guessed it, in the shape of a global map. Working four kilometres (2.5 miles) off shore between Port Rashid and the Burj Al Arab, dredgers began reclaiming the islands in 2003. The $1.8 billion project aims to attract the kinds of high-rolling investors who can set their sights on exclusively owning and living on, say, the 'UK' or 'Australia'. The degree to which the individual countries will be themed in terms of architecture and landscaping is still open to debate, but let's hope things don't get too realistic, for the sake of homeowners in, say, 'Iraq'.

Start

Finish

Culture & Customs

Dubai's myriad cultures embrace everything from the excesses of expat nightlife to conservative Islam.

Most young expats can recall a hard night's partying in Dubai coming to an end only as the dawn call to prayer starts up; indeed, the city's complex mix of liberalism and Islamic tradition defines the place. Tourists with preconceived ideas of Middle Eastern or Gulf austerity are surprised by Dubai's commitment to 'live and let live'. The beaches sport Emirati ladies in full burkha alongside Russian women in micro bikinis and no one bats an eyelid.

Western expats love to peddle urban myths about friends-of-friends rotting away in jail over some minor offence or conspiracy theories about the excesses of the Sheikhs but, cynicism aside, it is easy to misinterpret Dubai's liberalism. A night out guzzling cocktails and dancing on the tables, not to mention dodging kerb-crawlers on the way home, can leave you with the impression that the city has temporarily relocated somewhere far, far from the Muslim world. But if that's your impression, think again.

Religion is generally a private issue, but the UAE is an Islamic society. You're never far from the muezzin's call to prayer; cleavages and dateline chat numbers are blacked out in foreign newspapers; and, however benign and enlightened the rule, Dubai is a still a Sheikhdom and its leaders are treated with the utmost reverence. Still, bear this in mind, soak up Dubai's laid-back, polite and friendly ambience, and you'll negotiate, even appreciate, its intricacies with ease.

THE LOCAL POPULATION
Dubai's position at the crossroads of the Gulf, Indian subcontinent and Africa has always made it home or at least port of call – for expats from the region and beyond, but its transformation from a pearl-diving town to an economic powerhouse over the past 70 years has brought about a dramatic change in the city's ethnic make-up. The population of the UAE stands at around three and a half million, of which just over a million live in Dubai.

It is currently growing at around six per cent although, as Dubai builds up and up, and hopes to attract new, foreign home-owners, this rate is set to rise. There are about 2.5 men to every woman, and 80 per cent of the population is made up of foreigners, mostly workers from the Indian subcontinent and the Philippines, plus expats from the Middle East, Europe, Australasia and South Africa.

The distinction between 'workers' and 'expats' is telling. Even fly-by-night tourists can't fail to notice the bus-loads of labourers who graft all year round, building Dubai's new luxury hotels and homes. Most of them come from India, Bangladesh and Pakistan, live in what are openly called 'labour camps' and work long, round-the-clock shifts. While capitalist enthusiasts argue that the workers and are better off earning money for themselves and their families in the Gulf rather than struggling to find work back home, stories abound of workers arriving in Dubai under false pretences, collapsing in high summer temperatures and slaving away in dangerous conditions.

The city's service sector – the lower rungs of the tourist and entertainment industries, plus the maids and cleaners who look after local and expat families – tend to hail from the Philippines, Indonesia and Sri Lanka. Dubai's labouring classes survive for years on end, sending money back via the informal *hawala* system and visiting their families every two or three years. As every other taxi driver will tell you, many plan to come for a couple of years, but find themselves staying much longer; most can name the number of months and days until their next trip home.

'As AA Gill memorably observed, Dubai is the place where malls go on holiday.'

Their obvious exploitation contrasts strongly with the city's penchant for brash consumer luxury; for professionals, life in Dubai is a different story. Companies often include annual airline tickets and family memberships to beach clubs in their 'packages' and, while 'things ain't what they used to be', Dubai can still provide a classic expat lifestyle. But change is afoot: today's IT, media, tourist and property industries increasingly attract young Arabs, Iranians and Indians, as well as Brits, other Europeans, South Africans and Australasians, some of whom have an interest in the Middle East beyond its capacity for tax-free sunshine. The mantra is still 'work hard, play hard', but a new kind of sophistication is evident – and necessary, given Dubai's pace of development.

SOCIAL AFFAIRS

Dubai's glamorous clubbing scene – like its advertising and creative industries – is heavily influenced by the Arab world's party people, the Lebanese. A mix of Muslims and Christians, the Lebanese have always emigrated to far-flung lands, and there are substantial numbers in Dubai. Joining them are Palestinians, Syrians, other Levantine Arabs and Iranians, many of whom have been educated in Europe, the US or other Gulf states.

It's in the local passions of sport, business and shopping that Dubaians get together. The Thursday horseracing nights at Nad Al Sheba attract all levels of society; Arabs and Emiratis often support football teams in the English premier league as well as their local teams; and it's easy to tell when a major cricket match is on from the crowds that form outside the televisions set up at Indian and Pakistani cafés. Besides all things equine (racing, endurance riding, Arab horse racing and beauty contests), Emiratis are committed to their falconry – don't be surprised to see a row of hooded falcons coming through the airport's passport control, or a falconry in the garden of the palaces in Jumeirah and Umm Suqeim.

Families bond by hitting the shopping mall every Friday afternoon. There are around 32 malls in the emirate, with a new one being built every few months. As AA Gill memorably observed, Dubai is the place where malls go on holiday.

But, despite Dubai's generally harmonious and tolerant outlook, and its reputation as the most liberal of the emirates, some professionals do note a degree of subtle racism – from the patronising attitude of some expats towards the service classes, to club bouncers sometimes refusing entry to groups of Indian men. At times, compared to cities in Europe, Dubai can seem to be a collection of different ethnicities living in parallel, keeping themselves to themselves, rather than a mixed, multicultural society. Certainly, the old order that places Emiratis at the top of the pile, followed by Europeans and then other Arabs, has shown staying power. But increasing numbers of professional Indians, the creation of democratically elected local councils, and new laws allowing – even encouraging – foreigners to own property could change this, creating new 'stakeholders' in Dubai society.

While expats, particularly Westerners, might be highly visible, it's the local minority who define and rules the city. Many foreigners mistakenly believe that Emirati society is as uniform as its choice of dress, but dig beneath the surface and you'll find a complex, rapidly changing people. Young students and

Ramadan dos and don'ts

The exact timing of Ramadan, the ninth month in the lunar Muslim calendar, depends on the wisdom of the Moon Sighting Committee, but each year it tends to fall around 11 days earlier than the previous year; in 2004, the month should be called around mid October. Healthy, adult Muslims are required to fast from dawn until dusk – an imperative that's extended to Dubai as a whole, outside of screened-off cafés in hotels. Fasting, to re-focus the mind, is just one element of a month dedicated to prayer and *zakat* (charity), and the devout abstain from all drinks, cigarettes, sex and unclean thoughts during daylight hours. At the end of the day, the first food is taken at *Iftar* ('the breaking of the fast'), and the Maghreb prayers; then families and friends gather together for a major meal.

Dubai's frenzied commercial pace tends to come down a notch or two during the 30 days: live bands pack up their instruments and head off home, and many shops and businesses cut their hours or restrict opening to the morning and late evening. Non-Muslim expats and visitors can, nowadays, quietly drink alcohol in many hotels in the evenings to recorded music – although live music remains a definite no-no.

Be sure to make the most of the large *Iftar* tents that spring up around the city, where you can share the breaking of the fast with Emirati and other Muslim and non-Muslim hosts and guests. Many of the five-star hotels really go to town, erecting spectacularly decorated tents straight out of the *Arabian Nights* with lavish spreads of dates, sweets, mezze and rows of gleaming *shisha* pipes. The sweet smell of fruit-flavoured *shisha* smoke pervades the air and the click-clack of backgammon and chess games can be heard above familial chitter-chatter; for many locals

and visitors, Ramadan is a welcome taste of the old days. And to keep you on the straight and narrow, here are a few useful pointers...

DO...

● go with the flow, be sociable in the evenings and enjoy the public *Iftar* tents and festivities after sunset.

● if you're a non-Muslim, feel free to drink, eat and smoke in the privacy of your hotel at any time. Hotels usually serve food in the day in closed-off areas but alcohol is only available after 7pm. Some will allow tourists to get a takeaway to eat in their rooms.

● politely refuse food and drink in public during the day, even if it is offered by a Muslim friend.

● beware that office hours will change for the 30 days and that late morning is the best time to do business.

● join in Eid celebrations (see *p142*) and greet friends with a cheery 'Eid Mubarak!'

DON'T...

● smoke, drink or eat (including chewing gum) anywhere in public – shopping malls, souks, streets, beaches, taxis and public office spaces – between sunrise and sunset. If you're new to the area or a tourist, you'll usually receive a friendly warning from Muslims and/or the police, but take this advice as your first caution.

● dance or sing in public at any time. During Ramadan, nightclubs shut and even though bars open after sunset and sell alcohol, there are no live music, DJs, dancing or entertainment.

● play loud music at any time – especially at a level that might disturb your neighbours.

● wear tight or revealing clothes in public.

● swear in public. Blasphemy during Ramadan is particularly insulting.

professionals, whose grandparents may lived on camel milk and dates in the desert, deftly straddle Dubai's twin towers of capitalism and tradition. They are likely to combine an arranged marriage, the wearing of the *hijab* and other traditions with business acumen and an international education – and an absolute respect and love for the ruling Sheikhs with a deep knowledge of Hollywood film. An active programme of 'Emiratisation' aims to get more Emiratis into all areas of employment, but for now they tend to dominate only the public sector.

THAT FRIDAY FEELING

Government and other public offices open from Saturday to Thursday, and employees end the working week with a traditional Thursday family lunch. Many private companies take Friday and Saturday off instead, creating variable and confusing weekends. While Friday remains sacred, business is frenetic on every other day, with most of the population devotedly glued to their mobile phones. When scheduling appointments, however, be aware that you are dealing in 'Dubai time': most commitments, whether to have dinner or sign that multi-million dollar deal, are *Insha'allah* ('God willing'). An expression rather than an absolute, *Insha'allah* reminds us that not everything is in the hands of corporate earth-dwellers. Tourist activities and hotels tend to be international in standard, but take a detour into local life, and expect very little to happen resolutely on time, or to resolutely happen at all.

FAMILY FIRST

For Dubai's Emirati population – only two generations of separation from tribal living – the extended family is of crucial importance, from business dealings and traditional gatherings to trips to the mall or races. Names tend to define someone within their immediate family – as *bin* ('son of') or *bint* ('daughter of') – and within their tribe or extended family by the prefix *al*. Protocol dictates that respect and thanks should always be given to the older generations in each family, especially when it comes to official matters. The existence of *wasta*, the 'old boys' network' system of favours given to those with family and friends in high places, still happily resides alongside Dubai's new meritocracy.

HOSPITALITY

Emiratis are known for their warm hospitality and politeness. Traditionally, every guest who entered a Bedouin's tent or home had to be unconditionally fed and given shelter for three days. Nowadays, this kind of generosity is not essential for survival, but old habits die hard. If you're lucky enough to meet and be invited by locals (or other Gulf Arabs) for tea or coffee, do accept. The ritual of making and presenting coffee – strong, espresso-sized cups – is prized, and you'll be offered refill after refill. If your heart can't quite take it, just gently shake your cup from side to side; your host will know not to offer you any more. If you are doing the entertaining, make sure you press more refreshments on your guest – they may well refuse a few times out of politeness before caving in. If a meal presents itself, expect vast amounts of delicious food, much of which will end up being left – a sign of your host's generosity. Eat only with your right hand – the left hand is used for wiping the backside in the toilet.

NATIONAL AND INTERNATIONAL DRESS

Most Emirati men favour the traditional, practical *dishdasha* or *khandura* (a long, white shirt-dress), with *ghutra* (a white headdress) and *agal* (a black rope that holds the *ghutra* in place, traditionally used to hobble camels). In public, city women tend to wear an *abaya* (long black cloak) over a conservative dress, long skirt or tight designer jeans, with a *hijab* or

sheyla (a scarf that either wraps around the face and hair, or covers the whole face). Older women sometimes wear a black burkha that just leaves the eyes exposed, or a traditional hardened linen mask that sits on the nose. While obviously influenced by the Islamic tenet for modesty, the clothes are also deeply practical, as anyone who's survived the biting sandy winds of a desert *shamal* (northerly wind) can testify. As for Dubai's expat population, well, anything goes, but you're advised to dress to suit the occasion. Revealing or tight evening wear is tolerated in clubs, and a bikini is fine on the beach or by the hotel pool, but it's courteous (and advisable if you want to avoid getting stared at), to be more conservative when visiting heritage sites, the souks or anywhere in the city: no shorts is a good rule, and women should wear below-the-knee skirts and cover their shoulders. Beware that Sharjah has 'decency laws', and be sure to dress conservatively on any day trips there.

> **'Expect the melodic intonations of the muezzin to define your day and remind you that you're in Arabia.'**

Despite the flagrant exhibitionism of many expats, local police are quick to react to any complaints of harassment by men: should the generally harmless 'starers' at Jumeirah's public beach become anything more disturbing, you can report them to the beach patrols.

KEEPING THE FAITH

The call to prayer is likely to greet you upon landing in Dubai; once in the city, you're apparently never more than 500 metres (a quarter of a mile) away from a mosque – expect the melodic intonations of the muezzin to define your day and remind you that you're in Arabia. Most mosques are busy for the Friday 'sermon' – which is also broadcast from the minaret via loudspeakers – but Muslims can perform their five-times-daily prayers anywhere, from the side of the road to an office boardroom, as long as they are facing Mecca, to the west. Avoid walking in front of anyone praying, and don't stare; private yet public praying should be viewed as perfectly normal.

Compared to some other Gulf states, the UAE is tolerant and respectful of other religions – and hosts a number of temples and churches – but active promotion is frowned upon. Likewise with the consumption of alcohol: while visitors and non-Muslim residents are welcome to buy

Mosques: no shoes allowed.

duty free at the airport, or have big nights out in hotel bars, the hard stuff is tolerated rather than celebrated (*see p174* **Liquor and the law**). The nights before religious festivals are usually dry; there is pretty much zero tolerance for anyone found drink-driving; and members of CID tend to keep an eye on raucous parties. The two local importers – MMI and African & Eastern – serve hotels, residents who hold liquor licences and, increasingly, big outdoor entertainment and sporting events, but their outlets are understated and windowless. You may see Gulf Arabs, whether local or visiting from Saudi and other strict states, propping up the bar in quieter establishments, but generally, drinking is the preserve of expats.

Other *haram* (religiously forbidden) activities include the consumption of non-halal meat and pork products – which, typically for Dubai, are still sold to expats but from a separate 'pork shop' in supermarkets. Visitors should also resist any public displays of affection between men and women – and be aware that hand signals (beckoning with one finger, pointing directly, as well as the more international rude gestures) can be offensive. Displaying the soles of the feet in someone's direction can also be insulting. Don't be fooled into thinking that the common sight of men holding hands is evidence of a burgeoning gay scene – among Indians, Pakistanis and Arabs, this is merely a sign of friendship.

Generally, in Emirati society, outside of the family and private sphere, unmarried men and women tend to lead separate lives – although, for young people, the advent of the mobile phone, and the popularity of higher education, the cinema and mall, has facilitated a certain level of text message and other long-distance flirting. On public occasions, such as the racing, it's rare to see Emirati wives accompanying their husbands; at weddings, women, dressed in all their designer finery, usually hold separate celebrations to the men; some areas of life, such as local football matches, are still off-limits to women. These traditions, which extend to ladies' days in parks, female-only beaches, and women being served first or separately in bank or other queues, sit alongside the rise of the Emirati businesswoman and the prominent role taken by some of the Sheikhas.

While Emiratis are always forgiving of blunders, and tend to allow Western and Arab expats a different set of rules, it's advisable to be modest and wary of being too informal. For example, wait for a member of the opposite sex to extend their hand before going to shake theirs. An alternative to the handshake is simply to place your palm on your heart as a sign of your warmth or gratitude. Ask before taking a photograph of an Emirati woman and steer clear of snapping any military or government sites. Chances are that even if you do make a blunder, your Emirati hosts will be understanding – their warm manner, politeness and good sense of humour will keep you blissfully unaware.

HINGLISH AND OTHER DUBAI LINGOS

Dubai is pretty much bilingual these days – road signs, maps, even two local papers, are in English, and most Emiratis you'll meet will speak the language impeccably. Even if you're an Arabist, many business people will prefer to converse with you in English. However, some public sector workers or those behind the scenes in Emirati businesses don't always have the same finesse; at some time during your stay, a public official is bound to bark 'Yanni, give me passport' or 'I want form'. Combined with sometimes unfathomable levels of bureaucracy, inevitably requiring bundles of passport photos and forms in triplicate, public offices can be a tad confusing, but keep your cool (and remember it's much worse in most other developing countries) and local propriety will win through. Be sure to tune your ear to 'Hinglish' – a mix of Hindi or Urdu and English, or Indian English. The 'ethnic majority', many subcontinental Dubaians also manage their own blend of English plus some Arabic. Meeting them halfway is the least you can do.

GRAND LEISURE

Set in 37 acres of landscaped gardens, Grand Hyatt Dubai is an oasis of tranquility in the heart of the city. Enjoy world-class business and leisure facilities and an extensive choice of restaurants and bars.

FEEL THE HYATT TOUCH®

For reservations call your travel planner or Grand Hyatt Dubai at +971 4 317 1700

GRAND
HYATT
®

Where to Stay

Where to Stay 36

Where to Stay

Life is suite among the plush splendour of Dubai's luxury hotels, but don't expect much in the way of budget chic.

Hotels are a big deal in Dubai. Far more than mere doss-houses for visitors, the city's crash pads have been elevated to ostentatious exercises in luxury and, in the case of the **Burj Al Arab** (*see p43*), **Emirates Towers** (*see p38*) and **Jumeirah Beach Hotel** (*see p40*), iconic symbols of the city. Driven by the chains' desire to outdo one another, the rate of development over the past few years has been staggering and new properties appear to spring up on a daily basis. This boom is essential if the government is to achieve its stated aim of attracting 15 million tourists a year by 2010. With the first **Palm Island** project set to house between 30 and 70 five-star properties, the **Burj Dubai**, the world's tallest tower, renting rooms and **Hydropolis**, the first underwater hotel ever, set to open in 2006, it seems that no space on land, sea or air is free from the relentless development of the city, creating noise pollution and the occasional plumb of dust. (For all three of these new projects, *see p27* **Size matters**.)

So far supply has been met by demand, but with a tripling or quadrupling of available rooms over the next ten years, there are those who feel this could be a step too far. However, the doom merchants who proclaimed the end of the Dubai tourism dream in the wake of 9/11 and the Iraq war have already been proved wrong. Although occupancy rates plummeted for a short period after both incidents, Dubai bounced back within a few months – the tourist market here appears to be remarkably resilient. The majority of the hotels in the city are parts of the big chains, but a cut above your bog-standard franchises.

LOVE THY NEIGHBOURHOOD

When it comes to hotels, geography largely dictates style, with prices generally dropping the further you get from the shore. **Jumeirah**, with its astonishing beaches, plush malls and sun traps, is currently the most desirable district and is where you'll find the really ritzy resorts. While hotels here are far from cheap, you'll struggle to find one that doesn't send your jaw floorwards with its stunning views, fine facilities and general swank.

Sheikh Zayed Road is home to a shiny new breed of cloud-troubling business hotels, metaphorically miles away from its **Bur Dubai** mother district (for this reason, we have listed the reviews separately). Prices are as staggering as the architecture, but for location and style it's hard to beat.

Stretching from Creek to coastline, Bur Dubai offers some good value halfway houses between Jumeirah's polish and Deira's urban delights. But beware, while pockets such as **Oud Metha**, **Satwa** and **Karama** are some of the most charming in town, the central area is a heaving mass of high-rise towers and swirling exhaust fumes.

A colourful mix of souks, skyscrapers and shopping malls, **Deira** is one of the oldest areas of the city. Accommodation here varies from high-class Creek huggers such as the Hilton to the cheap and less-than-cheerful rooms that line the red-light district. Some way from the shoreline and containing the airport, the area is more geared to business than pleasure.

Those on a truly tight budget may struggle to find something suitable, as family-friendly low-end options are notable by their absence (*see p53* **Cut-price cribs**). But while many may baulk at the prices it is important to remember that your money goes a very long way indeed, and the level of services and facilities on hand at the top of the Dubai hotel tree are enough to make Europe or America's finest look like fleapits.

ABOUT THE LISTINGS

All hotels listed below are air-conditioned. The rates given are for rooms in high season (October to April). The categories are broken down by price of standard double room, with Luxury representing Dhs1,200 and above, Expensive Dhs600 to Dhs1,199 and Moderate below Dhs599. The rates quoted do not include ten per cent municipality tax and a ten per cent service charge, which will always be added to your bill. These rates are, however, very liable to change and it's well worth trying to see what you can negotiate when booking. Unless otherwise stated, rates include breakfast.

▶ For full reviews of hotel beach and health clubs, *see pp198-203*.
▶ For full reviews of hotel spas, *see pp203-6*.

Luxury

Bur Dubai

Grand Hyatt

Oud Metha Road (317 1234/fax 317 1235/
www.dubai.grand.hyatt.com). **Rates** Dhs1,200
single/double; Dhs1,800-Dhs10,000 suite.
Credit AmEx, DC, MC, V. **Map** p277 K3.
Currently the largest of Dubai's hotels, with 674
rooms, the Grand Hyatt is an impressive exercise in
hotel-based bombast. Housing a running track, three
outdoor pools, four tennis courts, a spa, 14 restaurants and bars and (gulp) its very own indoor rainforest with four-tonne dhows hung overhead, the
Hyatt is all about grand gestures. Rooms are light
and reasonably spacious, have a contemporary
Arabic decor and offer delightful views of either the
Creek or the Sheikh Zayed road. Bathrooms are
a tad small, although the massaging shower and
the colossal tub – which could happily house three
people plus the family pet – quickly subdue any
spatial quibbles. The Junior Suites are titanic, dwarfing most of its rivals, and can be extended yet further to create a three-bedroom apartment capable of
housing the Waltons.

A great deal of planning has gone into separating
the business and pleasure areas, with secluded
lounges and executive spaces ensuring the moneyminded don't have to contend with children playing
leapfrog. Big, bold and beautiful, the Hyatt is the
only true resort hotel in the centre of the city and
comes highly recommended.

The best Hotels

For sleeping by the beach
Jumeirah Beach Hotel *(see p40)*;
Le Meridien Mina Seyahi *(see p40)*.

For guaranteed romance
One&Only Royal Mirage *(see p44)*;
Ritz-Carlton Dubai (see *p44*).

For overwhelming opulence
Burj Al Arab *(see p43)*; Grand Hyatt
(see left).

For wheeler dealing
Hilton Dubai Creek *(see p54)*; Emirates
Towers *(see p38)*.

For bargain beds
Hilton Dubai Jumeirah *(see p54)*; Ibis
(see p52); Rydges Plaza *(see p52)*;
XVA *(see p45)*.

For old-school style and service
InterContinental Dubai *(see p39)*; Hyatt
Regency *(see p48)*; JW Marriott *(see p48)*.

For oriental class
Shangri-La *(see p38)*; Dusit Dubai
(see p47).

A Grand entrance: the luxurious lobby of the **Hyatt**.

The **Shangri-La.**

Hotel services *Babysitting. Bars. Beauty salon. Business services. Concierge. Gym. Internet access. Limousine service. No-smoking rooms. Parking. Pools. Restaurants.* **Room services** *Dataport. Minibar. Room service (24hrs). Telephone. Turndown. TV: satellite.*

Sheikh Zayed Road

Emirates Towers

Trade Centre side (330 0000/fax 330 3131/ www.jumeirahinternational.com). **Rates** Dhs1,400 single; Dhs1,450 double; Dhs2,800-Dhs6,500 suite. **Credit** AmEx, DC, MC, V. **Map** p276 H4.

The third Dubaian landmark (although some way behind the Burj and the Jumeirah Beach Hotel in the postcard stakes) Emirates Towers dominates Dubai's skyline. Occupying the taller of the two towers (the other being the most desirable office block in town), the hotel is a big hit with flashy powerbrokers the world over. A sophisticated lobby lounge and acres of atrium dominate the ground floor, while the glass lifts that shoot up and down the 52 storeys are a vertigo-inducing delight. Rooms are sizeable, with nice dark wood tables, gaudy soft furnishings and panoramas that would blow the socks off the most seasoned of travellers. Despite its business-oriented mentality, the Towers does have many tourist-friendly features, including a large swimming pool, health club and complimentary beach shuttle and entry to the Jumeirah Beach Club (*see p40*).

Hotel services *Babysitting. Bars. Beauty salon. Business services. Concierge. Gym. Internet access. Limousine service. No-smoking rooms. Parking. Pools. Restaurants.* **Room services** *Dataport. Minibar. Room service (24hrs). Telephone. Turndown. TV: satellite.*

Shangri-La

Satwa side (343 8888/fax 343 8886/www.shangri-la.com). **Rates** Dhs1,100 single; Dhs1,250 double; Dhs1,300 executive single; Dhs1,450 executive double; Dhs2,600-Dhs6,500 suite. **Credit** AmEx, DC, MC, V. **Map** p276 H4.

The new kid on the Sheikh Zayed block, the Shangri-La towers above its established competitors both literally and figuratively. The elegant and serene foyer is immaculate, visitors can skip between the 41 storeys via the super-speedy lifts and the breathtaking views out over the Jumeirah Beach or magnificent structures of Sheikh Zayed Road are incomparable. The spacious standard rooms impress with their minimalist chic, and the Aigner-equipped bathrooms feature separate tub, shower and toilet spaces. Business facilities are state-of-the-art and secluded, while the suites dazzle with their luxurious fittings and Bang & Olufsen entertainment centres. Pure class.

Hotel services *Babysitting. Bars. Beauty salon. Business services. Concierge. Gym. Internet access. Limousine service. No-smoking rooms. Parking. Pools. Restaurants. Spa.* **Room services** *Dataport. Minibar. Room service (24hrs). Telephone. Turndown. TV: satellite.*

Deira

InterContinental Dubai

Beniyas Road (222 7171/fax 228 4777/
www.dubai.intercontinental.com). **Rates** Dhs1,180
single; Dhs1,280 double; Dhs1,600-Dhs2,485 suite.
Credit AmEx, DC, MC, V. **Map** p279 J3.
Almost as old as the UAE itself, this 1970s monolith
was Dubai's first five-star and is the granddaddy of
the hotel scene. While impeccable service, brilliant
restaurants and (reception area aside) interesting
decor still make the InterContinental Dubai a fine
place to stay, time has taken its toll: the bathrooms
are small by contemporary standards, and the bedrooms, considered to be huge when the hotel was
constructed, should now be reclassed as reasonable.
On the plus side, recent renovations have success-
fully upgraded the place and the furnishings,
although plain, are very tasteful. Views are of either
the large hotel pool or the majestic Creek, and are
stunning regardless of the way your window faces.
The black marble-walled executive club is a little
cold but is a popular spot for businessmen to sit and
take in the colourful corniche views or listen to the
resident jazz band who toot their stuff (every night
except Friday). A fair option for travellers who want
to experience the city rather than baste themselves
on the beach, but in truth, you can get a lot more
for your money.
Hotel services *Babysitting. Bars. Beauty salon.*
Business services. Concierge. Gym. Internet access.
Limousine service. No-smoking rooms. Parking.
Pools. Restaurants. **Room services** *Dataport.*
Minibar. Room service (24hrs). Telephone.
Turndown. TV: satellite.

Le Meridien Dubai

Airport Road, Garhoud (282 4040/fax 282 4672/
www.lemeridien.com). **Rates** Dhs1,100 single;
Dhs1,300 double; Dhs1,400-Dhs9,000 suite.
Credit AmEx, DC, MC, V. **Map** p277 L2.
A large, low-lying, two-storey hotel situated near the
airport, but away from the flight path, the Meridien
caters mainly to shotgun visitors in Dubai who are
here for a quick shop or on an en-route layover.
Rooms could be described as 'grandma chic', with
dated decor and ageing white sofas, which are showing the marks of time. However, peer through the
nets and you'll be greeted with some surprisingly
pleasant views of the gardens and pool area. This,
plus the weighted-up health club, terrace balcony
rooms and swim-up bar, make the hotel a popular
choice with older American and European tourists
and businessmen.
  The grounds house Le Meridien Village, a culinary
tour de force with a throng of eateries set in their
own walkwayed gardens. The place comes alive at
night, with people eating and drinking al fresco into
the early hours. All that said, the steep room rates
are a turn-off.
Hotel services *Babysitting. Bars. Beauty salon.*
Business services. Concierge. Garden. Gym. Internet
access. Limousine service. No-smoking rooms.

Parking. Pools. Restaurants. **Room services**
Dataport. Minibar. Room service (24hrs). Telephone.
Turndown. TV: satellite.

Taj Palace Hotel

Between Al Maktoum Street & Al Rigga Road
(223 2222/fax 227 8222/www.tajpalacedubai.ae).
Rates Dhs1,000 single; Dhs 1,200-Dhs1,320
double; Dhs2,300-Dhs14,000 suite; Dhs1,500
single apartment; Dhs2,750 three-bed apartment.
Credit AmEx, DC, MC, V. **Map** p279 L3.
A haven of extravagance amid the drudgery of
downtown Deira, the Taj Palace is a grand mass of
glass and steel. Decked out with regal curtains, plush
sofas and deep carpets, it is keen to uphold traditional Arabian ideals and as such no women work
past eleven at night and it's the only five-star in the
city not to serve alcohol. These values have made
the Taj hugely popular with visitors from Gulf countries, particular Saudi Arabian businessmen. The
rooms are the largest in town and combine wooden
floors and stylish furnishings to comforting effect.
Health facilities are unisex and the rooftop pool and
tranquil and stylish Ayoma Spa (*see p203*) are well
used. An excellent option for those happy to forgo
location and a glass of wine with dinner.
Hotel services *Babysitting. Beauty salon. Business*
services. Concierge. Gym. Internet access. Limousine
service. No-smoking rooms. Parking. Pools.
Restaurants. **Room services** *Dataport. Room*
service (24hrs). Telephone. Turndown. TV: satellite.

Le Meridien Dubai, handy for the airport.

Jumeirah

Jumeirah Beach Club

Beach Road (334 5333/fax 334 6222/www.jumeirah international.com). **Rates** Dhs2,700 single suite; Dhs2,850 double suite; Dhs3,000-Dhs8,500 deluxe suite. **Credit** AmEx, DC, MC, V. **Map** p282 A15.

This beautiful collection of quality villa accommodation and top-notch facilities are set around lush gardens that lead to one of the most stunning beachfronts in town. Guests are put up in one of 50 luxurious suites, each of which has a private garden or balcony and a Jacuzzi. Thick foliage and subtle construction give the club a sense of tranquillity that is second-to-none in the city – and belies its location in the heart of Jumeirah. There's an excellent club for children, where you can offload the kids before heading off for some shore-side bronzing. In more active moments you can make use of the pools, tennis and squash courts and the limitless access to Wild Wadi, the city's finest water park (*see p148*). JBC is also home to the Satori Spa (*see p206*), a haven of pampering and plucking from which you'll emerge looking a million dollars before tripping over to Prasino's, the mainly Med restaurant (*see p98*). While by no means cheap, a stay at the Beach Club is a guaranteed hit for families looking for some serious downtime.
Hotel services *Babysitting. Bars. Beauty salon. Business services. Concierge. Garden. Gym. Internet access. Limousine service. No-smoking rooms. Parking. Pools. Restaurants. Spa.* **Room services** *Dataport. Minibar. Room service (24hrs). Telephone. Turndown. TV: satellite.*

Jumeirah Beach Hotel

Beach Road (348 0000/fax 348 2273/www.jumeirah international.com). **Rates** Dhs1,650 single; Dhs1,750 double; Dhs3,150-Dhs7,650 suite; Dhs4,000-Dhs5,300 villa. **Credit** AmEx, DC, MC, V. **Map** p274 B4.

A Dubaian landmark, the wave-shaped Jumeirah Beach Hotel is the city's best-known piece of architecture after the Burj Al Arab. For all its outer grandeur, however, it's a down-to-earth hotel patronised in the main by young European families in search of a spot of winter sun. In the shadow of its arching blue glass walls there's a decent children's club and a family adventure playground; just across the road lies the Wild Wadi flume park (*see p148*), home to aquatic tomfoolery on an epic scale. The hotel's beach hosts Beit Al Bahar, a series of luxury villas that offer an idyllic Gulfside retreat, overlooked by the lowering hulk of the Burj. Whether you decide to stay in the spacious, colourful rooms of the main hotel or in the refined chic of Beit Al Bahar, you'd be crazy not to tool up at the hotel's dive centre and pay a visit to the man-made coral reef just off shore.
Hotel services *Babysitting. Bars. Beauty salon. Business services. Concierge. Gym. Internet access. Limousine service. No-smoking rooms. Parking. Pools. Restaurants.* **Room services** *Dataport. Minibar. Room service (24hrs). Telephone. Turndown. TV: satellite.*

Le Meridien Mina Seyahi

Al Sufouh Road (399 3333/fax 399 5505/ www.lemeridien-minaseyahi.com). **Rates** Dhs1,200 single; Dhs1,300 double; Dhs1,400 Royal Club single; Dhs1,500 Royal Club double; Dhs1,700-Dhs 3,700 suite. **Credit** AmEx, DC, MC, V. **Map** p274 A5.

A gem of a beach property for familied-up tanhunters, the Mina retains a casual ambience that's at odds with its formal big brother, Le Royal Meridien. Rooms are simple but comfortable, with beach-side balconies overlooking Palm Island (specify a room with a view when you book). Bathrooms are standard rather than lavish, including nice little touches like an in-room radio. But it is outside that the Mina really comes into its own. With over 850m (2,800ft) of golden sand, the hotel has more front than any other in Dubai. And it utilises every inch of it with a host of water sports, four pool areas, a separate beach party zone and a popular beach bar, Barasti (*see p96*). The children's facilities, including the Penguin Club and dedicated pools, ensures that the sprogs don't interfere with the sun worshipping, while the glass-fronted gym allows you to look out to sea while shedding the pounds. The published room rate is pricey, but check for promotions, which make the possibility of staying here much more realistic.
Hotel services *Babysitting. Bars. Beauty salon. Business services. Concierge. Garden. Gym. Internet access. Limousine service. No-smoking rooms. Parking. Pools. Restaurants.* **Room services** *Dataport. Minibar. Room service (24hrs). Telephone. Turndown. TV: satellite.*

Le Royal Meridien

Al Sufouh Road (399 5555/fax 399 5999/www. leroyalmeridien-dubai.com). **Rates** Dhs1,500 single; Dhs1,600 double; Dhs3,000-Dhs8,000 suite. **Credit** AmEx, DC, MC, V. **Map** p274 A5.

Roses are a big deal at the Royal Meridien. In the rooms are finger bowls of water floating with petals to dip the digits; more rose residue scatters the bed and the bathroom has more blooms than a florist on 13 February. Such in-your-face opulence is typical of Le Meridien's flagship brand and the pools, gardens and great stretch of sand have been sculpted in a timelessly classic style. Accommodation is offered in either the main hotel or the stand-alone Tower or Club complexes; whichever you choose, all rooms are sea facing, large, bright and comfortable, with balconies to enjoy the view down the beach or over the Gulf. The 15-storey Tower is the newest and flashiest option, with panoramic windows and beds that could happily sleep a hippo. Sexy European clients flitter around the upmarket all-beige coffee spaces and bars, and it is doubtful that the pool has seen a full swimsuit in its life. For more decadence, head to the Caracalla Spa (*see p204*).
Hotel services *Babysitting. Bars. Beauty salon. Business services. Concierge. Garden. Gym. Internet access. Limousine service. No-smoking rooms. Parking. Pools. Restaurants.* **Room services** *Dataport. Minibar. Room service (24hrs). Telephone. Turndown. TV: satellite.*

The sky-bruising
Emirates Towers.
See p38.

Burj Al Arab

There are not enough superlatives in the world to adequately describe the extravagant and outrageous nature of the Burj Al Arab ('Arabian Tower'). Yes, at 321 metres (1,053 feet) it's the world's tallest hotel and, yes, it's the planet's only seven-star (albeit an honour that the Burj Al Arab bestows upon itself – international recognition stops at five) but nothing quite prepares you for the obscene affluence of its interiors. Set on its own island just off the coast from the Jumeirah Beach Hotel, the Burj's sail-like structure has become the definitive icon of this city – architectural wonder and cultural statement, it is to Dubai what the Eiffel Tower is to Paris, what Big Ben is to London.

The hotel is owned by Jumeirah International, which also counts in its portfolio the Jumeirah Beach Hotel and Jumeirah Beach Club (for both, see p40), Emirates Towers (see p38), Madinat Jumeirah (due to be completed in December 2004), and the Carlton Tower Hotel in London. Guests are picked up at the airport in one of a fleet of ten white Rolls-Royces and driven to the door across a bridge that shoots jets of flame to acknowledge the arrival of a VVVIP. A triumphant waterfall awaits in the lobby, which is flanked by floor-to-ceiling aquariums so vast the staff have to don scuba gear to clean them. Gold leaf covers almost every surface and huge golden pillars reach up into the atrium; greens, reds and blues all vie for prominence in a colourful reminder that style in Dubai is as much a case of volume as it is of taste. Everything is just as expensive as it looks; lavish decadence to satisfy those who can shell out Dhs3,850 a night for a duplex suite (the standard room).

Blatant sightseers are frowned upon and, away from the lobby, privacy is the order of the day. No floor houses more than 12 suites, and personal butlers cater to your whims round the clock. The spacious suites spread across two floors, with a staircase spiralling up to the sleeping quarters. This is very much a taste of modern Arabia: expect a printer, fax machine, scanner, internet access, wall-to-wall speakers and a 42-inch plasma screen TV.

The hotel that dominates so many photos of Dubai itself offers tremendous views. The best look at Dubai's coastline can be had from the restaurant Al Muntaha, suspended 200 metres (656 feet) above the Arabian Gulf (its name translating roughly into English as

'the highest'). And the Burj boasts the exclusive Assawan Spa & Health Club (see p203), also overlooking the sea. Be warned: treat yourself to a stay here and you may be reluctant to leave, the real world being too rude an awakening after such magnificence. If your budget won't stretch but you still want to take a look around, you'll be charged Dhs200 to set foot inside, but this can be redeem against food and drink. Truly a one-off.

Burj Al Arab

Beach Road, Jumeirah (301 7777/fax 301 7000/www.jumeirahinternational.com). **Rates** Dhs3,850 duplex suite; Dhs4,350-Dhs22,000 deluxe suite. **Credit** AmEx, DC, MC, V. **Map** p274 A4.
Hotel services. *Babysitting. Bars. Beauty salon. Business services. Concierge. Gym. Internet access. Limousine service. No-smoking rooms. Parking. Pools. Restaurants. Spa.* **Room services** *Dataport. Minibar. Room service (24hrs). Telephone. Turndown. TV: satellite.*

Mina A' Salam

Al Sufouh Road (366 8888/fax 366 7788/366 7777/
www.jumeirahinternational.com). **Rates** Dhs1,750
single; Dhs1,850 double; Dhs4,100-Dhs9,500 suite.
Credit AmEx, DC, MC, V. **Map** p274 A4.

Built around 3km (2 miles) of Venetian-style waterways filled with abras (*see p63* **Abra rides**)
that ferry guests around the resort, the Mina is a
gobsmackingly ambitious project that aims to
marry Dubai's modern-day opulence with its old-
world architecture. The sand-coloured buildings
are topped with legions of wind towers (*see p25* **The
world's first air-con**), and the interior is palatial.
Each of the 292 sea-facing rooms are styled in keeping with the Arabian theme: heavy studded doors
give way to Moorish arches hung with ornate
lanterns, and the beds are piled high with exotic
dark blue, red and gold fabrics. The real hook, however, are the large terraces which jut out towards the
water, ideal for sitting and sipping a leisurely G 'n'
T as the sun goes down. With walkways along the
harbour, al fresco restaurant terraces and a souk full
of lavish boutiques, Mina has a distinctly village feel
to it – albeit a village full of the deeply affluent.
Hotel services *Babysitting. Bars. Beauty salon.
Business services. Concierge. Garden. Gym. Internet
access. Limousine service. No-smoking rooms.
Parking. Pools. Restaurants.* **Room services**
*Dataport. Minibar. Room service (24hrs).
Telephone. Turndown. TV: satellite.*

One&Only Royal Mirage

Al Sufouh Road (399 9999/fax 399 9998/
www.oneandonlyresorts.com). **Rates** *The Palace*
Dhs1,330 single/double; Dhs2,560 suite. *Arabian
Court* Dhs1,520 single/double; Dhs3,470 suite.
Residence & Spa Dhs1,730 single/double; Dhs3,170
suite. **Credit** AmEx, DC, MC, V. **Map** p274 A5.

Styled on an Arabian fort, the Royal Mirage is a
uniquely impressive hotel experience. Where many
of Dubai's landmarks owe their success to a degree
of shock and awe, the Royal Mirage presents an illusion of days gone by with welcome subtlety. Many
travellers in the know leave more obvious Jumeirah
hotels to the tourists (and their kids) and head
instead for this haven of softly lit courtyards, thick
with shisha smoke and echoing to the faint beats of
Arabic music.

The Royal Mirage is in fact three hotels in one: the
Palace, the Arabian Court and the Residence, each
offering different levels of plush accommodation.
The complex's simple low-rise architecture holds
sumptuous interiors of rich fabrics and intricate
woodwork. Iron lanterns throw patterned candlelight onto sand-coloured walls, and pockets of rooms
are interspersed with Moorish arches and verdant
gardens. Add the delicate use of gold and warm
tones throughout and the scene is set for the ultimate
romantic getaway. The hotel is never more beautiful than at night, when couples emerge to take quiet
strolls down past the city's largest swimming pool
and on to the beach. Excellent facilities include the
clinically named Health & Beauty Institute (*see*

p204), al fresco sipping station the Rooftop (*see
p174*) and the Beach Bar & Grill, an exceedingly fine
waterfront eaterie (*see p97*). Deluxe rooms are sen-
sibly sized and full of wonderful examples of attention to detail, from the slippers by the bed to the
hand towel artfully folded into the shape of a swan.
Every inch of the Royal Mirage seems designed to
make you feel good about life, and, as such, it's well
worth the expense.
Hotel services *Babysitting. Bars. Beauty salon.
Business services. Concierge. Garden. Gym. Internet
access. Parking. Pools. Restaurants. Spa.* **Room services**
*Dataport. Minibar. Room service (24hrs). Telephone.
Turndown. TV: satellite.*

Ritz-Carlton Dubai

Al Sufouh Road (399 4000/fax 399 4001/
www.ritzcarlton.com). **Rates** Dhs2,150 single/
double; Dhs3,180 club; Dhs5,800-Dhs8,120 suite.
Credit AmEx, DC, MC, V. **Map** p274 A5.

The most classically stylish of Dubai's hotels, the
Ritz-Carlton is immaculately presented with a grand
marble lobby and gigantic windows offering unin-
terrupted views of the white sand and lapping
Arabian Gulf. Too traditional for those who get off
on Arabian chic, the hotel is all about European formality with luxury gently woven into its core. The
wooden-beamed tea lounge could happily host a
football match, the terrace is a delight at sunset and
the beach has cosy made-for-two sun loungers. A
separate adults-only pool offers peace for couples,
and even the family dip-pit is large and languid. All
the spacious rooms look out to sea and enjoy private
balconies, sumptuous soft furnishings and the most
comfortable beds in Dubai. The bathrooms again are
an exercise in comfort, with vast, glass-fronted
showers and baths deeper than Sartre. For a relaxed
stay with some old-world charm, this place is hard
to beat. For the Balinese-themed spa, *see p204.*
Hotel services *Babysitting. Bars. Beauty salon.
Business services. Concierge. Garden. Gym. Internet
access. Limousine service. No-smoking rooms.
Parking. Pools. Restaurants. Spa.* **Room services**
*Dataport. Minibar. Room service (24hrs). Telephone.
Turndown. TV: satellite.*

Expensive

Bur Dubai

Capitol Hotel

Mankhool Road, Satwa (346 0111/fax 346 0333/
www.capitol-hotel.com). **Rates** Dhs550 single;
Dhs660 double; Dhs1,250-Dhs1,750 suite.
Credit AmEx, DC, MC, V. **Map** p280 E7.

A nice alternative to Dubai's garish glitz, the Capitol
is marred by a surprisingly high room rate. Though
a tad prosaic, the standard rooms are a very good
size, with huge beds but banal views of built-up Bur
Dubai. Suites are large and welcoming, with a well-
decorated living space, and can be extended through
the use of an adjoining twin room. The hotel's

rooftop is home to a dying swimming pool, sadly departed fountains and a lonely café. The gym is poky but holds a good selection of equipment. Should the mood take you, you can request one of three masseuses to perform treatments in your room. Situated close to both Satwa's shopping streets and the beach, this remains a popular choice for leisure travellers from Eastern Europe, the Gulf States and India, as well as its more regular business guests. At this (published) rate you'd be wiser to pay less and stay at the Hilton Dubai Creek.

Hotel services *Babysitting. Bars. Beauty salon. Business services. Concierge. Gym. Internet access. Massage. No-smoking rooms. Parking. Pools. Restaurants.* **Room services** *Dataport. Minibar. Room service (24hr). Telephone. TV: satellite.*

XVA

This jaw-droppingly attractive property is unique in Dubai: built more than 70 years ago from coral and clay, it has been faithfully restored and reopened as a gallery, restaurant and boutique guesthouse. It lies nestled in the pocket of old Dubai known as Bastakia, a gorgeous if often overlooked area alongside the Creek, and is one of a handful of wind tower-topped buildings holding out against the lightning modernisation of the city. There's currently a new surge of interest in looking after the last vestiges of pre-oil Dubai, and Bastakia is at the crest of the preservation wave; the care lavished on the building, and the sense of time having slowed to a crawl within its walls, makes XVA (named after the number of the street it lies in) one of the most interesting and evocative places to stay in town. The guesthouse's facilities are minimalist, sparse even, but include a living room and studio where creative guests can put paint to canvas. There's also a gallery, which often exhibits work from local artists. Be sure to enjoy the rooftop terrace, where you can swing in suspended rocking chairs and look out over the skyline of old buildings and mosques to the bright lights of Bur Dubai proper.

XVA houses few guests at any one time, so book early. The unique atmosphere here is only heightened by the incredibly competitive rates. Just round the corner are the Majlis Art Gallery (*see p119 and p158*) and the excellent Basta Art Café (*see p102*).

XVA

Behind Basta Art Café, Al Fahidi Roundabout, Bastakia (353 5383/fax 353 5988/ xva@xvagallery.com). **Rates** Dhs500-Dhs600. **Credit** AmEx, MC, V. **Map** p278 H4. **Hotel services** *Concierge. Restaurant.* **Room services** *Minibar. Stereo.*

The **Ritz-Carlton Dubai**, a haven of old-school service and lavish luxury. *See p44.*

Mövenpick Hotel Bur Dubai

*19th Street (336 6000/fax 336 6626/www.
moevenpick-burdubai.com).* **Rates** Dhs600
single; Dhs660 double; Dhs1,500-Dhs5,000 suite.
Credit AmEx, DC, MC, V. **Map** p277 J3.

Modern and virtually scratch-free, the hotel formerly known as the Holiday Inn is comfortable without
being stuffy and while lacking the wow factor of the
beach hotels, it still offers an inviting ambience. The
panorama from the medium-sized rooms is all inner-
city Dubai, with the choice limited to apartment
blocks, empty stretches of sand or the hotel lobby.
That said, the orthopaedic beds are comfy and the
furnishings adequate. The suites and executive
rooms are a leap up from the standard ones and feature Jacuzzis in the bathrooms. Health fanatics are
well catered to: the gym is roomy and includes separate sex aerobics spaces and massage rooms, while
the rooftop boasts a large and lovely pool deck area
and jogging track (plus snack bar). Fine, but at the
time of going to press the Rydges Plaza was offering much more for considerably less.
Hotel services *Babysitting. Bars. Beauty salon.
Business services. Concierge. Gym. Internet access.
Limousine service. No-smoking rooms. Parking.
Pools. Restaurants.* **Room services** *Dataport.
Minibar. Room service (24hrs). Telephone.
Turndown. TV: satellite.*

Ramada Dubai

*Opposite Jumbo Electronics, Al Mankhool Road
(351 9999/fax 352 7589/www.ramadadubai.com).*
Rates Dhs570 single; Dhs650 double; Dhs1,200-
Dhs1,400 suite. **Credit** AmEx, DC, MC, V.
Map p280 E7.

Proud owner of the largest stained-glass window in
the Middle East, the twentysomething Ramada
Continental is just outside the more hectic heartland
of the Golden Sands area. The hotel is frequented by
both international guests and local residents, and its
shoreless location means that most of its clients tend
to be business folk. Rooms are spacious and most
have balconies that unfortunately overlook air con-
ditioning vents, building sites or the busy streets
below. Rooms are large and have pink-tiled bathrooms. Overall, the excellent service, competitive
corporate rates and size of the rooms make this a
good, comfortable choice for business guests but the
current rates are steep for what you get.
Hotel services *Babysitting. Bars. Beauty salon.
Business services. Concierge. Gym. Internet access.
Limousine service. No-smoking rooms. Parking.
Pools. Restaurants.* **Room services** *Minibar. Room
service (24hrs). Telephone. Turndown. TV: satellite.*

Sheikh Zayed Road

Crowne Plaza Dubai

*Satwa side (331 1111/fax 331 5555/www.ichotels.
com).* **Rates** Dhs1,100 single/double; Dhs1,450-
Dhs3,600 suite. **Credit** AmEx, DC, MC, V.
Map p281 G10.

Part of the InterContinental Group, the Crowne Plaza
is a comfortable city-centre business hotel that
does a nice sideline in the tourist trade. The prime
location on the Creek end of Sheikh Zayed Road
means that guests can be on the beach in 15 minutes
or anywhere in the city in ten. The grand and spacious lobby area, which is reached via steep and

skinny escalators, has aged well on the whole, although the originally swish decor needs to be bought up to speed as the '50s-style display cases are chipped and the carpet worn. Both the health club and pool are spacious and casual, and the club floor features an executive lounge and priority room, allowing VIP visitors to eat away from the chattering masses. Standard rooms are ridiculously small and crowded, while the itsy-bitsy bathrooms are dated even in the suites. The views, however, are as good as any in Dubai.

Hotel services *Babysitting. Bars. Beauty salon. Business services. Concierge. Gym. Internet access. Limousine service. No-smoking rooms. Parking. Pools. Restaurants.* **Room services** *Dataport. Minibar. Room service (24hr). Telephone. Turndown. TV: satellite.*

Dusit Dubai

Trade Centre side (343 3333/fax 343 4222/ http://dubai.dusit.com). **Rates** Dhs850 single/double; Dhs1,050 executive single; Dhs1,150 executive double; Dhs1,350-Dhs4,000 suite. **Credit** AmEx, DC, MC, V. **Map** p276 H4.

One of the most striking buildings on the street, the Dusit is a shiny marriage of glass and steel. Its Thai-style theming is evident throughout, from the Asian-chic decor of the rooms to the smart sarong-wearing staff. Rooms are lovely, with rich browns and sweeping views. Guests can work out in the well-stocked gym with its bird's-eye city views or laze in the 36th

Dusit Dubai, a bow-legged colossus.

floor open-air pool, before heading to the mini spa where they can get themselves primed for a night out. This is the closest you'll get to a high-class bargain on Sheikh Zayed Road.

Hotel services *Babysitting. Bars. Beauty salon. Business services. Concierge. Gym. Internet access. Limousine service. No-smoking rooms. Parking. Pools. Restaurants.* **Room services** *Dataport. Minibar. Room service (24hrs). Telephone. Turndown. TV: satellite.*

Fairmont Hotel

Satwa side (332 5555/fax 332 4555/www. fairmont.com). **Rates** Dhs800-Dhs1,050 single/double; Dhs1,000-Dhs2,000 suite. **Credit** AmEx, DC, MC, V. **Map** p281 G9.

An elegant beast of a hotel, the Fairmont juggles the requirements of both business and leisure guests in some style. Catering to the former, the hotel sets high-tech standards in the city, with wireless internet connection in all rooms and comprehensive in-house IT support. At the Fairmont's centre is a massive foyer graced with groovy leather sofas and a huge atrium, its walls splashed with every tone of colour to head-spinning effect. Bedrooms are spacious, with large beds, huge windows and well-chosen furnishings – although again they suffer from the 'more is more' approach to colour. The minimalist bathrooms, though large, will seem sterile by comparison.

A keen eye for detail is evident in the two pool areas on either side of the building – the sunset and sunrise decks – which have been decorated with stunning mosaics to reflect their respective themes. There's an impressive health club, plus the pricey but first-rate Willow Stream Spa (*see p206*). Because the hotel is situated as close to town as the Sheikh Zayed Road will allow, its lively restaurants pick up a lot of local trade. Oh, and you can't miss it: set directly across from the Trade Centre, it has four illuminated turrets which change colour throughout the week and have taken on a unique place in Dubai's cityscape.

Hotel services *Babysitting. Bars. Beauty salon. Business services. Concierge. Gym. Internet access. Limousine service. No smoking rooms. Parking. Pools. Restaurants.* **Room services** *Dataport. Minibar. Room service (24hrs). Telephone. Turndown. TV: satellite.*

Deira

Al Bustan Rotana

Casablanca Road, Garhoud (282 0000/ fax 282 8100/www.rotana.com). **Rates** Dhs700 single/double; Dhs850 Club Rotana single; Dhs950 Club Rotana double; Dhs1,500-Dhs6,000 suites. **Credit** AmEx, DC, MC, V. **Map** p277 K2.

Located within easy striking distance of Dubai's airport, the Al Bustan Rotana has positioned itself as a predominantly business hotel. Not that it's all work and no play – far from it: the Al Bustan offers a vast amount of leisure facilities for when the ties are loosened, including a spacious swimming pool, a popular nightclub and a well equipped, if poorly attended, gym.

Standard bedrooms are reasonably sized, with huge beds, but wardrobe space is limited and the bathrooms are dated, diminutive and low on amenities. A handful of rooms come with their own private terrace that face on to the pool deck, raising their appeal considerably. The executive club levels are a distinct improvement with larger rooms, a dedicated check in/out area, TV lounge, breakfast area and net access. A nice touch, but the hotel on the whole is somewhat pedestrian for the price.
Hotel services *Babysitting. Bars. Beauty salon. Business services. Concierge. Gym. Internet access. Limousine service. No-smoking rooms. Parking. Pools. Restaurants.* **Room services** *Dataport. Minibar. Room service (24hrs). Telephone. Turndown. TV: satellite.*

Hyatt Regency

Deira Corniche (209 1234/fax 209 1000/www.dubai. regency.hyatt.com). **Rates** Dhs800 single; Dhs875 double; Dhs1,300-Dhs3,000 suite. **Credit** AmEx, DC, MC, V. **Map** p279 J1.

Built in 1980, this vast 400-room stalwart sits close to the mouth of the Creek in downtown Deira. Tried and tested, the Regency is an unashamed courter of business guests, and a successful one at that. Wheeler-dealers, in particular those from East Asia, are wooed in their droves by the hotel's reputation, professionalism and plush suites. The out-of-the-way location – around 7km (4 miles) from the city and out of easy reach of Jumeirah's beaches – has

The **Al Bustan Rotana**. *See p47.*

created something of a siege mentality, and the hotel has every leisure facility going, including a revolving restaurant, nightclub, cinema, ice-skating rink, mini golf course and its very own shopping centre. The rooms are dominated by large glass windows offering fine views of Dubai, the Corniche and and Sharjah, with fresh flowers and plants to spruce the slightly dated furniture. A good hotel, but its location proves off-putting to many.
Hotel services *Babysitting. Bars. Beauty salon. Business services. Concierge. Gym. Internet access. Limousine service. No-smoking rooms. Parking. Pools. Restaurants.* **Room services** *Dataport. Minibar. Room service (24hrs). Telephone. Turndown. TV: satellite.*

JW Marriott

Muraqqabat Street (262 4444/fax 262 6264/ www.marriott.com). **Rates** Dhs750 single; Dhs850 double; Dhs1,500-Dhs9,000 suite. **Credit** AmEx, DC, MC, V. **Map** p277 K1.

Keeping in style with Marriotts the world over, this is an elegant and grand hotel attached to the Hamarain shopping centre. Huge sofas and lush cushions all but engulf guests at the lobby, and the enormous staircase is straight out of Cinderella. Strange, then, that the classy ambience is undermined somewhat by an assemblage of plastic palm trees. Rooms are comfortable and offer an old-world formality that's rare in Dubai hotels. As with most hotels in the downtown area, vistas are limited and there's little to please the eye in the neighbouring buildings or the busy main road. The pool and health facilities, aside from the massive gym and training area, are average at best. Where the hotel's attention to detail really comes to the fore is in the daily beach-bound shuttle buses. Before they leave, passengers are presented with a beach bag that provides towels, iced water and sun lotion and on return iced face towels to calm the sunburn.

Sheraton Dubai Creek

Beniyas Road (228 1111/fax 221 3468/www. sheraton.com/dubai). **Rates** Dhs690-Dhs765 single; Dhs750-Dhs825 double; Dhs1,560-Dhs8,280 suite. **Credit** AmEx, DC, MC, V. **Map** p279 K4.

The Sheraton is looking good after its multi-million dollar revamp in 2003. Stunning from the outside, with its tower and thrusting waterfront extension, it's slick but straightforwardly businesslike within. A huge escalator leads the way up to the dimly lit foyer, where suited executives sink cappuccinos and munch fresh-baked muffins. The tower rooms offer one of the most elevated views over the city, a panoramic snap of the Bur Dubaian shoreline framed by heavy curtains. The rooms are comfortable, and while they don't exactly ooze character you can cheer yourself with the fact that they're excellent value for money. The key advantage of this hotel for tourists is its location – though the Sheraton is far from the beach, it is a short skip away from the abra station, the gold souk and the cultural oasis of Shindagha, and within walking distance

Rooms with a view:
the **Sheraton Dubai Creek**.
See p48.

of a string of other hotels' restaurants and bars. If that sounds like too much effort, the Vivaldi restaurant (*see p92*) is one of the best Italians in town. All in all, it's a fantastic package. Nonetheless, at the advertised rates the Hilton Dubai Creek is better value.

Hotel services *Babysitting. Bars. Beauty salon. Business services. Concierge. Gym. Internet access. Limousine service. No-smoking rooms. Parking. Pools. Restaurants.* **Room services** *Dataport. Minibar. Room service (24hrs). Telephone. Turndown. TV: satellite.*

Jumeirah

Dubai Marine Beach Resort & Spa

Beach Road (346 1111/fax 346 0234/www. dxbmarine.com). **Rates** Dhs780 single; Dhs840 double; Dhs1,080-Dhs9,900 suite. **Credit** AmEx, DC, MC, V. **Map** p280 D8.

Situated at the beginning of the Beach Road in the built-up area of Jumeirah, the Dubai Marine Beach Resort & Spa is the only beachfront hotel in the city proper – the others start on the Al Sufouh Road, some 15km (9 miles) up. The property's great location, small but attractive beach, lush gardens and two swimming pools make it an ideal leisure venue, while its proximity to the city gives it the edge for beach-loving business travellers. Accommodation is scattered in 33 low-rise villa-style buildings spread throughout the resort, with each villa containing only six suites. Its quiet, green gardens and sun-drenched stretch of sand make Dubai Marine a per-

fect chill-out spot. While the rooms themselves could do with a facelift, the complex as a whole is a great place to relax. For the spa, *see p204*.

Hotel services *Babysitting. Bars. Beauty salon. Business services. Concierge. Garden. Gym. Internet access. Limousine service. No-smoking rooms. Parking. Pools. Restaurants. Spa.* **Room services** *Dataport. Minibar. Room service (24hrs). Telephone. Turndown. TV: satellite.*

Oasis Beach

Al Sufouh Road (399 4444/fax 399 4200/www. jebelali-international.com). **Rates** Dhs790 single; Dhs850 double; suites Dhs1,100-Dhs2,150. **Credit** AmEx, DC, MC, V. **Map** p274 A5.

The Oasis is the only four-star hotel on the beach (all the others are five or above) but it has two cards up its sleeve: affordable prices and one of the best beach clubs in town. These elements are enough to make it fiendishly popular with package holiday-makers from Europe and locals looking for a day on the sand. While the public areas are a touch rough and ready, the rooms are surprisingly attractive, decked out with a touch of oriental style. When booking, make sure to ask for a room on the shore side of the hotel: the other side overlooks a vast and ever-expanding building site. The private balconies offer tropical views over the palms and the pools, with the occasional jet-skier cutting up the waves in the mid-distance. Look out for price promotions that drop the rooms into the moderate category.

Hotel services *Babysitting. Bars. Beauty salon. Business services. Concierge. Gym. Internet access. Limousine service. No-smoking rooms. Parking.*

Pools. Restaurants. **Room services** Dataport.
Minibar. Room service (24hrs). Telephone.
Turndown. TV: satellite.

Sheraton Jumeirah Beach Resort
*Al Sufouh Road (399 5533/fax 399 5577/www.
starwoodhotels.com).* **Rates** Dhs750-870 single;
Dhs785-905 double; Dhs1,170 Tower single;
Dhs1,225 Tower double; Dhs1,680-4,000 suite.
Credit AmEx, DC, MC, V. **Map** p274 A5.
Currently the furthest beach property from the city
(although this is likely to change with Dubai's constant expansion) the Sheraton is a stylish resort
property with a good stretch of sand, decent beach
club, spacious gardens and a fine swimming pool.
Popular with European package tourists, the hotel
blurs the five-star lines with the overall feel more
comfortable than lavish; indeed, it's hard to believe
it belongs in the same class as the Mirage. Rooms
are large and overlook either the sea and resort
area or the rather less pleasing building sites of the
developing Dubai Marina and Jumeirah Beach
Residence. Still, it's a great-value place for those
looking to escape the trappings of inner-city vaca-
tions, which is just as well as a taxi ride into town
will set you back over Dhs30. Along with the Oasis
and Hilton Dubai Jumeirah, this is the best-value
spot on Al Sufouh Road.
Hotel services Babysitting. Bars. Beauty salon.
Business services. Concierge. Garden. Gym. Internet
access. Limousine service. No-smoking rooms.
Parking. Pools. Restaurants. **Room services**
Dataport. Minibar. Room service (24hrs).
Telephone. Turndown. TV: satellite.

Moderate

Bur Dubai

Jumeirah Rotana Dubai
*Al Dhiyafa Street, Satwa (345 5888/fax 345 8777/
www.rotana.com).* **Rates** Dhs350 single/double;
Dhs1000-Dhs1500 suite. **Credit** AmEx, DC, MC, V.
Map p280 F8.
The Jumeirah Rotana Dubai is cheekily and mis-
leadingly named: it is actually found in the shore-
free area of Satwa rather than beachy Jumeirah.
That said, this busy hotel has a casual atmosphere
and a 50/50 mix of business and leisure guests. The
spacious and light bedrooms come complete with
generously sized beds, plenty of wardrobe space and
entertaining views over the back streets. Decor
is typical bland Americana: although comfortable,
it's nothing to write home about. The hotel offers
a shuttle service to the Hilton beach club, Mercato
and Sahara shopping centres. With its reasonable
rates, the Jumeirah Rotana is the perfect place to stay
if you're on a family budget trip, and solitary business travellers will enjoy stretching their legs
outside on the ever-bustling Al Dhiyafa Street. But
if you have a peaceful weekend away or romantic
hotel escape in mind, look a little further down the
road, towards Al Sufouh.
Hotel services Bars. Business services. Concierge.
Gym. Internet access. No-smoking rooms. Parking.
Pools. Restaurants. **Room services** Dataport.
Minibar. Room service (24hrs). Telephone.
Turndown. TV: satellite.

Camel rides are one of the many beach-based activities available on the **Jumeirah** strip.

The beach club at **Oasis Beach**. *See p49.*

President Hotel

Trade Centre Road, Karama (334 6565/fax 336 8915). **Rates** Dhs200 single; Dhs300 double. **Credit** AmEx, MC, V. **Map** p281 J6.

Sat on one edge of the bargain-heavy Karama markets, this 50-room, two-star hotel seems as happy to offer knock-down prices as the traders who have set up shop behind it. The dark and dimly lit hallways lead into similarly gloomy rooms, with views of surrounding buildings and the busy road out front. The beds themselves are quite small, and the tiny bathrooms with their shampoo sachets are just enough to get by on. Staff are very friendly and helpful, although as there are so few of them, efficiency is notable by its absence and the guests, predominantly Indian and Gulf Coast families, seem to keep them teetering on the brink of a collective nervous breakdown. Dirt-cheap and centrally located, the President is a fair choice, but you're better off splashing out that bit more for the Jumeirah Rotana or, if you can live without a pool, opting for the Ibis.

Hotel services *Bars. No-smoking rooms. Parking. Pools. Restaurants.* **Room services** *Minibar. Room service (24hrs). Telephone. TV: satellite.*

Rydges Plaza

Satwa roundabout, Satwa (398 2222/fax 398 3700/www.rydges.com/dubai). **Rates** Dhs450 single; Dhs500 double; Dhs1,200-Dhs2,000 suite. **Credit** AmEx, DC, MC, V. **Map** p281 F8.

Occupying a city-centre location next to Satwa roundabout, this nine-storey hotel delivers far more in terms of comfort, style and facilities than its mundane exterior promises. The good position, attentive staff and faux classical pool area attract a repeat clientele of business travellers and elderly tourists. Bedrooms are spacious and comfortable but the furnishings, although unchipped and clean, match the somewhat dated style of the hotel. Most rooms have a clear view of the bustling street life below, and the suites come complete with 120-year-old stand-alone iron tubs that each weigh over a tonne. Along with the Hilton Dubai Creek, the Rydges is the best hotel in this price bracket.

Hotel services *Babysitting. Bars. Business services. Concierge. Gym. Internet access. Limousine service. No-smoking rooms. Parking. Pools. Restaurants.* **Room services** *Dataport. Minibar. Room service (24hrs). Telephone. Turndown. TV: satellite.*

Sheikh Zayed Road

Ibis

Behind World Trade Centre (318 7000/fax 318 7100/www.ibishotel.com). **Rates** Dhs350 single/double. **Credit** AmEx, DC, MC, V. **Map** p281 H9.

A rarity in Dubai, the Ibis is a fuss-free affair that caters to tourists seeking to spend their time in the city, rather than in their hotel rooms. Accommodation is cheap and without extras, breakfast is a flat Dhs35 and there's no pool. But by not trying to do it all, the hotel has invested its time and energy into the fundamentals, developing a high-class feel for a three-star property. The lobby is elegant, simple and dotted with Philippe Starck furniture. Rooms are comfortable – though at 20sq m (215sq ft) quite small – and offer pretty drab glimpses of the Dubai World Trade Centre apartments. A sound choice for the shoestring traveller who has no desire for fancy extras.

Hotel services *Bars. Internet access. No-smoking rooms. Parking. Restaurants.* **Room services** *Dataport. Telephone. TV: satellite.*

Novotel

Behind World Trade Centre (318 7000/fax 318 7100/www.novotel.com). **Rates** Dhs550 single/double; Dhs700-Dhs1,800 suite. **Credit** AmEx, DC, MC, V. **Map** p281 H9.

Built specifically to house the World Bank and IMF meetings held in Dubai in 2003, the Novotel boasts much higher standards in the budget market than the city is accustomed to. The lobby – all dark wood, open space and ordered sophistication – is a stylish reminder that this purpose-built cheapish hotel was nonetheless designed to impress some of the world's

Cut-price cribs

With five-star excess dominating the Dubai hotel scene, it might seem that putting a roof over your head has to be a pricey affair. This is not entirely true: the city does offer the economically minded traveller a few comfortable and cost-effective options, but they are relatively thin on the ground. The majority of the budget bunch are clustered around Al Fahidi Street and Bank Street in Bur Dubai, where you can pick up a clean if poky room for a couple of hundred dirhams. Do bear in mind, however, that Bank Street is at the heart of the less salubrious end of Bur Dubai, where it's not unheard of for female tourists to be propositioned while popping into the supermarket in the middle of the day.

Just off Al Fahidi Street you'll find the **Vasantam Hotel** (393 8006), a spartan lodging where a single room will set you back Dhs150 and a double costs Dhs180. While it's in no sense flashy, if you're here to see the city rather than hang out in your hotel it's the ideal launching point for exploring the most interesting end of town. Just around the corner, Dhs250 will secure you a single room (Dhs300 for a double) at the **New Peninsula Hotel** (393 9111), a smart and friendly towerblock hotel popular with Indian families and Arab businessmen. Alternatively, a night in one of the **Al Faris** group of studio apartments (336 6566), in Al Fahidi Street, Rolla Road or opposite Lamcy Plaza (*see p129*) is a good money-saving option. The cheapest apartments cost Dhs250 a day and are well maintained, with satellite TVs and mini gyms.

Bank Street is home to the **Rush Inn** (352 2235), a discount hostelry where you can expect to pay Dhs250 for a single room, Dhs300 for a double and only Dhs350 for a standard suite. The foyer is hung with slightly dismal snapshots of the karaoke stars working the plethora of themed in-house bars (one Pakistani, one Filipino and one African), but the rooms are none too shabby. However, if you're looking for a tranquil getaway, this place is probably not for you – the hotel's line-up of nightspots means it can be noisy until the wee small hours. Three minutes walk away from the Rush you'll find the **Golden Sands Hotel Apartment** chain (355 5553; *pictured*), a reasonable option if you're prepared to do without room service. Offering spacious and fully serviced self-catering flats from Dhs199 per night, the Golden Sands has a range of clean, furnished rooms stretching from one-bedroom studios to three-and four-bedroom apartments.

Across the Creek, the neighbourhood around **Al Rigga Street** in Deira is another reasonable hunting ground for cheap beds, but again suffers from less-than-salubrious nocturnal activities. Due to the varying vigilance by these hotels' managers when it comes to passing trade, we've refrained from recommending any specific properties in this part of town. Readers looking to stay in this area are advised to go door-to-door, ask to see rooms and make their own judgements: while we realise this isn't ideal it is the only way of assuring you find a room that fits.

There are pockets of accommodation around the noisy, but morally impeccable souk areas. At the time of writing, the **Gold Plaza Hotel** on Souk Deira Street (225 0240) was a fair option, with small but clean rooms for Dhs160. Slightly further out into Deira, the **Dubai Youth Hostel** (298 8161) on Qusais Road is more upmarket boarding house than hostel. Prices start from Dhs50, 'dormitories' contain a maximum of two beds and there are spruce, well-maintained family rooms for travellers with kids.

most important travellers. Although the rooms are small, they're not cramped and the facilities more than satisfy a budget-minded visitor. The hotel holds little appeal to sun-seeking holidaymakers and offers only a small pool and gym, but it will score highly with business visitors and those wishing to base themselves near Sheikh Zayed Road without paying through the nose.
Hotel services *Bars. Business services. Concierge. Gym. Internet access. No-smoking rooms. Parking. Pools. Restaurants.* **Room services** *Dataport. Minibar. Room service (24hrs). Telephone. Turndown. TV: satellite.*

Towers Rotana Hotel

Satwa side (343 8000/fax 343 8901/ www.rotana.com). **Rates** Dhs450 single/double; Dhs1,500 suites. **Credit** AmEx, DC, MC, V. **Map** p276 H4.
Surrounded by grander and considerably more expensive five-star properties, the Towers Rotana has a minimal design style and a younger clientele than its neighbours. Rooms are of average to cosy size but very comfortable and the views over Jumeirah and Satwa are enough to wobble the knees of most tourists. Decor is light and airy in both the bathrooms and bedrooms, and there's a large pool space and gym situated in a separate wing of the building. While pitched predominantly at business travellers, the Rotana is seconds away from the bars and restaurants on the Sheikh Zayed strip; not a bad option for holidaymakers who can't afford the lavishness of the Jumeirah strip yet want to avoid the drudgery of Deira.
Hotel services *Babysitting. Bars. Beauty salon. Business services. Concierge. Gym. Internet access. Limousine service. No-smoking rooms. Parking. Pools. Restaurants.* **Room services** *Dataport. Minibar. Room service (24hrs). Telephone. Turndown. TV: satellite.*

Deira

Hilton Dubai Creek

Beniyas Road (227 1111/fax 227 1131/www.hilton. com). **Rates** Dhs450 single/double; Dhs1,250 suite. **Credit** AmEx, DC, MC, V. **Map** p279 L4.
The classiest and most stylish city-centre hotel in Dubai, the Hilton Creek was designed by Carlos Ott (the brains behind the Opera de la Bastille in Paris) and has food by the world-renowned culinary master, Gordon Ramsay (*see p92*). Glide into the zen-like foyer where peaceful water features lap against glass and gleaming chrome and you enter a world of designer purity. For some people this exercise in modernism is just too cool, but if you want stylish urban chic, then this is the place for you. The large rooms are statements in contemporary luxury, and the huge comfortable beds and ultra-cool black and white bathrooms prove there is substance beyond the style. The room rates are remarkable for what you get and for downtown living, the Hilton Dubai Creek comes highly recommended.

Hotel services *Babysitting. Bars. Beauty salon. Business services. Concierge. Gym. Internet access. Limousine service. No-smoking rooms. Parking. Pools. Restaurants.* **Room services** *Dataport. Minibar. Room service (24hrs). Telephone. Turndown. TV: satellite.*

Millennium Airport Hotel

Casablanca Road, Garhoud (282 3464/fax 282 0627/www.millenniumhotels.com). **Rates** Dhs550 single/double; Dhs850-Dhs1,500 suites. **Credit** AmEx, DC, MC, V. **Map** p277 K2.
As you'd expect from the name, this comfortable crash pad is within spitting distance of Dubai's main airport terminal and attracts a great deal of fleeting business from European suits and crew. Kenny G muzak aside, the marble-heavy hotel foyer is elegant and inviting, while the large swimming pool and banks of green grass make it a low-key family favourite. Rooms are large (a twin share could easily sleep four cosy adults), airy and have pleasant views of the gardens. Wardrobe space and beds are both ample and a subtle Arabic touch runs throughout the decor and furnishings. The hourly airport bus service makes it an obvious choice for business travellers, but leisure visitors will also find the place a perfectly comfortable and decent place to stay – although it's a long way from the beach.
Hotel services *Babysitting. Bars. Beauty salon. Business services. Concierge. Internet access. Limousine service. No-smoking rooms. Parking. Pool. Restaurants.* **Room services** *Dataport. Minibar. Room service (24hrs). Telephone. Turndown. TV: satellite.*

Jumeirah

Hilton Dubai Jumeirah

Al Sufouh Road (399 1111/fax 399 1112/www. hilton.com). **Rates** Dhs450 single/double; Dhs750 suite. **Credit** AmEx, DC, MC, V. **Map** p274 A5.
A classic resort hotel, the Hilton Jumeirah is more package than out-and-out luxury: the decent-sized rooms are comfortable and functional rather than decadent, with cute little balconies and views over the endless blue of the Gulf. The hotel's large pool has a swim-up bar with underwater stools perched around the side so you can sit and slurp your cocktail while keeping cool. Pleasant terraced gardens lead down to the white sandy beach where a number of water sports are available, and a decent health club and gym add to the list of facilities on offer. While being family friendly, the hotel is also a great spot for couples, with sophisticated restaurants and one of the best bars in Dubai in Bice (*p97*). If you can get a room for the advertised rate or below then bite their arm off to do so: this is a bargain for the beachfront.
Hotel services *Babysitting. Bars. Beauty salon. Business services. Concierge. Gym. Internet access. Limousine service. No-smoking rooms. Parking. Pools. Restaurants.* **Room services** *Dataport. Minibar. Room service (24hrs). Telephone. Turndown. TV: satellite.*

Sightseeing

Introduction

How to discover the hidden depths of Dubai.

Vibrant and eclectic, Dubai the city gives visitors the impression of being brand new. The skyscrapers that line the city's main artery, Sheikh Zayed Road, were all built within the past 20 years, and some of the most famous and striking buildings are just a few years old – with new additions springing up all the time. Expansion is underway on a massive scale and hardly a week goes by without a new building or road being opened.

The fact that Dubai is a city that is perpetually under construction means that it can be both unattractive and tiresome to navigate. Its sights are mainly new, or recently renovated, so much of the character of old Dubai has been lost. Those in search of history and tradition will have to search far harder than those wishing to enjoy the glitz of 21st-century Dubai. The city is not rich in historic or cultural sights but, if you know where to look, there are dozens of worthwhile excursions.

LAYOUT AND ORIENTATION

Dubai sits on the Arabian Gulf, which is key to the city's tourism success today and has been a source of both food and trade for centuries. Historically Dubai was two settlements built on either side of the Creek, a 15-kilometre (9½-mile)

inlet around which the city's trade developed. **Deira** is a catch-all term for the area to the north of the Creek, and **Bur Dubai** refers to the south. The terms 'Deira side' and 'Bur Dubai side' are still used to differentiate between the areas north and south of the Creek. A little further along the coast, Bur Dubai merges with **Jumeirah**, where residential, retail and tourist development stretches for some 15 kilometres (9½ miles) southwards. The recommended sights mentioned in these pages are categorised by these three areas.

When petro-dollars began to flow into the emirate in the 1960s Deira and Bur Dubai developed rapidly, the former becoming the trade centre and the latter the residential area. Today, however, all the major developments in the city are taking place on the Bur Dubai side, with projects such as Knowledge Village and Media City springing up alongside **Sheikh Zayed Road**. This thoroughfare runs from Abu Dhabi, the UAE's capital, to Bur Dubai and feeds Deira with traffic via two bridges, dubbed Garhoud, after a district, and Al Maktoum, after the ruling family. For getting from one end of the city to another, Sheikh Zayed Road is a faster if less scenic option than the Beach Road.

Heritage & Diving Village: a memory lane with plenty of tourist regalia. *See p60.*

GETTING AROUND

Dubai is not well served by public transport. There are plans for a rail system, and a bus service called 'Mass Rapid Transport' has evolved. However, the best way to get around the city is by car and, as a result, traffic problems are increasing. Dubai's road network is mostly new and, for the most part, easy to navigate, but many additions to the network are under construction, which frequently cause traffic chaos. *See also p243* **Navigation**.

In your quest for Dubai's more rewarding sights, taxis are the best way of getting around. The government recently introduced competition into this previously state-run service, and the effect has been a dramatic improvement in quality. Drivers are generally courteous and knowledgeable, and all cars have meters. A growing number of taxis accept credit cards. The exceptions to the rule are cabs that hail from the neighbouring emirate of Sharjah, who'll happily pull over for tourists as part of an opportunistic foray into Dubai even though the government frowns upon them. Despite the plush interiors, these often odorous cars are private vehicles and lack meters. If you'd rather face the hassle of an independent operator than wait for Dubai's finest to show, negotiate a price with the driver and make sure that he knows how to reach your desired destination before pulling away. Generally speaking, taxis loiter outside any building that will provide a steady stream of customers, or can be hailed on almost any street corner, day or night. *See also p243* **Taxis**.

Choosing to drive yourself means dealing with all other road users. Drivers from other Middle Eastern or subcontinental countries will find driving a breeze, but those arriving from the West will be alarmed by the weaving motorists who drive too fast then too slow, too close to each other and never with the use of indicators. *See also p244* **Driving**.

Dubai's lack of effective street addresses will also become painfully obvious. Residents offer and receive directions according to landmarks such as parks, banks and, predominantly, hotels. It pays to have a well-known spot in mind if you're looking for somewhere off the beaten track. *See also p246* **Addresses**.

TOWN AND COUNTRY

Urban Dubai is alive with sights and smells. What it lacks in ancient architecture it makes up for in character and ambition; in the shadow of proud, uncompromising hotels and office structures nestle heaving souks and forlorn shipyards, reminding one of the small fishing village swallowed up by the big city forever. But while it is a mistake to shrink from

The best Sights

Sights

For Dubai's earliest settlement
The oasis town of **Hatta** slumbers in the foothills of the Hajar mountains (*see p69*).

For Islamic understanding
Go beyond the beach with an eye-opening account of **Jumeirah Mosque** (*see p67*).

For ancient crafts
Witness a day in the life of early weavers and pearl divers at **Heritage & Diving Village** (*see p60*).

For cutting-edge architecture
Stop for coffee at the **Burj Al Arab** (*see p65*). Try not to gawp.

For a blast from the past
Wander unhurried around **Bastakia** (*see p59*) and stop by the **Dubai Museum** (*see p60*).

For souk heaven (or hell)
Get your bearings, plunge into **Deira** and bedeck yourself with gold (*see p62*).

For off-road thrills
Have a qualified driver take you on a **desert tour** into the dunes for a barbecue and belly dance (*see p74*).

For four-legged racing
Find out why the world's fastest horses and camels call **Nad Al Sheba** home (*see p71*).

For cooling down
Little kids (and big ones) can soak up the views of Jumeirah from the slides at **Wild Wadi** (*see p65*).

For luxury in the desert
$1,300 per night buys life's finer things, like views of the oryx, at **Al Maha** (*see p68* **Magic Al Maha**).

Dubai the city, to spurn a glimpse of the Creek entirely for the sanitised joy of your hotel room would be madness.

While desert driving requires a masterful hand, those not yet skilled can turn to nearly any local tour operator for a 4x4 safari with barbecues and belly dancing thrown in for good measure. Further afield still lie Dubai's sister emirates (*see pp208-240*); sleepier, but prettier, and replete with opportunities to walk along deserted shorelines or laze at the feet of cool, quiet mountains.

Sightseeing

Urban Dubai

The modern city is short on history but big on tradition.

Sightseeing

Measuring time in Dubai is a strange business. This is a city with deep roots, where evidence of settled communities stretches back as far as the 5th century AD. Westerners tasting the warm hospitality of today's Middle East for the first time – enticed by tales of luxury and, ultimately, the marketing savvy of Dubai's rulers – are often enchanted by the timeless serenity of old Arabia. Europe and beyond can seem as distant in years as it is in miles when listening to the Arabic call to prayer. And yet there are few tangible examples of history in the city itself, where the little amount of traditional architecture has been largely renovated or lost. Among the thousands of sun-worshippers arriving in Dubai each year are many travelling salespeople, engineers and consultants, who return to the city after a business trip many years ago only to discover so much has changed: high-rise towers and austere glass structures now stand where once there was nothing but sand.

So Dubai is not a city for sightseeing in the classic sense. There are few museums of note here, and no galleries aside from commercial ventures showcasing work from contemporary Arabic artists. For those in search of history, it is far better to view Dubai as a living museum, a place founded on strong Arabic values but where the world's cultures interweave together and change unfolds at a blistering pace. The resulting city offers tourists a wealth of rich experiences and goes some way to explaining Dubai's stellar rise to prominence as a travel destination of choice; not bad for a village once viewed as a mere stop-off point for traders, sailors and pilots.

Bur Dubai

As Dubai was settled, a residential area developed along the sandy southern banks of the Creek and became known as Bur Dubai. It is here that the emirate's rulers made their home in sea-facing fortifications, and the district remains the seat of the Diwan (the Ruler's Office), Dubai's most senior administrative body. As the city grew, the area became home to embassies and consulates, creating an atmosphere of regal calm, with commercial activity centred on the mouth of the Creek. Today the situation is changing fast and, while the banks of the Creek are still free from development, Bur Dubai has sprawled inland, with tower blocks springing up on practically every available inch of sand. Small nuggets of history persist, but the vast bulk of Bur Dubai is a characterless concrete jungle that offers little of interest to the visitor.

As the residential community has grown, so commerce has developed to support local residents. The once tiny souk has expanded dramatically, supermarkets and shopping malls have opened, and highways traverse the area.

Dubai Museum (*see p60*) makes a good starting point for exploration of Bur Dubai, and visitors with cars can park in the adjacent space. From the museum, make your way northwards towards the Creek and enjoy **Bur Dubai souk** (Map p278 H4) on foot. A curious

Pockets of the old town survive in **Bastakia**.

mixture of old and new, it lacks the traditional charm of Deira's **old souk** (*see p62*) but does boast a vast array of goods. At worst this lesser-known area could be described as tacky and cheap; at best it would be fair to say it's a haphazard market-style collection of shops.

Be sure to pass through the **textile souk** (*see p116*). This is a great place to buy traditional Arab clothing, Pakistani and Indian saris and salwar kameez, the traditional baggy shirt and trouser outfits worn by women in Pakistan, Afghanistan and to a lesser degree in India. These can be tailored from the fabric of your choice in a matter of hours at very reasonable prices.

Streets filled with fabric and tailoring shops soon lead you to the covered area of the **Bastakia souk**, which is filled with Arabic curios and souvenirs. The best prices and bargains are to be found in the less attractive streets beyond the renovated centre. A walk through the covered area ends at the abra crossing point, where a left turn will lead you to the collection of shops known as the **watch souk**. Hefty doses of caution and scepticism are advised, but some of the watches on display are genuine and prices are hard to beat. If you head west from this point you will reach the electrical souk (also known as **Electrical Street**, *see p120*), a great place to buy camera and video

equipment or even white goods. As with most of Dubai's souks, the boundaries are hazy, but those in search of computers, software or games would do well to explore its southern streets.

Bur Dubai sprawls southwards to merge with the coastal development of **Jumeirah** and westwards to **Port Rashid** on the coast, but the most rewarding sights are to be found where it all began – along the Creek.

Bastakia

Between Al Fahidi Street & the southern bank of the Creek. **Map** p278 H3.

One of Dubai's most picturesque heritage sights, Bastakia is being carefully renovated and turned into a pedestrianised conservation area. By the end of 2004 some 50-plus houses will have been completed and a museum, more restaurants and a cultural centre are planned. The name Bastakia comes from the first people to settle the area, who were traders from Bastak in southern Iran. The ruler of Dubai encouraged such immigration in the early 1900s by granting favourable tax concessions. Many came and most stayed, which explains why so many Emiratis are of southern Iranian descent.

Stepping into the narrow alleyways of Bastakia is to step into Dubai's past. Many buildings sport wind towers, a surprisingly efficient form of natural air-conditioning designed to capture the breeze and funnel the cooler air into the rooms below (*see p25* **The world's first air-con**). Many older Emirati

Sightseeing

Al Dhiyafah Street at night

There is hardly a moment in any 24 hours when Al Dhiyafah Street in Satwa (Map p280 F8) can be described as quiet, but at night this bustling social thoroughfare really comes into its own. Effectively the border between Bur Dubai and Jumeirah, Al Dhiyafah Street is the palm-lined main street that marks the outer boundary of the Satwa area.

Once a village in its own right, and home to the building in which the treaty that created the United Arab Emirates was signed in 1971, Satwa is in danger of being swallowed up by the burgeoning residential metropolis of Bur Dubai. But it has retained its character and exudes an atmosphere of Arabic and Asian bohemian chic. Shops and cafés line the pavements, making it Dubai's ultimate people-watching location.

Al Dhiyafah Street is largely dominated by chain restaurants and fast-food outlets, but there is also a smattering of traditional cafés that serve fresh juices and Arabic tea and coffee laced with honey and cardamom.

nationals tell of summers spent in Bastakia when entire families would gather to sleep outside on raised platforms to escape the heat of indoor rooms.

Dubai Museum

Al Fahidi Fort, Bastakia (353 1862/www.dubai tourism.co.ae). **Open** 8.30am-8.30pm Sat-Thur; 2.30-8.30pm Fri. **Admission** Dhs3; Dhs1 concessions; free under-5s. **No credit cards. Map** p278 H4.
Considered by many residents to be a must for visitors, the museum is undoubtedly one of Dubai's best efforts and is well worth a visit. The Al Fahidi Fort was built in 1787 as Dubai's primary sea defence and also served as the ruler's residence. In 1970 it was renovated so the museum could be housed within its walls. Inside, the displays are creative and imaginative, allowing you to peek into an Islamic school, walk through a 1950s souk, watch traditional craftsmen at work and even to experience (almost) the tranquil beauty of an Arabian night in the desert. *See also below* **Old Dubai in a day**.

Heritage & Diving Village

Al Shindagha (393 7151/www.dubaitourism.co.ae). **Open** 10am-midnight Sat-Thur; 4pm-midnight Fri. **Admission** free. **Map** p278 G3.
This pleasant 'living' museum by the Creek, staffed by guides, potters, weavers and other craftspeople, focuses on Dubai's maritime past and depicts the living conditions of original seafarers, who harvested the Arabian Gulf for pearls and fish to trade. Static but entertaining displays chart the history of Dubai's pearling industry, and a tented village gives a glimpse into the Bedouin way of life that remained unchanged until well into the 20th century. During religious holidays, such as Eid Al Fitr (usually in Nov) and Eid Al Hadha (usually in Feb), and throughout the Dubai Shopping Festival (mid Jan-mid Feb), traditional ceremonies are laid on, including sword dancing and wedding celebrations. At these times old pearl divers are often on hand to recount tales of adventure and hardship.

Old Dubai in a day

Take a shiny new bouncing babe of a city, overly warm temperatures and a healthy distrust of anyone who would rather walk than drive, and it's hardly surprising that Dubai should lack the sort of historical circuit that overly enthusiastic tourists mark out as must-do. Which is not to say that visitors can't taste the past in a neat afternoon-sized package. It is perfectly possible to immerse yourself in the tale of Dubai's extraordinarily rapid development, if your journey begins in the **Dubai Museum** (*see above*).

The museum is housed in **Al Fahidi Fort**, Bastakia, which dates from the late 1700s; in its previous lives, Dubai's oldest building has acted as a fort, the seat of government, the ruler's residence, an ammunition depot and a jail. In the courtyard stands a traditional winter reed *arish* hut, erected next to an old wooden dhow. Galleries off the main courtyard celebrate the Bedouin predilection for weaponry with an array of spears, armour, brass wristguards, *khanjar* knives, swords and old guns, many beautifully inscribed with calligraphy and etched with the maker's name.

Inside, more recent galleries mark out key stages in Dubai's history: in 1580, an explorer described Dubai as a prosperous, pearl-diving town; in 1894, foreigners were granted tax-exempt status, fuelling the transformation to expat haven. A slightly surreal, larger-than-life souk, where dozens of wax-figure tailors, blacksmiths, coffee-drinkers and *shisha* smokers are portrayed to the background of a

clattering soundtrack, makes for a fairly spooky experience, as does a display of skeletons recovered at archaeological sites in Al Qusais and Jumeirah, dating from the first millennium BC. Other rooms spotlight desert wildlife and take you beneath the ocean for fishing and pearl-diving. All in all, the museum is entertaining, occasionally bizarre and offers some great factoids.

At this point, you will probably be in need of some refreshment. Pop into the **Basta Art Café** (*see p102*), just around the corner, where a fresh lime and mint juice and souk salad will get you back on your feet. Next door is the delightful **Majlis Gallery** (*see p158*), and around the corner, down an alleyway overshadowed by wind towers, is **XVA**, a newly restored guesthouse and art gallery (*see p45*). Each modern venture sits in an old building true to Bastakia's traditional architecture; it's well worth stretching your legs and letting your imagination wander.

Abras to take you across the Creek are a five-minute walk away through the start of the textile souk, or you could continue on the heritage trail to **Sheikh Saeed Al Maktoum House** (*see p62*), home to evocative old photographs and documents, many signed by Dubai's former ruler himself. Also in the same area is the **Heritage & Diving Village** (*see above*), best experienced in the evenings, particularly at Eid when local dance troupes entertain visitors. For details call Dubai Tourism Information Centre (228 5000).

Al Fahidi Fort, home of
Dubai Museum. *See p60.*

Modern mall meets working wharf in **Deira**.

Sheikh Saeed Al Maktoum House

Al Shindagha (393 7139/www.dubaitourism.co.ae).
Open 8am-10pm Sat-Thur; 3-10pm Fri. **Admission**
Dhs2; Dhs1 concessions; free under-8s. **No credit
cards. Map** p278 G3.

Built in 1896 out of coral covered in lime and sand
plaster, this traditional house was the home of
Dubai's former ruler until his death in 1958 – hence
its strategic position at the mouth of the Creek. Now
restored and converted into a museum, it displays
small exhibitions of old documents, stamps, curren-
cies and a collection of old photographs of Dubai and
its ruling family. Guided tours are available.

Deira

Deira is a bustling, chaotic, dusty commercial
hub where plate-glass office blocks tower over
the single-storey buildings of the old souks. It
is most definitely an area best explored on foot.
Broadly speaking the term Deira is used to
describe everything north of the Creek that, in
reality, is an amalgam of sub-districts. The
most exciting part for the visitor, however, is
the original 'Deira' on the Creek – the heart and
soul of old Dubai.

The best way to start to discover Deira is to
walk along the Creek where old meets new with
full force. Five-star hotels such as the Sheraton
and InterContinental are situated just yards
away from wharfs that haven't changed in the

past 60 years. On the roads, limousines and
4x4s jostle for road space with pick-up trucks,
while sharp-suited businessmen and women
wait at zebra crossings alongside sarong-clad
workers from the subcontinent pushing
handcarts, and fishermen in work-stained
kandouras. Traditional dhows still line the
Creek wharf and, day and night, seamen unload
goods destined for the many tiny shops that
make up Dubai's oldest trading area.

It's here that you'll find **Deira old souk**,
sprawling around the mouth of the Creek on the
north shore, where the waterway widens at the
entrance to the Gulf (Map p278 H3). The area is
best explored during late afternoon or evening,
when temperatures are lowest and the traders
are at their busiest. The entrance to the old
souk stands under renovated buildings with
traditional wind towers. Like most markets, it
has evolved into sections defined by the goods
sold in each and criss-crossed by alleyways. In
this case the areas are known individually as
the **spice souk** (*see p116*), **antique souk** and
textile souk (*see p116*).

Step into the spice souk and you instantly
breathe in the scents of Arabia and the East.
Chillis, cardamom and saffron are piled high
outside spice shops; ornately decorated glass-
stoppered bottles line shelves in traditional
perfume shops; and the sweet aroma of
frankincense fills the air. At one time more
valuable than gold, frankincense (a gum resin
obtained from trees of the genus *Boswellia*)
remains one of Arabia's most prized perfumes
and is the base for some of the world's most
expensive scents. Traditionally, crystals are
placed in a frankincense burner and heated over
a flame, allowing the resulting aromatic smoke
to waft through clothes and rooms alike.
Shopkeepers are happy to demonstrate the
custom and both frankincense crystals and the
burners can be bought at very reasonable prices
throughout the souk.

The original coral-stone shops have been
renovated and, sadly, much of the dusty charm
of the souk has been lost, but it is now a far
cleaner place to visit. Take the time to make
your way through the myriad alleyways to
explore the many shops selling Arabic curios
and antiques.

Once you reach the antique shops you know
that you are approaching the renowned **gold
souk** (*see p118*). Its centre is a wide alley
covered by a roof and supported by carved
wooden pillars, but the souk extends into the
adjoining streets. It's worth venturing beyond
the main plaza-like area to explore the outer
alleys where many specialist shops trade in
silver, pearls and semi-precious stones.
'Bargaining' (haggling) is expected in all souks;

Abra rides

One of the best ways to view the Dubai Creek is by abra – traditional wooden water taxis that cross the Creek day and night. These apparently rickety but watertight boats have been ferrying residents and traders across the Creek since Dubai was first settled; originally they were rowing boats, but are now powered by smelly diesel engines. Even now, almost 15,000 people still cross the Creek by abra every day.

To take a ride on an abra, look for the clearly marked boarding points on both sides of the Creek: in Deira by the dhow wharfage near the entrance to the old souk, and in Bur Dubai at the end of Al Seef Road by the entrance to the renovated part of the Bastakia Souk. The crossing takes a few minutes and costs 50 fils per person. The abras are commuter vehicles

for manual and low-paid workers, and boarding can be chaotic at peak times when hundreds of workers jostle for space on the stone steps that the boats pull up to. You are likely to find yourself pulled across the decks of several boats by helpful abra captains, who are quick to extend welcoming but rather soiled hands to anyone hesitating or looking for a space on the bench seating.

The basic crossing allows you to take in the atmosphere of the Creek and gives a great insight into how the city operated in the past. For a more comprehensive tour of the Creek it's well worth hiring your own abra – simply ask a boat captain and agree a price and the length of the tour before you set out. A journey up and down the Creek should cost no more than Dhs50.

Carry on up the Creek

Sightseeing

A thriving business thoroughfare by day, the Dubai Creek slips into a quieter, romantic atmosphere at sunset. In early evening families make their way to the water's edge to walk and enjoy the cool breeze that comes off the water. Dhows decked with fairy lights cruise the waterway and reflections from windows glint on the rippled waters as yachts drift back to the marina.

The night-time Creek experience can be enjoyed from the shore or from the water. Our advice is to walk up an appetite and then enjoy the heart of Dubai by making a meal of it: for good food and one of the best air-conditioned views in town, the **Vivaldi** restaurant in the Sheraton Dubai Creek (*see p92*) is highly recommended; if you prefer an al fresco experience and a little less luxury, **Fatafeet** (*see p80*), opposite the British Embassy in Bur Dubai, is one of the best places to lap up the ambience from the water's edge. Fresh juices, a range of Arabic dishes and *shisha* (the traditional Arabic 'hubbly-bubbly' pipes through which flavoured tobacco is smoked) are all available.

Cruises are plentiful and range from trips aboard fully air-conditioned dhows to the more basic but equally enjoyable abra.

If you begin your tour from the dhow wharfage in Deira, your first views will be of the Bastakia area on the southern banks of the Creek with its wind tower houses. As you journey inland, look out for the expansive frontage of the **British Embassy** on the southern banks, before casting your eyes to the north shore towards the high-tech splendour of two award-winning buildings: the bow-fronted **National Bank of Dubai** and sharply angled **Dubai Chamber of Commerce** building. Views of old Dubai and the Creek, reflected in the convex front of the National Bank of Dubai building, make for a great photo opportunity.

If your tour extends beyond the Al Maktoum Bridge, look out for the famed white sails of the clubhouse at the **Dubai Creek Golf Club** on the north shore and, towards the south shore, a close-up view of Dubai's past at the **Dhow Building Yard**.

There are several companies cruising the Creek. Creekside Leisure (336 8406) offers a mighty fine two-hour dinner cruise aboard the *Floating Majlis*. Other companies include Creek Cruises (393 9860), Danat Dubai Cruises (351 1117), Al Boom Tourist Village (324 3000; not licensed to serve alcohol) and Al Mansour (205 7333; not licensed to serve alcohol).

Sole searching: handmade shoes from **Deira old souk**. *See p62*.

don't be afraid to leave a shop to try next door if you cannot reach a price that you consider reasonable. Most shopkeepers will offer tea or cold drinks while a deal is struck – a sign of traditional hospitality and an indication that negotiations are progressing well.

What Deira lacks in refinement it makes up for in energy and character. And to experience it at first hand all you have to do is to walk along the corniche that borders the Creek. Note that Deira is by no means pristine: despite the Dubai Municipality's efforts, litter abounds and spitting in the street is commonplace.

Al Ahmadiya School & Heritage House

Near Gold House building, Al Khor Street, Al Ras (226 0286/www.dubaitourism.co.ae). **Open** 8am-8pm Sat-Thur; 2.30-8pm Fri. **Admission** free. **Map** p278 G3.

Established in 1912, this was the first school in Dubai and was renovated as a museum in 1995. Next door is the Heritage House, a traditional house with interiors from 1890. Guides and touch screens take you through the tour of the two small museums.

Jumeirah

Just half a century ago, Jumeirah was a fishing village several kilometres outside Dubai. Today it is one of the most high-profile areas of the city and residents often refer to it, with tongue placed firmly in cheek, as the Beverly Hills of

Dubai. A few original villas survive and are much sought after by expatriate residents as (almost) affordable beachside homes. The area commonly referred to as Jumeirah – though Jumeirah is only a part of it – stretches along Dubai's southern coast for some 16 kilometres (10 miles), incorporating the suburb of **Umm Suqeim**. It is serviced by two main roads: the **Beach Road** that runs along the coast and the **Al Wasl Road** that runs parallel a few blocks inland. A haphazard network of streets lined with luxury villas links the two.

Jumeirah developed southwards from the Satwa borders and the oldest part, known as **Jumeirah 1**, remains one of the most sought-after addresses in Dubai. It is here that the first chic malls and coffee shops grew up, and it is still a popular choice today for residents in search of a latte or manicure. At this end of the Beach Road the **Jumeirah Mosque** (*see p67*) welcomes non-Muslims.

Along the Beach Road are **Dubai Zoo** (*see p67*), various shopping malls (of which Mercato Mall can boast the most fashionable clientele) and several public beaches. The beaches run from Jumeirah 1 to the far end of Umm Suqeim, where the **Jumeirah Beach Hotel** (*see p40*) and **Burj Al Arab** (*see p43*), next to **Wild Wadi** water park (*see p148*) mark the beginning of the resort strip. The chances are that if you're heading to the beach, you're heading to Jumeirah.

EveryDay Diamonds

Capture the moment...forever

Moments
Diamond Moments

• **Wafi City**, The Link   Tel: 971 4 3242855 • **Gold and Diamond Park**, Sheikh Zayed Road   Tel: 971 4 3478034
• **Eternity Jewels**, Gold land, Near Gold Souk, Deira Tel: 971 4 2290945 • **Al Khen Jewellers**, Lamcy Plaza, 1st Floor Tel: 971 4 3350044
• **Taif Jewellers**, Al Ras Centre, Opp Deira Bus Stand Tel: 971 4 2254142

Dubai Zoo

Beach Road, Jumeirah 1 (349 6444). **Open** 10am-6.30pm Sat-Mon, Wed-Fri. **Admission** Dhs3. **No credit cards**. **Map** p280 C10.

The animals at the Dubai Zoo are the survivors, and progeny, of a private collection now owned by the Dubai Municipality. It has been heavily criticised as it is old-fashioned and the animals are caged so they enjoy little freedom. There are plans to move the zoo to a far more spacious site out of town but, for the moment it's still in Jumeirah. The range of species is surprisingly wide and includes lions, tigers, giraffe, bears, reptiles and birds, but it's up to your conscience as to whether you would enjoy a visit.

Gold & Diamond Park Museum

Gold & Diamond Park, Interchange 4, Sheikh Zayed Road (347 7788/www.goldanddiamondpark.com). **Open** 10am-10pm Sat-Thur; 4-10pm Fri. **Admission** free. **Map** p274 B4.

The Gold & Diamond Park features examples of Arabian, Italian and indian jewellery, and conducts guided tours to the manufacturing plant, showing visitors how diamonds are cut and how gold is produced. There are plenty of opportunities to purchase, although you may get a better deal in the souks.

Jumeirah Mosque

Beach Road, Jumeirah 1. **Map** p280 D9.

Arguably the most beautiful mosque in Dubai, the Jumeirah Mosque stands at the northern end of the Beach Road. Non-Muslims are not normally allowed inside mosques, but the Sheikh Mohammed Centre for Cultural Understanding (*see below*) organises visits to the Jumeirah Mosque at 10am Sunday and Thursday mornings. You'll get a chance to walk through the mosque with a small group of fellow sightseers before putting questions to your guide about the mosque and more generally the Islamic faith. You must wear modest clothing (no shorts) and ladies, a headscarf please (*see p22* **Dome truths**). Both men and women will be asked to remove their shoes before entering. A worthy destination in its own right, this also makes a good start point from which to explore Jumeirah.

Majlis Ghorfat Um Al Sheef

Beach Road, Jumeirah 4; look for the brown heritage signposts (394 6343). **Open** 8.30am-1.30pm, 3.30-8.30pm Sat-Thur; 3.30-8.30pm Fri. **Admission** Dhs2. **No credit cards**. **Map** p274 B4.

Built in simple traditional style from coral and stone, the two-storey *majlis* was used by the late ruler of Dubai, Sheikh Rashid bin Saeed Al Maktoum, the founder of modern Dubai (*see p8*). *Majlis* means 'meeting place' in Arabic and is where matters of business or other importance are discussed. This particular one has been carefully preserved by the Dubai Municipality. The ground floor is an open veranda, and the first floor *majlis* room is furnished with cushions and Arabic antiques. The open-air rooftop terrace was used for sleeping, as the height ensures the platform enjoys a stiff sea breeze.

The fact that many of the visionary plans for modern Dubai were probably hatched in such a simple structure, by a man who had known nothing of 20th-century luxury for most of his life, is remarkable. A visit to the *majlis* highlights the dramatic development and the extent of the changes that Dubai has undergone in just a matter of decades, particularly as you can see the Burj Al Arab hotel from the rooftop. That said, the *majlis* only really merits a short visit: it's fascinating as a contrast between old and new Dubai, but does not rate as a significant cultural experience.

Sheikh Mohammed Centre for Cultural Understanding

Beach Centre mall, Beach Road (344 7755/smccu@emirates.net.ae). **Open** 8am-3pm Sat-Thur. **Admission** free. **Map** p280 D10.

Founded by Dubai's Crown Prince, HH Sheikh Mohammed bin Rashid Al Maktoum (*see p16*), to promote cultural awareness and understanding, the Centre organises a variety of activities and visits that are aimed at helping to break down cultural barriers. Young volunteers from the Centre conduct hour-long English-language tours of Jumeirah Mosque (*see above*) on Thursdays and Sundays (free, no booking necessary, just turn up at the mosque a little before 10am). In a city where many visitors, and perhaps surprisingly, many expatriate residents, do not have the opportunity to get close to the local community, the centre is invaluable and its work is acclaimed by locals, visitors and expatriates.

Criticised **Dubai Zoo** is cleaning up its act.

Further Afield

Enjoy quieter times in the emirate of Dubai, far from the madding city.

Modern Dubai owes much to its coastal origins, but there is life beyond the densely populated areas clustered around the Creek – albeit at a greatly slowed pace. Desert parks, towering dunes and mountain pools await the more adventurous traveller. What follows in these next few pages are recommended sights beyond the city boundaries, all an easy ride away. Unfortunately, Dubai's lack of public transport makes driving the only viable option. Taxis are not cost-effective over longer journeys (across to Hatta, for example), not to mention the impracticality of hailing a cab for the return journey. Hiring wheels for excursions during your stay is a much better idea; *see p244*.

Miscellaneous sights

Jebel Ali Beach

Sheikh Zayed Road, between Jebel Ali Hotel & Ghantoot.

Dubai's most remote and unspoiled beach lies some 40 minutes' drive south of the city, towards Abu Dhabi, and stretches, unencumbered by development, for some 15km (9½ miles) to the Abu Dhabi/ Dubai border. This expanse of unbroken sand represents Dubai's only remaining 'natural' beach, yet there are strong rumours that, despite the fact that it is a nature reserve, development plans are under-

way. The area will most certainly be affected by the Jebel Ali Palm (*see p27* **Size matters**) and there are fears that this valued area will soon be damaged or lost forever. A favourite with beach-loving residents and kite surfers, who relish the freedom of the emirate's longest free stretch of coastline, the beach is open to all, but those who wish to camp on the beach must apply for a permit from Dubai Municipality.

Take the exit signposted for the Jebel Ali Hotel off the Sheikh Zayed Road. Turn left at the roundabout before the hotel and follow the tarmac road that runs along the coast behind the dunes. Pick your spot and turn right towards the sea – the beach is straight ahead. A 4x4 is essential to get on to the beach itself, although hard-packed sand tracks enable two-wheel-drive vehicles to reach the northern edge of the beach. There are showers (not all of which work) and *barasti* (palm-leaf) sunshades, but no other amenities; this is not a beach for those who enjoy luxury or need facilities to be close at hand.

Khor Dubai Wildlife Sanctuary

Ras Al Khor industrial area. **Map** p277 J4.

Head south from Dubai on the Ras Al Khor Road and you'll soon skirt the edge of the Creek. There's little to see on your journey through the Ral Al Khor industrial area, but glance back over your shoulder and you'll see an unassuming stretch of land. Dedicated as a nature reserve, the marshy ground is

Magic Al Maha

The exclusive Al Maha resort is situated about 50 kilometres (30 miles) east of Dubai on the road to Al Ain. Effectively in the middle of nowhere, Al Maha – formally known as the Dubai Desert Conservation Reserve – is a set of stunningly luxurious individual villas with private pools, established on a conservation reserve whose land mass takes up five per cent of the emirate of Dubai. No private vehicles are allowed on the reserve, but you'll be collected and returned to your hotel or home (a Dhs250 transport fee is added to all Bedouin suite bookings).

The hotel accommodation is impeccable – you're paying for it – and the 24-hour service outstanding; Al Maha employs at least three staff per guest at any given time. Offering traditional activities such as falconry and

camel riding to 4x4 desert safaris, Al Maha is the ultimate get-away-from-it-all ecotourism spot. The site cultivates indigenous flora and fauna, encouraging you to soak up the atmosphere over fine food and vintage wines. At dusk, sitting on your private balcony with gin and tonic in hand, you can watch rare and endangered Arabian oryx – *maha* in Arabic, hence the resort's name – as they come to drink at the watering hole, just a couple of hundred metres from your chalet.

Al Maha

Al Ain Road (303 4222/fax 343 9696/ www.al-maha.com). **Rates** Bedouin suites from $1,300 (inclusive of breakfast, lunch, dinner & two activities). **Credit** AmEx, DC, MC, V.

There's nothing remotely mad about Hatta, or the town's **Hatta Fort Hotel**. *See p70.*

home to thousands of flamingos, waders and other birds, many of which migrate to Dubai seasonally. A favourite spot for photographers, the reserve affords spectacular views of flamingos against a backdrop of the Dubai skyline. The only way to preserve nature here is to protect it from people, so the reserve is closed to the public. It is, however, easily viewed from the Ras Al Khor Road or the road that runs from the Bu Kidra roundabout (also known as the Polo Club roundabout) towards Dubai.

Mushrif Park

On the airport road towards Al Khawaneej, near Mirdif (288 3624). **Open** 8am-11.30pm daily. **Admission** Dhs3; Dhs10 per car. *Swimming pool* Dhs10; Dhs5 concessions. *Train* Dhs2. **Map** p275 F3. The park is approximately ten minutes drive out of town, close to the residential suburb of Mirdif. It is so huge that you can drive around it or take the miniature train that tours every afternoon. The variety of themed displays include miniature houses from around the world. Camel and pony rides are available in the afternoons. Wildlife such as deer and gazelle roam the farthest corners of the park, where landscaped gardens give way to sand dunes covered with indigenous vegetation. Dogs are not allowed.

Hatta

Snugly tucked between Dubai and Oman, the oasis town of Hatta is a welcome change of pace from Dubai's fast-lane living and is a popular day trip for tourists with wheels. An excursion to Hatta offers plenty of off-road action and just a dash of heritage, making for a varied day out.

From Sheikh Zayed Road, Dubai, take either the Trade Centre roundabout, or Interchange 1 or 2, and turn inland. From here you will see signs to Hatta. As you continue along the highway, you will notice the landscape change colour slowly, from a washed-out pale yellow to a rich red ochre. It's the iron oxide present in the sand that gives it this unusual warm glow; in the right light it can be spectacular.

Shortly after the village of Madam (expect a large roundabout and little else) you will pass through a small patch of Oman. Be aware that most hire-car insurance will not cover trips outside of the UAE and you will be uninsured for this section of road should you have an accident, even though there are no official border posts to notify you.

Pool position

To get to Hatta Pools from Dubai:

● Turn right at the Fort roundabout at the entrance to Hatta.

● Take a left towards the Heritage Village; the road curves round past the village and ends at a junction.

● Turn left, then immediately to your right on a small road which you follow for two kilometres (1¼ miles).

● Continue along the main road and take the next main road to your right, over a series of speed bumps and past a row of dilapidated shacks on the left.

● Continue along this road through a few villages for the next six kilometres (3½ miles) until the tarmac peters out.

● At this point, take a right on a graded gravel track and into the foothills of the Hajar mountains. The track is easily manageable in a typical saloon car if you drive carefully and stick to the main drag. Of course, opting for a 4x4 gives you the freedom to explore some of the subsidiary tracks, of which there are many.

● The turnoff to the main pools is just after you drive up and over a large hill, beyond the signpost for Bon.

● You'll have driven just over 4½ kilometres (2½ miles) along the main gravel track by the time you turn left to a smaller track, which doubles back on itself before heading directly for the pools.

● If you are in a saloon car, park and walk the rest of the way. In a 4x4 you can drive the next few hundred metres to an expanse that serves as a parking area. From here it is an easy walk over the *falaj* irrigation system, following the path down into the wadi (riverbed).

The views are spectacular, and the layers of jagged peaks fading off into the distance across the gravel plains and the acacia trees gives the area something of an African air.

At last you will reach the town of Hatta, considered to be the oldest village in the emirate of Dubai. The town is overlooked by two defensive towers built in the 1880s and boasts a real old-world country charm. Its tranquil setting in the foothills of the Hajar Mountains, the rocky range that spans the eastern flank of the UAE, is compelling, and the location offers numerous routes to explore on foot, by mountain bike or 4x4.

Hatta Fort Hotel

Hatta (852 3211/www.hattaforthotel.com). **Rates** from Dhs495; Dhs1,440 suites. **Credit** AmEx, DC, MC, V.

One of the country's oldest hotels, this is the only place to stay in Hatta and well worth a stop-off for a sundowner even if you're not planning to stay the night. The building houses two food options, Café Gazebo, whose terrace has great views over the mountains, and the more formal Jeema Restaurant.

The 50 individual chalet-style rooms offer rustic, high A-frame wooden ceilings and all look out over the rolling green lawns of the 80-acre property. The grounds are home to a teeming wealth of birdlife: keep an eye out for the brilliant turquoise flash of the elusive Indian roller. The facilities include a swimming pool, nine-hole golf course, jogging track, tennis court, archery and experienced guides for 4x4 mountain and desert excursions.

Breakfast is included in the basic rate and there are excellent offers during the summer months, with rates as low as Dhs300 per room for weeknights throughout the low season. But be warned: while the mountains escape the humidity endured by coastal areas, temperatures can still rise well above 50°C.

Hatta Pools

The major tourist draw in this corner of the Emirates are Hatta's natural pools, a 45-minute drive from Hatta Fort Hotel (*see above*). No matter how hot the weather, there is always cold, clear water flowing here. Deep gorges have been eroded by the rushing river over countless centuries, and if you walk downstream you'll reach an area where the wadi widens and you can loll in the shallows or swim up the gorge to a waterfall.

Visiting the pools for a picnic or swim is an inspirational experience, but it can get very busy at weekends. It also suffers from the same problem as other beauty spots in the UAE – the unwelcome attentions of litter louts and vandals.

Heritage Village

Hatta (852 1374). **Admission** free. **Open** 8am-5pm daily.

A subdued slice of culture, The Heritage Village was established to commemorate a traditional mountain village set in an oasis and makes for a nice morning expedition. The village is bordered by two round towers built to protect the town from attacks during the rule of Sheikh Hasher bin Maktoum bin Butti in the late 1880s. The village consists of various Omani-styled fortified and public buildings (including a 200-year-old mosque) and holds about 30 houses fully restored to their original architectural style, with primary materials including mud and *barasti* (dried palm leaves tied together) used for authenticity. The village strives to educate visitors in the multiple uses of palm-tree products and dates, such as date honey. To find the Village, turn right at the Fort roundabout and follow the brown signboards.

Nad Al Sheba

The Nad Al Sheba area, a ten-minute drive inland from Dubai, is home to two of the sports at the heart of Arab heritage – horse- and camel-racing – and one beloved of Western expats, golf. By taking in both the Nad Al Sheba golf and racing clubs, and the camel souk and racetrack, it's possible to experience the extremes of modern-day luxury and traditional Arabia in one visit, as well as watch sports at polar ends of the financial spectrum.

Nad Al Sheba Club & Racecourse
336 3666/3031. **Map** p274 C4.

Home of the world's richest horse-race and Dubai's best-known fashion parade, the Dubai World Cup (*see p139*), Nad Al Sheba Club incorporates both a racecourse and a floodlit 18-hole golf course. The club is surrounded by racing stables that house some of the world's most valuable bloodstock: for the price of a drink, it's possible to catch a glimpse of the finest fillies being put through their paces every morning from the vantage point of the Spike Bar. Between November and March the club hosts race meetings on Thursdays and Saturdays, the

Big Red

About half an hour outside Dubai, in the direction of Hatta, you will come to a huge sand dune on your right hand side affectionately known by expats as Big Red. It's a majestic, looming sight, a fiery orange-red mass set against a brilliant blue sky. But if you've made it this far, don't sit lovingly by the roadside in your 4x4. Big Red is a playground for big kids with big engines: by far the best way to enjoy this stretch of desert is to get stuck right in.

Nearby is a popular quad-biking centre, which is great fun but somewhat chaotic and accidents there are commonplace. You have a choice of 50cc, 80cc and 200cc bikes. Prices range from Dhs15 for 15 minutes on a 50cc to Dhs200 for an hour on the 200cc bike. You can even hire a Land Cruiser for Dhs50 per 30 minutes for a shot at getting to the summit of Big Red itself. Rentals operate

from 8am to sunset daily, and should you require sustenance a supermarket, restaurant and toilets are on hand.

Most tours operators run trips to Hatta via Big Red but you can always set your own schedule and hire a 4x4. One of the best places to do so is Budget (285 8550), which offers Toyota Land Cruisers fully kitted out and complete with steel bumpers and roll bar for Dhs550-Dhs600 per day, including insurance. If you choose to drive yourself, remember that it is not safe to venture off road with just one vehicle; get someone else to hire another vehicle and accompany you. Mobile phone coverage is extremely poor in the mountains and you are likely to be out of touch. You should carry at least one full cool-box of water for every two people (10-12 litres), plenty of food, a first aid kit, some tow rope and a shovel (*see also p221* **Four by four play**).

Grand stands at **Nad Al Sheba**. *See p71.*

most prestigious of which are the Dubai Racing Festival meets, held over nine weeks, starting in January onwards (*see p142*).

Nad Al Sheba Racing Tour & Godolphin Gallery

336 3666/ www.nadalshebaclub.com. **Open** *Sept-June* from 7am Mon, Wed, Sat. **Tour admission** Dhs130; Dhs60 concessions. **Credit** AmEx, DC, MC, V. **Map** p274 C4.

Take this unique tour for an up-close and personal glimpse into the horse-racing world. After watching the noble beasts training, the tour moves to the clubhouse for a full cooked breakfast. After coffee and questions, it's time for a behind-the-scenes look at the grandstands, jockeys' room, steward's enquiry room and a walk through the trophy-laden Godolphin Gallery – a shrine to the phenomenal success story of Godolphin, Sheikh Mohammed bin Rashid Al Maktoum's international racing operation. The tour takes around four hours, and you must phone in advance to book.

Nad Al Sheba Camel Souk & Racetrack

Map p274 C4.

Opposite the splendour of the horse racecourse you will find a less glamorous, but no less spectacular activity going on: camel racing. Also known as the 'ships of the desert' and prized by locals, camels might have earned a reputation for trudging miles without water in the harshest of environments but

there's nothing plodding about a racing camel. They can reach surprisingly high speeds at full gallop, and some fine specimens are even worth as much as their equine counterparts.

The schedule of camel races is somewhat erratic and hard to come by but the area is worth a visit anyway, since camel training takes place throughout the day and well into the night. The entrance to the track is adjacent to the camel souk, a small cluster of shops selling everything that the camel owner could need. Don't be put off if you are *sans* dromedary – traditional camel blankets make fantastic throws for sofas and racing ropes are superb dog leads. The whole area is a hive of hump-related activity day and night. Trainers follow their charges in 4x4s shouting instructions in guttural Arabic to the young jockeys, and most jockeys are happy to pose for photos (but always ask first to avoid causing offence).

Across the road from the camel racetrack you will find the camel farms. The sand is soft and deep so a 4x4 is essential if you wish to venture into 'Camel Farm Alley' but, if you're properly equipped, it's well worth making the effort. Simply follow the camel trains as they cross the road from the racetrack to see where they live. If you're desperate to see them in full stride, your best chance to watch a race will be when the major meetings take place in the early morning during the Eid holidays (usually in November, and February) – again, you'll need a 4x4 to follow all the action. *See also p142.*

Guided Tours

Let the experts show you the way.

There is lots to see and do beyond the luxury of Dubai's hotels. But if you don't know where to start, or are unwilling to strike out on your own, one of the best ways to experience the emirate of Dubai is to take a tour. Numerous operators run a vast array of organised tours that range from guided city trips to overnight desert camping adventures. While we've recommended reliable tour operators (*see p75*), it's a disappointing fact that many companies in the UAE seem to employ drivers with little local knowledge who are ill-equipped to act as tour guides.

City tours

For a summarised (and air-conditioned) account of the sights of the city, and to ensure that you don't get lost, it's a good idea to take an organised trip. Tour operators run a variety of forays into Dubai, with the general themes being either heritage or shopping. Heritage tours will provide a time-efficient overview of new and old Dubai, taking in the souks, the mosques, Bastakia wind tower houses and the Creek. A shopping tour will combine visits to Dubai's ultra-modern shopping malls with starkly contrasting stops at traditional souks. Shopping tours normally last for half a day and run during the daytime and in the evening.

Few tour operators specialise in any given trip, but rather run various tours of the city as well as more adventurous outbound adventures.

BUS TOURS

The arrival of the **Big Bus Company** (324 4187) in Dubai in 2002 gave the city its own double-deckers from London. As with all the company's tours worldwide, you have the option to hop off at specified points of interest in order to explore in your own time, before catching a subsequent bus to continue your sightseeing journey. There is a live and informative commentary in English on every bus. The distinctive vehicles leave from outside Biella restaurant at **Wafi City** mall (*see p115*) on the hour every hour from 9am to 5pm, seven days a week, all year round. Ticket prices (Dhs75; Dhs45 concessions; Dhs195 families) include entry to the **Dubai Museum** (*see p60*) and **Sheikh Saeed Al Maktoum House** (*see p62*).

Desert tours

The 'absolute must' for all visitors is a trip to the desert. For UAE nationals and resident expatriates the desert is a big playground, a practically unrestricted adventure park in which all are free to frolic. Dune driving and overnight camping trips are popular with those who live in the emirate, for good reason. The desert can be breathtakingly beautiful and there is tremendous fun to be had in the rolling dunes. The high number of 4x4s on UAE roads testify to the fact that most residents spend at least some of their leisure time in the desert. Of course, there is a downside to the freedom that all enjoy in Dubai's deserts: there is no doubt that desert driving is damaging the region's eco-structure. Much of what should be pristine wilderness is heavily littered and, as yet, nothing comprehensive has been done to clean up the mess.

All aboard the **Big Bus Company**.

Arabian adventures: raiders of the lost park.

Most tour operators run a selection of desert safaris, comprising half-day and full-day trips or overnight stays. Experienced desert drivers (some tour companies run their own desert driving schools) will collect you from your hotel in an immaculate 4x4 and whisk you 45 minutes inland. Here, the gold of coastal sands gives way to deep red, originating from the rock of the Hajar mountains that run from north to south across the country.

The desert adventure typically begins close to an outcrop known as **Fossil Rock** that rises above the desert some 30 kilometres (20 miles) from the Dubai–Hatta road. A brief stop allows the driver to deflate the vehicle's tyres (think 'high heels on grass' – fully inflated tyres sink into soft sand, whereas partially deflated ones allow the vehicle to pass over all but the softest surfaces). Your journey will then take you past ramshackle camel and goat farms, over small scrub-covered dunes and into the mountainous ranges of the red desert.

After a rollercoaster ride up and down more demanding dunes, and with heart firmly in mouth (less steadfast stomachs should skip fried breakfast), you will visit a purpose-built Arabic campsite for lunch or dinner and, depending on the length of your tour, traditional Arabic festivities. These are very likely to include belly dancing and the chance to ride a camel – if only for twenty yards or so. It's all good fun, but staged purely for the tourists and the displays bear little resemblance to traditional Emirati life. In fact, the camel handlers are normally Sudanese, while the belly shaking so energetically in front of you is invariably Russian or Lebanese in origin.

Tour operators normally require a minimum of four people to embark on a trip, and will often group couples and individuals together in order to make up the numbers. Typically (with the exception of full-day tours), safaris begin in the afternoon as temperatures drop towards the end of the day. Many overnight safaris will combine a desert tour with a wadi-bashing mountain trip the following morning. Wadis are river beds that are dry for the majority of the year and form wonderfully rugged tracks to follow in your 4x4 – an act known to expats as 'bashing'.

Tour operators

All tour operators offer desert, mountain and wadi, and activity tours. Call for details.

Africa Connection 339 0232.
Arabian Adventures 303 4888.
Arabian Link Tours 572 6666.
Desert Rangers 340 2408.
DTTS 343 2221.
East Adventure Tours 355 5677.
Gulf Ventures 209 5509.
Khasab Tours 266 9950.
Lama Tours 273 2240.
Net Tours 266 6655.
Off-Road Adventures 343 2288.
Planet Travel Tours 282 2199.
Royal Tours 223 1274.
Voyagers Xtreme 345 4504.

Wadis are the UAE's best natural attraction.

In some places pools of water remain all year round and it can even be possible to go swimming in them.

Expect to pay in the region of Dhs350 for an overnight desert safari. Normally all food and beverages are included, but check before you set out. In the UAE you are never far from a main road and mobile phone coverage extends everywhere but the most mountainous areas. Tour groups rarely travel without back-up vehicles too, but it is still wise to take a few precautions. Carry at least a small bottle of water with you and a few basics such as plasters and sunscreen. Long, loose clothing is recommended (long shorts are acceptable for both men and women) and you should take a hat. The most practical headgear is the traditional Arab headdress (*ghutra*), which both protects from the sun and can be wrapped Bedouin-style around your face to keep off blowing sand. If you are staying overnight it's wise to take a sweater as the desert can cool rapidly in the night. To tackle the hot desert sand, opt for boots over flip-flops or sandals.

MOUNTAIN AND WADI TOURS
Towards Dubai's eastern border with Oman lie the Hajar mountains. Frequently referred to as the 'backbone of the Arabian peninsula', this spectacular mountain range runs from the Empty Quarter in Oman across the length of the UAE before rising to its zenith in the north in the Musandam, above the Straits of Hormuz.

Traditionally, Dubai's ruling Al Maktoum family would escape the coastal humidity of the summer in the oasis mountain village of Hatta, close to the Omani border (*see p69*). Today a small and slumbering town, Hatta still boasts some of the most dramatic scenery in the emirate. Storms can lash the mountains at any time of year creating flash floods that turn wadis into raging torrents. Over the centuries, water has carved paths into the limestone and Hatta is perhaps best known for its crystal clear freshwater pools (*see p70*). Mountain and wadi tours explore this charming, desolate region over a full day, with lunch either eaten picnic-style in the mountains or in the Hatta Fort Hotel during the sticky summer months. As with the desert, long, loose clothing is recommended and boots are preferable to beach footwear. Sunscreen and a hat are essential. Expect to pay up to Dhs350 for a mountain and wadi tour including lunch.

ACTIVITY TOURS
Most tour operators also offer supervised activities that allow you to experience the thrill of the desert first-hand. No firm specialises solely in activity tours, but it's worth contacting our recommended operators (*see p75*) to try the bizarre sport of sand-skiing (effectively snowboarding in the desert) or to get the adrenaline pumping by racing a dune buggy against your mates. Some operators will even tailor-make trips to individual requirements.

Eat, Drink, Shop

Restaurants

Variety and innovation are the hallmarks of Dubai's eateries.

The oddest thing about dining in Dubai is how much of it takes place in hotels. As the only booze-licensed buildings in town, they have something of a monopoly on the eat-out scene, and unless you're prepared to forgo a soothing glass of wine with your meal, you'll spend a lot of time swanning through lobbies on your way to dinner. Happily, however, Dubai's aim of becoming a hub of world tourism, combined with its flabbergasting oil wealth, means that the city's hotels are ploughing vast resources into creating original, innovative restaurants.

Competition is unbelievably fierce: the city already has 35 five-star hotels, and 2004 should see them joined by the world's first underwater hotel, the world's tallest hotel and Palm Island, a manmade leisure behemoth and home to endless new eateries. All this construction hands the power to the customers – you'll find that you can afford to eat in incredibly luxurious settings and not feel the pinch too much.

It also means that in order to succeed, new restaurants have to do something a bit different: whereas five years ago, hotels would roll out a franchised, faceless Italian, Lebanese and Japanese outlet and have done with it, they

now have to be far more adventurous to survive. These days you can now get hold of almost any cuisine, from Singaporean to Filipino and from Tunisian to Vietnamese. The one rather gaping deficiency is in local food – Emirati cuisine is not widely available outside the homes of UAE nationals. Although the national dish is whole baked lamb or camel, in a country where the vast majority of the population are expats, Iranian *baba ganouj* and Keralan biryanis are far more widely consumed. Vegetarian restaurants are also hard to come by in Dubai – while vegetarian food is available in most places, a veg-only outlet is yet to open.

Despite not being able to serve booze, independent restaurants still flourish in Dubai. Steer clear of the affluent beach communities of Jumeirah and head to downtown Bur Dubai and Deira and you can eat yourself silly for a pittance. Indian and Pakistani curry houses abound, serving delightful street food in spartan settings, and you can pick up a freshly sliced *shoarma* (a spicy chicken doner kebab) for mere peanuts at any roadside grill. European-style cafés are also mushrooming, especially among the high towers, bright lights and fast-food joints of the Sheikh Zayed Road.

Practicalities and payment

In this chapter, we have split the restaurants up by area (Bur Dubai, Deira, and Jumeirah, which covers Jumeirah Beach Road and the so-called 'golden mile' of beach hotels starting at the Burj Al Arab). We've also divided them by broad cuisine categories (for a more detailed breakdown, *see p101* **Restaurants by cuisine**) and have included the 'average' price of a meal. This is the typical price of a three-course dinner for two with drinks: a glass of house wine per person if the restaurant is licensed, a glass of juice if it isn't.

You'll find that all restaurants have air-conditioning, and that in fine-dining restaurants dress codes are laxer than in many Arab and Western countries. While you won't be welcome in shorts and a T-shirt in the top-end restaurants, only the Burj Al Arab demands that jackets and no jeans be worn

at dinner. Reservations are essential when eating in hotels, both because popular restaurants get incredibly oversubscribed and because they have an annoying habit of changing their opening hours on a near-weekly basis.

During Ramadan (which normally falls in the month of November; *see p31 and p140*), you'll find that restaurants aren't open for lunch and many have different opening times in the evenings. You will, however, be able to indulge in the pleasures of *Iftar*, the fast-breaking tents where expats and locals congregate to eat meze, nibble dates, olug back coffee and puff on *shishas* over a game or two of backgammon. Wherever and whenever you eat in Dubai, don't forget to tip: 10-15 per cent is standard, and in many restaurants the waiting staff will receive all profits from cigarette sales.

Arabic

Awtar

Grand Hyatt Dubai, Oud Metha Road (317 1234).
Open 12.30-3pm, 7.30pm-3am Sun-Thur. **Average**
Dhs250. **Credit** AmEx, DC, MC, V. **Map** p277 K3.
Barbecued meat is the house aroma at Awtar. The
scent of smoking wood and flame-grilled lamb hits
you the moment you enter and works your hunger
to fever pitch in seconds. The decor is reminiscent
of an ultra-lavish Bedouin tent: opulence and Arabic
style spiral out from the swathes of lush fabric to
the vibrantly coloured glass lanterns. Plough
through fresh meze: hot chicken livers in sassy
lemon-infused sauce, deep-fried cheese, white bean
salad and spicy sausages are all impeccable. The
tender chops and *shish taouk* (marinated chicken
kebab) also hit the spot.

Damyati

Opposite Little Hut, Karama (396 5280). **Open**
7.30-11am, 1pm-1am daily. **Average** Dhs50.
No credit cards. **Map** p277 K3.
Damyati is a cheapskate carnivore's paradise and a
well-guarded secret among grill devotees. Forget
such luxuries as a menu or cutlery, it's not that kind
of place. However, the *shoarma*, kebabs and lamb
chops are mouth-wateringly marinated, and the
falafel scarily moreish. Complimentary pickles, houmous, salad and bread are thrown in, and you'll
emerge with change from Dhs20.

Fakhreldine

Mövenpick Hotel Bur Dubai, 19th Street (336 6000).
Open noon-3pm, 6pm-3am daily. **Average** Dhs250.
Credit AmEx, MC, V. **Map** p277 J3.
This modern restaurant concept has come to Dubai
from the UK: named after Prince Fakhreldine II, it's
London's best-known and most popular Lebanese
restaurant. The decor in Dubai's version is stunning,
an astonishing mix of classic and contemporary.
Take a seat on the huge cushions in the *majlis* area
or in a cosy booth and get stuck into topnotch
Lebanese cuisine (be sure to order some charcoal-
grilled kebabs) to the sound of live entertainment.

Fatafeet

Al Seef Road (397 9222). **Open** 7.30pm-2am daily.
Average Dhs100. **Credit** AmEx, DC, MC, V.
Map p279 J4.
This open-air eaterie on the creekside lays on a huge
number of Egyptian classics. Try the stuffed roast
pigeons, delicious fish tajen stew and the 'tarb', a
plate of delicately spiced lamb sausages. A round
of thick *manaeesh* unleavened bread topped with
melted cheese and some *fatafeet foul* (a garlicky,
beany mix) are also mandatory. Round off with
flaky *fiteer mishaltit* bread, filled with cream and
covered in bitter-sweet honey. Wash it all down with
mugs of *sahlab*, a sweet custard-like drink with nuts,
and puff on *shisha* as the dhows float by. Bliss.

Marrakech

Shangri-La Hotel, Sheikh Zayed Road (343 8888).
Open 1-3pm, 8pm-12.30am daily. **Average** Dhs380.
Credit AmEx, DC, MC, V. **Map** p283 F12.
From the low armchairs, booths and fountain to the
crockery and beaten-metal serving dishes, the
Marrakech is elegantly themed around whites, blues
and silvers, and the food is generally blessed with
the light touch too. The menu features the usual
selection of soups, salads, *bastilla* (flaky pastry pies),
couscous and tagines, but has made concessions to
fish-friendly Dubai – hammour (the local version of
cod), grilled and otherwise, makes a regular appearance, and fishy *bastilla al bahra* – easily enough for
two – is packed with rustic, citrus flavour. Dishes of
carrot, roasted aubergine with preserved lemon and
melt-in-the-mouth lentils all have a garlicky, tangy
tone that give the taste buds a wake-up call.

Al Nafoorah

*Emirates Towers Shopping Boulevard, Sheikh Zayed
Road (330 0000).* **Open** noon-3pm, 7.30-midnight
daily. **Average** Dhs250. **Credit** AmEx, DC, MC, V.
Map p276 H4.
This is unquestionably one of the best Lebanese
restaurants in the emirate. After nibbling on pista-
chios, iced almonds and deliciously acidulated carrot,
get stuck into some unstoppably good meze: a purée
of roasted garlic potatoes, houmous with warm
pine kernels, tangy *labneh* yoghurt and chicken
livers with pomegranate sauce. The *shish taouk* is
the finest in town and the dessert stands, filled with
green dates and honey, fresh fruit and Arabic
sweets, are divine.

Olive House: Lebanese nibbles. *See p81.*

Olive House

Tower No.1, Sheikh Zayed Road, opposite Emirates Towers (343 3110). **Open** 9am-1am daily. **Average** Dhs80. **No credit cards. Map** p283 F12.

A glass-fronted café with a small delicatessen and bakery counter, Olive House is a cosmopolitan hangout combining low prices with sophisticated Leb-Med cuisine. It's got a loyal coterie of professional loungers and office workers and becomes so popular in winter that it has to colonise the adjacent pavement space. The menu is a well-planned mix of salads, pizzas and grills: before any orders arrive, hot pouches of bread turn up with helpings of soft cheese, oily black tapenade and sun-dried tomato paste. Avoid ruining your appetite on the freebies: it would be a travesty to miss out on the chicken and beef kebabs, dunked in houmous, *moutabel* and lashings of chilli sauce.

Al Tannour

Crowne Plaza Hotel, Sheikh Zayed Road (331 1111). **Open** 8.30pm-3am daily. **Average** Dhs250 before 11pm; after 11pm Dhs220 minimum charge per person (set menu & entertainment included). **Credit** AmEx, MC, V. **Map** p281 G10.

If you're looking for an authentic meal with live entertainment, we advise a late-night trip to this Lebanese eaterie at the Crowne Plaza. Ignore the odd entrance hall and make your way to the fourth floor, where a huge restaurant and moderately friendly welcome await you. Enjoy fresh bread cooked over the saj, tabouleh full of crunchy ground wheat and lemon, rounds of halloumi cheese and lightly fried lamb's brain. Round it all off with plenty of kebabs while the belly-dancing kicks in.

European

The Exchange

Fairmont Hotel, Sheikh Zayed Road (332 5555). **Open** 7pm-1am daily. **Average** Dhs500. **Credit** AmEx, DC, MC, V. **Map** p281 G9.

The Exchange's design is a little frosty, and the refined atmosphere is perhaps more conducive to genteel muttering than to convivial chat, but it has established itself as a home of fine steak. The 200g (7oz) filets mignons are well aged, seasoned to perfection and come with a choice of ten mustards. The regular sampling menus are extremely good value.

Links

Nad al Sheba Club, off the Dubai–Al Ain road (336 3666). **Open** 6-10pm Sat-Thur. **Average** Dhs270. **Credit** AmEx, DC, MC, V. **Map** p274 C4.

An outdoor restaurant at the world-famous Nad al Sheba Club, where on race nights world-class horses thunder by as you dine. The salad buffet is the only starter on offer, and although limited, the selection is fabulous: *pipirade* salad of roasted vegetables with whole cloves of divinely smooth garlic, a self-assembly Caesar salad with bags of parmesan, Waldorf salad with massive chunks of apple and not a limp leaf in sight. Then move on to the main focus of juicy

The best Restaurants

For creekside eating
Fatafeet (*see p80*) for roast pigeon; **The Boardwalk** (*see p89*) for European snacks; and the **Al Mansour Dhow** (*see p88*) if you want to eat on the creek in a big old boat.

For romantic meals
Verre (*see p92*) for a taste of Gordon Ramsay's finest; **Vivaldi** (*see p92*) for excellent Italian food; and the **Beach Bar & Grill** (*see p97*) for beachside views.

For fresh fish
Peppercrab (*see p85*) for Singaporean dishes; **Sea World** (*see p82*) for pick 'n' mix fish and a view; **Sammach** (*see p96*) for cheap, Lebanese-style food; and **Al Mahara** (*see p97*) if you've got money to burn.

For budget eats
The Chalet (*see p96*) for Arabic; **Damyati** (*see p80*) for Egyptian; and **India House** (*see p87*) for, erm, Indian.

For crazy flavours
Indochine (*see p83*), a top Vietnamese spot; **Eau Zone** (*see p99*) for Asian fusion; or **Trader Vic's** (*see p87*), a Polynesian joint.

For beautiful views
Vu's (*see p82*) on the 50th floor at the Emirates Towers; and **Al Dawaar** (*see p88*) for 360-degree views over Deira.

For boozy dinners
All-you-can-eat-and-drink deals are on offer at **Spice Island** (*see p92*) at the Renaissance Dubai; and the **Market Place** (*see p91*) at the JW Marriott Hotel.

and tender fillet steaks and melt-in-your-mouth Hokubee tenderloins. These fabulous hunks of top-quality meat arrive plain and char-grilled with a choice of sauces: hollandaise with mint, red wine sauce sweetened with raisins, and chickpea purée. Polish them off with a cheery paper cone of crunchy roasted new potatoes and finish things off with a decent helping of sweet and tangy apple crumble.

Medzo

Wafi Pyramids at Wafi City mall, off Oud Metha Road (324 0000). **Open** 12.30-3pm, 7.30-11pm daily. **Average** Dhs250. **Credit** AmEx, DC, MC, V. **Map** p277 J3.

Dining on the terrace of Medzo is a decidedly post-modern experience. Thanks to the joys of globalisation you can enjoy Italian haute cuisine served by

Eat, Drink, Shop

a French-speaking Filipino waiter at a table surrounded by faux Egyptian artefacts. In contrast to the hotchpotch surroundings the food is an exercise in subtle harmony. Pasta is Medzo's forte, and though it doesn't always get it 100 per cent right, it packs in enough jaw-to-the-floor dishes (check out the chilli linguine with sautéed garlic prawns and lime) to make it a lasting favourite.

Il Rustico

Rydges Plaza Hotel, Satwa roundabout, Satwa (398 2222). **Open** noon-3pm, 6pm-midnight daily. **Average** Dhs200. **Credit** AmEx, DC, MC, V. **Map** p281 F8.

A snug, low-lit place with a wood-burning pizza oven offering hearty soul food at extremely reasonable prices. Their cheese-packed tortellinis and carbonaras are guaranteed to put you in a good mood, and the comfy settings are conducive to long-drawn-out chats over espressos and shots of grappa.

Sea World

Above Safestway supermarket, Sheikh Zayed Road (321 1500). **Open** noon-3.30pm, 7pm-midnight Sat-Wed; noon-midnight Thur, Fri. **Average** Dhs300. **Credit** AmEx, MC, V. **Map** p283 D15.

This bright, spotless, 500-seat restaurant's claim to fame is the huge 'market' of fresh fish and seafood on ice along one end. An elegant waitress with a small shopping trolley will help you to select fish, veg, cooking style and sauces. The food is good enough to tempt you back, but a little overpriced for an unlicensed establishment.

Vu's

Emirates Towers Hotel, Sheikh Zayed Road (330 0000). **Open** 12.30-2.45pm, 7.30-11.15pm daily. **Average** Dhs500. **Credit** AmEx, DC, MC, V. **Map** p276 H4.

The view from the 50th floor of Emirates Towers is staggering. All the tables look out to sea, and nothing obscures your outlook over Satwa, Jumeirah and Umm Suqiem. Far to the right is Deira, and on a crystal-clear day you can even see Sharjah. The food has always had an immaculate fine-dining pedigree and under the new award-winning chef, Nancy Kinchela, it just keeps getting better. Round off your evening at the bar on the floor above (*see p170*).

Western Steak House

Crowne Plaza Hotel, Sheikh Zayed Road (331 1111). **Open** noon-3pm, 7-11.30pm daily. **Average** Dhs500. **Credit** AmEx, DC, MC, V. **Map** p281 G10.

In a cosy corner of the Crowne Plaza, manned by attentive if somewhat over-zealous staff, the Western Steak House is an excellent venue for a night of carnivorous indulgence. It stakes its reputation on the quality of its meat and the menu is varied enough to satisfy the most adventurous of steak connoisseurs. Try the tournedos rossini, topped with duck liver and mushrooms, bursting with husky juices and pepped up with a *périgourdine* sauce.

Far Eastern

Benjarong

Dusit Hotel, Sheikh Zayed Road (343 3333). **Open** 7-11pm daily. **Average** Dhs300. **Credit** MC, V. **Map** p276 I14.

Serenity rules at Benjarong: all the rage of Sheikh Zayed Road is left at the door and any remaining personal stress surely dissolves as you enter the dark, temple-like interior. Pretty wooden pillars inlaid with mother-of-pearl frame a small stage where traditional dancers perform. By the time your cocktail-filled pineapples and melons have arrived,

Know your meze
Make like a local with kibbeh and foul.

Along with kebabs and biryanis, Arabic cuisine in the Gulf is heavily reliant on meze, bite-sized snacks brought in endless waves and accompanied by freshly cooked bread. Lebanese, Iranian and Egyptian menus are dotted with worrying items such as brain sandwich and raw tongue, which may deter the less courageous. If you want to advance beyond houmous and falafel but avoid anything too adventurous, get stuck into some of the following:

Fatayer – small fried pastry parcels, often filled with spinach

Fattoush – a green salad made with strips of toasted pitta bread and vinegar dressing

Foul medames – a piquant mix of fava beans, olive oil, garlic, red onions, tomato and hot pepper

Halloumi – delicious cheese made of lamb and goat's milk. It's often seared for a charcoal taste and has what can only be described as a 'squeaky' texture

Kibbeh – small balls made of minced lamb and wheat, crisp on the outside and crumbly within

Labneh – minted yoghurt

Manakish – discs of bread baked with cheese

Moutabel – a puréed aubergine mix

Sambousik – flaky pastries filled with oozing cheese or tart spinach

Tabbouleh – a parsley salad with ground wheat and lemon juice

Hoi An: Franco-Vietnamese heaven.

a state of Thai tranquillity is pretty much guaranteed. Staples like *tom yam goong* and beef green curry are all flawless and the crispy crayfish salad, dressed and mixed with green mango at the table, is a flavour-, scent- and texture-teaser.

ET Sushi

Emirates Towers Hotel, Sheikh Zayed Road (330 0000). **Open** 12.30-3pm, 7.30pm-midnight daily. **Average** Dhs200. **Credit** AmEx, DC, MC, V. **Map** p276 H4.

At 12.30pm on the dot a sushi carousel fires into life, trundling round dispensing its colour-coded wares, from yellow plates of crab stick at Dhs9 through to black platters of freshwater eel at Dhs28. Slurp on icy fruit drinks such as pineapple shakes while you swipe plastic-hatted saucers filled with maki and sushi from the rolling display. Giant seaweed-lined rounds of sweet omelette, slabs of succulent reddish-pink tuna and wonderful spicy salmon and avocado wraps all score highly. For those in need of less fishy fare, a la carte offerings include a mean chicken teriyaki and super-refreshing soba noodles.

Ginseng

Wafi Pyramids at Wafi City mall, off Oud Metha Road (324 4777). **Open** 7pm-1am daily. **Average** Dhs250. **Credit** AmEx, DC, MC, V. **Map** p277 J3.

Hip and contemporary, Ginseng is lounge, bar (*see p164*) and restaurant all in one. The space is small and the decor has that minimal look that you know

must have cost a fortune to achieve. Exotic fusion cocktails and Asian tapas are the name of the game: try thick wedges of *aloo tikki* potato cake dunked in cooling yoghurt, sticks of shrimp roll zipped through spice-studded dip, and moreish goat's cheese samosas. The perfect warm-up before a night throwing shapes at the Planetarium club next door.

Hoi An

Shangri-La Hotel, Sheikh Zayed Road (343 8888). **Open** 7.30pm-1am daily. **Average** Dhs400. **Credit** AmEx, DC, MC, V. **Map** p283 F12.

Hoi An's menu is a wily combination of Vietnamese and classic French styles. Barring major seafood allergies, you should get some Dungeness crab, a super-subtle blend with seams of exotic flavour served in green bamboo tubes. When it comes to picking mains, the smart money's on an order of wok-cooked beef tournedos. Served in a rustic French casserole pot, the cognac-marinated meat is tear-jerkingly good and layered with sweet onions, watercress and spice to deliver a sophisticated thump to the palate. Round off with an orange filled with kaffir lime mousse: exquisite.

Indochine

Grand Hyatt Hotel, Oud Metha Road (317 1234). **Open** 7pm-midnight Tue-Sun. **Average** Dhs350. **Credit** MC, V. **Map** p277 K3.

Trip down the curving slate steps of the Grand Hyatt foyer, through a vast crop of lanky trees and outlandish shrubbery, and you'll hit Indochine, a beautifully decorated Vietnamese joint filled with light lacquered wood and Asian knick-knacks. Nibble on rice crackers slathered in soy, hot sauce and unfeasibly moreish chicken dip before hitting the intriguing menu, which bulges with wonderful dishes and exotic ingredients, from lotus root to cotton fish and papaya to banana flower.

Lemongrass

Next to Lamcy Plaza mall, Oud Metha (334 2325). **Open** noon-11.30pm daily. **Average** Dhs200. **Credit** MC, V. **Map** p277 J3.

This beautiful, bright, contemporary Thai restaurant with attitude is an independent establishment, and it shows – the all-Thai staff are more attentive and the decor quirkier than at many hotel-bound joints. Lemongrass also has the massive advantage of being open from noon to midnight so if you get a Thai food craving mid-afternoon, it's on hand to help. Special highlights include the *tod man talay* fish cakes, the whole deep-fried hammour and the lemongrass juice, a clear, sweet, orchid-topped drink, the liquid equivalent of a Turkish delight.

Noodle House

Emirates Towers Boulevard mall, Sheikh Zayed Road (330 0000). **Open** noon-midnight daily. **Average** Dhs150. **Credit** AmEx, DC, MC, V. **Map** p276 H4.

Noodle House is a slice of cosmopolitan chic in the slickest building in town. It's perfect for a lunch date: the noise, bustle and super-fast service will minimise

Eat, Drink, Shop

Who am I getting all dressed up for?

those embarrassing gaps in conversation and the communal tables lend the place an easy, ice-breaking kind of atmosphere. Whizz through the tick 'n' mix pad and order both of you some moreish Thai chicken with cashew nuts, a portion of Shanghai beef noodles and a sturdy helping of Cantonese duck with all the hoisin trimmings.

Peppercrab

Grand Hyatt Hotel, Oud Metha Road (317 1234).
Open 7pm-midnight Sat, Mon, Tue, Fri; 7pm-1am Wed, Thur. **Average** Dhs500. **Credit** AmEx, DC, MC, V. **Map** p277 K3.
Fish-heads rejoice: Peppercrab is a place of inspired piscine creation where you can soothe your meat-weary soul. It's notionally a Singaporean joint and offers not only fantastic, innovative food, but also a charming setting both inside and out. The menu's an exhilarating read and main courses of crustaceans and fish are plucked directly from the tank. Start off with a light, fluffy omelette, stuffed with cooked oysters, and move on to the house speciality, 1.5kg (some 3lb) of mud crab in hot sauce: get your hands messy digging out the soft white meat before digging into a whole spiced hammour.

Sakura

Crowne Plaza Hotel, Sheikh Zayed Road (331 1111).
Open 7pm-midnight daily. **Average** Dhs300. **Credit** AmEx, DC, MC, V. **Map** p281 G10.
Sakura was an early bird on Dubai's five-star Asian restaurant circuit; in the noughties, it's beginning to look a little tired around the edges. The restaurant is stylish, but all that shiny monochrome lacquer and pop muzak is just, well, sooo '80s. However, come teppanyaki time, it springs into life: the hot-plate chef gets into some serious Tom-Cruise-in-*Cocktail*-style antics with spatulas and eggs, and knocks up piles of tossed and seared prawns, hammour and lobster tail, not to mention delicious fresh-fried rice and sizzling hunks of sliced beef, all for a set meal price of Dhs125.

Shang Palace

Shangri-La Hotel, Sheikh Zayed Road (343 8888).
Open 12.30-3pm, 8pm-midnight daily. **Credit** AmEx, DC, MC, V. **Average** Dhs400. **Map** p283 F12.
Diners can choose between an inner sanctum of tables, shielded by a wall of antiques and a tornado of gold roses, or a place on the main balcony overlooking the foyer below. The chef hails from Hong Kong and lays on *echt* Chinese food. This is sometimes good: nail-on-the-head hits include beancurd with spring onion and crunchy nuggets of fried shrimp, strips of honey-sweet Shanghainese smoked fish and on-the-bone wedges of tender roast pigeon. Avoid the 'fujian' fried rice, however – it's heaped with a fishy, beefy sauce that's authentic but utterly underwhelming.

Teatro

Towers Rotana Hotel, Sheikh Zayed Road (343 8000). **Open** 6.30pm-2am daily. **Average** Dhs300. **Credit** AmEx, DC, MC, V. **Map** p276 H4.

The fame game

Dubai has an increasingly exciting food scene: as Gordon Ramsay said on a recent trip over, 'There's no shadow of a doubt that Dubai can become a culinary hub like Paris or London in the next five to ten years.' He does admittedly have a vested interest in bigging-up the place – his **Verre** restaurant (*see p92*) is among the best fine-dining establishments in town, and regulars at Pétrus and Claridge's often pop in for dinner on their Middle Eastern junkets.

Ramsay is by no means the only celebrity chef with links to Dubai: Michel Rostang, the double Michelin-starred owner of some of the best bistros in Paris, has set up the excellent **Café Chic** (*see p89*) at the Meridien Dubai, and Freddie Forster, another big gun, holds court at the Royal Mirage. Ken Hom and Gary Rhodes both come over for regular cheffing jaunts, and sommeliers such as Jancis Robinson and Oz Clarke are helping to promote the burgeoning wine market.

Home-grown celebrities are also starting to emerge in Dubai. First among these is John Wood, the executive chef at the **Burj Al Arab** (*see pp97-8*), who is emerging as something of a media darling. Endless involvement with magazines and public events have made him a well-known local figure, and rumours abound of a move into international television shows and product launches in the near future. Jamie Oliver beware…

Teatro is one of Dubai's favourite fusion restaurants, and reliably excellent if you're looking for some intriguing flavour combinations. The kitchen, sushi bar, bar and well-stocked wine cellar are artfully integrated into the dining area and the chef takes centre stage, conducting his culinary orchestra: a Western kitchen to his left, an Eastern kitchen to his right. An unusual but exciting mix of food is prepared in the clay tandoor, the wok, the wood-burning pizza oven, the lavastone grill, the rotisserie and the Chinese smoke oven.

Thai Chi

Wafi Pyramids at Wafi City mall, off Oud Metha Road (324 4100). **Open** 12.30-3pm, 7.30pm-midnight daily. **Average** Dhs275. **Credit** AmEx, DC, MC, V. **Map** p277 J3.
Two restaurants – Thai and Chinese – have come together under one roof at Thai Chi, each with its own distinct interior: bamboo decoration for the casual Chinese area and a more formal, traditional

Shang Palace, home of rigorously authentic Chinese food. *See p85.*

setting for the Thai dining room. The glass noodle salad with raw chilli spice and zesty lime juice is an artful creation, and the stir-fried crab, roughly chopped in a sweet and spicy curry with (believe it or not) scrambled eggs, satisfies at ten different levels. The sticky coconut rice pudding is another lick-the-plate-clean winner.

Yo! Sushi

BurJuman Centre, Trade Centre Road (359 5479). **Open** noon-11pm Sat-Wed; 2pm-midnight Thur, Fri. **Average** Dhs110. **Credit** AmEx, DC, MC, V. **Map** p279 J5.

Despite a less than edifying location – backing on to the Bur Juman car park, with lines of 4x4s clearly visible through the glass – this turquoise-beamed space is pretty, and filled with hustling waiters in branded caps and aprons. Settling into a trackside booth, you can order an unlimited soda at Dhs5 or bottomless egg-cups of green tea for only Dhs3. Pluck soba noodles with green and purple pickles, immaculate hand-rolls, top-notch *edamame* and *nigiri* directly from the circling conveyor belt. The freshly cooked katsu and teriyaki, however, are far less impressive.

Zheng He's

Mina A' Salam Hotel, Al Sufouh Road (366 8888). **Open** noon-3pm, 7-11.30pm daily. **Average** Dhs400. **Credit** AmEx, DC, MC, V. **Map** p274 A4.

Sitting above the ludicrously pretty manmade harbour of the Mina A'Salam with its gliding electric dhows and views out over the Arabian Gulf beyond, Zheng's offers some of the finest Chinese food this side of Shanghai. Try the authentic selection of dim sum – melt-in-the-mouth scallop numbers packed with fresh flavour, fabulous crystal shrimp dumplings and juicy pork and pak choy dumplings – and

follow with an excellent half of Beijing duck with all the trimmings. You'll shell out for the experience (expect to pay big if you want to splash out on fresh seafood or multiple main course dishes) but it's worth every last fils.

Indian

Asha's

Wafi Pyramids at Wafi City mall, off Oud Metha Road (324 0000). **Open** 12.30-3pm, 7.30pm-12.30am daily. **Average** Dhs300. **Credit** AmEx, DC, MC, V. **Map** p277 J3.

This ultra-successful Indian restaurant is the brainchild of the singer Asha Bhosle, and three distinct cuisines are on offer – traditional fare, contemporary fusion, and Ms Bhosle's personal favourites. The food is excellent: try the *murg biryani awadh*, stuffed with dried fruit and nuts and cooked with basmati rice, and the seared red snapper with garam masala. In wintertime, the terrace is idyllic.

Bikanervala

Behind Bombay Chowpatty in Karama (396 3666). **Open** 9.30am-midnight Sat-Thur; 9-11.30am, 1.30pm-midnight Fri. **Average** Dhs50. **Credit** AmEx, DC, MC, V. **Map** p277 J2.

The diners at Bikanervala are not particularly worried about the oddball service and lamentable aircon. They come for a taste of home: the *chatpatta* taste of Rajasthan, crammed with roadside faves such as *raj kachori, bhalla papri* and *papri chaat*. These *chaat* combinations (small papadis, corn kachoris and lentil vadas topped with hot and sweet chutneys, potatoes and masala) are beautifully, authentically rendered, and should be rounded off with some pancakey *malpua*.

Coconut Grove

Rydges Plaza Hotel, Satwa roundabout, Satwa (398 3800). **Open** noon-3pm, 7pm-1am daily. **Average** Dhs60. **Credit** AmEx, DC, MC, V. **Map** p281 F8.

If you crave comfort, quiet and Keralan food then Coco Grove is your place. Located on the ninth floor of Rydges Plaza, it offers leisurely service and bird's-eye views over Satwa. Load up on freshly cooked appam pancakes, thick-gravied meen made with tamarind, coconut-milk fish *moilee* steamed and dosa rolls stuffed with spicy vegetable sambar. Wash it down with kurumba punch made with lime, mint and honey, and your bill will still be laughably petite.

Delhi Darbar

Opposite the post office, Karama (334 7171). **Open** 8am-1am Sat-Thur; 7.30-11.30am, 1.30-3.30pm Fri. **Average** Dhs40. **No credit cards. Map** p277 J2.

Delhi Darbar is the classic Indian cheap eat. It's slightly more upmarket than other local curry houses, and boy do the prices reflect this: delicious vegetable dishes such as palak paneer and malai kofta come in at a whacking Dhs7.50 and mutton kadai at Dhs9.50. Even with naan and rice, you're unlikely to hit the Dhs20 mark. The chicken tikka masala (Dhs13.50), rivals the Fairmont Hotel's version, which costs four times as much. The dahl is intriguing, packed with all sorts of beans and lentils, including a tiny black variety that pop in your mouth.

India House

Al Fahidi Street (352 6006). **Open** 7am-1am Sat-Thur; 7.30-11.30am, 1.30pm-12.30am Fri. **Average** Dhs50. **No credit cards. Map** p278 H4.

One of the few restaurants on Al Fahidi Street in the Bur Dubai electronics souk (halfway down, next to Choitram Supermarket, opposite Sheeba Electronics), India House is one of the finest and cheapest Indian restaurants in the city. In among the extraordinary range of dosas, puris and individual Punjabi dishes, it is the thali that is king. Efficient waiters repeatedly fill your seven (Dhs7) or eleven (Dhs13) stainless steel dishes of gorgeous curries, piping hot puri, rice and sweets until you can eat no more. Accept no substitute.

Mohanlal's Taste Buds

Behind the Karama fish market (336 2001). **Open** 12.30-3pm, 7-11.30pm daily. **Average** Dhs100. **Credit** MC, V. **Map** p277 J2.

Its location, combined with the traditionally fish-heaviness of Keralan cuisine means seafood dishes are in the majority at Mohanlal's. Only an ultra-greedy or chronically short-sighted diner could describe the opening dishes as 'starters'. Try out a massive helping of spicy prawns, a handsome, slow-cooked dish dressed in roasted chilli paste and spice, and follow up with an equally ogre-sized helping of tandoori pomfret, a subtly flavoured pair of marinated fish. The fish *moilee,* awash with coconut milk and sweetened by a sturdy helping of *idiappam,* is also a winner.

Ravi's

Satwa High Street (331 5353). **Open** 5am-3am daily. **Average** Dhs60. **No credit cards. Map** p281 F8.

Craig David's favourite Dubaian curry house is one of the cheapest in the city and well-loved by expats in search of a discount spice-fest. It offers straightforward tandoori dishes with lashings of dal, biryani and nan to back them up, all freshly made to order in the tiny open kitchen. Sit on garden furniture outside or in the super-spartan interior and eat yourself silly for next to nothing.

International

Manhattan Grill

Grand Hyatt Hotel, Oud Metha Road (317 1234). **Open** 7pm-midnight Sun, Mon-Fri. **Average** Dhs680. **Credit** AmEx, DC, MC, V. **Map** p277 K3.

Manhattan Grill lands a killer blow when it comes to hunks of sizzling Nebraska cow. The interior nods towards the downtown 1950s diner, with red leather banquettes filling one wall, but otherwise the Grill's style is totally uptown – all aluminium shelving, open kitchens, wine-filled glass cabinets and stiff white tablecloths. For sheer indulgence, order the monolithic tenderloin, with sides of sautéed mushrooms, creamed spinach, garlic mash and roasted root vegetables.

Trader Vic's

Crowne Plaza Hotel, Sheikh Zayed Road (331 1111). **Open** noon-3pm, 7-11pm Sat-Thur; 7-11pm Fri. **Average** Dhs300. **Credit** AmEx, DC, MC, V. **Map** p281 G10.

Upmarket curry house **Asha's.** *See p86.*

Eat, Drink, Shop

Ravi's, popular for its cheap and cheerful curries. *See p87.*

A wood-lined Polynesian haunt adorned with voodoo statues and model boats. While the food can be variable, the cocktails and mocktails remain outstanding at any time. We prescribe Samoan fogcutters all round and some nibbles: a couple of platters filled with mozzarella balls, lamb slices and barbecued chicken should do the trick. If you stick around for mains, the ragout of snails in creamy peppercorn sauce is worth a punt. *See also p170.*

Deira

Arabic

Al Dawaar
Hyatt Regency Hotel, Deira Corniche (209 1100). **Open** 12.30-3pm, 7-11pm daily. **Average** Dhs320. **Credit** AmEx, MC, V. **Map** p279 J1.
Dubai's only revolving restaurant is getting a little old (the Hyatt Regency was built in 1980) but remains impressive: a full revolution takes a little under two hours and is a spectacular way to view Dubai from 25 storeys above the Creek. A different Dhs160 deal is served every night, and the international mix (Arabic, Mediterranean, Japanese) is a cut above most buffet spreads.

Al Mansour Dhow
InterContinental Hotel, Beniyas Road (222 7171). **Sails** 1.30pm, 8.30pm daily. **Average** Dhs330. **Credit** AmEx, DC, MC, V. **Map** p279 J3.
This big, pretty, happily licensed boat cruises off on regular dinner voyages, sculling down as far as the gold souk before turning back to Maktoum bridge. At nighttime, the river is utterly beautiful, and the

would justify the fare on its own: the run-of-the-mill international buffet is just the icing on the cake. After dinner, soak up the stunning views over a post-prandial *shisha* pipe. Don't even think of booking a cruise in the summer months, though, unless you're keen on nibbling in a waterborne sauna.

Al Mawal
Al Bustan Rotana Hotel, Casablanca Road, Garhoud (282 6530). **Open** 12.30-3.30pm, 8pm-12.30am daily. **Average** Dhs300. **Credit** AmEx, DC, MC, V. **Map** p277 K2.
Alive with evocative music, gyrating bellies and masses of revellers clouded in a sweet *shisha* haze, Al Mawal has a deservedly great reputation. The waiters love a bit of showmanship, the tabouleh is vibrant and piquant, and the mixed grill impressive. The food is excellent; flavours are fresh and linger in the mind for days. The pricing is very reasonable for food of this calibre, and the entertainment certainly draws in the crowds.

Al Mijana
Le Meridien Dubai, Airport Road, Garhoud (282 4040). **Open** 12.30-3pm, 8-11.30pm daily. **Average** Dhs300. **Credit** AmEx, DC, MC, V. **Map** p277 L2.
A high-end home to the best of Lebanese cuisine. Al Mijana's menu is split into three set sections, each of which houses more food than your local supermarket. Service is uniformly superb, with a barrage of helpful and amusing waiting staff more than happy to guide you through the maze of meze on offer. The highlight of the cold dishes is the *kibbeh nayee*, an emulsified paste of the freshest raw lamb and burghul wheat – the meat dissolves beautifully on the tongue, leaving a satisfying tang.

Shahrzad

Hyatt Regency Hotel, Deira Corniche (209 1200).
Open 12.30-3pm, 8pm-midnight Sun-Fri. **Average**
Dhs300. **Credit** AmEx, DC, MC, V. **Map** p279 J1.
A Persian restaurant, beautifully decked out with
carved wooden screens, patterned walls, Iranian
rugs and stunning copper lamps. The open-plan
kitchen, with a traditional tandoor oven and charcoal grill under a beaten copper canopy, adds extra
ambience and fabulous smells to the restaurant. Top
meze, bread cooked fresh and delivered to the table
by the in-house baker, beautiful stews and kebabs
all hit the spot.

European

The Aquarium

*Dubai Creek Golf & Yacht Club, Garhoud Road (295
6000).* **Open** 12.30-3pm, 7.30-11pm Sat-Thur;
11.30am-3pm, 7.30-11pm Fri. **Average** Dhs500.
Credit AmEx, DC, MC, V. **Map** p277 K3.
The Aquarium has the feel of an elaborately decorated watchtower. This thick-carpeted glasshouse
of leaning metal columns looks out at the Creek and
down over the heads and sloped shoulders of diners
at the Boardwalk (*see below*). The Aquarium's major
attraction is the vast tube of gleaming blue water,
where schools of yellow-finned tiddlers scull their
way round. As you'd expect, seafood rules here and
you'll be won over by the dazzling array of à la carte
fish on offer.

The Boardwalk

*Dubai Creek Golf & Yacht Club, Garhoud Road (295
6000).* **Open** 8am-midnight daily. **Average** Dhs200.
Credit AmEx, DC, MC, V. **Map** p277 K3.
A triumph of style over substance, the Boardwalk's
stunning creekside views more than compensate for
the mediocre menu. Avoid the harsh lighting and
uncomfy chairs at the bar and head over to the terrace, warmed by Paris café-style heaters in cool
evenings. The setting is romantic, the surroundings
interesting, and the water only half a footstep away.
The menu is fine although not exciting: lots of solid,
stodgy dishes like Chinese noodles and fish and
chips. The steaks are good and the fajitas fine but
the views and reasonable price tag are what really
make this place special.

Bodega

*Le Meridien Dubai, Airport Road, Garhoud
(282 4040).* **Open** 12.30-2.30pm, 8-11.30pm daily.
Average Dhs250. **Credit** AmEx, DC, MC, V.
Map p277 L2.
Only a rabidly committed Hispanophobe could possibly disapprove of Bodega, the airport Meridien's
glorious Spanish joint. A lushly appointed main
room leads into a lantern-lit quad, sealed in by sloping tiled roofs. Try the paella: a vast, fragrant dish
filled with clumps of pungent, crispy-topped rice.
Three versions of this classic Spanish dish exist at
Bodega, all served steamingly fresh in enormous
metal containers. Entertainment comes courtesy of

a pair of roving Spanish guitarists, who get a certain amount of atmosphere going with a string of
La Bamba-esque hits.

Café Chic

*Le Meridien Dubai, Airport Road, Garhoud (282
4040).* **Open** 12.30-2.45pm, 8-11.45pm Sat-Thur;
8-11.45pm Fri. **Average** Dhs340. **Credit** AmEx,
DC, MC, V. **Map** p277 L2.
Offering an authentic range of French cuisine, Café
Chic is très, très chic. Intimate yet airy, the bar and
lounge areas offer a quiet venue for an aperitif or
late-night coffee and cigar. Michel Rostang, of two-
star Michelin fame, has created a catalogue of
authentic French ensembles, presented with flair on
a series of fine white plates. Munch your way
through a perfect asparagus salad followed by striking duck carpaccio, but make sure to leave enough
room for a killer chocolate soufflé.

Casa Mia

*Le Meridien Dubai, Airport Road, Garhoud
(282 4040).* **Open** 12.30-2.45pm, 8-11.45pm daily.
Average Dhs300. **Credit** AmEx, DC, MC, V.
Map p277 L2.
This restaurant has a well-deserved reputation for
excellent Italian cuisine, and the authentic dishes
stand head and shoulders above most trattoria offerings. Wood is imported from Italy for the pizza oven,
and the wine list heaves with good bottles. The rab-
bit leg stuffed with Italian sausage is a guaranteed
crowd-pleaser.

The Aquarium.

Eat, Drink, Shop

reflections of pleasure

Häagen-Dazs
Belgian Chocolate

The purest dark Belgian chocolate
flakes combined with tender
chocolate ice cream.
Try this temptation of Häagen-Dazs
chocolate ice cream with
Belgian chocolate flakes.

The Boardwalk. *See p89.*

Focaccia

Hyatt Regency Hotel, Deira Corniche (209 1600).
Open 12.30-3pm, 7.30-11.30pm Sat-Thur. **Average**
Dhs320. **Credit** AmEx, DC, MC, V. **Map** p279 J1.
A cavernous restaurant, complete with piazza, conservatory, private dining room, library and wine cellar, Focaccia is a Cluedo board brought to life. The snug library is the best bet, offering the warmth of an English country manor. Starters are a speciality, with the baked snails and beef carpaccio heading the pack, while the cheesecake tart is a serious contender for best dessert in Dubai.

Glasshouse

Hilton Dubai Creek Hotel, Beniyas Road (227 1111). **Open** 12.30-3.30pm, 7pm-midnight daily.
Average Dhs250. **Credit** AmEx, DC, MC, V.
Map p279 L4.
Glasshouse at the Hilton Dubai Creek is a well-groomed big-city restaurant, filled with Carlos Ott curves and waiters in black pyjamas. Go à la carte and load up on school dinner-chic: tuck into fish and chips, bangers and mash with shallot gravy and apple tart with ice-cream, all backed up with a wonderful half bottle of Louis Roederer.

JW's Steakhouse

JW Marriott Hotel, Muraqqabat Street (262 4444).
Open 12.30-3pm, 7.30-11.30pm daily. **Average**
Dhs400. **Credit** AmEx, DC, MC, V. **Map** p277 K1.
JW is restlessly inventive with meat, turning out complex dishes that regulars rave about; we're amazed the place is still not besieged by ravenous carnivores. Seating is in super-comfy armchairs and the steaks cut like butter. Savour the filet mignon complete with a beautiful béarnaise sauce, one of the finest couples since Fred first twirled Ginger. Accompaniments of baked potatoes with soured

cream and crisp vegetables satisfy the breaks between meaty mouthfuls, but leave little doubt as to the star of the show.

Legends Steakhouse

Dubai Creek Golf & Yacht Club, Garhoud Road (295 6000). **Open** 7-11pm daily. **Average** Dhs340.
Credit AmEx, DC, MC, V. **Map** p277 K3.
In a break from the dark, leatherbound steakhouse norm, Legends is a high-ceilinged, pastel-coloured space with wide-open views over the golf club, the perfect setting for a serious meatathon. The jaunty-angled main room combines classic and modern styles to good effect and opens on to an expansive terrace, guaranteeing a superior al fresco dining experience. Pick of the mains is the peppercorn tenderloin steak, flambéed in brandy and red wine before your eyes.

Market Place

JW Marriott Hotel, Muraqqabat Street (262 4444).
Open 12.30-3pm, 7.30-11.30pm daily. **Average**
Dhs280. **Credit** AmEx, DC, MC, V. **Map** p277 K1.
The Market Place is is a cut above many all-you-can-eat deals in Dubai. Floppy-hatted chefs cook up fresh pasta, chicken and curry to order and there's plenty of good-quality sushi, antipasti and oysters on offer. A wall of fresh bread and an array of salads pad things out nicely. Load up on flame-grilled mini-steaks, gratin potatoes and osso bucco, and by the time you hit the enormous dessert colony, you'll be too full to be disappointed at the synthetic sponginess of it all.

M's Beef Bistro

Le Meridien Dubai, Airport Road, Garhoud (282 4040). **Open** 12.30-2.45pm, 8-11.45pm daily.
Average Dhs300. **Credit** AmEx, DC, MC, V.
Map p277 L2.

Room with a view: **Legends Steakhouse**. See p91.

M's makes you feel so at home you could turn up in pyjamas and no one would bat an eyelid. Dining takes place outside on the attractive terrace, inside by candlelight or up at the bar, and minimal tables make for an intimate atmosphere and attentive service. The menu itself holds few surprises: cow is the top dog here, though soups and seafood are also on hand to whet the appetite.

Oxygen
Al Bustan Rotana Hotel, Casablanca Road, Garhoud (282 0000). **Open** 6pm-3am daily. **Average** Dhs120. **Credit** AmEx, DC, MC, V. **Map** p277 K2.
In the bowels of the Al Bustan Rotana hotel lies the wonderfully stylish yet refreshingly unpretentious Oxygen restaurant. The ritzy decor takes its cue from a more decadent era, and is stuffed with mouldings, candelabras and candles the size of the Burj. You'd be forgiven for thinking it costs the earth to dine here, but Oxygen offers exceptional value for money as well as laying on some quirky treats: try tequila shots of gazpacho, strawberry bruschetta and exotic fruit heaped on dry ice. *See also p171.*

Seafood Market
Le Meridien Dubai, Airport Road, Garhoud (282 4040). **Open** 12.30-2.45pm, 7.30-11.30pm daily. **Average** Dhs300. **Credit** AmEx, DC, MC, V. **Map** p277 L2.
The best of the pick-your-own restaurants in Dubai: trot over to the ice-packed shelves which heave with fresh fish, pick your favourite and have it cooked and sauced to your specifications. Cold bottles of white and rosé wine are set next to the fish, so it's very convenient to choose drinks at the same time.

Spice Island
Renaissance Dubai Hotel, Salahuddin Road, just by the JW Marriott Hotel (262 5555). **Open** 7-11.30pm Sat-Thur; 10am-3pm, 7-11.30pm Fri. **Average** Dhs260. **Credit** AmEx, DC, MC, V. **Map** p277 K1.

Pulling in the punters with its regular all-you-can-eat-and-drink gorge-athons, Spice Island is chaotic and noisy; more like a bustling market than a remote and exotic isle. You have to be assertive in making your way through the determined hordes of grazers to get your share of the food. The choice is vast, with every corner of the culinary world covered at different feasting stations. However, it is undoubtedly the 'all you can drink' part of the bargain that draws the crowds.

Verre
Hilton Dubai Creek, Beniyas Road (227 1111). **Open** 7pm-midnight Sun-Fri. **Average** Dhs500. **Credit** AmEx, DC, MC, V. **Map** p279 L4.
Gordon Ramsay's own Middle Eastern outpost, Verre is a serious contender for finest restaurant in Dubai. The restaurant manager charms his way around the tables, making all the guests feel like the evening has been laid on for them alone, and a sommelier is permanently on hand to recommend the perfect bottle. The contemporary cuisine is immaculate and will convince your mouth it's died and gone to tastebud heaven. An evening here doesn't come cheap, but it gives many fine-dining restaurants in London or Paris a run for their money

Vivaldi
Sheraton Dubai Creek, Beniyas Road (207 1717). **Open** 6.30am-1.30am daily. **Average** Dhs250. **Credit** AmEx, DC, MC, V. **Map** p279 K4.
From its views up the Creek to the much-lauded food, and from the immaculate service to the fantastic wine selection, Vivaldi is now established as one of the best and most romantic Italian restaurants in town. The grilled beef tournedos is particularly fine – tender and moist, oozing with salacious flavour and marooned on a bed of spinach, surrounded by a thick and extravagant gorgonzola sauce. Italian heaven, pure and simple.

Brunching out

Friday is the first day of the Dubaian weekend and Friday brunch is a big deal, particularly among the Western expat community. Almost every hotel restaurant lays on a special buffet where you can meet up with your mates and kick back for a few hours, idly picking at fried breakfasts, roast meals and meze, possibly washed down with pint-sized beverages. Here are five of Dubai's favourites:

The Alamo
Dubai Marine Beach Resort & Spa, Beach Road, Jumeirah (346 1111). **Map** p280 D8. Buck's fizz, omelettes, pastries and waffles are the order of the day at this classic pub brunch. The full works come for Dhs66, and the relaxed atmosphere makes it tempting to segue into a leisurely afternoon's drinking. *See also p177.*

The Aquarium
Dubai Creek Golf & Yacht Club, Garhoud Road (295 0000). **Map** p277 K3. This beautiful restaurant has fabulous views over the creek and a highly popular Dhs75 brunch. Expect an international spread of food and lots of fish.

Carter's
Wafi Pyramids at Wafi City mall, off Oud Metha Road, Deira (324 0000). **Map** p277 J3. Help yourself to Dhs65-worth of cold cuts and sushi, cereals and salads, pasta and puddings. Take your booty outside and enjoy it on the pretty terrace.

Glasshouse
Hilton Dubai Creek, Beniyas Road, Deira (227 1111). **Map** p279 L4. A pricey option at Dhs120, but this is one of the classiest brunches in Dubai. The continental buffet breakfast is fine and the à la carte hot dishes are appealing, but the real hook is the free-flowing complimentary champagne. *See also p91.*

Waxy O'Conner's
Ascot Hotel, Khalid Bin Al Waleed Road (Bank Street), Bur Dubai (352 0900). **Map** p278 H4. The Friday Funky Brunch is incredible value: for Dhs50, you get one full Irish breakfast, five pints and a buffet carvery – a great deal, but gourmets beware, the food plays a firm second fiddle to the booze. *See also p171.*

Brunch till you drop at **The Alamo.**

Eat, Drink, Shop

wagamama

delicious noodles, fabulous rice dishes and freshly squeezed juices

wagamama dubai

**ground floor, crowne plaza dubai
sheikh zayed road**

for menu / locations and chatroom visit: www.wagamama.com

positive eating + positive living

Far Eastern

Blue Elephant
Al Bustan Rotana Hotel, Casablanca Road, Garhoud (282 0000). **Open** 11am-3pm, 7pm-midnight daily. **Average** Dhs290. **Credit** AmEx, DC, MC, V. **Map** p277 K2.
The Elephant's decor has something of an al fresco feel: sloping roofs, ponds, bridges and a cascading waterfall all give the illusion of the outside in. Although it's by no means innovative, the food is fine: try the herby *muak lek* corn cakes followed by an explosive dish of *himmapan* vegetables with stir-fried tofu and potentially a Bangkok fish, a huge slab of hammour smothered in a pungent chilli mix.

China Club
InterContinental Hotel, Beniyas Road (222 7171). **Open** 1-3.15pm, 8-11.30pm daily. **Average** Dhs300. **Credit** AmEx, DC, MC, V. **Map** p279 J3.
A high-design establishment with elegant service, intimate atmosphere and ambitions to fine-dining status. Sliding into a side booth you'll be immediately impressed by the musical backdrop – instead of lobe-wrenching panpipes, the sultry crooning of Sinatra takes centre stage, interwoven with some Ella Fitzgerald. While it doesn't hit the mark every time, the food is inventive and some dishes truly excel: try the *jin ling* duck soldiers or the top quality Szechuan prawns.

Kiku
Le Meridien Dubai, Airport Road, Garhoud (282 4040). **Open** noon-3pm, 7-11.45pm daily. **Average** Dhs250. **Credit** AmEx, DC, MC, V. **Map** p277 L2.
In contrast to its high-design fellow outlets at the Meridien, Kiku looks just a little scruffy: conference room furniture and shower-glass partitions make for mediocre decor in the main room. This should not detract from the fine food however, particularly the wonderful steak miso set. The meat is dreamily good, sizzling hot and packed with marinated flavour, backed up with pickles and dim sum-esque Chinese cabbage.

Long Yin
Le Meridien Dubai, Airport Road, Garhoud (282 4040). **Open** 12.30-2.45pm, 7.30-11.45pm daily. **Average** Dhs300. **Credit** AmEx, DC, MC, V. **Map** p277 L2.
A haven of Cantonese kitsch, complete with Chinese bridges, ponds of goldfish and tanks full of doomed lobsters, but the menu is thankfully more refined. The spare ribs are chin-wiping, finger-sucking success, and the crispy duck the best in Dubai. Long Yin is by no means cheap, with starters at around Dhs45 and mains at Dhs60, but it is excellent for a sophisticated Chinese feed.

Minato
InterContinental Hotel, Beniyas Road (205 7333). **Open** 1-3pm, 7-11pm daily. **Average** Dhs300. **Credit** AmEx, DC, MC, V. **Map** p279 J3.

Minato serves some of the most imaginative Japanese dishes in town, so it's a smart choice if you want to experiment with something other than run-of-the-mill sushi and yakitori. Star of the menu is the sukiyaki hotpot, a huge brim-filled cauldron of goodness housing beef sirloin cut in bacon-like strips, baby mushrooms, noodles, seared cabbage, onion (both spring and regular) and huge hunks of tofu. A top choice for a foray into the exotic. Round the evening off with a cocktail or two at the tattoo-themed Kubu bar downstairs.

Miyako
Hyatt Regency Hotel, Deira Corniche (209 1234). **Open** 12.30-3pm, 7-11pm daily. **Average** Dhs 400. **Credit** AmEx, MC, V. **Map** p279 J1.
The Dubai branch of the famed Japanese restaurant chain is unquestionably one of the finest dining attractions in the city. You'll have to decide which of the two seating choices to go for: table-service for à la carte sushi, sashimi and shabu-shabu, or a theatrical performance around the teppanyaki grill. Teppanyaki is clearly the real joy of Miyako, and they've got it down to a fine art: the freshest possible ingredients, the best cuts of meat and priceless live-cooking entertainment.

Sukhothai
Le Meridien Dubai, Airport Road, Garhoud (282 4040). **Open** 12.30-2.45pm, 7.30-11.45pm daily. **Average** Dhs300. **Credit** AmEx, DC, MC, V. **Map** p277 L2.

China Club: Sinatra meets Szechuan.

Duck with fruit is a universally beautiful combination. The lychee variation at Sukhothai is without doubt the best thing happening to duck in a two-mile radius: wonderfully tasty pieces of bird come simmered in spicy red curry sauce with nuggets of soft fruit. Other dishes of note include the chilli and coriander fish cakes and the fresh pan-fried prawns. The carved wood and Kim-music provide the perfect backdrop to some of the best Thai food in town.

Jumeirah

Arabic

The Chalet

Beach Road, just after Al Manara Road (348 7557). **Open** 11.30am-2am daily. **Average** Dhs40. **No credit cards. Map** p274 B4.

The Chalet was interior-designed by pixies – toadstool tables topped with strawberries, indoor trees and enormous blue sunflowers abound. The same woodland folk have produced a menu of budget grills, seafood and pasta, most of which romps in firmly under the Dhs20 mark. Follow up your friendly welcome with a huge Dhs14 lamb biryani, a vast bed of rice with four marinated mutton chops and three bowls of sauce – salsa, raita and chicken broth. Very filling.

Al Khaima

Le Royal Meridien Beach Resort & Spa, Al Sufouh Road (399 5555). **Open** noon-4pm, 8pm-midnight, daily. **Average** Dhs400. **Credit** AmEx, DC, MC, V. **Map** p274 A5.

A large wooden deck extends out from this idyllic beachside restaurant towards the sea, with a stretch of lawn leading onwards to the sand. Sit under huge umbrellas enjoying the cool breeze and sipping fruit cocktails before heading to the lunchtime barbecue buffet. Start off at the chilled, sealed salad bar (at the press of a button plastic domes lift up to allow access) then choose a little seafood or poultry for grilling. In the evenings there's a decent Lebanese à la carte selection.

Majlis Al Bahar

Opposite Wild Wadi & the Burj Al Arab, Beach Road (301 7777). **Open** 10am-midnight daily. **Average** Dhs400. **Credit** AmEx, DC, MC, V. **Map** p274 A4.

Flickering candles and uplit palm trees fringe the seating area at Majlis al Bahar, inches from the immaculate beach and the lapping Gulf beyond. Atmosphere is courtesy of poker-faced musicians in moustaches and fez hats, and the whole ensemble is completed by the ultimate eye-candy of the Burj Al Arab. The large tables are laid with appetising cushions of fresh bread with flavoured mayonnaise and fat green olives. A diverse selection of Arabic and European food is all done well, but it's clear you're paying most of your money for the crazily romantic views. Be sure to book in advance or security may get shirty at the gate.

Sammach

Beach Centre mall, Beach Road (349 4140). **Open** 12.30-11.15pm daily. **Average** Dhs100. **Credit** AmEx, DC, MC, V. **Map** p282 B13.

Sammach is trying desperately hard to re-create a little harbourside Lebanon in shopping-mall Dubai. Pick fresh red snapper and African hammour from the iceboat, and while they're grilling, savour the revelatory fish tajen, an aubergine and tahina base with chunks of hammour, pine nuts and shreds of sweet, smoky fried onion. Food this cheap hasn't tasted so good in a long while.

Tagine

One&Only Royal Mirage Hotel, Al Sufouh Road (399 9999). **Open** 7.30-11.30pm Sat, Sun, Tue-Fri. **Average** Dhs600. **Credit** AmEx, DC, MC, V. **Map** p274 A5.

A fine Moroccan experience awaits at Tagine. The interior is candlelit, the music is live and the waiters are all done up in traditional dress. The menu is full of classic dishes, with the emphasis, unsurprisingly, on tagines and couscous. Visitors would do well to start with harira soup and fresh bread, perked up by a dollop or two of red-hot harissa. You can't go wrong on main courses, the chicken maasel tagine being a particular winner – tender chicken in a beautiful, rich sauce filled with dates and nuts.

European

La Baie

Ritz-Carlton Hotel, Al Sufouh Road (399 4000). **Open** 7-11pm Mon-Sat. **Average** Dhs350. **Credit** AmEx, DC, MC, V. **Map** p274 A5.

La Baie offers smart, formal dining in a stylish setting cheered up by rampant candles and bowers of fresh blooms. Waiters insinuate their way round the room, a pianist tinkles elegantly in the corner and the menu heaves with hearty meat dishes served with indulgent sauces and creamy mash: the sort of food that makes you feel glad to be alive. Try the beef tenderloin with onion reduction but make sure to save room for the masterly baked cheesecake.

Barasti

Le Meridien Mina Seyahi Hotel, Al Sufouh Road (399 3333). **Open** 8am-2am daily. **Average** Dhs200. **Credit** AmEx, DC, MC, V. **Map** p274 A5.

Better known for its beach parties and poolside barbecue, Barasti is also a first-class spot for an elegant meal in laid-back surroundings: on the outside terrace, you sit mere metres away from the lapping Gulf. The clientele ranges from the smartly dressed to the bermuda-shorted and the atmosphere is relaxed, lending itself equally to a few early evening drinks or to a full three course meal. The menu features plenty of innovative comfort food like pancetta-wrapped prawns, blackened cajun chicken with mango salsa and mash or delicious fried calamari with sea salt, chilli and minted mayonnaise. The deeply alcoholic Long Island ice-tea sorbet is also a winner. *See also p177.*

The Chalet. *See p96.*

Beach Bar & Grill

*One&Only Royal Mirage Hotel, Al Sufouh Road
(399 9999).* **Open** noon-4pm, 7.30pm-midnight
daily. **Average** Dhs300. **Credit** AmEx, DC, MC, V.
Map p274 A5.

The name is instantly forgettable, but the setting is
among the most romantic in the city. As well as
being well known for its views, the Beach Bar has
something of a reputation as a proposal spot, and
many a question has been popped on its terrace seating. Take a table on this dining platform, from which
vantage point you can admire the broad sweep of
the moonlit beach and hear the waves lapping at the
shore a stone's throw from your plates of fresh warm
bread. The food is good rather than outstanding –
lots of reasonably executed grill classics like seared
fresh water prawns and lamb loin with roast fennel
– but the location makes it perfect for dating, doting
or even popping the big one.

Bice

Hilton Dubai Jumeirah, Al Sufouh Road (399 1111).
Open noon-3pm, 7-11pm daily. **Average** Dhs300.
Credit AmEx, DC, MC, V. **Map** p274 A5.

Run by a Riminian restaurant manager who keeps
it real by importing top-class ingredients from Italy,
Bice is a sophisticated and authentic joint. Start with
pots of grissini and focaccia loaded with pungent
black tapenade and order at will: you can't put a foot
wrong. From ruffles of bresaola with crumbling
aged parmesan to veal and beef ragú draped on
home-made spaghetti, and from rich risottos hum-
ming with truffle oil to the teak-brown chocolate
soufflé, it's all masterfully well done.

Boudoir

*Dubai Marine Beach Resort, Beach Road (345
5995).* **Open** 7.30-11pm daily. **Average** Dhs500.
Credit AmEx, DC, MC, V. **Map** p280 D8.

From the outsize pomanders of red roses to the elaborate chandeliers and purple satin padded walls, this
haven of French frippery has 'Moulin Rouge' written all over it. By evening, it's an elaborate yet warmly inviting restaurant; come midnight the central
tables are cleared to allow the Beautiful People to
boogie away, champagne glasses in hand. Never
mind cake, at Boudoir Marie Antoinette would've
indulged on the likes of Omani prawn lollipops with
tomato jus slammers, electric green chicken with the
zing of kaffir lime leaves, roast salmon with saffron
noodles and other innovative dishes that fuse
flavours of the east and west. *See also p174.*

Celebrities

*One&Only Royal Mirage Hotel, Al Sufouh Road (399
9999).* **Open** 7-11pm Sun-Fri. **Average** Dhs600.
Credit AmEx, DC, MC, V.

Stunning views down a palm-lined avenue towards
a gazebo and the beach beyond leave you in no
doubt you're luxuriating in a stunning corner of the
Arabian Peninsula. The restaurant is home to
Freddie Foster, one of the big names in Dubai's eat-
out scene, and serves up some of the best fine-dining food in the city, at great expense and to the
accompaniment of over-loud musicians.

Al Mahara

Burj Al Arab Hotel, Beach Road (301 7600). **Open**
12.30-3pm, 7pm-midnight daily. **Average** Dhs600.
Credit AmEx, DC, MC, V. **Map** p274 A4.

This is the only restaurant in Dubai to be entered via a submarine. Guests enter a padded capsule with all-round video screens filled with pixelated fish and steered down to the main room, a stylish corridor encircling an enormous illuminated aquarium. The beauty of the place, combined with the subtle service and gentle music, guarantees an atmosphere of serenity and romance, and the fish-centric menu pushes the experience to the heavenly. Start with six fat oysters and follow up with imaginative creations like pan-fried halibut with white chocolate or sweet and sour lobster. Beware, though, the price tag is as hefty as they come.

Al Muntaha

Burj Al Arab Hotel, Beach Road (301 7777). **Open** 12.30-3pm, 7pm-midnight daily. **Average** Dhs800. **Credit** AmEx, DC, MC, V. **Map** p274 A4.

You may need a bank loan to pay off any excessive indulgences, especially an extravagant foray into the wine list – but the food at Al Muntaha is simply fabulous. Dining in this multicoloured, skyward restaurant is an extraordinary experience not only because of the location; all the combinations and flavours are stunning, from the Caesar salad with lobster to the pot-roasted loin of veal with pan-fried breads. It would be a shame not to leave room for the apple brioche tatin with lavender ice-cream.

Prasino's

Jumeirah Beach Club, Beach Road (344 5333). **Open** 12.30-3pm, 7.30-11pm daily. **Average** Dhs400. **Credit** AmEx, DC, MC, V. **Map** p282 A15.

Cocktails at **Pachanga**. *See p99.*

Prasino's is a classy joint with a parade of quirky twists: one corner hosts a mad voodoo wardrobe, a hundreds-and-thousands chandelier hangs from the roof and a big stone sits in the corner looking inscrutable and holy. The first port of call is the bar, where you can give your order and kill time over a cold beer while the chefs get busy on your dinner and a pianist knocks out some moody jazz classics. The international menu often changes, but is always crammed with enticing, well-prepared dishes, from slow-cooked swordfish in goose fat to prosciutto-wrapped pork with smoked apple chutney.

Retro

Le Meridien Mina Seyahi Hotel, Al Sufouh Road (399 3333). **Open** 7-11pm daily. **Average** Dhs400. **Credit** AmEx, DC, MC, V. **Map** p274 A5.

Although Retro prices are high, an al fresco evening on the terrace is worth investing in. The tables have great views towards the sea and while at night you can't see the waves, they still beckon diners for a romantic after-dinner stroll along the beach. The bread is freshly baked, the mainly Med menu is innovative (think Barbary duck with foie gras ravioli, and lobster cake with fresh coconut) and the sticky toffee pudding is ambrosial. A trolley-load of irresistible aromatic cheeses is wheeled out after dinner.

Signatures

Jebel Ali Hotel, off Exit 13 on Sheikh Zayed Road (883 6000). **Open** 7-11pm Sat, Sun, Tue-Fri. **Average** Dhs300. **Credit** AmEx, DC, MC, V. **Map** p274 A5.

This neo-rustic eaterie is filled with candles and floored with slate, backed with a show kitchen where chefs are visible beavering away over their pots. The menu is modern French, offering both à la carte and five-course gourmet selections, and the wine list is an intelligent mix of old and new world bottles. The terrace is ideal for a pre-dinner sharpener and the food is fine-dining: try the lobster salad with lightly sautéed foie gras or the seared sea bass on a bed of braised red cabbage. Beware, though, it's a fair old bop out of the centre of town.

The Wharf

Mina A' Salam Hotel, Al Sufouh Road (366 8888). **Open** noon-3pm, 7-11pm daily. **Average** Dhs400. **Credit** AmEx, DC, MC, V. **Map** p274 A4.

The Wharf occupies one of the most attractive locations in town, a hotel which combines a beachside spot with Arabian decoration and Venetian waterways. While the restaurant's Gothic chandelier, exposed brickwork and barrel-filled interior is unexciting, the canalside terrace is blissful in winter. The Wharf seafood is truly excellent – consider marinated salmon with blini, potatoes and an affable dollop of chive-flavoured cheese or the grilled fish salad, a munificent spread of scallops, squid and hammour with a wonderful avocado and sweet tomato salad. The real winner, however, is a genius of a paella: a thoroughbred panful of fat prawns, thick chorizo and wickedly moreish rice.

Al Mahara – liquid lunch with a difference. *See p97.*

Far Eastern

Eau Zone

*Arabian Court at the One&Only Royal Mirage Hotel,
Al Sufouh Road (399 9999).* **Open** noon-3.30pm,
7-11.30pm daily. **Average** Dhs450. **Credit** AmEx,
DC, MC, V. **Map** p274 A5.

Eau Zone is without a doubt one of Dubai's most
dreamily romantic restaurant settings: head down
one of the boardwalks that spider out from the main
restaurant and take a table in the middle of a lagoon-
like pool. Dim lights make reading the menu a tad
tricky but the decor is superb and the ambience –
even down to the soft, somehow funky muzak –
is spot on. The cuisine is contemporary with an
Asian twist: spicy papaya salad, John Dory with
wafer-thin slices of anis star fused in orange juice,
and robata yaki duck with crunchy Vietnamese rice
and pomegranate.

Indian

Nina

*Arabian Court at the One&Only Royal Mirage Hotel,
Al Sufouh Road (399 9999).* **Open** 8pm-midnight
Sat-Thur. **Average** Dhs250. **Credit** AmEx, DC,
MC, V. **Map** p274 A5.

Decorated in deep red and purple tones, Nina draws
diners down the stairs with the twinkle of diwali
candles: once inside, it's all subtle lighting, showers
of delicate silver beads and velvety curtains. As
befits its clientele of seniors, families, trendies and
skinny Bollywood starlets, Nina offers a wide choice,

from tasty morsels to hefty meals; main courses
range from small vegetarian stir-fries and curries for
Dhs20 to lobster wrapped in banana leaf for Dhs90.
The head chef is Australian, but his team are Indian:
the delicate use of fresh herbs in Thai cooking, so
beloved down under, has been applied here to high
Indian cuisine with maximum effect.

International

Pachanga

Hilton Jumeirah, Al Sufouh Road (399 1111).
Open 4pm-midnight daily. **Average** Dhs350.
Credit AmEx, DC, MC, V. **Map** p274 A5.

Challenge: sit in Pachanga and try not to wiggle,
grind and generally swivel your hips to the sounds
of the super-cool band who play as you dine. It's no
easy task – their beat gets into your booty like only
the South Americans know how. The menu draws
on Argentina, Brazil and Mexico, and while not overly authentic, it all works pretty well. Delightful gua-
camole is knocked up at the table and served with
tortilla chips; the Brazilian fried goose liver, while
more French than Latino, is a toothsome beauty; and
the skillet of sirloin is worth every peso.

La Parilla

Jumeirah Beach Hotel, Beach Road (348 0000).
Open 12.30-2.30pm, 7-11.30pm daily. **Average**
Dhs400. **Credit** AmEx, DC, MC, V. **Map** p274 B4.

The starters are uninspired, the prices high and the
atmosphere irritatingly gung-ho. However, this
Argentinian grill room does have one major redeem-
ing factor – the steak. Unutterably wonderful slabs

FORGET EVERYTHING YOU KNOW ABOUT STEAK RESTAURANTS

THINK CONTEMPORARY INTERIORS. EXPERT STAFF. IMAGINATIVE CHEFS.

A CHARCOAL GRILL. THE FINEST CUTS OF BEEF. FRESH SEAFOOD.

AND A WINE SELECTION THAT DEFIES DESCRIPTION.

WELCOME TO PALM GRILL - NOT JUST ANOTHER STEAKHOUSE.

CONTEMPORARY STEAKHOUSE

INTERCONTINENTAL.
DUBAI
CALL 205 7333/7444

of prime South American meat turn up flame-grilled, as thick as a brick and a thousand times tastier – Order a wedge of this wonder-meat for your main course, accompanied by a glass or two of fruity red. Kick back after dinner and watch the vigorous Latino rope-dancing, which is either flamboyant or laughable depending on your perspective.

Prime Rib
Le Royal Meridien Hotel, Al Sufouh Road (399 5555). **Open** 7pm-midnight daily. **Average** Dhs500. **Credit** AmEx, DC, MC, V. **Map** p274 A5.

It's well worth getting down Sheikh Zayed Road to eat in this pretty restaurant that offers a hint of 1920s decadence: art deco lighting, ol' Satchmo playing away in the background and waiters determined to supply you with champagne aperitifs. American Angus beef is the mainstay, but there's plenty of veg and seafood on offer, all pitched at prime prices. Apart from the outstanding Alaskan king crab legs in chive butter sauce, however, many of the non-steak options are disappointing: quit messing around and order yourself 600g (22oz) of rib-eye with spicy horseradish sauce: steak heaven, pure and simple.

Restaurants by cuisine

Chinese
China Club (*see p95*), Long Yin (*see p95*), Shang Palace (*see p85*), Zheng He's (*see p86*).

Egyptian
Damyati (*see p80*), Fatafeet (*see p80*).

French
La Baie (*see p96*), Café Chic (*see p89*), Verre (*see p92*), Vu's (*see p82*).

Fusion
Boudoir (*see p97*), Eau Zone (*see p99*), Ginseng (*see p83*), Oxgen (*see p92*), Teatro (*see p85*).

Indian
See Indian sections, pp86-87, p99.

Iranian
Shahrzad (*see p89*).

Italian
Bice (*see p97*), Casa Mia (*see p89*), Focaccia (*see p91*), Medzo (*see p81*), Il Rustico (*see p82*), Vivaldi (*see p92*).

Japanese
ET Sushi (*see p83*), Kiku (*see p95*), Minato (*see p95*), Miyako (*see p95*), Sakura (*see p85*), Yo! Sushi (*see p86*).

Lebanese
Awtar (*see p80*), The Chalet (*see p96*), Al Dawaar (*see p88*), Fakhreldine (*see p80*), Al Khaima (*see p96*), Majlis al Baher (*see p96*), Al Mansour Dhow (*see p88*), Al Mawal (*see p88*), Al Mijana (*see p88*), Al Nafoorah (*see p80*), Olive House (*see p81*), Sammach (*see p96*), Al Tannour (*see p81*).

Mediterranean
The Beach Bar & Grill (*see p97*), Celebrities (*see p97*), Glasshouse (*see p91*), Market

Place (*see p91*), Al Muntaha (*see p98*), Prasino's (*see p98*), Retro (*see p98*), Signatures (*see p98*), Spice Island (*see p92*).

Moroccan
Marrakech (*see p80*), Tagine (*see p96*).

Noodle Bar
Noodle House (*see p83*).

North American
The Boardwalk (*see p89*).

Polynesian
Trader Vic's (*see p87*).

Seafood
The Aquarium (*see p89*), Barasti (*see p96*), Al Mahara (*see p97*), The Seafood Market (*see p92*), Sea World (*see p82*), The Wharf (*see p98*).

Singaporean
Peppercrab (*see p85*).

South American
Pachanga (*see p99*).

Spanish
Bodega (*see p89*).

Steakhouses
The Exchange (*see p81*), JW's Steakhouse (*see p91*), Legends Steakhouse (*see p91*), Links (*see p81*), Manhattan Grill (*see p87*), M's Beef Bistro (*see p91*), La Parilla (*see p99*), Prime Rib (*see p101*), Western Steak House (*see p82*).

Thai
Benjarong (*see p82*), Blue Elephant (*p95*), Lemongrass (*p83*), Sukhothai (*p95*), Thai Chi (*p85*).

Vietnamese
Hoi An (*see p83*), Indochine (*p83*).

Eat, Drink, Shop

Cafés & Bars

From low-key coffee houses to cosmopolitan tippling dens.

Although Dubai has its fair share of pubs and bars, disappointingly few of them excel when it comes to food. While new cafés are increasingly investing in well-crafted, intelligent menus, most bars are still serving up the same uninspiring stodge they were five years ago. Certain areas are particularly poor for gastro-pubbing – Jumeirah, with its endless five-star hotels, has almost nowhere good for a booze and a bite. There are, as always, a few exceptions to the rule – **Vintage** at the Wafi Pyramids (*see p106*) has worked out the perfect mix of dishes for its booze list, and **Zinc** (see *p106*) and **The Agency** (see *p105*) are following suit.

Dubai has a large and sophisticated café society, in part because for a large portion of the population, hanging out in places where alcohol is served is anathema. The influence of traditional Arabic hospitality also plays a role – sitting and chatting over endless coffees, dates and the occasional *shisha* pipe is an integral part of life in the Gulf, and there are countless outlets where you can do just that. Floating in this sea of caffeine and nibbles, certain groups can be readily identified. Swaggering media types 'do lunch' in caffs at Dubai Media City and Garhoud, Lebanese businessmen preen themselves in chi-chi joints on Sheikh Zayed Road and expat wives meet for gossip in coffee houses up and down the Jumeirah Beach Road.

Along with contact details and map references, we've included the 'average' price of a meal. This is the typical price of a one-course meal for two people, with drinks: a glass of house wine per person if the bar or café is licensed, a glass of juice if it isn't. As in the West, it's customary to leave a ten per cent tip when eating in cafés and the posher bars, and this is particularly important in Dubai where wages for waiters can be incredibly low, often only Dhs2,000 a month.

Bur Dubai

Cafés

Aroma Garden Café
Oud Metha Road, next to Dubai TV (336 8999). **Open** 10am-1.30am Sat-Thur; noon-1.30am Fri. **Average** Dhs60. **Credit** AmEx, MC, V. **Map** p277 J2.
Ethereal, enigmatic and aromatic, Aroma Garden café is the ultimate place to unwind and de-stress. There's soft lighting, the sound of running water and a lot of greenery. Filled with locals, it has quickly become a popular meeting place for a snack and a *shisha*, and the air is thick with apple and strawberry smoke. The food's fine, but it's the atmosphere that swings this place into the premier league.

Basta Art Café
Al Fahidi roundabout, next to the Majlis Gallery (353 5071). **Open** 10am-8pm Sat-Thur. **Average** Dhs90. **No credit cards**. **Map** p278 H4.
This wonderful courtyard café offers a cool respite from the Bur Dubaian hurly-burly outside. It's perfect for spending a long afternoon on your own, flicking idly through a paperback as you sip at an icy mocktail (try the zing-filled lime and mint juice). The salads and wraps are unfeasibly good: check out the souk salad with crunchy cashews, wedges of tomato, chicken strips and couscous, or the 'wind towers', lavished with cheddar cheese, apple and sweetcorn, all beefed up with thick chunks of turkey bacon.

Courtyard dining at **Basta Art Café**.

The big smoke

Shishas, also known as hookahs and hubbly-bubbly pipes, are an everyday sight in Dubai. Lumps of perfumed tobacco are heated by sucking air through red-hot embers, and the smoke is channelled to the customer through an elaborately decorated pipe. Less harmful and addictive than cigarettes (the tar and nicotine content is far lower), they're an integral part of Arab culture and wheeled out for guests after most meals. While the experience can be a novel one, if you're used to ciggies, you may get bored after the first 15 minutes or so – the embers burn incredibly slowly and are regularly replaced by waiters armed with tongs, so you can make a shisha last for hours if you feel so inclined. They are, however, built to share, so you can spread the smoking load among your friends, each of whom will be presented with their own disposable mouthpiece.

The tobacco used comes in a variety of exotic flavours, from the traditional apple to the less conventional bubblegum and cola. You can indulge in a puff in almost any Arabic café or outlet: our recommendations for a hubble and a bubble are **Fatafeet** (see p80), the Egyptian restaurant down by the Creek, which does a delicious fruit cocktail version, and **Shakespeare & Co** (see p104) on Sheikh Zayed Road, whose apple shisha is a Granny Smith-scented delight.

The Chippy

Sheikh Zayed Road, opposite the Dusit Hotel (343 3114). **Open** 5pm-midnight daily. **Average** Dhs50. **No credit cards. Map** p283 F13

A black and white office-furnished '80s joint, with a wide choice of delicacies, including deep-fried Mars Bars, haggis, Scotch pie and white pudding as well as decent fish and chips. Not for the romantics among us (no music, little atmosphere, counter service) but a nice choice for lovers of newspaper-wrapped batter.

Dôme

Burjuman Centre, Trade Centre Road (355 6004). **Open** 7.30am-11.30pm daily. **Credit** MC, V. **Average** Dhs60. **Map** p279 J5.

A pleasant Australian caff serving wonderful focaccia sandwiches; try the club and the smoked salmon with avocado and capers. Larger dishes such as Indonesian spicy noodles also excel, and the restful atmosphere and rack of mags make it the perfect place to put your feet up after a shopping spree.

Elements

Wafi City mall, Oud Metha Road (324 4252). **Open** 10am-midnight Sat-Thur; noon-midnight Fri. **Average** Dhs100. **Credit** AmEx, MC, V. **Map** p277 J3.

Elements has three levels of cool: industrial chic in the riveted battleship walls and exposed rigging of pipes and vents; Ikea chic in the platoon of teardrop lamps and curvy art-deco leather seats; and sushi chic up at the Zen-style coffee bar. Quirky touches abound: menus are mounted on lumps of granite, a flowerbed runs round the café perimeter and a pair of swings dangle from the roof. Mix and match from the menu as outlandishly as you like, although we advise staying simple with a made-at-table chicken Caesar or some pesto-laced pasta. There's also a kooky little tacked-on bakery where you can grab yourself oven-fresh rolls, croissants and loaves to take away.

French Bakery

Defence roundabout, Sheikh Zayed Road (343 6444). **Open** 24 hours daily. **Average** Dhs80. **Credit** MC, V. **Map** p283 F13.

Brightly lit, spacious and with a slightly clinical feel to it, the French Bakery is the home of fine continental pastries. Heaps of glistening cellophane candy bags, sugared almonds tied up with coloured ribbons and ornate displays of exclusive chocolates form an integral part of the decor. The line of gleaming glass-fronted display fridges and freezers is filled with ice-cream, gateaux, pastries and savouries. Head down and let your sweet tooth drive you to mammoth excess.

French Connection

Al Wafa Tower, Sheikh Zayed Road (343 8311). **Open** 7am-midnight daily. **Average** Dhs70. **Credit** MC, V. **Map** p283 F12.

The decor's fresh and relaxing – shades of beige and baby blue, with pale wood floorboards and fittings complemented by plenty of natural light – and the ambience informal. Paninis, strawberry tartlets and hot chocolate with marshmallows all do good service, as do the freshly baked croissants.

Goodies
Wafi City mall, Oud Metha Road (324 4433).
Open 9.30am-midnight daily. **Average** Dhs150.
Credit AmEx, DC, MC, V. **Map** p277 F3.
Make your way through racks of gold-wrapped chocolates, tanks full of fresh goat's cheese, mountains of truffle-dashed black olives and intricately shaped marzipan sweets to place an order at the long chilled counter. Goodies' daily specials are universally excellent, but staff are particularly gifted at chickpea and pine nut baked fish and cheese-capped moussakas and lasagnas. The mall-hugging eaterie also has an entire corner devoted to the making and grilling of gourmet kebabs: pick your stick from a platoon of multicoloured meats and match it with some special raisin-filled rice.

Häagen-Dazs Café
Al Diyafah Street, near Jumeirah Rotana Hotel, Satwa (345 6199). **Open** 1pm-midnight daily.
Average Dhs50. **Credit** AmEx, DC, MC, V.
Map p280 F8.
Al Diyafah Street in Satwa has more than its fair share of ice-cream cafés, and this is by far and away the best. The service can be a mite abrupt, but the concept is flawless – stock a wide range of HD ice-creams, from Strawberry Cheesecake to Pralines & Cream, and provide sauces, sprinkles, wafers and milkshakes to back them up. Stop by on a baking afternoon and pick your favourite scoops, slather them in fudge and plonk them on top of a Belgian wafer cone. Maaaarvellous.

Al Reef Lebanese Bakery
Karama Zabeel Road, next to Karama post office (396 1980). **Open** 24 hours daily. **Average** Dhs40.
No credit cards. Map p277 J2.
Open around the clock, the Al Reef bakery is an excellent place for breakfast, lunch or a late-night snack. Whenever you go it's sure to be busy, as punters queue up for the fine and filling sandwiches on offer. There's a long list of combinations, but the sausage and egg (Dhs 5) is highly recommended. The mass of customers makes it a confusing place, so remember to order at the counter first and then pay at the register. While you wait, sneak a look through the serving hole to watch the *zataar* bread inflating in the oven behind.

Shakespeare & Co
Kendah House, Sheikh Zayed Road (331 1757).
Open 7am-1am daily. **Average** Dhs100. **Credit** AmEx, DC, MC, V. **Map** p283 F11.
Shakespeare is battling a world of hotel uniformity with quirkiness and flair. The decor is vaguely old lady's living room-esque, there are sofas to loll around in, books and magazines to browse and a

Cheerful chic. **French Connection.** *See p103.*

charming outside area built around a large cage filled with brightly plumed birds. It's the sort of place you could eat at every day for a week and not get bored: particular favourites are the gnocchi with a nutty cheese sauce, the magically creamy mushroom soup and the super-light rice and tuna salad.

Tagpuan
Opposite the Golden Fork, Karama Shopping Centre, off Za'abeel Road, Karama (337 3959). **Open** 9.30am-midnight daily. **Average** Dhs40. **No credit cards. Map** p277 J2.
Tagpuan – a little corner of Manila in Karama – is the kind of tiny, bustling local café that attracts just about everyone. Everyone Filipino and in the know, that is. Groups of young lads slug Dhs5 banana shakes, couples chat over steaming plates of *bihon guisado* glass noodles, kids tuck into ice-cream and older guys slurp bowls of *tinolang manok* (chicken in delicious broth) with their eyes on the obligatory blaring TV.

Zyara
Union Tower (National Bank of Abu Dhabi building), Sheikh Zayed Road (343 5454). **Open** 8am-midnight daily. **Average** Dhs120. **Credit** AmEx, MC, V.
Map p283 F12.
Zyara is part of a clutch of young upstarts striving to inject some Franco-Lebanese bohemia into the unforgiving, angular avenue of skyscrapers that makes up Sheikh Zayed Road. The decor is charming: beaten-up wooden chairs and tables compete for your attention with sink-in sofas covered in flowery

fabrics; the wooden floors are covered in Iranian kilims and the walls feature regular exhibitions by local artists. The sandwich-and-snacks menu is original (look out for the Gloo Gloo salad), but the quality's reasonable rather than outstanding.

Bars

The Agency
Emirates Towers Hotel, Sheikh Zayed Road (330 0000). **Open** 12.30pm-1am Sat-Thur; 3pm-1am Fri. **Average** Dhs100. **Credit** AmEx, DC, MC, V. **Map** p276 H4.
The Agency is an upmarket London/New York style wine bar, made for conversation with its low-lit and chilled-out interior. Match your bottle of chilled white with fondues, charcuterie and booze-snacks ranging from bruschetta to chilli prawns. More sophisticated tapas are constantly being added: try Italian Roma tomatoes infused with basil oil and stuffed with gorgonzola, a round of creamy French goat's cheese topped with chopped olives and walnuts, and a citrus seafood cocktail of uncertain but tasty origin. Dishes more loyal to the home of tapas include plates of crispy chorizo on a bed of spicy tomatoes, deliciously fresh, brackish rolls of marinated anchovies and prawns properly soaked in deep orange chilli oil that'll have you reaching for gulps of chilled Pinot Grigio. *See also p168.*

Aussie Legends
Rydges Plaza Hotel, Satwa roundabout, Satwa (398 2222). **Open** 3pm-3am Sat-Wed; Fri; 1pm-3am Thur. **Average** Dhs70. **Credit** AmEx, DC, MC, V. **Map** p281 F8.
There's no overlooking this bar's antipodean heritage. Aussie flags hang from the roof and chalkboard drawings of wombats, emus and kangaroos line the walls. A good place for a game of pool and a quiet pint. The 'international' selection of Cajun, Mexican and British tucker is rather patchy and plays a firm second fiddle to the drinking. *See also p169.*

Boston Bar
Jumeirah Rotana Hotel, Al Dhiyafa Street, Satwa (345 5888). **Open** noon-3am daily. **Average** Dhs70. **Credit** AmEx, DC, MC, V. **Map** p280 F8.
Based on the pub in *Cheers*, the Boston is a well-known haunt for middle-aged expat drinkers, who perch on stools round the circular bar. Although it still attracts a crowd on discount-drinks nights, the Boston no longer enjoys the popularity it did in the days when alternatives were limited. A reasonable atmosphere is matched with basic snacks like nachos and cheese, burgers and buffalo wings. *See also p177.*

Henry J Bean's
Capitol Hotel, Mankhool Road, Satwa (345 8375). **Open** noon-3am daily. **Average** Dhs70. **Credit** AmEx, DC, MC, V. **Map** p280 E7.
A wood-lined burger joint with vicious air-con and nostalgic piped-in pop. The barbecue cheeseburger is a fulsome Dhs27 beauty, as big as a bus and at

The best Cafés

For funky atmosphere
Aroma Garden Café (*see p102*) for the eating-in-a-greenhouse feel; **More** (*see p107*) for rampant quirkiness; and **Elements** (*see p103*) for indoor swings and build-your-own-dish dining.

For gourmet lunches
Consider **Goodies** (*see p104*), the luxury foodstore at Wafi (choose at the counter and eat on the terrace); and **Lime Tree Café** (*see p108*) in Jumeirah for fresh, original delicatessen treats.

For outside dining
Next to the huge birdcage at **Shakespeare & Co** (*see p104*); in the hidden courtyard at **Gerard's** (*see p108*); or in the backyard at **Basta Art Café** (*see p102*).

For fresh pastries
Try **Paul** (*see p109*), the Parisian bakery at the Mercato Centre, for strawberry tarts; and **Al Reef Lebanese Bakery** (*see p104*) for Arabic cakes.

For discount nibbles
There's **Tagpuan** (*see p104*) for Filipino snacks; or the **Oasis Restaurant** (*see p108*) for some pre-beach burgers and mocktails.

For discreet liaisons
The softly lit **Vienna Café** (*see p107*) at the JW Marriott; or the low-key **Skywalk Café** (*see p107*).

For icy treats
Visit the **French Bakery** (*see p103*) for cakes with your ice-cream; or the **Häagen-Dazs Café** (*see p104*) on Al Diyafah street for conefuls of the good stuff.

Eat, Drink, Shop

least three times as tasty, a fine accompaniment to a bottle or two of Beck's. Average Tex-Mex combos are also on offer. Although Henry J can't shake off that franchise feeling, it's fine for a spot of yankee-doodle dining.

Red Lion
Metropolitan Hotel, Interchange 2, Sheikh Zayed Road (343 0000). **Open** noon-1am daily. **Average** Dhs70. **Credit** AmEx, DC, MC, V. **Map** p274 C3.
One of the oldest bars in Dubai, this pseudo-English pub is decked out in all the traditional regalia: mock-Tudor beams, stained-glass windows and, bizarrely, models of German castles adorned with plastic sausages. The menu, however, is the key factor,

Purple patch: **More**'s decor is a brave attempt at arty chic. *See p107.*

offering well cooked pub-style lunches and dinners. No surprises here: you get perfectly adequate steak and kidney pie, chicken curry, fish and chips, and no skimping on portions.

Vintage

Wafi Pyramids at Wafi City mall, off Oud Metha Road (324 0000). **Open** 6pm-1am daily. **Average** Dhs180. **Credit** AmEx, DC, MC, V. **Map** p277 J3.
Through the imposing, sphinxy doors at Wafi Pyramids lies Vintage, a cosmopolitan wine bar with a legendary list of bottles, printed in a book-sized menu. As well as having more drink on offer than you could comfortably work through in three lifetimes, Vintage also supplies perfect tippling food: ham, fondue, gourmet pies and a beautiful assortment of cheeses. The sort of place you could happily settle in for the evening.

Zinc

Crowne Plaza Hotel, Sheikh Zayed Road (331 1111). **Open** 7pm-3am daily. **Average** Dhs250. **Credit** AmEx, DC, MC, V. **Map** p281 G10.
Turning an identity crisis (is it a bar, is it a restaurant, is it a club?) into an attribute (it's a brilliant mix of all three) Zinc is the ideal place to dance away a broken heart or nurture a new infatuation. The food is surprisingly good: the barbecued duck starter and seafood soup are particular tasty. The mains show Zinc to be a meat-market of the highest order: the fine selection of generously sized steaks is accompanied by an extensive range of sauces to fuel your bopping ardour. *See also p165.*

Deira

Cafés

Café Mozart

Next to Twin Towers shopping centre (221 6565). **Open** 8am-midnight daily. **Average** Dhs80. **No credit cards.** **Map** p279 J3.

Tucked away in a side alley in the shadow of the Twin Towers shopping centre, Café Mozart is largely unmolested by the light of day. Inside, with its plush velours seating it exudes an air of faded grandeur, and as a remedy to Dubai's standard ultra-modern mall experience, it's hard to fault. Given the café's slightly run-down feel, the menu comes as a surprise, featuring ambitious dishes such as lobster thermidor and veal steak. For the less daring, a selection of sandwiches is backed up by a reasonably priced choice of coffees.

Caravan Café

Hyatt Regency Hotel, Deira Corniche (209 1300). **Open** 24hrs daily. **Average** Dhs70. **Credit** AmEx, DC, MC, V. **Map** p279 J1.
An extremely comfortable place to top up your caffeine levels, the Caravan is filled with tasteful soft sofas and armchairs upholstered in local fabrics. The international spread of food may be pricey but is immaculately prepared and presented. The choice of coffees is limited, but a full range of teas is available, all served in an individual pot with spare hot water and petits fours on the side. Service is a little rushed, but that seems to suit the mainly business clientele down to the ground.

Lexus Café

Deira City Centre mall, Garhoud (295 3200). **Open** 10am-9.30pm daily. **Average** Dhs80. **Credit** MC, V. **Map** p277 K2.
The Lexus Café is a masterpiece of modern branding; don't even think of entering if you have a problem with aggressive product placement. There are Lexus placemats, embossed Lexus menus, 'Lexus surprise' mocktails and – less subtle – a huge great Lexus car in the middle of the room. The menu is light, focusing on salads, fat sandwiches, sushi and soup. As you wait for your food you can mull over the thoughtfully provided, entirely Lexus-based reading material, and wolf down excellent zesty mocktails. Ideal for a mid-shop coffee break if you can take the product placement.

More

next to Welcare Hospital, behind Lifco supermarket, Garhoud (283 0224). **Open** 8am-10pm daily. **Average** Dhs150. **Credit** AmEx, DC, MC, V. **Map** p277 K3.

A wonderful place to come for relaxed meals with friends, or a long-drawn-out coffee and cake on your own, More is lunch venue of choice for many an office worker. The main room is a warehouse of kookiness, filled with melons on pedestals and ball-bearing-studded sofas under a purple ceiling. Clients sit in comfy leather seats and take their time eating at huge mahogany tables scattered with papers and magazines. Dishes to choose from range from Canadian salmon to Australian beef and Dutch *pannekoeken* to Iranian chicken.

Skywalk Café

Tower A, Marriott Executive Apartments, Riggat Albuteen Street (213 1220). **Open** 7am-11pm daily. **Average** Dhs70. **Credit** AmEx, DC, MC, V. **Map** p277 K2.

You're unlikely to stumble across this café, but you won't regret setting out to find it. Shelves of Heinz beans, washing powder and magazines adorn the entrance (the place doubles as grocery store for apartment residents) but beyond that is a lovely, bright café with free internet terminals at the back. The fittings are wooden, and shelves of freshly baked bread and pastries form an integral part of the decor, as does the open-plan pizza prep area. Perfect for a cheeky Caesar salad, a fresh pizza and a hot chocolate with lashings of cream before checking your emails.

Vienna Café

JW Marriott Hotel, Muraqqabat Street (262 4444). **Open** 24hrs daily. **Average** Dhs70. **Credit** AmEx, DC, MC, V. **Map** p277 K1.

With its dark wooden panelling and cosy booths set against the window, the Marriott's ground-floor café is long on atmosphere and short on daylight. A popular haunt of businessmen, its gloomy interior and secluded seating also makes it perfect for clandestine liaisons. In keeping with the Viennese concept, all coffees bear German or pseudo-German names, with plain white coffee masquerading as a Wiener mélange. Alcoholic Irish coffees are also available.

Bars

The Cellar

The Aviation Club, Garhoud Road (282 4122). **Open** noon-4pm, 7pm-midnight daily. **Average** Dhs100. **Credit** AmEx, MC, V. **Map** p277 L3.

Dubai loves the Cellar for its smoking club nights, but it's also making a name for its upstanding booze food. The fondues are outstanding, and Dutch meat balls, smoked salmon ruffles and other upmarket nibbles are all more than welcome after a hard evening's drinking.

Dubliners

Le Meridien Dubai, Airport Road, Garhoud (282 4040). **Open** noon-midnight daily. **Average** Dhs70. **Credit** AmEx, DC, MC, V. **Map** p277 L2.

'De Dub, de pub, wid de grub' is the slogan, and it's not far wrong. This cosy, faux-Oirish watering hole is home to some top Guinness-food: doorstop sandwiches with home-made bread, Irish stew, fish and chips and a hefty Dhs39 all-day brekker with buttered toast and tea. *See p173.*

The Irish Village

Dubai Tennis Stadium, Garhoud Road (282 4750). **Open** 11am-1.30am daily. **Average** Dhs60. **Credit** AmEx, DC, MC, V. **Map** p277 L3.

Eat, Drink, Shop

Feel the squeeze

Dubai is packed to the gills and beyond with cheerful mocktail merchants, eager to whip up bananas and purée grapes on your behalf. **Fruitesca** at Deira City Centre (294 9150) has a top range of juices and cocktails, from chunky meals-in-a-cup with lashings of muesli to healthier options with alarmingly frank names. The 'bladder-cleansing tonic' with watermelon, grape and cranberry is perhaps the winner, but the 'pain remover' or 'cancer-killer' run close seconds.

At the pricier end of things, the **Sol Bar** at the Fairmont Hotel (332 5555) does lovely smoothies: its Be Berry version is wonderful, filled with raspberries, blueberries, strawberries, a squeeze of lemon and a hint of mint in an icy-cold yoghurt and milk blend.

However, if it's not dairy you desire you could always DIY a juice – mix a selection of up to 12 fruits for just Dhs20 a glass.

If you're not prepared to splash out on your juice, the **Al Ijaza Cafeteria** on Jumeirah Beach Road (344 4874) does a decent line in super-cheap mocktails. No fewer than 59 options are on offer: try a 'George Armani' juice, the perfect partner for a Dhs2 cheese and honey sandwich. Equally fine is the **Sport Athletic Café**, behind Lal's supermarket in Satwa (349 1980), where a straightforward fruit cocktail will set you back only Dhs5 a pop and will be knocked up in seconds. Their other mixes appear to have been named entirely at random: indulge in a cup of 'Nokia', 'Miami', 'Computer' or 'Bin Ladin' juice.

One of Dubai's most popular watering holes, and probably your best bet for fine pub fodder: toasted BLTs, light and fluffy cheese omelettes, and a daily roast. Boasting a massive outdoor area and live music from one-man-warbler Degsy, the IV is perfect for al fresco boozing during the winter months. *See also p173.*

Jumeirah

Cafés

Café Céramique
Town Centre mall, Beach Road (344 7331). **Open** 8am-midnight daily. **Average** Dhs65. **Credit** AmEx, MC, V. **Map** p282 C12.
This chilled art and craft eatery is an utter joy. It's the café equivalent of a long soaky bath: relaxing, peaceful and full of bright yellow ducks. People come here to work out their artistic demons on ceramic plates and pottery animals. Menu options include lasagna of smoked salmon, Japanese style, and 'mixed salad on a crispy brick'. Their designer bagels are fresh, simple and tasty, as well as very reasonably priced. *See also p151.*

Gerard's
Magrudy Centre, Beach Road (344 3327). **Open** 7am-11.30pm daily. **Average** Dhs80. **Credit** AmEx, DC, MC, V. **Map** p280 D9.
A Dubai institution. Gerard's lies in a small but cunningly constructed mall with an open-air courtyard at its heart. Inside the feel is upmarket, and the background music soothing classical, making this a popular venue for people trying to finish reading that novel or simply meeting Jumeirah-based friends for a mid-morning gossip. The snacks, cakes and sarnies are nothing to write home about but the mint tea, iced coffee and cappuccinos all hit the spot.

Japengo
Palm Strip mall, opposite Jumeirah Mosque (345 4979). **Open** 10am-1am daily. **Average** Dhs100. **Credit** AmEx, MC, V. **Map** p280 D9.
Japengo is a curious hybrid – part coffee shop, part pizzeria, part noodle bar and part sushi bar – yet somehow it works. The staff in these elongated premises are friendly, and keen for you to try something from the peculiar menu, which includes a huge selection of fruit smoothies in addition to the Italian and Japanese snacks.

Johnny Rocket's
Beach Road (344 7859). **Open** noon-midnight daily. **Average** Dhs80. **No credit cards.** **Map** p280 D9.
Johnny Rocket's offers 1950s US diner chic and enormous home-made burgers. Finish one of these mustard and relish-filled goliaths and you'll feel like you've run a cow-eating marathon. The long, thick shakes are sheer indulgence. Alternatives for burger sceptics include peanut butter and jelly sandwiches and hotdogs.

Lime Tree Café
Beach Road, next to The One shop (349 8498). **Open** 7.30am-8pm daily. **Average** Dhs80. **Credit** AmEx, MC, V. **Map** p280 D9.
If you're in the mood for a light lunch, the Lime Tree Café serves indisputably the best deli-style meals in town in perky, dayglo settings. Tuck into some vinegar-drizzled French beans with pine nuts and fat strips of smoked bacon, a bowlful of fruit-filled couscous or a chunky pair of red onion-stuffed chicken kebabs with spicy nut sauce. Take a comfy armchair in the main room or, if you are a sun-seeker or a smoker, head to the upstairs balcony.

Lobby Lounge (Ritz-Carlton)
Ritz-Carlton Hotel, Al Sufouh Road (399 4000). **Open** 11am-1.30am daily. **Average** Dhs120. **Credit** AmEx, DC, MC, V. **Map** p274 A5.
Teatime at the Ritz sees fresh-baked scones served to customers so deeply entrenched in their sofas that they may well never leave. On the ocean side of the lounge, the furniture is less well sprung, but any decrease in comfort is made up for by the glorious picture-postcard sea views, complete with waving palm trees. In winter, an outdoor terrace provides a perfect place to sip and watch the waves lap the shore. A range of cakes is on offer, as are snacks such as chicken tikka, which is cooked at your table on a heated rock.

Lobby Lounge (Royal Mirage)
One&Only Royal Mirage Hotel, Al Sufouh Road (399 9999). **Open** noon-12.45am daily. **Average** Dhs150. **Credit** AmEx, DC, MC, V. **Map** p274 A5.
The lobby lounge in the Royal Mirage is breathtaking, but the veranda overlooking the sea takes the biscuit. Sink into deep chairs outside in the cool, late afternoon breeze and feast on the fabulous view while contemplating which of the three waist-expanding tea options (Arabic, British or chocolate, all at Dhs75) to try. Head over towards the end of the day and enjoy watching the sun sinking into the sea over the rim of a fine teacup.

La Marquise
Palm Strip mall, opposite Jumeirah Mosque (345 8433). **Open** 10am-1am Sat-Thur; 3pm-1am Fri. **Average** Dhs70. **Credit** MC, V. **Map** p280 D9.
La Marquise styles itself as an upmarket *salon de thé* and upholsters itself to match; its regal blue armchairs are comfortable and decorated with gold stars. Perhaps because the walls of the café are all glass, this place has the feel of a hotel lobby, although the outside tables on a veranda overlooking the mosque are an option in cooler weather. The main food menu is extensive, stretching from Italian dishes and sandwiches to French specialities via juicy burgers.

Oasis Restaurant
21c Street, off Al Wasl Road, towards Al Sufouh in Umm Suqeim 1 (394 9353). **Open** 8am-2am daily. **Average** Dhs20. **No credit cards.** **Map** p274 B4.

The One Café, home of the self-saucing chocolate cake.

Between a mosque and a sandy place lies the Oasis, crown prince of all things cheap and cheerful, the ideal spot to pick up some bargain lunch before skipping off down the beach. Whether they tend you at your car or at the Formica tables within, the greenclad waiters waste no time doling out some of the best chicken *shoarma* in town. Double up with a small banana juice and it's yours for the laughable sum of Dhs4.50.

The One Café

The One shop, Beach Road, next to Jumeirah Mosque (345 6687). **Open** 9am-10pm Sat-Thur; 2-10pm Fri. **Average** Dhs70. **Credit** AmEx, DC, MC, V. **Map** p280 D9.
The first floor of a giant furniture store may not sound like the most promising location, but The One café makes great use of its limited space, separated from the rest of the shop by floor-length muslin curtains that lend the place a soft, tranquil atmosphere. The menu changes constantly, with new themes (such as Caribbean, Cajun or Creole) all carried off with relative aplomb. The self-saucing chocolate cake is pure sin.

Paul

Mercato Mall, Beach Road (344 4161). **Open** 8am-11pm daily. **Average** Dhs120. **Credit** MC, V. **Map** p282 C12.
Occupying a side wing at this Italianate mega-mall, Paul is a pretty enough gallic caff with an inviting dark wood decor. Heart-rending French pop from the '70s is upsettingly loud inside, but you're fairly safe in the outer courtyard. Freshly baked pastries,

breads and quiche are the keynote here: all are outstandingly good. Cheesy, hyper-calorific tourtes, creamy gratins and ham-topped tartines all come with dressed salad and just-baked olive and sesame rolls. Service is slower than a tortoise, but for a spot of Parisian lunch the place is ideal.

Sahn Eddar

Burj Al Arab Hotel, Beach Road (301 7600). **Open** 7am-10am daily. **Average** Dhs200. **Credit** AmEx, DC, MC, V. **Map** p274 A4.
From your tables at Sahn Eddar you can watch the performing fountain at the front entrance to the Burj Al Arab, set against a backdrop of beach and sea. Cream teas with all the trimmings push all the right buttons, especially if you take them 'with champagne'. As with everything at the Burj, however, a meal here is very expensive and you must book ahead to get in at the front gate.

Bars

Dhow & Anchor

Jumeirah Beach Hotel, Beach Road (348 0000). **Open** 12.30-11.30pm daily. **Average** Dhs100. **Credit** AmEx, DC, MC, V. **Map** p274 B4.
This small hostelry tucked away to the side of the main Jumeirah Beach Hotel lobby is a neat and tidy version of an English country local. The split-level terrace outside with sea and Burj al Arab views is idyllic in the cooler months. Food is classic pub grub: fish and chips, pies and puddings, all in giant-sized portions, and there's a special kids' menu on hand.

bayti بيتي

ROBERTO & LEONARDI

Talk smart,
walk smart, look smart
and shop smart.

عركـز المـارينـا
MARINA MALL

Customer Service: 02 6812310 - E-mail: info@marinamall.ae

Shops & Services

From malls to markets, gold to Gucci, this city is a consumer's paradise.

Dubai has a reputation for being 'the shopping capital of the Middle East', with most shops located in vast air-conditioned malls. Yet despite the city's tax-free status, prices in the malls aren't generally any cheaper than you might find in any other major city. Genuine bargains are really only to be had during the month-long **Dubai Shopping Festival** (*see p141*), when posters declaring discounts of anything up to 75 per cent are the norm. A more permanent source of deals can be found in the guise of Dubai's souks, but you'll have to barter hard to get the costs down. Nonetheless, the city's malls do run year-round promotions and raffles with great prizes to be won, from a bar of gold to a new car. To enter, all you usually have to do is hand over your till receipt.

What Dubai does offer the customer is a great deal of choice: the main shopping malls are full of international brands, designer labels and speciality stores and come equipped with adequate parking and fierce air-conditioning (take a sweater even if it's 100 degrees outside). Malls don't follow traditional opening hours – the majority open from Saturday to Thursday from 10am to 10pm, while on Friday they open

at 4pm and close at 11pm. During the holy month of Ramadan, shop hours vary: most will be open 9am-1pm and 7-10pm Saturday to Thursday. On Friday they will only open in the evening, from 7-11pm. Opening hours also change radically during the Dubai Shopping Festival (*see p141*).

Don't forget the streets and souks for shopping as bargains are up for grabs here – it's worth braving the heat for them. **Karama** market area (*see p130* **Instant Karama**) is the place to go for all your fake designer handbags and shoes, the gold souk (*see p118* **Going for gold**) is a must if you're after jewellery, and the textile souk has plenty of fabrics, which one of the city's many tailors will transform into a top-notch suit. Shops in these areas generally follow traditional opening hours, so expect to find them closed at lunchtime (between 1pm and 4pm) and on Friday until 4pm.

In the malls, all major retailers accept credit cards including American Express, Visa, MasterCard and Diners Club, and many also have foreign currency exchange centres and ATM machines. Small traders, souks and local convenience stores will, however, only accept

Deira City Centre, Dubai's most popular mall. *See p115.*

Eat, Drink, Shop

cash. American dollars are widely accepted, but the best bargains are to be had using the local currency. Being equipped with dirhams will make shopping a whole lot easier, quicker and, if you haggle hard, cheaper too.

Thursday is the busiest shopping day, since for many people here it's the start of the weekend. Unless you enjoy the competition, you may find the inevitable crowds unbearable.

'BARGAINING'

Haggling is a tradition in Dubai's souks and independent shops, and it really is rare to pay the full price on the tag – if there is one. Most shopkeepers will quote you a figure saying that it is the price 'before discount'. Even the 'best price' isn't necessarily as low as you can go. The trick to haggling is to take your time, be polite and to decide what you are happy to pay for the item. A common rule is to initially offer half the quoted price. If you can't get the price down, simply walk away; many shop assistants will literally chase you out into the street to secure a purchase. Bargaining is not common practice in malls, although it doesn't hurt to ask for a discount, especially if you're paying cash.

The best Malls

Deira City Centre
Easily the most popular mall in Dubai, with everything from handbags and jewellery to cosmetics and trendy clothes. Brace yourself for the crowds. See p115.

Mercato Mall
The best mall in Dubai for hip, young fashion. Funky independent clothes shops and the trendiest high street labels dominate. See p115.

BurJuman Centre
It's a mammoth mall with plenty of upmarket appeal, offering designer clothes, high-end jewellery and top leather goods. See right.

Wafi City
Eclectic in look with its stained-glass ceiling and Egyptian features, Wafi City boasts an excellent range of designer clothes outlets, unique home furnishing shops and top-quality electronic stores. See p115.

Al Ghurair City
Lacks the glitz and glamour of the other big malls, but has plenty of quirky, attractive gift items at reasonable prices. See p115.

SHIPPING

To export goods home contact a cargo or shipping agency directly, *see p247* **Courier companies** or consult the Yellow Pages under 'Shipping'. A good agency will give you a quote for shipping bulk items home and most operate globally. The price of exporting goods varies depending on the item (electronic goods can be more expensive) and quantity. In the end visitors may find it isn't worth the money to ship items home, as export tax makes the process very expensive. During the **Dubai Shopping Festival** (*see p141*) and **Dubai Summer Surprises** (*see p140*) a few courier and shipping companies have special rates which are worth checking out.

REFUNDS

There are no laws, codes or regulations in Dubai to protect customers, which means that it is up to the store whether they offer refund or an exchange on faulty goods. Faulty goods are more easily exchanged than refunded, especially if you have kept the receipt. If you are returning an unwanted gift you'll have more luck if the item has not been worn or used and is still in its original packaging. To be on the safe side, always check the refund and exchange policy before making a purchase.

Malls

Bur Dubai

BurJuman Centre
Trade Centre Road (352 0222/www.burjuman.com). **Open** 10am-10pm Sat-Thur; 4-10pm Fri. **Map** p279 J5.
The BurJuman centre is a classy affair, with plenty of exclusive outlets selling designer brands: Donna Karan, Christian Lacroix, Calvin Klein, Cartier, Tiffany and Louis Vuitton. A Dhs1.4 million extension is taking BurJuman to four times its current size; when it's finished the Middle East's flagship Saks Fifth Avenue will sit next to Prada and Chanel in the extension. Electronics, home furnishings, perfume and cosmetic retailers can also be found. Entertainment features include a multi-screen cinema complex, a leisure arcade for younger shoppers, a food court and numerous cafés and restaurants. For outdoor seating – and top-notch sarnies – head to the Dôme café (*see p103*) at street level.

Emirates Towers Boulevard
Sheikh Zayed Road (330 0000). **Open** 10am-10pm Sat-Thur; 4-10pm Fri. **Map** p276 H4.
The Shopping Boulevard links the Emirates Hotel and Office towers, and is mapped out over two floors. As befits the location, this is a place for some serious, smart shopping. Designer-label boutiques – superstars Gucci, Giorgio Armani, Yves Saint Laurent and leather accessory store Bottega Veneta

Eat, Drink, Shop

Eat, Drink, Shop

Mercato Mall: Grand entrance. *See p115.*

Cool for suits at Mercato's **Massimo Dutti**.

– dominate the ground floor. Upstairs there's anchor shop Villa Moda, housing top-notch designs from the likes of Prada, Alexander McQueen and Stella McCartney. For glamorous shoes and bags to accessorise, head to Jimmy Choo, before rounding off your spree with some seriously sexy lingerie from Janet Reger next door.

Lamcy Plaza
Oud Metha (335 9999). **Open** 10am-10pm Sat-Wed; 10am-10.30pm Thur. **Map** p277 J3.

Lamcy is not an especially good-looking mall – the decor is dated, the layout is muddling, the huge waterfall at the entrance is tacky and the replica Tower Bridge is just extraordinary. Escalators connect the levels, but they're well hidden, so finding your way round can be tiresome. However, if you're looking for cheap 'n' cheerful goods, from footwear to home accessories, Lamcy is the place to go. High-street fashion outlets include Dorothy Perkins, Tammy and Jeffrey Rogers, while cut-price outlets encompass Shoemart, Fashion Factory and Mr Price. The feng shui shop on the ground floor, with its oriental knick-knacks, candles, wall hangings

and Buddha statues, is also worth a visit. Lamcy is always full of shoppers taking advantage of the constant promotions, so be prepared for the crowds. If it all gets too much, the Pizza Hut and Mongolian BBQ should help to keep you going.

Oasis Centre
Between Interchanges 2 & 3, Sheikh Zayed Road (339 5459). **Open** 10am-10pm Sat-Thur; 2-10pm Fri. **Map** p274 B4.

This glass-fronted, elongated mall is often overlooked because it's located away from the hub of Dubai action, a ten-minute drive along Sheikh Zayed Road heading towards Jumeirah. Shops are spread over two floors, with the focal point being the large Home Centre stocking top-quality furniture, accessories and furnishings at affordable prices. The Lifestyles store is also good for bargain brand-name cosmetics, bath accessories and gift items, while other cheap outlets include fashion store Splash and sensible footwear shop Shoemart. There's also a jungle-themed food court and free play area for children, plus Cyborg, a noisy, neon venue with a ten-pin bowling alley.

Abu Dhabi Trade Center
Shop in Style and Stay in Luxury

- A City Conference Resort
- The Beach Rotana Hotel & Towers features 558 luxurious Rooms and Suites
- 10 International dining venues
- Beach club with all leisure and fitness facilities
- Exclusive passageway connects the Hotel to the prestigious Abu Dhabi Mall
- Over 200 shops and restaurants at the Abu Dhabi Mall
- 9 cinemas and a children's entertainment complex at Abu Dhabi Mall
- Over 3000 covered car parking spaces

BEACH ROTANA
HOTEL & TOWER
ABU DHABI

مركز أبوظبي
ABU DHABI MALL

closer to y

For more information and reservations please contact
Beach Rotana Hotel & Towers
Tel: +971 2 644 3000, Fax: +971 2 644 2111, e-mail: beach.hotel@rotana.com or
Abu Dhabi Mall
Tel: +971 2 645 4858, Fax: +971 2 645 7737, e-mail: admall@emirates.net.ae

Gardens Shopping Mall

The Gardens Mall is due to open late September 2004, and will be located along Sheikh Zayed Road, between Interchanges 5 and 6. The single-level mall, which will be the largest in the UAE, will have five themed shopping zones with influences taken from Morocco, Egypt, Persia, India and China. Entertainment, restaurants and family activities will all be found here, together with retail outlets including Next, River Island, Top Shop and Dorothy Perkins. French hypermarket Géant will offer customers groceries, textiles, fashionwear, electronics and household items.

Wafi City

Oud Metha Road (352 0222). **Open** 10am-10pm Sat-Thur; 4-10pm Fri. **Map** p277 J3.
Wafi is easy to spot, thanks to the three concrete pyramids (the Wafi Pyramids) surrounding it. A quiet, upmarket mall, it is spread over four floors. Modern and elegant in design, it competes with BurJuman on the chic label front. Chanel, Givenchy and Jaeger are just some of the international names that share floor space with regional designer labels. On the first floor are shops with more affordable price tags, such as Miss Sixty, Jumbo Electronics and shoe store Connexion. There's a good range of coffee shops and restaurants, from the much-loved Indian eaterie, Asha's (*see p86*), to the laid-back Elements café (*see p103*). There's also Lebanese delicatessen Goodies (*see p104*), dishing out Arabic and continental cuisine to take away or enjoy on the terrace. The children's entertainment centre, Encounter Zone, is on the third floor, and there are pizzas and burgers at the food court next door.

Deira

Al Ghurair City

Al Rigga Road (223 2333). **Open** 10am-10pm Sat-Thur; 2-10pm Fri. **Map** p279 K3.
This 20-year-old mall (the oldest in Dubai) combines Arabic decor with modern design. Popular outlets include French Connection, Guess, Nine West, Virgin Cosmetics and Book Corner. The mall is a bit of a maze and spread over two floors, with corridors branching out at all angles, but it's worth persevering: tucked in the alleyways are excellent speciality stores selling everything from Arabic jewellery and rugs to South African beauty products and children's Italian dresses. There are also an eight-screen cineplex and numerous food and coffee outlets.

Deira City Centre

Garhoud (295 1010). **Open** 10am-10pm Sat-Thur; 2-10pm Fri. **Map** p277 K2.
The most popular mall in Dubai has more than 280 shops, two food courts, an entertainment centre and cinema multiplex spread over three floors. Chain stores include Debenhams and Ikea, and high-street fashion names Top Shop and River Island; independent outlets sell local artefacts. For such a vast mall it's surprisingly simple to navigate, with giant hypermarket Carrefour dominating the first floor. The mall also contains plenty of corridors leading to miniature themed courts including the Jewellery Court, Textile Court and Arabian Treasures, selling carpets, antiques and gifts. Among the 30-plus eateries are Burger King, McDonald's, Starbucks and Costa Coffee. There's even an 11-screen multiplex cinema and an eight-lane bowling alley. Children can go wild in the sprawling amusement centre, Magic Planet. On the lower floor is Citygate, which houses more than 40 electronic shops. Note that parking here can become ridiculously congested at peak times, even though there are 4,000 spaces.

Jumeirah

Jumeirah Centre

Beach Road (349 9702). **Open** 10am-9pm Thur-Sat; 5-9pm Fri. **Map** p280 D9.
This small, attractive mall is very popular with Jumeirah residents. Outlets are arranged over two floors and include Benetton, Emirates Sport and Body Shop downstairs, while upstairs discounted designer fashions can be found at Blue Cactus and local handicrafts at Sunny Days. Textiles and Persian rugs are further highlights. Or just sit back with a coffee at La Brioche and soak up the quiet, calm surroundings.

Jumeirah Plaza

Beach Road (349 7111). **Open** 10am-10pm Sat-Thur; 5-10pm Fri. **Map** p280 D9.
A small shopping centre with an eye-catching pink front. Stores include gift shop Susan Walpole and the excellent second-hand bookshop House of Prose. There are also a few craft and rug shops upstairs, plus a safe play area for children.

Mercato Mall

Beach Road (344 4161). **Open** 10am-10pm Sat-Thur; 2-10pm Fri. **Map** p282 C12.
When it comes to looks this brave new mall takes top prize, with its richly coloured walls and Venetian murals. The building is themed on a medieval Italian town, so there are plenty of meandering passageways and mock town squares, Mercato being the Italian word for market. While Spinneys supermarket caters for foodies, and Home Centre offers a range of furnishings, the mall has developed a reputation for innovative clothes stores, drawing the young and trendy. Make sure you check out the funky swimwear at Moda Brazil, the *Sex and the*

Shopping by design

BurJuman Centre

Calvin Klein, Christian Lacroix, Donna Karan/DKNY, Louis Vuitton, Ralph Lauren, Salvatore Ferragamo. See p112.

Deira City Centre

Burberry, Dolce & Gabbana, Tiffany & Co. See p115.

Emirates Towers Boulevard

Bottega Veneta, Bulgari, Cartier, Giorgio Armani, Gucci, Janet Reger, Jimmy Choo. See p112.

Mercato Mall

Fleurt (Betsey Johnson), Emporio Armani, Hugo Boss. See p115.

Wafi City

Chanel, Designers' Club at St John. See p115.

City-style dresses at Fleurt and the cute, affordable shoes at PrettyFIT. Starbucks in the downstairs foyer is a popular meeting spot, while those seeking a quieter caffeine fix should head to tea shop Paul (*see p109*), with its quaint French snack menu. Every fashion taste is pretty much catered for at Mercato: Junior Armani for designer kids, Top Shop and Mango for mainstream trends, Massimo Dutti and Hugo Boss for the more mature shopper. Other stores worth visiting are funky home interiors shops Kas Australia and Living Zone, and cosmetic outlets Areej and MAC. This is also a good place for Persian and Iranian carpets, gold jewellery and local artefacts, although prices are higher than in the souks. There's a Virgin Megastore for all music and DVD needs, a food court on the first floor, and a seven-screen cinema.

Palm Strip

Beach Road (346 1462). **Open** 10am-10pm Sat-Thur; 5-10pm Fri. **Map** p280 D9.
This small whitewashed mall is the only open-air shopping centre in Dubai. Shops are set back from the road and arranged over two levels. Downstairs is dominated by the monolithic Mango clothes store, Starbucks coffee shop and Japengo restaurant (*see p108*), while upstairs you'll find CD shop Music Master and the N-Bar (nail bar). Other fashionable outlets include Karen Millen, Young Designers Emporium and Escada Sport. Because it's an open-air mall there's no dire piped music, but there is also no air-con, making it quite uncomfortable in the peak summer months.

Souks

Dubai is awash with local markets, and the creekside souks are a remnant of its days as a thriving port for smugglers and traders in the 19th century. While much has changed since then, the Deira and Bur Dubai souks still have plenty of goods that are worth haggling over, from spices and silks to electronics and gold.

Food

Food souk

Opposite the gold souk, Deira. **Open** 9am-1pm, 4-10pm Sat-Thur; 4-10pm Fri. **Map** p278 H2.
Dubai's bustling fruit and veg souk shares an enormous hangar-like space with the fish market in Deira. A quick tour of the pungent fish section will get you stocked up in seconds, as salesmen force their wares on you – sometimes going to the extent of slipping fish in your basket and then demanding cash. Having haggled over hammour (the local version of cod) and bartered over barracuda, head to the much less frantic fruit and vegetable arena. Huge piles of melons, guava and onions are all there for the taking (for a small price).

Spices

Spice souk

Between Al Nasr Square & the Creek area at the gold souk, Deira. **Open** 9am-1pm, 4-10pm Sat-Thur; 4-10pm Fri. **Map** p278 H3.
Buying food at the markets and souks of Dubai isn't necessarily much cheaper than supermarket shopping, but it's a million times more fun. Entering the spice souk by the main abra station on the Deira side of the Creek, you plunge into a cobweb of thin alleyways filled with mainly Iranian shops piled high with fragrant goods. Spend some time wandering around, absorbing the atmosphere, and be prepared to haggle when you find something you want. Big barrels of cumin, dried lemons and coriander seed surround you on all sides and vie for space alongside baskets of star of anise, stacks of cinnamon sticks and oodles of frankincense. Heaven for food lovers.

Textiles

Textile souk

Al Fahidi Street, Bur Dubai. **Open** 9am-1pm, 4-10pm Sat-Thur; 4-10pm Fri. **Map** p278 H4.
With so many textile shops in Dubai, it makes financial sense to buy material here and have it made up into the style of your favourite trousers or shirt. Tailors can copy from an original item or from a pattern, with simple designs costing about Dhs30 and taking only a day or two to complete. A good tailor will advise on how much cloth you need (buy a little extra to be on the safe side) and offer you at least one

Souks: the spice of Dubai life. *See p116.*

Going for gold

The gold souk near the Hyatt Regency in Deira is the place to go for exotic, unique jewellery. The shaded walkway is flanked by shop windows full of gold (and, to a lesser extent, silver) bracelets, rings, pendants and necklaces. Designs are both modern and traditional, heavy and delicate. Gold in Dubai is crafted in India and comes in several shades; the most popular jewellery is 24-carat and orangey in colour, but you can also get 18, 21 and 22 carat. Some of the antique shops also sell genuine silver Omani Bedouin silver – which is not only beautiful but increasingly rare (and valuable) as demand outstrips supply.

There are very strict laws involving authenticity of gold, so if a shop attendant tells you a piece of jewellery is 24-carat, then it probably is. Prices fluctuate depending on whether the piece was made by a craftsman or a machine, and the price of gold on that day. Most items are sold by weight but you should bargain hard.

There are plenty of alleyways leading off to little shops (the best of which are listed below), so allow plenty of time to explore throughout. Benches in the covered walkway are perfect for resting on in between browsing, but sit for more than a second and you will get jumped on by traders attempting to flog counterfeit watches.

In the unlikely event that you can't find a design you like among the thousands on offer, take in a photo or drawing of what you want and a craftsman will make it up for you. As well as rings and bracelets, you can get money clips, touristy knick-knacks and even gold tiaras. For something more unusual, have your name cut on to a necklace in English or Arabic, or bargain over *shisha* pipes, backgammon sets and voluminous black *abayas*.

Aries Trading
Old Gold Market, opposite gold souk main entrance (225 9891). **Open** 9am-1.30pm, 4-10pm Sat-Thur; 9-11.30am, 4.30-10pm Fri. **No credit cards**. **Map** p278 H3.
Bargains galore are to be found at this silver jewellery store. Heavy chokers, chunky chain bracelets and tarnished Indian toe rings are all stocked, as are more unusual pieces.

AST
Next to Aries Trading, Old Gold Market, gold souk (225 5727). **Open** 9.30am-2pm, 4-10pm Sat-Thur; 4-10pm Fri. **Credit** AmEx, MC, V. **Map** p278 H3.
AST is good for cheap pashminas that look far more expensive than they are – prices start at Dhs15. There's no shortage of variety, from plain or printed to embroidered or decorated with beads and tassels. If you want to spend a bit more cash, the store manager will happily produce attractive but more expensive pashminas costing around Dhs2,500.

Gulf Novelties
Turn right at main entrance to gold souk, shop in an alleyway on the left (226 4720). **Open** 9am-1pm, 4-9.30pm Sat-Thur; 4-9pm Fri. **Credit** AmEx, MC, V. **Map** p278 H3.
This crammed shop is a great place for gifts and curiosities, including wooden camels, marble chess sets, *shisha* pipes, *dishdashes* (men's ankle-length shirts) and ultimately tacky Burj Al Arab miniatures.

Al Jaber Gallery
Turn right at main entrance to gold souk, shop at far end (226 8092). **Open** 9am-1pm, 4-10pm Sat-Thur; 4-10pm Fri. **Credit** AmEx, MC, V. **Map** p278 H3.
A good source of *shisha* pipes (Dhs45-Dhs100 depending on your haggling skills), wooden backgammon sets (Dhs50), and heavy, silver Arabic bracelets.

Eat, Drink, Shop

fitting before the final stitching. If you're not completely happy with the way your finished garment looks, don't be shy to ask them to make alterations.

For a good range of textile shops in a single area, head to Al Fahidi Street in Bur Dubai (the two below are the best). It's a good place to pick up material for your suit, shirt or skirt. Most of the shops close around lunchtime, so get there early morning or late afternoon. Avoid taking a car, as parking is a nightmare and the one-way road is guaranteed to be congested with taxis, pedestrians and cyclists. If you get caught short of cash there are ATM machines and a Thomas Cook exchange bureau.

Meena Bazar
Meena Bazar Lane, off Al Fahidi Street, Bur Dubai (352 1374). **Open** 9.30am-1pm, 4.30-10pm Sat-Thur; 4.30-10pm Fri. **Credit** AmEx, MC, V. **Map** p278 H4.
The best-known textile shop in the area, Meena Bazar is the place all the taxi drivers will take you to if you ask for the 'textile souk'. The store stocks raw silk, Burberry silk, chiffon, metallic net and plain cotton, as well as plenty of more expensive embroidered material. Prices vary, but be prepared to haggle.

Rivoli
Al Fahidi Street, Bur Dubai (353 5448). **Open** 9.30am-1pm, 4.30-10pm Sat-Thur; 4.30-10pm Fri. **Credit** AmEx, MC, V. **Map** p278 H4.
A smart textile shop with men's fabrics downstairs and ladies' materials upstairs. Swiss cotton, French chiffon and silk are all stocked, and the shop assistants are keen to offer 'best discount'. There's also a good range of Italian cotton in plain and check design that is ideal for shirts. Textiles purchased here can be made up by the Rivoli tailor shop over in Karama at a discount.

Antiques

Creative Art Centre
Behind Choithram supermarket, Beach Road, Jumeirah (344 4394). **Open** 8am-6pm Sat-Thur. **Credit** MC, V. **Map** p282 C12.
This gallery set in two villas displays local fine art, antiques, gifts and souvenirs. Among the collector's items are chests, old Omani doors made into coffee tables and Bedouin silver, while gift items – starting from Dhs15 – include freshwater pearls.

Lucky's
Industrial Area no.11, Sharjah (06 534 1937). **Open** 9am-1pm, 4-8.30pm Sat-Thur; 9am-noon, 4-8.30pm Fri. **Credit** MC, V. **Map** p275 F1.
Based in Sharjah's industrial area, Lucky's is the best place to head for large pieces of Indian antique furniture at bargain prices.

Majlis Gallery
Al Fahidi roundabout, Bastakia, Bur Dubai (353 6233). **Open** 9.30am-1.30pm, 4.30-8pm Sat-Thur. **Credit** AmEx, MC, V. **Map** p278 H4.
This old courtyard and series of exhibition rooms

hosts regular shows by local and international artists and craftspeople. It's a bit hit and miss, but the occasional treasure can be found. *See also p158.*

Marina
Al Barsha, Interchange 4, Sheikh Zayed Road, Bur Dubai (347 8940). **Open** 9.30am-8.30pm Sat-Thur; 3-8.30pm Fri. **Credit** AmEx, MC, V. **Map** p274 B5.
A warehouse jam-packed with Indian, Indonesian and Italian furniture – both original items and reproductions – all at low prices.

Petals
Wafi City mall, Oud Metha Road (324 6266). **Open** 10am-10pm Sat-Thur; 4-10pm Fri. **Credit** AmEx, MC, V. **Map** p277 J3.
Shopping at Petals is a unique experience, to say the least. With its chic leopard-print chaises longues, lavish coloured chandeliers and fancy chairs covered in crushed- velvet, it's well worth a browse.

Showcase Antiques, Art & Frames
Beach Road, off Interchange 3, Sheikh Zayed Road, Umm Suqeim (348 8797). **Open** 10am-1pm, 4-8pm Sat-Thur; 4-8pm Fri. **Credit** AmEx, MC, V. **Map** p274 B4.
The wonderful display of antiques, art and collectibles on offer at this shop includes local dowry chests, silver Bedouin jewellery (such as fabulous chunky rings), silver *khanjars* (daggers), and antique coffee pots and coffee tables, plus furniture from Europe. A selection of British antiques is housed upstairs.

Books

Censorship laws in Dubai mean that all books coming into the country are checked, and anything too controversial regarding politics or Islam is likely to be banned, as are any art (or other) books containing nudes. You can buy most international magazines here, but any revealing photos will be blacked out by a thick, black marker pen.

Book Corner
Al Ghurair City mall, Al Rigga Road, Deira (228 2835). **Open** 10am-10pm Sat-Thur; 2-10pm Fri. **Credit** AmEx, MC, V. **Map** p279 K3.
This is the largest bookshop in the Middle East and as such stocks titles on everything imaginable, from architecture to zoology. It's usually quick to get in the latest releases, and often offers good discounts. **Other locations**: Dune Centre, Satwa (345 5490).

Books Plus
Lamcy Plaza mall, Oud Metha (336 6362). **Open** 10am-10pm Sat-Thur. **Credit** AmEx, MC, V. **Map** p277 J3.
A wide selection of books, international newspapers and magazines in both English and Arabic. It also has a decent range of fiction and non-fiction titles, plus new arrivals and bestsellers.

Eat, Drink, Shop

BookWorld

Al Hudaiba Street, Satwa (349 1914). **Open** 10am-1pm, 5-9pm Sat-Thur; 5-9pm Fri. **Credit** AmEx, MC, V. **Map** p280 E9.

The biggest and best range of second-hand books in Dubai, all in good condition and arranged in alphabetical order on sliding bookshelves, and a selection of old international and local magazines. Buy, read, then return to get a percentage of your money back.

Book Worm

Near Park'n'Shop, Al Safa Complex, Jumeirah (394 5770). **Open** *Summer* 10am-1pm, 4-7pm Sat-Thur. *Winter* 10am-8pm Sat-Thur. **Credit** AmEx, MC, V. **Map** p276 F5.

The only bookshop in Dubai dedicated to children's books, in English, French and Arabic.

House of Prose

Jumeirah Plaza mall, Beach Road, Jumeirah (344 9021). **Open** 10am-10pm Sat-Thur; 5.30-8pm Fri. **No credit cards. Map** p280 D9.

This second-hand bookshop is not as big as BookWorld (*see above*), but titles are all in good condition. You'll find children's books, classics, contemporary fiction and travel guides, all neatly arranged in alphabetical order. The shop will also buy your used books.

Magrudy's

Deira City Centre mall, Garhoud (295 7744). **Open** 10am-10pm Thur-Sat; 2-10pm Fri. **Credit** AmEx, MC, V. **Map** p277 K2.

Magrudy's is the best bookshop in the Emirates: if you can't find it here you're unlikely to find it anywhere else. In worst-case scenarios you can always request that a title be ordered in. Browse through the hundreds of shelves covering everything from biographies to blockbusters. There's also a small stationery section and a coffee shop.
Other locations: Magrudy Centre, Beach Road, Jumeirah (344 4192).

Virgin Megastore

Mercato Mall, Beach Road, Jumeirah (344 6971). **Open** 10am-10pm Sat-Thur; 2-10pm Fri. **Credit** AmEx, MC, V. **Map** p282 C12.

The pounding beat from the vast music section makes this an impossible place to stand and browse. It's more impressive for its range of glossy coffee-table reading matter rather than serious literature. *See also p135.*

Computing & electricals

For a real bargain, the past and present collide headlong in so-called '**Computer Street**', a flurry of shops selling today's electronics in a modern twist on yesteryear's souks. Found on **Khalid Bin Al Waleed Road** (Bank Street), Bur Dubai (Map p278 G4), it's more of a concept than a physical street and every bit a colourful, neon experience. Start where the road intersects

with Mankhool Road and you'll soon see the large **Computer Depot store** (355 1515), an open-plan showroom that stocks PCs and peripherals from all the big brands. From here you'll discover about a mile of shops squeezed along one side of the road with their small, glass fronts stacked with the latest computers, printers, scanners and almost every other conceivable networking toy.

Interspersed are Arabic cafés with plastic tables and chairs on the pavement. Once you've stocked up on refreshment turn down **Al Raffa Street** and you'll see yet more shops with billboards offering both new and used computers at wholesale and retail prices.

Just a blip on your GPS system awaylies **Electrical Street**, sharing space with the textile souk on Al Fahidi Street. In the evenings its shopfronts blaze with fluorescent and flashing lights, proudly proclaiming such manufacturers as Sharp, Sony, Panasonic and Philips. There's a vast range of electrical goods to choose from, and over-eager shop assistants will do their best to entice you in. Take your time and look for the best deal. On the whole prices are competitive, owing to the number of places offering the same or similar products, so you should be able to pick up a bargain DVD player, digital camera or stereo if you haggle hard. And do plug in your purchase in the shop to make sure it works properly. Most shops close for prayers between 1pm and 4pm and open again in the late afternoon until 11pm.

It pays to do a little research before heading out to hunt for electrical goods, as shop attendants are not always knowledgeable about their stock. If you are planning to take your item back home with you, check that you are buying a model that will operate in your home country (TVs are set to operate at different frequencies in different parts of the world, and DVD players are restricted to play discs from a certain region, so what works in Dubai won't necessarily work in London and Lahore).

Carrefour

Deira City Centre mall, Garhoud (295 1600). **Open** 10am-10pm Sat-Thur; 2-10pm Fri. **Credit** AmEx, MC, V. **Map** p277 K2.

At the best of times Carrefour is a bit of a scrum, but this vast hypermarket can't be beaten for its wide range of bargain electronics. Alongside the cameras and music systems are plenty of cheap, quality household items. You can pick up a microwave for as little as Dhs169 and a small fridge for just Dhs285.

CompuMe

Near Dubai Tennis Stadium, Zalfa Building, Garhoud Road, Garhoud (282 8555). **Open** 10am-10pm Sat-Thur; 4-10pm Fri. **Credit** AmEx, MC, V. **Map** p277 K2.

Chip shops: **Khalid Bin Al Waleed Road**, aka '**Computer Street**'. *See p120.*

The giant cubic greenhouse rising out of Garhoud is in fact home to one of the city's few dedicated IT stores. A broad range of hardware features laptops, PCs, PDAs and printers, including big-name vendors like HP, IBM, Dell and Toshiba. The self-titled 'megastore' includes a PC clinic, where repairs and upgrades are carried out while you wait, and sells specialist software programs, computing magazines and books.

Emirates Computers
Near Chilis Restaurant, Garhoud Road, Garhoud (282 5800/www.etechnoworld.com). **Open** 10am-10pm Sat-Thur; 4-10pm Fri. **Credit** AmEx, MC, V. **Map** p277 K2.
Known for its year-round sales promotions and raffles, EC typically has a deal or two to be struck on products from its primary brands Nokia and Dell. The UAE-wide distributor also stocks Proxima, Lexmark and Apple, and complements its IT range with high-tech toys like joysticks and a host of mobile phone accessories. It also has particularly generous discounts on its battery of gadgets during the Dubai Shopping Festival (*see p141*).

Jacky's Electronics
Airport Road, Garhoud (282 1822). **Open** 9am-1pm, 4-9pm Sat-Thur; 4-9pm Fri. **Credit** AmEx, MC, V. **Map** p277 K2.
Jacky's Electronic stocks a good range of white goods and electrical equipment at better-than-average prices. Its audio-visual choice is limited, but includes more popular Japanese brands as well as

the odd unit assembled on an Asian production line for less. There's a useful camera department with multiple digital camcorders and snap-shooters.
Other locations: Deira City Centre mall, Garhoud (294 9480).

Jumbo Electronics
Opposite Ramada Hotel, Al Mankhool Road, Bur Dubai (352 3555). **Open** 10am-1pm, 4.30-10pm Sat-Thur; 4-10pm Fri. **Credit** AmEx, MC, V. **Map** p278 H5.
Jumbo Electronics is big (so to speak) in Dubai, and popular for its exhaustive range of well-known brands such as Palm, Sony and Panasonic. It's particularly reliable for entry-level home theatres, games consoles, DVD players and simple but effective hi-fi systems.
Other locations: Wafi City mall, Oud Metha Road (324 2077).

Plug-Ins
Deira City Centre mall, Garhoud (295 0404). **Open** 10am-10pm Sat-Thur; 2-10pm Fri. **Credit** AmEx, MC, V. **Map** p277 K2.
This trusted store picks up a lot of passing trade from its prime spot in City Centre mall, but many more shoppers single out Plug-Ins for its friendly, well-informed staff. The broad range of kit extends from household consumer giants such as Panasonic and JVC, to more specialist items like Bose home theatre and Denon amplifiers. Expect to find everything from printers to laptops and digital cameras to plasma screens.

Step into Mercato.

The Good Life

Sharaf Enterprises

Opposite Astoria Hotel, Al Fahidi Street, Bur Dubai (353 4978). **Open** 9am-1pm, 4.30-10pm Thur-Sat; 9am-noon Fri. **Credit** AmEx, MC, V. **Map** p278 H4.
Filling the niche between bargain basement and reputable store, this place has every type of electrical equipment and home appliance you could wish for, from Sony CD Walkmans to Kenwood car radios, via Olympus cameras to Panasonic stereo systems. It even has an area selling gold and silver watches.

Swistar

Al Fahidi Street, Bur Dubai (353 9646). **Open** 9-11.30am, 2-11pm Thur-Sat; 9am-11pm Fri. **Credit** AmEx, MC, V.
Electrical equipment of all kinds is stacked in boxes by the shop entrance, with PlayStation 2s, Gameboys and numerous radio cassette players and portable TVs all on offer.

VV & Sons

Al Fahidi Street, Bur Dubai (353 2444). **Open** 9am-1pm, 4.30-9.30pm Sat-Thur. **Credit** AmEx, MC, V. **Map** p278 H4.
If you want to create some serious sound, this is the place to go. A vast range of speakers is displayed at the back of the shop, while upstairs there's a selection of high-quality DVD players and amplifiers for heavy-duty home theatre systems. In terms of names, lesser-known brands such as Jamo and Sherwood sit next to international favourites like JBL. Turntables and professional DJ sound equipment are not stocked in the shop, but can be ordered.

Department stores

Bhs

Al Ghurair City mall, Al Rigga Road, Deira (352 5150). **Open** 10am-10pm Sat-Thur; 2-10pm Fri. **Credit** AmEx, MC, V. **Map** p279 K3.
Most British expats will pinch themselves upon discovering a branch of Bhs thriving in Dubai. But thrive it does, with quality ranges at affordable prices. In practice, however, it's more of a children's clothing retailer than department store as the womenswear, home furnishing and lighting departments, which have transformed the brand elsewhere in the world, are yet to be launched in the UAE.

Debenhams

Deira City Centre mall, Garhoud (294 0011). **Open** 10am-10pm Sat-Thur; 2-10pm Fri. **Credit** AmEx, DC, MC, V. **Map** p277 K2.
The Dubai branch of Britain's biggest department store stocks all the things you would expect from this comprehensive retailer. As well as housing a perfumery and its own brand of clothing, Debenhams is home to concessions from the likes of TopShop and Oasis, and designer collections by John Rocha, Jasper Conran and Pearce Fionda. Also on sale is the entire Debenhams home line, including soft furnishings, fashion accessories and kitchen appliances.

Jashanmal

Wafi City mall, Oud Metha Road (324 4800). **Open** 10am-10pm Sat-Thur; 4-10pm Fri. **Credit** AmEx, DC, MC, V. **Map** p277 J3.
The Gulf's leading home-grown retailer. Both Dubai branches contain home furnishings, electrical appliances and home accessories. The Dubai branch also houses clothing collections by Thomas Burberry, Mexx and Clarks.
Other locations: Al Ghurair City mall, Al Rigga Road, Deira (227 7780).

Marks & Spencer

Salahudin Road, Deira (222 2000). **Open** 10am-10.30pm daily. **Credit** AmEx, DC, MC, V. **Map** p277 K1.
One of only eight M&S stores outside the UK to launch per una, the women's fashion brand and brainchild of design guru George Davies. This Dubai branch delivers on the same quality underwear, clothing and home accessories that loyal fans have come to expect from the brand. It lacks the variety and quality in the food hall, however – just one or two aisles offer up a trivial selection of dry and frozen goods.

Fashion

Beachwear

Heatwaves

Town Centre mall, Beach Road, Jumeirah (342 0445). **Open** 10am-10pm Sat-Thur; 5-10pm Fri. **Credit** AmEx, MC, V. **Map** p282 C12.
Heatwaves is reliable for basic, simple bikinis and swimsuits in a range of plain colours. Swimwear tends to be on the conservative side, but there are usually designs with high-cut bikini bottoms and strapless bikini tops added to the mix.

Moda Brazil

Mercato Mall, Beach Road, Jumeirah (344 3074). **Open** 10am-10pm Sat-Thur; 3-10pm Fri. **Credit** AmEx, MC, V. **Map** p282 C12.
This boutique stocks the widest selection of fashionable bikinis in town, from racy swimsuits to tropical-coloured bikinis. Sizes are on the small size, but designs are straight off the catwalk.

Sun&Sand Sports

Deira City Centre mall, Garhoud (295 5551). **Open** 10am-10pm Sat-Thur; 2-10pm Fri. **Credit** AmEx, MC, V. **Map** p277 K2.
Sensible swimwear for sporty types.

Women'secret

Deira City Centre mall, Garhoud (295 9665). **Open** 10am-10pm Sat-Thur; 2-10pm Fri. **Credit** AmEx, MC, V. **Map** p277 K2.
Although it's essentially an underwear shop, Women'secret also stocks a range of patterned swimsuits, pretty halterneck and string bikinis in a variety of colours.

Eat, Drink, Shop

Boutiques and bikinis: cornerstones of Dubai's shopping scene.

Boutiques

Abiti
Dana Centre, Al Maktoum Street, Deira (222 3383).
Open 9am-1pm, 4-9pm Sat-Thur. **Credit** AmEx,
MC, V. **Map** p279 K3.
This super-glamorous boutique is the place for dramatic evening dresses and hand-embroidered jeans, with the emphasis on feathers and sequins.

Blue Cactus
Jumeirah Centre mall, Beach Road, Jumeirah (344 7734). **Open** 10am-9pm Sat-Thur; 6-9pm Fri. **Credit** AmEx, MC, V. **Map** p280 D9.
The selection at Blue Cactus is small but covers a mix of top-quality chain-store labels and designer womenswear. Kay Unger dresses, Prada short-sleeve shirts and DKNY outfits are all offered at a fraction of their usual retail price.

Century 2000
Next to Carpetland, Za'abeel Road, Bur Dubai (336 6654). **Open** 9am-1pm, 4-8.30pm Sat-Thur. **Credit** AmEx, MC, V. **Map** p277 J3.
Century 2000 is considered to be a wholesale rather than retail shop, so all the designer shoes, mens- and womenswear are sold at lower than usual prices. The emphasis is on Italian labels, including Versace, D&G and Roberto Cavalli. It's also a good place to find the latest 'must-have' designer handbag.

Eve Michelle
Magrudy Centre, Beach Road, Jumeirah (342 9574).
Open 9.30am-8pm Sat-Thur. **Credit** AmEx, MC, V.
Map p280 D9.

A boutique selling costume jewellery, fashionable, glamorous tops and a selection of casual clothes. Many items are imported from London, and deliveries are regular, so you can normally chance upon some up-to-the-minute hip clobber. Hats and shoes are further draws.

Fleurt
Mercato Mall, Beach Road, Jumeirah (342 0906).
Open 10am-10pm Sat-Thur; 2-10pm Fri. **Credit**
AmEx, MC, V. **Map** p282 C12.
This sassy store has a small but desirable selection of sexy Betsey Johnson dresses, glam Kosiuko outfits, colourful leather handbags and stylish, modern jewellery. A great one-stop shop.

Moda Brazil
Mercato Mall, Beach Road, Jumeirah (344 3074).
Open 10am-10pm Sat-Thur; 3-10pm Fri. **Credit**
AmEx, MC, V. **Map** p282 C12.
A candy-coloured boutique with outlets in New York and Rio, Moda Brazil is a good place for sexy summer dresses and strappy tops with flirty fringes and motifs.

Childrenswear

Armani Junior
Mercato Mall, Beach Road, Jumeirah (342 0111).
Open 10am-10pm Sat-Thur; 2-10pm Fri. **Credit**
AmEx, MC, V. **Map** p282 C12.
Deck your little darling out in some seriously cool casuals; Armani jeans, T-shirts and hats are arranged neatly along the shelves.

Barbie Shop

Mercato Mall, Beach Road, Jumeirah (349 3490).
Open 10am-10pm Sat-Thur; 2-11pm Fri. **Credit**
AmEx, MC, V. **Map** p282 C12.
An ultra-girly, pink store, dedicated to the plastic
fantastic one. Barbie dolls and accessories are
stocked on one side, children's roller skates, pink
sunglasses, sweatshirts, beach shoes and beauty
sets on the other.

Little Bunnies

*BurJuman Centre mall, Trade Centre Road, Bur
Dubai (351 7955).* **Open** 10am-10pm Sat-Thur;
4-10pm Fri. **Credit** AmEx, MC, V. **Map** p279 J5.
Little Bunnies is home to pretty pinafore dresses,
cute romper suits, practical hooded tops, tracksuits
and jeans for girls and boys from 0-14. The highlight, though, has to be the fabulous range of silk
and linen party dresses from Dhs1,250.

Little Castle

Wafi City mall, Oud Metha Road (324 6525).
Open 10am-10pm Sat-Thur; 5-10pm Fri.
Credit AmEx, MC, V. **Map** p277 J3.
Cute designer dresses, trendy T-shirts and smart
suits for kids can all be found here. The shop stocks
Italian labels only, including Young Versace, Diesel,
Moschino and Mona Lisa, and caters for three-
month-old babies up to eight-year-olds. To complete
the stylish look, there are dinky rucksacks, belts,
casual and party shoes.

Lugean

*Al Ghurair City mall, Al Rigga Road, Deira (228
4317).* **Open** 10am-10pm Sat-Thur; 2-10pm Fri.
Credit AmEx, MC, V. **Map** p279 K3.
The place to go for lovely girly party dresses and
handsome tiny-tot suits. Items aren't cheap (frocks
from Dhs200), but they're so cute you'll want to keep
them forever.

Tom Tailor

Wafi City mall, Oud Metha Road (324 1170). **Open**
10am-10pm Sat-Thur; 4-10pm Fri. **Credit** AmEx,
MC, V. **Map** p277 J3.
Tom Tailor is a no-nonsense, affordable fashion
store for pre-teen girls. You won't find any glittery
tops, just lots of casual clobber, from trendy jeans
to hip body jackets. There's also a smaller collection
for early teens.

Designer

Bugatti

*Falcon Tower, behind Hilton Dubai Creek (Beniyas
Road), Deira (228 5109/5118).* **Open** 10am-10pm
Sat-Thur; 5-10pm Fri. **Credit** AmEx, MC, V.
Map p279 L4.
Tucked away in downtown Deira, this sparkling
white boutique is a label lover's dream, a glittering
paean to all things modish. Clothes are exclusive to
Bugatti, with shoes, bags and daywear downstairs,
evening gowns, corsets and grown-up glamour

upstairs. Also hanging gracefully from the rails are
clothes from other designers, including Dolce &
Gabbana, Jean Paul Gaultier and Ben de Lisi.

Chanel

Wafi City mall, Oud Metha Road (324 0464). **Open**
10am-10pm Sat-Thur; 5-10pm Fri. **Credit** AmEx,
MC, V. **Map** p277 J3.
This shop has a small selection of the latest suits,
dresses, bags, shoes and jewellery from the chic
French label. Chanel's make-up also features.

Gianni Versace

Al Maktoum Street, Deira (227 3741). **Open**
9.30am-1pm, 5-9.30pm Sat-Thur. **Credit** AmEx,
MC, V. **Map** p279 K3.
This spacious, quiet store has sharp suits for men
downstairs and daywear for women upstairs, with
Moschino shirts and skirts sitting among Versace
offerings. There are also plenty of bags, shoes, belts
and bikinis, and a small selection of killer dresses
for those red-carpet occasions.

Giorgio Armani

*Emirates Towers Boulevard mall, Sheikh Zayed
Road, Bur Dubai (330 0447).* **Open** 10am-10pm
Sat-Thur; 4-10pm Fri. **Credit** AmEx, MC, V.
Map p276 H4.
This vast shop is full of all the latest Armani
designs: suits and shoes for men, lots of well-cut
skirts and smart jackets for women. If you have cash
to splash, check out the hugely expensive gowns.

Gucci

Al Maktoum Street, Deira (221 5444). **Open** 10am-
1pm, 5-9.30pm Sat-Thur; 5-9.30pm Fri. **Credit**
AmEx, MC, V. **Map** p279 K3.
Stretching over two floors, this boutique is much
larger than the outlet in the Emirates Towers
Boulevard. Women get a large range of ladieswear
and accessories, while gents can browse through the
collection of smart suits, shoes and briefcases.
Other locations: Emirates Towers Boulevard mall,
Sheikh Zayed Road (330 3313).

Podium

Al Maktoum Street, Deira (222 8688). **Open**
9.30am-1pm, 5-9.30pm Sat-Thur; 5-9.30pm Fri.
Credit AmEx, MC, V. **Map** p279 K3.
This shop is just for the ladies, with sexy Dolce &
Gabbana stilettos, fashionable Roberto Cavalli
clothes and Iceberg jeans. Whether you're after a
glam evening dress or designer T-shirt, it's all here.

Villa Moda

*Emirates Towers Boulevard mall, Sheikh Zayed
Road, Bur Dubai (330 4555).* **Open** 10am-10pm
Sat-Thur; 4-10pm Fri. **Credit** AmEx, MC, V.
Map p276 H4.
Nicknamed the Harvey Nicks of the Middle East,
this is the one-stop shop for designer fashion. All the
latest designs from Prada, Marni, Alexander
McQueen and Stella McCartney hang next to Lulu
Guinness bags and Gina shoes. The men's range is
smaller than the women's.

Lingerie

There are plenty of shops selling luxury lingerie in Dubai, but the majority of their wares are underwhelming, frilly number put together with little erotic flair. Truly classy designs are few and far between, and sizes are tailored to the waifishly built. No-nonsense, everyday underwear is also difficult to come by, and prices are often heavily marked up. The following stores struggle against mediocrity.

Designer Deals
Al Mina Road, opposite the Capitol Hotel, Satwa (398 7600). **Open** 10am-2pm, 5-10pm Sat-Thur; 5-10pm Fri. **Credit** AmEx, DC, MC, V. **Map** p280 F7.
It's a clothes store rather than lingerie shop, but if you have time to rummage you'll find Victoria's Secret lingerie at lower-than-usual prices. Pretty slip dresses cost a mere Dhs65, and sheer bras sell at Dhs15. New designs arrive every month, but they are often bunched together with less attractive non-designer pieces.

Inner Lines
Deira City Centre mall, Garhoud (295 0627). **Open** 10am-10pm Sat-Thur; 2-10pm Fri. **Credit** AmEx, MC, V. **Map** p277 K2.
You can't really go wrong with Calvin Klein underwear, and at Inner Lines you'll find a small but attractive selection, encompassing sexy, lacy knickers and bras in every colour. Other brands stocked at Inner Lines include BodySlimmers, which give quick-fix solutions to sagging bums and tums; and the Princess Tam Tam range, which offers support for the fuller chest.

Janet Reger
Emirates Towers Boulevard mall, Sheikh Zayed Road, Bur Dubai (330 0660). **Open** 10am-10pm Sat-Thur; 4-10pm Fri. **Credit** AmEx, MC, V. **Map** p276 H4.
Established in the 1960s but new to Dubai, this store offers camisole tops, French knickers, silk nightwear and beautiful corsets and suspenders. Sophisticated, sexy, top-quality stuff.

Nayomi
Mercato Mall, Beach Road, Jumeirah (344 9120). **Open** 10am-10pm Sat-Thur; 4-10pm Fri. **Credit** MC, V. **Map** p282 C12.
The leading Middle Eastern retailer of quality lingerie, Nayomi stocks lacy dressing gowns from Dhs845 and rather less sexy neck-to-ankle nightdresses from Dhs325.

La Perla
BurJuman Centre mall, Trade Centre Road, Bur Dubai (355 1251). **Open** 10am-10pm Sat-Thur; 4-10pm Fri. **Credit** AmEx, MC, V. **Map** p279 J5.
Every woman deserves a piece of La Perla, the ultimate in luxury lingerie. This small store has lacy Italian bras, satin, silk and cotton bodywear and sexy corsets, at top-end prices.

Mid-range

Diesel
Mercato Mall, Beach Road, Jumeirah (349 9985). **Open** 10am-10pm Sat-Thur; 2-10pm Fri. **Credit** AmEx, MC, V. **Map** p282 C12.
This well-known store sells trendy beachwear dresses, denim jeans and casual clobber for demanding teenagers and dressed-down twentysomethings. It's all very hip, though not exactly cheap.
Other locations: Deira City Centre mall, Garhoud (295 0792).

Karen Millen
Palm Strip mall, Beach Road, Jumeirah (346 1106). **Open** 10am-10pm Sat-Thur; 5-9.30pm Fri. **Credit** AmEx, MC, V. **Map** p280 D9.
This English chain stocks a fine selection of ultra-sexy, strappy dresses and beaded, halter-neck and strapless tops.
Other locations: Deira City Centre mall, Garhoud (295 5007).

Mango
Palm Strip mall, Beach Road, Jumeirah (346 1826). **Open** 10am-10pm Sat-Thur; 5-10pm Fri. **Credit** AmEx, MC, V. **Map** p280 D9.
Like its Spanish sister Zara, Mango is strong on trendy casual pieces that are easy to mix and match. Further fortes include smart trouser suits, grown-up summery dresses, shoes, bags and belts.
Other locations: Deira City Centre mall, Garhoud (295 0182).

Massimo Dutti
Deira City Centre mall, Garhoud (295 4788). **Open** 10am-10pm Sat-Thur; 2-10pm Fri. **Credit** AmEx, MC, V. **Map** p277 K2.
Popular with the mature shopper, Massimo Dutti is reliable for well-cut leather and suede jackets, glamorous eveningwear and sophisticated suits in fabrics such as corduroy and linen.
Other locations: Mercato Mall, Beach Road, Jumeirah (344 7158).

Miss Sixty
Wafi City mall, Oud Metha Road (324 1998). **Open** 10am-10pm Sat-Thur; 4.30-10pm Fri. **Credit** AmEx, MC, V. **Map** p277 J3.
Plenty of sassy clothes are up for grabs here, from funky fitted jeans to sexy micro minis. There's also a small selection of trendy trainers and thigh-high boots to wear with attitude.

Top Shop
Mercato Mall, Beach Road, Jumeirah (344 2677). **Open** 10am-10pm Sat-Thur; 2-10pm Fri. **Credit** AmEx, MC, V. **Map** p282 C12.
A popular spot for catwalk fashion at high-street prices, from hipster jeans to vintage-style dresses. The collection changes regularly, but always includes a range of cheeky underwear.
Other locations: Debenhams, Deira City Centre mall, Garhoud (295 1010).

Zara

Deira City Centre mall, Garhoud (295 3377). **Open**
10am-10pm Sat-Thur; 2-10pm Fri. **Credit** AmEx,
MC, V. **Map** p277 K2.

Part of the well-known Spanish chain, this is the
largest fashion store in Dubai and probably the most
popular. The back of the shop houses funky, retro
garments and kids' clothes, while the front has all
the latest in fashionable tops and bottoms for men
and women. There's also a small but attractive selection of shoes and belts. Great value for money.
Other locations: BurJuman Centre mall, Trade
Centre Road, Bur Dubai (351 3332).

Sportswear

Adidas

*BurJuman Centre mall, Trade Centre Road, Bur
Dubai (359 0995)*. **Open** 10am-10pm Sat-Thur;
4-10pm Fri. **Credit** MC, V. **Map** p279 J5.

All the latest Adidas trainers, tracksuits, shorts and
T-shirts for men, with a smaller range of gymwear
and footwear for women. Adidas watches round out
the collection.
Other locations: Adidas Factory Shop, Airport
Road, Garhoud (282 5868).

Golf House

*BurJuman Centre mall, Trade Centre Road, Bur
Dubai (351 9012)*. **Open** 10am-10pm Sat-Thur;
4-10pm Fri. **Credit** AmEx, MC, V. **Map** p279 J5.

A shop dedicated to golfing equipment and clothes.
You'll find a good selection of irons, plus plenty of
men's and ladies' clothing, including a popular line
of Burberry hats, shirts, trousers and shorts.

Intermilan

*Near Lal's supermarket, Al Hudaiba Street,
Satwa (349 7765)*. **Open** 9am-11pm Sat-Thur;
9am-11.30am, 3-11.30pm Fri. **No credit cards**.
Map p280 E9.

Al Maktoum Street

Before the development of the malls, Al
Maktoum Street was the most fashionable
shopping area in Dubai. Although it could
never be likened to Bond Street in London
or Fifth Avenue in New York, Al Maktoum
Street was once famous for its share of
designer stores. Today most glamour stores
have been lured away, but there are a handful
of outlets still worth visiting. Start from the
Deira clock tower and work your way up the
road towards Garhoud and you'll pass

designer fashion shops Gianni Versace and
Bugatti Men, haute couture boutique Walid
Atallah, jewellery outlets Damas and Bulgari
and extravagant furniture emporium Majestic
Palace. If you're looking for some absolutely
fabulous frocks, stop off at Abiti (*see p124*),
a boutique upstairs in the quiet Dana Centre.

Most shops on Al Maktoum Street adhere
to traditional hours, opening for business
from 9am-1pm and 4.30-9pm, and closing on
Friday for the day.

The tailors of the **textile souk**, **Al Fahidi Street**, will replicate designs for a snip. *See p116.*

This is the best place in town for cheap football shirts, tracksuit bottoms and mens' trainers. Check the Dhs10 rail at the front of the shop for Oakley shorts and Fox T-shirts.

Sports Market
Opposite Jumeirah Centre mall, Beach Road, Jumeirah (344 3799). **Open** 10am-1pm, 4-10pm Sat-Thur; 2-10pm Fri. **Credit** AmEx, MC, V. **Map** p280 D9.
You'll find equipment for most general sports here, from golf clubs to tennis racquets, bikes to rollerblades. There's also plenty of sports and gym clothing for men and women, with international brand names Nike, Dunlop and Slazenger.

Sun&Sand Sports
Khalid Bin Al Waleed Road (Bank Street), Bur Dubai (351 6222). **Open** 10am-10pm Sat-Thur; 2-10pm Fri. **Credit** AmEx, MC, V. **Map** p279 J5.
Sun&S and Sports is the biggest sports shop in Dubai, and it stocks everything from gym equipment to tennis gear. Trainer addicts might not find the very latest styles, but prices are generally reasonable, and Nike, Adidas and Puma are just three of the brands available.
Other locations: Deira City Centre mall, Garhoud (295 5551).

Tailors

For textiles, *see p116* **Textile souk**.

Century Tailoring
Shop no.25, Block C, Karama market area (337 6610). **Open** 9am-10.30pm Sat-Thur; 9am-11am, 4-10.30pm Fri. **No credit cards**. **Map** p281 J7.
These tailors in the Karama market area specialise in men's suits, trousers and shirts. It takes two days to make up the clothes, with one fitting. Prices start at Dhs30.

Coventry Tailoring
Next to Deepaks material shop, Al Hudaibah Road, Satwa (344 7563). **Open** 9.30am-1pm, 4-9.30pm Sat-Thur. **No credit cards**. **Map** p280 E9.
These Satwa tailors have built up a fine reputation in an area already swamped with cloth-cutters. Their workmanship is second to none, and they're pretty quick, usually knocking out a well-crafted copy a pair of trousers in about a week.

Dream Girl Tailors
Opposite Emirate Bank International, across from Satwa roundabout, Satwa (349 5445). **Open** 9.30am-1.30pm, 3.30-10pm Thur-Sat; 6-8pm Fri. **No credit cards**. **Map** p281 F8.
This popular place is always busy, so you may have to wait a couple of weeks for a garment to be made up. If you bring in a pair of your favourite trousers, they will copy them exactly. Evening dresses come out particularly well, and cost from about Dhs200.

Gents Tailors
Near the Astoria Hotel, Al Fahidi Street, Bur Dubai (353 1460). **Open** 9.30am-2pm, 4.30-10pm Sat-Thur; 4-10pm Fri. **Credit** AmEx, MC, V. **Map** p278 H4.
At Gents Tailors, stick figures scrawled on scraps of paper are swiftly transformed into beautifully fitting, good-value clothes – staff can also carbon copy anything you bring along. The suits, dresses and shawls hanging from lofted steel racks reflect the tremendous talent of these tailors.

Kachins
Cosmos Lane, Meena Bazaar, Bur Dubai (352 1386). **Open** 9am-1.30pm, 4-10.30pm Sat-Thur; 4-10.30pm Fri. **Credit** AmEx, MC, V. **Map** p278 H4.
Kachins has a good reputation for turning out smart suits. Tailoring for a two-piece is about Dhs550, while shirts are Dhs35 to Dhs40.

Walid Atallah

Al Maktoum Street, next to Al Khaleej Palace Hotel, Deira (222 6172). **Open** 10am-2pm, 5-10pm Sat-Thur. **No credit cards. Map** p279 K3.

If you're after a frock for a special occasion or even a wedding dress, you really should consider making an appointment at this Lebanese boutique. They will work with you from start to finish, from sketching the design to helping you to shop for the fabric. It all takes about two weeks, but staff say they can do it in one if it's urgent. Prices start at Dhs3,000, increasing depending on the amount of detail.

Fashion accessories

Hats

Blue Cactus

Jumeirah Centre mall, Beach Road, Jumeirah (344 7734). **Open** 10am-9pm Sat-Thur; 5-9pm Fri. **Credit** AmEx, MC, V. **Map** p280 D9.

The selection of hats here is small from January to March, but among the lampshade headwear you can sometimes find the odd show-stopping design that doesn't cost a fortune.

Designers' Club at St John

Wafi City mall, Oud Metha Road (324 0028). **Open** 10am-10pm Sat-Thur; 4.30-10pm Fri. **Credit** AmEx, MC, V. **Map** p277 J3.

A good range of expensive stylish, dressy and sophisticated headwear. Prices start from Dhs990 and rise to Dhs1,500.

Oasis Fashion

Wafi City mall, Oud Metha Road (324 9074). **Open** 10am-10pm Sat-Thur; 4.30-10pm Fri. **Credit** AmEx, MC, V. **Map** p277 J3.

Not a place for shrinking violets, Oasis excels in hats with feathery, frilly and flowery appendages, all at affordable prices.

Sunny Days

Jumeirah Centre mall, Beach Road, Jumeirah (349 5275). **Open** 10am-9pm Sat-Thur; 5-9pm Fri. **Credit** MC, V. **Map** p280 D9.

Local milliner Lynn Holyoak often sells her colourful creations at Sunny Days in the run-up to the World Cup, when demand skyrockets. Prices are reasonable – expect to pay around Dhs400.

Jewellery

The gold souk (*see p118* **Going for gold**) is the best place to go for jewellery as it offers a wide range of designs to suit different tastes and budgets, but for designer jewellery and international brands like Graff and Cartier, head to the major shopping malls. All the latest pieces arrive in Dubai as soon as they become available elsewhere in the world, so collections are always up to date.

Cartier

Emirates Towers Boulevard mall, Sheikh Zayed Road, Bur Dubai (330 0034). **Open** 10am-10pm Sat-Thur; 5-10pm Fri. **Credit** AmEx, DC, MC, V. **Map** p276 H4.

Gorgeous gems, from opal to sapphire, set delicately in rings, bracelets and necklaces.

Damas

Deira City Centre mall, Garhoud (295 3848). **Open** 10am-10pm Sat-Thur; 2-10pm Fri. **Credit** AmEx, DC, MC, V. **Map** p277 K2.

There are Damas outlets all over Dubai; in fact, there's one in nearly every major shopping mall. The jewellery is predominantly chunky and gold, and has a definite Arabic flavour. New collections arrive regularly but the overall emphasis here is on heavy rings, sparkly necklaces and big diamonds and pearls.

Other locations: throughout the city.

Gold & Diamond Park

Gold & Diamond Park, Interchange 4, Sheikh Zayed Road (347 7574). **Open** 10am-10pm Sat-Thur; 4-10pm Fri. **Credit** AmEx, MC, V. **Map** p274 B4.

A great place to buy gold, with shops selling diamonds and all manner of gold (yellow, white, even purple) arranged around a central square. Alternatively, you can have your own design made up while you wait.

Graff

Wafi City mall, Oud Metha Road (324 4221). **Open** 10am-10pm Sat-Thur; 4.30-10pm Fri. **Credit** AmEx, DC, MC, V. **Map** p277 J3.

If you're in the market for diamonds, it's worth stopping at this hugely attractive shop. Graff's is the only company that produces, manufactures and retails its own gems, so the dazzling range changes every day rather than with the seasons. Necklaces, earrings and rings are classically beautifully rather than garish.

Tiffany & Co

Deira City Centre mall, Garhoud (295 3884). **Open** 10am-10pm Sat-Thur; 2-10pm Fri. **Credit** AmEx, DC, MC, V. **Map** p277 K2.

Tiffany's outlet may be small, but it still squeezes in a selection of classy jewellery, chic accessories and gift items.

Other locations: BurJuman Centre mall, Trade Centre Road, Bur Dubai (359 0101).

Shoes

Al-Fareed Shoes

Musalla Road, opposite Special Ostadi Restaurant, Bur Dubai (359 2862). **Open** 8.30am-2pm, 4-11pm Sat-Thur; 3-11pm Fri. **No credit cards. Map** p278 H4.

Khalid Javed, owner of Al-Fareed Shoes, is a famed master shoe-maker. Nowadays, his tiny shop is more concerned with repairs, but hanging in the windows are exquisite, soft leather, gold or silver embroidered

Eat, Drink, Shop

slipper-shoes. Each pair is uniquely decorated and if your size isn't available he'll happily make up a bespoke pair within 24 hours. Best of all, it'll set you back a mere Dhs30.

Jimmy Choo

Emirates Towers Boulevard mall, Sheikh Zayed Road (330 0404). **Open** 10am-10pm Sat-Thur; 4-10pm Fri. **Credit** AmEx, MC, V. **Map** p276 H4.
Fabulously chic boots and desirable heels, though be prepared to flex the plastic.

Land of Shoes

Shop 153, Block N, Karama market area (335 6145). **Open** 9am-1.30pm, 4-10.30pm Sat-Thur; 4-10pm Fri. **No credit cards. Map** p279 J5.
Land of Shoes carries makes such as Timberland and Dockers at low prices – but be warned, the area is notorious for its fakes.

Milano

Mercato Mall, Beach Road, Jumeirah (344 9517). **Open** 10am-10pm Sat-Thur; 2-10pm Fri. **Credit** AmEx, MC, V. **Map** p282 C12.
There's something at Milano to suit every woman's footwear mood, occasion and price range, from vampish heels to everyday flats. There's also a selection of men's leather shoes, which are a little more conservative.

Nine West

Deira City Centre mall, Garhoud (295 6887). **Open** 10am-10pm Thur-Sat; 2-10pm Fri. **Credit** AmEx, MC, V. **Map** p277 K2.
This familiar chain is great for day-to-day basics as well as sparkly sandals. It's also one of the few shops in Dubai that offers shoes in large sizes.
Other locations: Town Centre mall, Beach Road, Jumeirah (344 0038).

Instant Karama

If it's fake designer T-shirts, handbags and shoes you want, head for Karama. The market area is spread out over a network of streets and courtyards, with racks of funky T-shirts, cheap tracksuit bottoms and trendy skatewear lining the walkways. Shopkeepers compete with each other to attract passers-by into their stores, offering 'best price' for fake Rolex watches, Gucci handbags and pirate DVDs. You'll see plenty of bargain-hunting tourists clutching grey plastic bags, evidence that they've been busy spending – their new purchases virtually indistinguishable from the real designer goodies toted by rich locals.

If you're after a bag, make sure you ask to see the rest of the stock. Many places have 'secret' back doors or attic rooms crammed with products they are not allowed, by law, to show off. There's plenty of good copy Christian Dior, Bulgari and Louis Vuitton to be had, as well as the usual souvenirs such as fluffy camels, backgammon boards and *shisha* pipes.

Many of the outlets follow traditional shop opening hours, so your best bet is to arrive early in the morning or late in the afternoon. Allow plenty of time to wander around, and remember to bring your bargaining skills: polite but firm haggling is very much the order of the day here.

If all that jostling leaves you hungry, nesting between the fake designer accessory shops are small restaurants serving Indian and Arabic food. Alternatively, grab a samosa or falafel to go from one of the street vendors.

PrettyFIT

Mercato Mall, Beach Road, Jumeirah (344 0015).
Open 10am-10pm Sat-Thur; 2-10pm Fri. **Credit**
AmEx, MC, V. **Map** p282 C12.
Shoes at PrettyFIT are neither glam nor staid, but a
working average somewhere in between. Flats and
heels, strappies and slip-ons all come in a variety of
colours and are usually decorated with stripes, polka
dots, checks or flowers. Prices start at around the
Dhs80 mark.

Stuart Weitzman/Moreschi

*BurJuman Centre mall, Trade Centre Road, Bur
Dubai (359 0568).* **Open** 10am-10pm Sat-Thur;
4-10pm Fri. **Credit** AmEx, MC, V. **Map** p279 J5.
Celebrity designer Stuart Weitzman offers shoppers
seriously glam shoes at this store, with every foot
size well catered for. In the same shop sits a smaller line of high-quality Moreschi leather footwear.

Florists

Blooms

Beach Road, Jumeirah (344 0912). **Open** 9am-1pm,
4-9pm Sat-Thur. **Credit** AmEx, MC, V. **Map** p276 G3.
As well as indoor plants and dried flowers, Blooms
has carved out a niche for silk flower craft, offering
unique flower arrangements and frilly matching
decorative items for the home. The store also boasts
a small selection of fresh flowers.

Desert Flowers

*Near the Iranian Hospital, Al Hudaiba Road, Satwa
(349 7318).* **Open** 8am-1.30am, 4-10pm Sat-Thur;
4-10pm Fri. **Credit** AmEx, MC, V. **Map** p280 E9.
There are lots of flower shops on Al Hudaiba Road,
but Desert Flowers is the best. From the outside it
looks like a market stall, with potted plants laid out
on the pavement, but there are plenty of fresh, artificial and dried flower arrangements and stems
tucked away inside.

Oleander

*Century Plaza mall, Beach Road, Jumeirah (344
0560).* **Open** 8am-9pm Sat-Thur; 4-9pm Fri.
Credit AmEx, MC, V. **Map** p280 D9.
Oleander's is more of a garden accessory shop than
a dedicated florist's, but go to the back of the store
and you'll find some beautiful, perfumed bunches of
flowers hidden behind the huge green plants and
outdoor furniture.

Spinneys

Mercato Mall, Beach Road, Jumeirah (349 6900).
Open 10am-10pm Sat-Thur; 2-10pm Fri. **Credit**
AmEx, MC, V. **Map** p282 C12.
This flower shop might be hidden away in a supermarket but it provides a good selection of perfumed
stems and bouquets, as well as talented staff who
are quick to tie up your purchase with a ribbon or
bow. Look out for market-day promotions, when
flowers are ridiculously cheap (15 roses for a mere
Dhs10, for instance).

Food shops

Dolce Antico

Mercato Mall, Beach Road, Jumeirah (344 0028).
Open 10am-10pm Sat-Thur; 5-10pm Fri. **Credit**
AmEx, MC, V. **Map** p282 C12.
This small but elegant Italian food shop caters mainly to the sweet of tooth – head over to stock up on
handmade chocolates and preserved fruit in beautiful heavy glass jars.

Goodies

Wafi City mall, Oud Metha Road (324 4433). **Open**
10am-10pm Sat-Thur; 4-10pm Fri. **Credit** AmEx,
DC, MC, V. **Map** p277 J3.
Dubai's favourite gourmet goods shop, Goodies is
stocked to the rafters with Arabian cheeses and
sweets, ringed by baskets of fat olives, truffles and
dates. The home-made ice-cream is delicious and the
luxury chocolates worth every fils.

Nutty Nuts

*Taj Palace Hotel, between Al Maktoum Street &
Al Rigga Road, Deira (223 2222).* **Open** 10am-11pm
daily. **Credit** AmEx, MC, V. **Map** p279 L3.
Ignore the mad-as-a-bicycle name and trip round
this cosy store loading up on nougat chunks, dried
fruit, designer dates and turkish delight. There's a
little cake shop in the neighbouring lobby if you
want a slab of gateau to go.

Pronto

*Fairmont Hotel, Sheik Zayed Road, Bur Dubai (332
5555).* **Open** 7am-11pm daily. **Credit** AmEx, MC, V.
Map p281 G9.
A reasonable mini deli selling nice-looking mustards
and jams, cold meats and cheeses. Confidence in the
place's gourmet credentials is slightly undermined
by the sight of shelves of baked beans and bran
flakes, but the parma ham and smoked salmon are
worth queuing up for.

Sweety Sweets

Al Musallah Road, Bur Dubai (397 1380). **Open**
9am-1.30pm 4.30-10.30pm Sat-Thur; 9.30-11.30am
Fri. **No credit cards.** **Map** p278 H4.
A nibble-lovers paradise: saunter round inhaling the
chilli-laced air and lose yourself in the rows of
papads (mini poppadoms), pickles, puri, vada pav
(spicy fried potato) and Bombay mix. Pick up half a
kilo of methi chakli for Dhs15 – the crispy, fenu-
greek-flavoured fried rice-flour is most addictive
snack you can imagine.

Health & beauty

Cosmetics & perfume

Every major mall has at least one perfume or
cosmetics shop. New fragrances are available as
soon as they are launched in their country of
origin, but prices can be high, so you're better
off stocking up at the airport duty-free.

Eat, Drink, Shop

Ajmal Perfumes

Deira City Centre mall, Garhoud (295 3580). **Open** 10am-10pm Sat-Thur; 3-10pm Fri. **Credit** AmEx, MC, V. **Map** p277 K2.

Ajmal specialises in Arabic perfumes, which are stronger and spicier than Western scents. Of course, there is a large selection of ready-mades, but you can also have fun blending your own perfume with the help of the in-store perfumer.

Areej

Mercato Mall, Beach Road, Jumeirah (344 6894). **Open** 10am-10pm Sat-Thur; 2-10pm Fri. **Credit** AmEx, MC, V. **Map** p282 C12.

All the international perfumes, cosmetics, lotions and potions are stocked at this huge store, including Lancôme, Estée Lauder and Calvin Klein.

MAC

Deira City Centre mall, Garhoud (295 7704). **Open** 10am-10pm Sat-Thur; 2-10pm Fri. **Credit** AmEx, MC, V. **Map** p277 K2.

This is the city's largest MAC branch, with an impressive range of foundations and nail, eye and lip colours.

Other locations: Mercato Mall, Beach Road, Jumeirah (344 9536).

Mikyajy

Deira City Centre mall, Garhoud (295 7844). **Open** 10am-10pm Sat-Thur; 2-10pm Fri. **Credit** AmEx, MC, V. **Map** p277 K2.

Mikyajy's range of international fragrances and quirky cosmetic brands isn't huge, but it's worth checking out for its own-brand make-up boxes and cosmetic palettes, which are cheaper than most other high street brands.

Paris Gallery

Deira City Centre mall, Garhoud (294 1111). **Open** 10am-10pm Thur-Sat; 3-10pm Fri. **Credit** AmEx, MC, V. **Map** p277 K2.

With two locations in Deira City Centre (the Level 2 store is the bigger and better of the two), Paris Gallery stocks an array of international perfumes and cosmetics, plus a good range of designer sunglasses and watches.

Red Earth

Deira City Centre mall, Garhoud (295 1887). **Open** 10am-10pm Sat-Thur; 2-10pm Fri. **Credit** AmEx, MC, V. **Map** p277 K2.

This trendy brand of make-up covers everything from shimmery foundations to canary-yellow eyeshadows, with an especially big choice of lip and nail colours. Prices are reasonable.

Rituals

Deira City Centre mall, Garhoud (294 1432). **Open** 10am-10pm Sat-Thur; 2-10pm Fri. **Credit** AmEx, MC, V. **Map** p277 K2.

The range of Dutch bodycare products at this store is small but covers items for both men and women, along the lines of body scrubs, shower gels and, to complete your healthy lifestyle, tea.

Blend your own scent at **Ajmal Perfumes**.

Villa Moda

Emirates Towers Boulevard mall, Sheikh Zayed Road (330 4555). **Open** 10am-10pm Sat-Thur; 4-10pm Fri. **Credit** AmEx, MC, V. **Map** p276 H4.

Vila Moda is a clutch of pricey boutiques artfully dotted around the equally classy Emirates Towers Shopping Boulevard. The list of brands available covers almost every designer name imaginable, from Prada to Stella McCartney and from Alexander McQueen to Antonia Marras.

Salons

Curve

BurJuman Centre, Trade Centre Road, Bur Dubai (355 3788). **Open** 10am-10pm Sat-Thur; 4-10pm Fri. **Credit** AmEx, DC, MC, V. **Map** p279 J5.

Every girl in Curve seems to be called Nadia but whether you get Nadia #1 or #4, chances are you're going to get a great haircut or beauty treatment for a bargain price (the typical cost of a hair cut is a mere Dhs100). This is a no-nonsense operation, with staff that forgo the holiday chit-chat to work wonders quickly on head and body.

Nail Station

Town Centre Mall, Beach Road, Jumeirah (349 0123). **Open** 9am-9pm Sat, Thur; 2-9pm Sun-Wed. **Credit** AmEx, DC, MC, V. **Map** p282 C12.

Although the all-white, almost futuristic interior looks a little cold at first, the smiling staff and friendly French owner more than make up for it. Technicians are quick and competent at all manner of manicures, and with a huge plasma screen showing feel-good movies and a pedicure corner with comfy armchairs, even impatient customers will be happy to sit still. As well as regularly increasing their own lines of varnishes, the Nail Station plans to offer a wider selection of waxing and beauty treatments in the very near future.

Reflections

Villa no.3, past Spinneys Centre, Al Wasl Road, Jumeirah (394 4595). **Open** 9am-6pm Sat, Thur; 9am-8pm Sun-Wed. **Credit** MC, V. **Map** p276 F5.

Based in a house on Al Wasl Road, Reflections certainly proves a welcoming and homely experience. Split over two levels, Fleckies, as the salon is affectionately known, offers a range of beauty treatments including facials and tanning on the first floor, while down below a small but intimate hair salon sees mops chopped with no little style. More interested in cups of tea and a healthy chinwag than the high (lights) fashion, the staff are friendly, warm and personable. While Reflections may not be the hippest, most cutting edge salon in Dubai, its staff are well trained in the latest, styles, techniques and trends and the informal ambience is a breath of fresh air.

Le Salon

Dubai Marine Beach Resort & Spa, Jumeirah (346 2266). **Open** 10.30am-8.30pm Sat-Thur; 4-8.30pm Fri. **Credit** AmEx, MC, V. **Map** p280 D8.

This friendly Jordanian-run salon is the perfect place to get your barnet whipped into shape. Despite the upmarket surroundings, prices are competitive – Dhs100 for a men's cut and blow-dry, Dhs185 for a women's, and upwards of Dhs200 for highlights. Tip – if they say you need to go short, trust them.

Toni & Guy

Emirates Towers Boulevard mall, Sheikh Zayed Road (330 3345). **Open** 10am-10pm Sat-Thur; 4-8pm Fri. **Credit** MC, V. **Map** p276 H4.

If you only trust one salon with your crowning glory, it's has to be Toni & Guy. Don't expect to find your bog-standard hairdressers or, god forbid, barbers here, these guys are self-appointed hair technicians and each one has graduated through the T&G ranks. A visit here will cost you (a wash, cut and blow-dry will cost you between Dhs150 and Dhs250), but you know you are in safe hands. As well as all the usual cuts, highlights, low-lights and blow-dries for girls, boys can also place their tresses in the staff's hands. Throw in a well-stocked mag rack, some funky staff and you have the total hair experience.

Home furnishings

Bayti

Deira City Centre mall, Garhoud (294 9292). **Open** 10am-10pm Sat-Thur; 2-10pm Fri. **Credit** AmEx, MC, V. **Map** p277 K2.

The place for quirky home accessories, funky crockery, kitchen fragrances, candles and vases.

Home Centre

Mercato Mall, Beach Road, Jumeirah (344 2266). **Open** 10am-10pm Sat-Thur; 2-10pm Fri. **Credit** AmEx, MC, V. **Map** p282 C12.

The kitchenware and other home furnishings here are cheaper and plainer than at Ikea, but the bonus is that they're pre-assembled, so you don't have the hassle of doing it yourself.

Other locations: Oasis Centre mall, between Interchanges 2 & 3, Sheikh Zayed Road (339 5217).

Ikea

Deira City Centre mall, Garhoud (295 0434). **Open** 10am-10pm Sat-Thur; 2-10pm Fri. **Credit** AmEx, MC, V. **Map** p277 K2.

This well-known store stocks plenty of self-assembly kitchen, bedroom and bathroom accessories.

Kas Australia

Mercato Mall, Beach Road, Jumeirah (344 1179). **Open** 10am-10pm Sat-Thur; 2-10pm Fri. **Credit** MC, V. **Map** p282 C12.

Kas Australia is an excellent supplier of citrus-coloured cushions and brightly coloured, trendy throws to liven up any room.

The Living Zone

Mercato Mall, Beach Road, Jumeriah (344 5994). **Open** 10am-10pm Sat-Thur; 2-10pm Fri. **Credit** MC, V. **Map** p282 C12.

Three outlets rolled into one. American-owned Bombay is the place for luxurious bedroom accessories, velvet-crushed cushions and expensive feathered lampshades; Danish outlet the Zone has attractive stainless steel and chrome kitchen utensils; Swiss store Bodum is tiny in comparison, but has enough cafetières and colourful coffee mugs to kit out your home.

Majestic Palace

Al Maktoum Street, Deira (222 6160). **Open** 9am-1pm, 4.30-9pm Sat-Thur. **Credit** AmEx, MC, V. **Map** p279 K3.

The Majestic is a great place if you're after some seriously luxurious Italian furniture. Items are large and expensive, so bring your plastic and be prepared to ship goods home.

The One

Beach Road, Jumeirah (345 6687). **Open** 9am-10pm Sat-Thur; 2-10pm Fri. **Credit** AmEx, DC, MC, V. **Map** p280 D9.

Established in 1995, this local company has become the most popular home accessories shop in Dubai. The home furnishings, gifts and decorating products are attractive, as are the prices.

Port of Call

4th floor, Kendah House, Sheikh Zayed Road, Bur Dubai (332 6006). **Open** 4.30-7.30pm Sat-Thur. **Credit** MC, V. **Map** p283 F11.

A friendly gallery atmosphere prevails at the Port of Call, which showcases oriental antiques and furniture alongside contemporary art and accessories. It's a small operation with limited opening hours, but a good place for unearthing the occasional gem. While you're there, don't miss the opportunity for a refreshment at the quirky Shakespeare & Co café in the same building (*see p104*).

Eat, Drink, Shop

All day
shopping in
the City

for fashion

Pride of
Kashmir.

Rugs

If it's rugs and carpets you're after, Dubai has a vast range of them, from contemporary to traditional, antique to new, and cheap to expensive. They also come from a vast number of countries including Iran, Turkey, Pakistan and Central Asia.

If you're planning on purchasing an antique rug, the best way to spot a good one is to check its reverse side. The more knots there are on the underside, the better the rug's quality and the longer it's likely to last. On the whole, silk is more expensive than wool, and rugs from Iran are generally more valuable than the equivalent from Turkey or Kashmir.

There are plenty of carpet shops around town, so it pays to shop around to get a feel for the range on offer (remember to haggle). Be sure to visit Global Village during the Dubai Shopping Festival (*see p141*) for Afghan, Iraqi and tribal designs at low prices. **Deira Tower** on Al Nasr Square is also worth a look, with around 40 shops offering a wide variety of rugs from all over the region.

Al Madaen

Near Iranian Hospital, Pagoda House, Satwa (345 4488). **Open** 10am-1.30pm, 5-10pm Sat-Thur; 5-10pm Fri. **Credit** AmEx, MC, V. **Map** p280 E9.
A small shop selling Iranian carpets in all sizes. Prices start at Dhs1,500 but can go up to Dhs100,000 for antique rugs (which come with gold frames – these are collector's pieces to be hung on the wall rather than thrown on the floor).

Carpetland

Za'abeel Road, Bur Dubai (337 7677). **Open** 9am-1.30pm, 4.30-8.30pm Sat-Thur. **Credit** AmEx, MC, V. **Map** p277 J3.
A great place for contemporary rug designs in bold colours, at a range of prices.

Pride of Kashmir

Deira City Centre mall, Garhoud (295 0655). **Open** 10am-10pm Sat-Thur; 2-10pm Fri. **Credit** AmEx, MC, V. **Map** p277 K2.
This shop is part of the covered 'mock souk' in Deira City Centre. There's a wide selection of rugs from Iran, Kashmir and Turkey, both antique and modern, starting from around Dhs200 and going up to Dhs60,000. You can even order a reproduction of the world's oldest surviving rug, the Pazyryck rug.

Toshkhana Trading

Behind Al-Anwar Jewellery, gold souk, Deira (225 4440). **Open** 9.30am-10pm Sat-Thur; 4-10pm Fri. **Credit** AmEx, MC, V. **Map** p278 H3.
Located down one of the alleyways in the gold souk, Toshkhana has plenty of expensive carpets. Handmade silk and cotton rugs cost from Dhs1,500 to Dhs15,000, while wool carpets are between Dhs800 and Dhs1,500. For something more unusual, embroidered velvet-trimmed rugs with decorative jewels are around Dhs2,500.

Total Arts

The Courtyard, between Interchanges 3 & 4 of Sheikh Zayed Road, Al Quoz (228 2888). **Open** 10am-1pm, 4-8pm Sat-Thur. **Credit** AmEx, MC, V. **Map** p274 C4.
Total Arts is a gallery rather than a shop, but it holds regular exhibitions of tribal weavings and rugs from Iran that are available to buy. Every piece is clearly labelled with details of its age and origin, and the knowledgeable staff are on hand to answer any queries you might have.

Music

Ohm Records

Opposite BurJuman Centre mall, Trade Centre Road, Bur Dubai (397 3728). **Open** 2-10pm daily. **Credit** DC, MC, V. **Map** p279 J5.
Ohm Records is the first record shop in the Middle East to sell vinyl shipped in from London, New York, France and Belgium. All the records come from independent labels, with not a mainstream tune in sight. Professional and bedroom DJs gather at the weekends to play on the decks for free. For the complete look, the shop also sells record bags and a small line of streetwear.

Virgin Megastore

Mercato Mall, Beach Road, Jumeirah (344 6971). **Open** 10am-10am Sat-Thur; 2-10pm Fri. **Credit** AmEx, MC, V. **Map** p282 C12.
As elsewhere around the globe, all musical tastes are catered to at Virgin, from international bands to Arabic music and Bollywood films. But despite the wide range of DVDs, CDs and videos, all material

Eat, Drink, Shop

has to be screened and, if required, censored. So don't be surprised if you can't find the latest Hollywood blockbuster or must-have CD.
Other locations: BurJuman Centre mall, Trade Centre Road, Bur Dubai (351 3444); Deira City Centre mall, Garhoud (295 8599).

Opticians

Most malls have at least one optician's; eye tests are often free if you buy glasses or contacts.

Al Jaber Optical Centre
Deira City Centre mall, Garhoud (295 4400).
Open 10am-10pm Sat-Thur; 2-10pm Fri.
Credit AmEx, MC, V. **Map** p277 K2.

Optic Art
BurJuman Centre mall, Trade Centre Road, Bur Dubai (352 8171). **Open** 10am-10pm Sat-Thur; 4-10pm Fri. **Credit** AmEx, MC, V. **Map** p279 J5.

Yateem Opticians
Beach Centre mall, Beach Road, Jumeirah (349 0909). **Open** 10am-10pm Sat-Thur; 5-10pm Fri. **Credit** AmEx, MC, V. **Map** p280 D10.
Other locations: Al Ghurair City mall, Al Rigga Road, Deira (228 1787).

Ohm Records: spin city. *See p135.*

Outdoor equipment

Ace Hardware
Near Oasis Centre mall, between Interchanges 2 & 3, Sheikh Zayed Road, Bur Dubai (338 1416). **Open** 9am-9pm daily. **Credit** AmEx, MC, V. **Map** p274 B4.
The largest hardware store in Dubai, with everything from DIY to outdoor accessories. This shop also has the best range of barbecues, tents, sleeping bags and camping equipment, including cool bags, compasses and water carriers.

Al Hamur Marine & Sports Equipment
Opposite Jumeirah Centre mall, Beach Road, Jumeirah (344 4468). **Open** 8.30am-1pm, 4.30-9pm Thur-Sat; 8.30am-11am, 4.30-9pm Fri. **Credit** MC, V. **Map** p280 D9.
An excellent shop for underwater equipment. Wetsuits, diving equipment, masks and fins are all here, alongside a good range of fishing rods, body boards and beach balls.

Carrefour
Deira City Centre mall, Garhoud (295 1600). **Open** 10am-10pm Sat-Thur; 2-10pm Fri. **Credit** AmEx, MC, V. **Map** p277 K2.
The place to go for cheap outdoor gear. A three-person Sundome tent costs Dhs199, a disposable barbecue costs around Dhs10 and an adult snorkelling kit will set you back Dhs99. There's also a huge range of sleeping bags and outdoor game sets, including volleyball and badminton nets.

Picnico
Al Bahr Marine, Beach Road, Jumeirah (394 1653). **Open** 9am-9pm Sat-Thur; 4.30-9pm Fri. **Credit** AmEx, MC, V. **Map** p280 D9.
Picnico specialises in camping equipment, and has a decent range of tents, sleeping bags and barbecue sets. Rounding out the stock are handheld GPS systems, penknives and gadgets galore.

Souvenirs

See also p118 **Going for gold**.

Gift World
Shop no.209, Block T, Karama market area (335 8097). **Open** 9am-10.30pm Sat-Thur; 4-10.30pm Fri. **Credit** AmEx, MC, V. **Map** p281 J7.
Gift World is a good place to buy handicrafts. Expect to find colourful, embroidered bedspreads from India and thick table covers from Syria, plus silver trinkets and ornamental features.

Gifts Tent
Shops nos.52 & 53, Block D, Karama market area (335 4416). **Open** 9am-10.30pm Sat-Thur; 4-10.30pm Fri. **Credit** AmEx, MC, V. **Map** p281 J7.
This shop is full of touristy knick-knacks and souvenirs: *shisha* pipes, backgammon boards, pashminas from Dhs10 and even cuddly, singing camels – how can you resist?

Eat, Drink, Shop

Arts & Entertainment

Festivals & Events

The city's burgeoning social calendar: sport, more sport and a little shopping.

Dubai's thirst to become the tourism capital of the Middle East is unquenchable. The emirate has poured considerable money and effort into fledgling events, particularly in the sporting field, which have since grown into star-studded fixtures on the global calendar. The likes of the **Dubai Rugby Sevens** and the **Dubai World Cup** – the richest horse race in the world – are first-class events by anyone's standards. And the latter epitomises the city's commitment to 'live and let live': Western and Levantine expats teeter about in their finery, sipping champagne in the many bars and eateries; serious Emirati racehorse owners in gold-trimmed *dishdashes* (ankle-length shirts) celebrate the return of their winning jockeys to the enclosure; and Sudanese,

Easily **Suede**: Dubai is luring top performers

Indian and Yemeni race-goers cheer from the stands, ripping up their programmes into confetti in honour of celebrity jockeys and winning members of the Maktoum family. Whatever your bag, the atmosphere is electric.

When it comes to cultural events, Dubai is only just getting going. The (hopefully annual) Gig on the Green – the emirate's answer to Glastonbury or Woodstock – was a resounding success in October 2003, while the **Dubai International Film Festival** is all set for December 2004 (*see p153* **Fest behaviour**). Otherwise, if you're after a little tradition, the holy month of **Ramadan**, followed by the celebration of **Eid Al Fitr**, allows a glimpse of the real Arabia. For non-Muslim residents and tourists, Ramadan is only a dry-ish month nowadays – alcoholic drinks are served after sundown in most hotels – and atmospheric *Iftar* (fast-breaking) tents offer a rare opportunity to share the evening with Emirati, Arab and other Muslim hosts and guests. Dubai's Heritage Village and other traditional spots come into their own over the festive days at Eid, which is celebrated with fireworks, dancing, singing, huge platters of dates and other delicacies, and hour upon hour of *shisha* smoking.

Meanwhile, Dubai's 'ethnic majority', the Indian population, makes the most of **Diwali**, dressing up apartment blocks in bright lights and candles and partying family-style in the streets and restaurants of subcontinental neighbourhoods such as Karama and Satwa.

And then there's Dubai's other religion: shopping. What other city in the world would dare, with a straight face, to put on a festival dedicated to the art of consuming goods? Nevertheless, it's become a true success: the month-long extravaganza that is the **Dubai Shopping Festival** packs flights, hotels and malls with keen shoppers intent on hoovering up bargains.

The big events are crammed into the high season (October to May), although steps have been taken to attract visitors in the hot summer months, especially families from other Gulf states, with its kids' festival, **Summer Surprises**. Here we've focused on the best annual events; many are dependent on the international sporting calendar or Ramadan, so precise dates tend to vary each year. Other one-off events featuring visiting bands, musicians

Speed humps: **Camel Racing** is a must-see. *See p142.*

and theatre companies tend to take place in the winter months outside Ramadan – pick up a copy of the monthly *Time Out Dubai* magazine for further details. Tickets are available from the venues listed below or from the *Time Out* ticketline (800 4669/www.itptickets.com).

Spring

Dubai Duty Free Tennis Open

Dubai Tennis Stadium, Aviation Club, Garhoud Road (282 9166/316 6969/www.dubaitennis championships.com). **Map** p277 K3. **Date** mid February Mar.
The Dubai Duty Free Tennis Open is a fantastic opportunity to see the world's top players slamming it out in a laid-back atmosphere devoid of the queues, rain and soaring ticket prices typical of Wimbledon and the Australian Open – tickets for the Dubai Open cost from Dhs30. Regular members of the Aviation Club suddenly find themselves changing alongside the likes of Henman and Roddick, and players can often be spotted strolling through the Irish Village 'pub garden' – which lays on champagne and strawberries for the occasion. The fortnight-long event begins with the Women's Tennis Association's Women's Open and continues with the Association of Tennis Professionals' $1 million Men's Open.

Dubai Desert Golf Classic

Emirates Golf Club, off Interchange 5, Sheikh Zayed Road (295 6440/www.dubaidesertclassic.com). **Map** p274 A5. **Date** 4 days in early Mar.

Dubai's greening of the desert – the city has eight golf courses, and more are planned – attracts golfers from around the world. Come March each year, fans welcome the likes of Tiger Woods, Colin Montgomerie (who has his own course, The Montgomerie, in Dubai) and previous winner Ernie Els for the Dubai Desert Classic, part of the European Professional Golf Association Tour, where they compete for a total of £1.2 million. Tickets cost Dhs130 for a day pass, Dhs450 for a season ticket (concessions half price).

Dubai World Cup

Nad Al Sheba horse-racing stadium, off the Dubai–Al Ain Road (332 2277/336 3666/ www.dubaiworldcup.com/www.emiratesracing.com/ www.drc.co.ae). **Map** p274 C4. **Date** late Mar.
The Dubai World Cup is famed as the richest horse-race in the world: prize money in 2003 totalled $15 million, with the seventh and most prestigious race netting the competitors a cool $6 million. Over the years the meet has expanded to include a month-long 'Racing Carnival', taking in four racing evenings and plenty of social and fashion events before the big day itself. This is when you'll see Dubai at its finest: all facets of UAE society attend, in all manner of dress and level of sobriety, and the atmosphere in the stands is truly electric – never more so than when a member of Godolphin (the royal family's stable) romps home first, ridden by beloved celebrity jockey Frankie Dettori. Admission to the stands if free, but tickets for the (licensed) International Village start from Dhs150. For information on how to see the horses being put through their paces, *see pp71-73* **Nad Al Sheba**.

Arts & Entertainment

Late-night *shisha* smoking during **Ramadan**.

Summer

Dubai Summer Surprises

Various venues (www.mydsf.com). **Date** early June-late Aug.

A three-month effort to draw in the crowds over Dubai's stifling summer, DSS, as it's known locally, features bargains and an endless stream of children's entertainment, mainly taking place in the city's shopping malls. DSS is presided over by the slightly irksome Modhesh, a bright yellow cartoon character that appears in 'person' in the various malls and in caricature at every street corner and roundabout. Still, keeping the kids happy during the summer months can't be knocked – and, if you can take the heat, now's the perfect time to snap up bargain-rate flights and hotel rooms. *See also p145*.

Autumn

Desert Challenge

Various venues (www.uaedesertchallenge.com). **Date** 5 days in Oct.

The largest motorsport event in the Middle East (at least until the 2004 Formula One race in Bahrain trod on its toes), the UAE Marlboro Desert Challenge pits the world's finest endurance riders and cross-country drivers against each other. The last round of both the FIA Cup and FIM World Championship for Cross Country Rallies, the UAE Challenge is the final shakedown before January's Paris–Dakar Rally. While it's the cars that grab the headlines, there are separate categories for an assortment of trucks and bikes. The five-day event begins with a

prologue stage – which in 2003 took place on Palm Island – and continues with four other stages, starting on the Corniche in Abu Dhabi and continuing across the remote deserts of Abu Dhabi and Dubai emirates, with the bivouac (tented nightstop) sited at Mizaira'a in the Liwa Oasis, at the edge of the Rub Al-Khali (Empty Quarter). Grab a spot at the finish line – at the Dubai International Marine Club (DIMC) – and take in the awards ceremony, or head out to Liwa to see some determined motorheads tackle some of the world's biggest sand dunes (*see p221* **Four by four play**).

Ramadan

Various venues. **Date** varies; starts mid Oct in 2004, early Oct in 2005.

The ninth month in the lunar Muslim calendar, Ramadan tends to fall some time between mid October and mid November, around 11 days earlier than the previous year. Muslims are required to fast from dawn until dusk – an imperative that's extended to non-Muslims in public areas in Dubai, apart from some screened-off cafés in hotels.

Non-Muslim expats and visitors can, nowadays, quietly drink alcohol in many hotels in the evenings – although live music remains a definite no-no. Be sure to make the most of the large, canvas *Iftar* tents that spring up around the city, where you can share the breaking of the fast every evening with Emirati and other Muslim hosts and their guests. (For further tips on how to behave, *see p31* **Ramadan dos and don'ts**.) Many of the five-star hotels really go to town, erecting beautifully decorated tents straight out of *Arabian Nights*, with lavish spreads of dates, sweets, mezze and rows of gleaming *shisha* pipes – try the Ritz-Carlton's Bedouin village which includes four types of tent (Moroccan, Syrian, Iranian and Egyptian). The sweet smell of fruit-flavoured *shisha* smoke pervades the air and the click-clack of backgammon and chess games can be heard above familial chat; for many locals and visitors, Ramadan is a welcome taste of the old days.

Diwali

Various venues. **Date** varies, mid Oct-mid Nov.

The five-day Hindu 'Festival of Lights' – the equivalent of the Western New Year or Muslim Eid Al Fitr – is celebrated during the month of Ashwin, and normally falls between mid October and mid November. The Indian population lays on colourful, noisy celebrations that go on for around five days. Entrances to villas, restaurants and shops are decorated with Rangoli designs (symmetrical images depicting gods, goddesses, dancers and other figures) and candles to welcome Lakshmi, the goddess of wealth and prosperity, and drive away evil spirits. Come evening time, kids race down from apartment blocks to let off firecrackers, and communal firework parties take place all over town. You might manage to wangle an invitation to a party but if not, soak up some of the atmosphere in one of Dubai's Indian neighbourhoods, preferably over a cheap-as-chips meal in one of Karama or Satwa's many curry houses (*see pp86-7*).

Dubai Shopping Festival

Only Dubai, with its recent, zealous conversion to the art of consumerism, could pull off dedicating a festival to the art of shopping. But pull it off it has: the month-long extravaganza (mid January to mid February) sees flights and hotels – not to mention shopping malls – packed with bargain hunters.

Depending on your level of shopalholism, it's either a dream come true or the worst holiday imaginable. Some airlines even offer excess baggage allowance as well as two-seats-for-one and other deals. Towards the end of the festival, the airport begins to resemble a warehouse, with shoppers struggling to check in box-loads of fridges, electronic goods and clothes – not to mention bags of frozen chickens and other bizarre must-haves. The most enthusiastic shoppers tend to hail from the former USSR, the Gulf states and India but, cynicism aside, there's something in it for everyone.

In recent years, some of the more upmarket boutiques have declined to join in but most of the bigger shops have sales, some with discounts of up to 75 per cent. The malls lay on entertainment, kids' activities and more raffles than you can wave a credit card at. There's also a huge fun fair by the Creek, and firework displays every evening.

More bohemian shoppers will marvel at the bargain seekers' scrum of the **Global Village** – a vast, glorified, global souk featuring kitsch pavilions from 32 Middle Eastern, African and Asian countries. In 2004, the Village was on the Creek by Garhoud Bridge, at the site of the proposed Dubai Festival City, but in 2005 it is due to move to a permanent site off the Emirates Road. Beware: take a taxi, limber up beforehand, sharpen your elbows and – especially in the evenings – prepare to experience shopping hell. Around three million people visited in 2003, many with sugar-pumped kids in tow.

But the crush is worth it – you can load up on gifts (for yourself or others) for years. From India there are chic chiffon coats and cheap summer pashminas; from Thailand, beautiful silk handbags; from Yemen, silver *khanjar* (traditional knives) and antique jewellery; from Palestine, top quality olive oil and traditional crockery; from Iraq, Afghanistan and Iran, a massive selection of contrasting styles of low-priced carpets, plus an array of unusual antiques.

Throughout the month, the Heritage Village and museums lay on special activities, including an Arabian Bedouin Lifestyle Festival, and there are exhibitions, concerts and other shows (see *Time Out Dubai* magazine for details), but these are merely a pretence that the event is about something more than snapping up suitcase-loads of bargains. If you can take the pace, it's all yours. See www.mydsf.com for further details.

Arts & Entertainment

Eid Al Fitr

Various venues. **Date** 3 days at end of Ramadan; dates vary, usually Nov.

The timing of Eid Al Fitr – 'Feast of the Breaking of the Fast' – depends on the conclusion of Ramadan (*see p140*): in 2004 the three-day Eid festival should fall around mid November, and in 2005 at the beginning of the month. Taking advantage of the longest Muslim holiday, many Dubai residents head off on camping trips or abroad, but staying in town is no bad thing. The end of the month of abstinence is celebrated in time-honoured Arabian style. Unless you are lucky enough to be invited to a family party by Emiratis or expat Arabs, it's best to celebrate at one of the restaurants along the Creek (such as Fatafeet, *see p80*) or at the Heritage & Diving Village (*see p60*), which has a shisha and mezze café and an Emirati restaurant. There are fireworks displays every evening, and Emiratis and other Muslims gather to sing and dance to traditional bands, and stalls sell traditional foods, including fresh oysters, and handicrafts. *See also below* **Eid Al Adha.**

Camel Racing

Nad Al Sheba camel racetrack, off the Dubai–Al Ain Road (338 2324). **Map** p274 C4. **Date** early Nov-Apr.

The camel racing and horse-racing seasons begin in early November and continue through to April. Whether it's the sport of kings or the ungainly efforts of the ships of the desert that grab you, the races attract all strata of UAE society and are a must for visitors. Camel races tend to take place on Thursdays and Fridays, around 7am; you can watch training sessions most mornings around 10am (*see p73*). The season reaches its peak in March, with prize-races attended by the ruling Emirati families.

Horse-racing

Nad Al Sheba horse-racing stadium, off the Dubai–Al Ain Road (336 3666/www.nadalshebaclub.com/ www.drc.co.ae). **Map** p274 C4. **Date** every Thur from 7pm during winter (9pm during Ramadan).

Horse-racing at the grand Nad Al Sheba track, featuring local and international steeds and their jockeys, takes place each week during winter, with races every 30 minutes. Betting is not allowed, although various competitions offer cash prizes. Entrance is free to the Maktoum and Millennium stands; a day membership with access to the clubhouse and Del Mar bar is Dhs60; otherwise, beg, borrow or steal an owner's badge to hobnob with the binoculared in the more exclusive boxes and bars. *See also p71.*

Dubai Rugby Sevens

Dubai Exiles Club, 6km (4 miles) east of Dubai on the Al Awir Road (321 0008/www.dubairugby7s.com). **Map** p277 K5. **Date** 3 days in early Dec.

Granted International Rugby Board status a few years ago, this annual World Sevens Series tournament features 16 international and huge numbers of

local and regional teams competing for a variety of trophies. Rugby fans can spot their sporting idols and then watch a local game featuring teams from around the Gulf. Much loved by residents and overseas visitors alike – some 20,000 people attended in 2003 – Dubai (or its expats at least) properly lets its hair down in the Rugby Village; festivities culminate in Rugby Rock, a huge party with live bands on the final day. Tickets to the matches cost from Dhs80 for a day pass, Dhs150 for a season ticket.

World Offshore Powerboat Championship & Lifestyles Festival

Dubai International Marine Club, Le Meridien Mina Seyahi Hotel, Al Sufouh Road, Jumeirah (399 4111). **Map** p274 A5. **Date** 2 days in mid Dec.

The UIM Class I World Offshore Powerboat Championship races, to give them their full name, take place over two days in mid December. Top teams from around the world compete for a place on the podium, and while much of the racing takes place out to sea, it's quite something to see the boats race in and out of the pier. This aquatic version of Formula One attracts some glamorous teams, from Hollywood directors to local stars, the Victory Team. The racing is accompanied by a classy festival on the pier that includes fashion shows and cafés by day, and a string of international bands by night.

Dubai Shopping Festival

Various venues (www.mydsf.com). **Date** mid Jan-mid Feb.

Dubai's month-long festival of bargain shopping, with various entertainment thrown in (*see p141*).

Dubai International Jazz Festival

Dubai Media City, off Sheikh Zayed Road (391 1196/ www.chilloutproductions.com). **Map** p274 A5. **Date** 3 days in Jan.

Who would've thought that a love affair between a Gulf state and that all-American music form, jazz, could be struck up so quickly? The first Dubai International Jazz Festival in January 2003 was a resounding success, attracting world-class musicians such as Stanley Gordon, Archie Shepp and Billy Cobham to the main stage, plus a host of local bands to a smaller arena. After the outdoor concerts (day pass Dhs145, 3-day pass Dhs 195), jam sessions continue at hotel bars into the small hours.

Eid Al Adha

Various venues. **Dates** vary, usually Feb.

The Festival of the Sacrifice takes place on the tenth day of the Islamic month Dhul-Hijjah (the last month of the Islamic calendar, usually falling around February). Although only the pilgrims in Mecca can participate fully, all other Muslims in the world join with them by celebrating and in Dubai the dates are marked with a four-day holiday. Celebrations tend to be based in individual homes and are far less ostentatious than those that mark the Eid Al Fitr (*see above*). No alcohol will be served on the day preceding Eid Al Adha.

Arts & Entertainment

Dubai Rugby Sevens.
See p142.

Children

Beaches, water slides, junior snorkelling and a mass of mall fun.

Dubai is a children's paradise – for eight months of the year, at least (October to May). A family-oriented society, safe beaches, an array of kids' clubs at the hotels offering activities as diverse as treasure hunting and scuba diving (yes, for the little ones), and child-friendly shopping and leisure malls make the city an ideal option for parents in search of a worry-free holiday.

Not that the four summer months are a complete write-off: the government's campaign to get families holidaying between June and September has resulted in a wealth of indoor 'edutainment' and other less worthy activities (*see pp148-151*), and hotels offer some imaginative ways to keep the little ones busy and out of the midday sun. Travel companies and hotels also offer special deals, which can be especially attractive to families.

The celebrated hospitality of the Arabs will become even warmer if you're visiting with kids, and their presence can be a great

Children's City.
See p148.

ice-breaker. Meanwhile, Dubai's service class, predominantly made up of waiters, taxi drivers and maids from child-centred India and the Philippines, ensures that young offspring are always the centre of attention.

Dubai Museum and other heritage centres are not particularly child-oriented, but Dubai does boast a fantastic, dedicated **Children's City**, a vast construction in Creek Park billed as the world's fifth-largest 'infotainment' facility.

Older kids and teenagers can can be pretty much guaranteed to be kept busy with the massive range of water sports at the beaches and beach clubs, gaming areas and activities at the malls; there are also skates park, wave pools and arts and crafts at independent centres. The clothes stores in Karama and Satwa should be full of imitation designer gems for the teenage shopper (*see p130* **Instant Karama**). For mid to late teens, look out for 'rain parties' and other non-alcoholic raves listed in *Time Out Dubai* magazine.

The importance of keeping kids covered up and sunscreened can't be overstated at any time of year. Otherwise, Dubai has few potential pitfalls for parents. Some of the city's more chi-chi bars and restaurants (especially licensed establishments in hotels, and particularly in the evenings) do not seem to accommodate children particularly well, but outdoor eating in the winter months can be ideal for restless younger kids, and independent, cheap restaurants with 'family rooms' are always welcoming. Many cafés and restaurants, particularly those in hotels and malls, have children's menus, but are not always equipped with high chairs – remember to check when making a reservation. Hotels offering Friday brunches tend to be much more geared up towards visiting families (*see p151* **Do play with your food**).

Likewise, be sure to ask your hotel in advance about babysitting services and kids' clubs (*see pp36-54*). If you're stuck for ideas during a holiday visit, need advice or are planning a longer stay, the local community group **Expat Mum** (www.expatmum.com) will be of help. Another useful resource to check out is **Rent-A-Crib** (050 588 7917, www.angelfire.com/in4/rentacrib), which will rent out everything from children's car seats and cots to toys.

Exploring the city

Bastakia & the Creek

Dubai's heat, hard edges and multi-lane roads can make urban exploring a nightmare, especially with kids in tow. However, there are spots where you can leave the highways behind and take off on foot, interspersing your journey with brief taxi rides. The Creek, with its abra stations and dhow wharfage, plus Children's City, makes for an ideal half-day family wander.

While energy levels are high, you could begin at **Dubai Museum** (*see p60*) in Bastakia, Bur Dubai side. Some displays of artefacts can be a little boring for younger kids – although older ones might enjoy the traditional weaponry – but the mock souk, halfway through the museum, is spooky enough to grab the attention of wandering minds, and the pearl-diving display is also interesting. Entrance is a mere Dhs1 for children (under-fives free, adults Dhs3).

Further round on the Bur Dubai side is the **Heritage & Diving Village** (*see p60*) – particularly worth visiting in the winter evenings, when children can take donkey and camel rides and watch traditional singing and dancing. Both the Heritage and Diving Villages can be sleepy during the summer and some weekday evenings: phone in advance to check whether special activities are taking place.

A five-minute walk from the museum down to the Creek will take you to the abra stations – kids will love packing on to the water taxis with Dubai's workers and chugging across to the Deira side (costs Dhs1), although little ones will need hanging on to as there's not much protection. Abras can be hired for longer trips (around 30 minutes) up and down the Creek; this is a fun way to check out the Deira cityscape, Bastakia wind towers, and dhows packed with goods bound for Iran. You have to haggle for the cost of the trip but don't agree to pay more than Dhs50.

Teenagers will enjoy the souks in Deira, but you may be better off catching the abra back again with younger ones and heading upstream by (road) taxi to the lush, green Creek Park and **Children's City** (*see p148*), a brilliant interactive 'edutainment' centre aimed at five- to 15-year-olds. One highlight is the giant, open-backed computer and the larger-than-life internal phones.

Further upstream, just before Garhoud Bridge, is **Wonderland Theme & Water Park** (*see p148*), a kids-oriented leisure centre that includes a 'Desert Extreme' skate park, funfair rides, karting, paintballing and Splashland, complete with nine water rides and several pools. It's good clean fun but – compared to Children's City – is definitely beginning to show its age.

Dubai Summer Surprises

Childless Dubai residents have been known to scoff at the unashamedly uncool Dubai Summer Surprises, with its weeks of mall-oriented 'surprises' and rather annoying mascot Modhesh ('surprise' in Arabic), a cuddly, bright yellow, punk-haired cartoon character. But step out of August's 40°C-plus temperatures and into a chilled shopping mall, and you'll come across bevies of grateful adults sipping coffee while their little ones are entertained. Singletons may mock, but it can be a godsend for parents at a loss as to how to entertain cooped-up kids.

DSS runs from the middle of June through to the end of August. Each week is themed, with activities, shows, competitions and giveaways taking place in malls and around the city, organised by different government departments. Children can look forward to baking cakes, making sweets, creating various 'works of art', getting showered in petals and being crowned flower queen of the day, not to mention performing in an ice show and hunting for treasure. As a further incentive, many shops and malls feature sales or special discounts throughout the summer.

The programme of activities changes each year, but you can expect Colour Surprises, featuring laser and light shows, the very popular Ice Surprises, with sporting events and a daily ice show, and Heritage Surprises, including falconry, mock Bedouin wedding ceremonies and other elaborate folkloric entertainment. For information, go to www.mydsf.com.

Fast fun!

Do you love defying gravity and thrive on fast fun? At Wild Wadi you can enjoy your day exactly the way you like it. We've got 23 rides and attractions that can relax you or get your adrenalin pumping. And you can meet Leila, General Mahmar, Ali and the rest of the Wild Wadi gang. So come and have a fundamentally fun time!

Jumeirah & Umm Suqeim

Jumeirah and its long strip of public and private beaches (*see p201* **City suntraps: beaches and parks**) might be Dubai's best-heeled neighbourhood, but its seaside lifestyle and residential, family-oriented atmosphere makes it an ideal base for holidaying with children. Jumeirah public beach can fill up quickly at weekends – an alternative is to head up the coast to Wollongong or Umm Suqeim beaches, or to pay a Dhs5 entrance fee to Jumeirah Beach Park, a green, shady area with showers and picnic tables (Saturdays are for women and children only).

Dubai Zoo (*see p67*), on Beach Road, is long overdue a transfer to more spacious grounds in the desert and, for now, the animals tend to be a little cramped in small cages, which can make for unpleasant viewing. Still, it remains a popular distraction for some families. The various malls along the Beach Road – **Mercato Mall** (*see p115*), **Palm Strip** (*see p116*), Town Centre, Beach Centre – all offer fast food, coffee bars and other refreshment options, plus shopping and some games centres for kids. The more arty visitor might prefer to indulge in some painting at **Café Céramique** (*see p151*), where kids and adults can pick a ceramic bowl, plate, mug, piggy bank or other item, and paint and glaze it while enjoying a coffee, juice or bagel. Children can be left for a couple of hours if booked into a workshop, or there's a great terrace with sea views to while away the hours. Jumeirah is also home to the **Dubai International Arts Centre** (*see p151*), which has classes in everything from pottery to marble mosaics for children, teenagers and adults – although classes need to be booked in advance.

Heading up the coast to Umm Suqeim, next to Dubai's most recognisable landmark, the Burj Al Arab, is **Wild Wadi** water park (*see p148*). With 23 rides, a wave pool, eateries and a shipwreck, this is a day's activity in itself – and kids will no doubt hassle you to return.

Outdoor fun

Aside from the few notorious months of soaring temperatures, which see Dubai's residents dive desperately for air-conditioned environments, the sun-drenched city offers excellent opportunities to get outdoors. Many an expat parent will tell you that their child's ability to play outside almost all year round is reason enough to relocate to Dubai. Adults can enjoy immaculate beach parks (*see p201* **City suntraps: beaches and parks**) and various water sports (*see pp186-197*), but there are plenty of activities for kids too.

Green and pleasant **Al Safa Park**.

Parks & play areas

Al Mamzar Park

Al Mamzar Creek, by the Sharjah border (296 6201). **Open** 8am-11pm Sat-Wed; 8am-11.30pm Thur, Fri. **Admission** Dhs5. **No credit cards. Map** p275 D1. Looking out over a blue lagoon to the emirate of Sharjah, this park has large grassed areas, three beaches and plentiful barbecue areas, providing one of the most entertaining places for children in the city. There is also a large wooden fort and an amphitheatre that often lays on family shows. On Fridays the park has a fantastic laid-back atmosphere, filled with Indian, Arab and Emirati families enjoying barbecues and celebrating their day off by singing and playing drums. Note that on Wednesdays the park is open to women and children only.

Al Safa Park

Near Choithram supermarket on Al Wasl Road, Jumeirah (349 2111). **Open** 8am-11.30pm daily. **Admission** Dhs5. **No credit cards. Map** p276 G5. Al Safa Park, a firm favourite with the prosperous, villa-dwelling Jumeirah crowd, has large stretches of grass that are perfect for games of football or cricket, plus plenty of shady areas and trees to relax under. Weekends are often extremely busy with barbecuers and sauntering couples, and the amusingly bouncy tarmac path running around the perimeter attracts pre- and post-work joggers and power-walkers in their droves. The tiny boating lake, miniature funfair (with a small Ferris wheel) and play areas dotted around are perfect for children. The slightly run-down but ludicrously cheap tennis courts are handy for older kids, but you may have to wait your turn before getting on to one. The park is open to women and children only on Tuesdays.

Umm Suqeim Park

Near Jumeirah Beach Hotel, off Beach Road, Jumeirah (348 4554). **Open** 8am-10.30pm Sat-Wed; 8am-11pm Thur, Fri. **Admission** free. **No credit cards**. **Map** p274 B4.

Situated opposite the public beach, this modest, if slightly tired-looking, park has an array of educational apparatus for children and pleasant shaded gazebo areas for parents. It's ideal as an alternative to the beach.

Theme & water parks

Luna Park

Al Nasr Leisureland, Oud Metha (337 1234). **Open** 9am-10.30pm daily. **Admission** *Leisureland, incl Luna Park* Dhs10; Dhs5 concessions. **Credit** AmEx, DC, MC, V. **Map** p277 J3.

A permanent funfair offering a range of rides suitable for four-year-olds upwards, including bumper cars, go-karts and a rollercoaster. Leisureland also includes an ice rink and a giant outdoor pool with three-foot-high waves and a tiled 'beach', plus six slides and a water playground with water cannons (admission to the pool is an additional Dhs40 for adults and Dhs20 for children).

Wild Wadi

Next to Jumeirah Beach Hotel, Beach Road, Jumeirah (348 4444/www.wildwadi.com). **Open** *Winter* 11am-6pm daily. *Summer* phone for times. **Admission** Dhs120; Dhs100 concessions; free under-3s. **Credit** AmEx, DC, MC, V. **Map** p274 B4.

Dubai's Arabian-themed premier water park has 23 fun-filled rides for kids and adults. Wind your way in leisurely fashion round Whitewater Wadi, propel yourself up Summit Surge, then fly down the 33m-high (108ft) Jumeirah Sceirah (read scarer). A word of warning: hold on to your shorts! Plenty of lifeguards are on hand to make sure you and your rubber ring don't part company. Kids love the shipwreck with squirting canons, and there are plenty of fast-food restaurants to feed them up in afterwards. Parents, meanwhile, can take turns to chill out in Breaker's Bay for the day.

Wonderland Theme & Water Park

Creekside Park, near Garhoud Bridge, Garhoud (324 1222). **Open** *Theme Park* 2-10pm Sat-Wed; noon-11pm Thur, Fri. *Splashland* 10am-7pm daily. **Admission** *Whole park* Dhs75; Dhs55 concessions. *Splashland only* Dhs45; Dhs35 concessions. **Credit** AmEx, DC, MC, V. **Map** p277 K3.

Wonderland includes a theme park, Splashland and the Desert Extreme skate park, which has half-pipes, trick boxes, rail slides and ramps for BMXers, skateboarders and inline skaters (over-fives only). Helmets are compulsory and all equipment can be hired. Besides Splashland, with its nine water rides and activity pools, there's a huge variety of indoor and outdoor rides, food outlets, paintballing, go-karting and, for the less adventurous, camel rides. Timings are liable to change, so phone to check.

Scuba diving & snorkelling

Al Boom Diving

Near the Iranian Hospital, Al Wasl Road, Satwa (342 2993). **Cost** *Bubblemaker course* Dhs250. *Seal course* Dhs1,000. *Junior Open Water course* Dhs1,700. **Credit** MC, V. **Map** p280 E9.

Al Boom runs the PADI Bubblemaker courses (a 60- to 90-minute basic introduction to diving for over-eights), PADI Seal courses (basic principles for over-eights; over 12 hours) and PADI Junior Open Water courses (ten years and over; 30 hours) in two fully equipped classrooms and a swimming pool.

Scuba Arabia

Le Meridien Mina Seyahi Hotel, Al Sufouh Road, Jumeirah (399 3333/2278). **Cost** *Seal course* Dhs800. *Junior Open Water course* Dhs1700. **Credit** AmEx, DC, MC, V. **Map** p274 A5.

Eight- to ten-year-olds can become PADI Seal team members and discover the thrill of underwater diving in the safety of the Club Mina pool at the hotel. Over-tens can move on to the Open Water course (they must be accompanied by an adult), which gains them a certificate that allows them to dive anywhere in the world.

Indoor fun

Activity centres

Children's City

Creek Park, entrance on Riyadh Road (334 0808). **Open** 9am-9.30pm Sat-Thur; 4-9.30pm Fri. **Admission** Dhs15; Dhs40 family; Dhs10 concessions. **Credit** AmEx, DC, MC, V. **Map** p277 K3.

Children's City is a huge Duplo-esque centre in Creek Park, a brightly coloured blocky building that boasts a myriad of educational zones, designed to stimulate the curiosity of toddlers and teenagers alike. These areas of 'edutainment' include the Toddler area, Discovery Space section, Physical Science zone, Computer & Communication Gallery, The Way We Live area and Nature Centre, plus culture blocks dedicated to the history of the UAE and profiles of Arab intellectuals, a planetarium and an amphitheatre. The displays are imaginative, interactive and highly entertaining (our favourite is the giant computer with rideable mouse). The centre also features a Malik Burger joint for refreshments, a library and an early-learning shop.

Encounter Zone. *See p150.*

There are more than 20 water rides at **Wild Wadi** water park. *See p148.*

Encounter Zone

Level 3, Wafi City mall, Oud Metha Road (324 7747/ ezone@emirates.net.ae). **Open** 10am-10pm Sat-Tue; 10am-11pm Wed, Thur; 1-10pm Fri. **Admission** *Galactica* Dhs25/hr; *LunarLand* Dhs20/hr; *all zones* Dhs45/day. **Credit** DC, MC, V. **Map** p277 J3.

Encounter Zone has two parts. LunarLand, for under-eights, has a Snow Capsule, Komet roller-coaster and the slides and tunnels of Skylab. Galactica, for over-eights, has network games, an indoor skate park, chamber of horror house, 3-D cinema, anti-gravity racing simulator and the mentally challenging Crystal Maze, with medieval, future and ocean zones. Kids can be left under the drop 'n' shop deal. Enquire about other packages.

Fun City

Oasis Centre mall, Sheikh Zayed Road (339 1302). **Open** 10am-10pm Sat-Thur; 2-11pm Fri. **Admission** free; rides & games Dhs2 each. **Credit** AmEx, DC, MC, V. **Map** p274 B4.

Fun City has a lot to offer children of all ages. The area for under-fives ('Fun and Learn') features several make-believe areas, including a kitchen, a library, fair, art studio and shop. For slightly older children there's a good-size two-tier soft-play maze (at the Oasis and Mercato branches), a substantial bouncy castle, and a smallish area for bumper cars. **Other locations**: Mercato Mall, Jumeirah (349 9976); BurJuman Centre mall, Bur Dubai (359 3336).

Magic Planet

City Centre mall, Beach Road, Jumeirah (295 4333). **Open** 10am-midnight daily. **Admission** free; rides & games from Dhs2; unlimited-ride wristband Dhs50. **Credit** AmEx, DC, MC, V. **Map** p277 K2.

Whizzing and whirring, Magic Planet is possibly the noisiest of Dubai's indoor play areas. It boasts literally dozens of arcade games, fairground rides (including a Ferris wheel, a traditional carousel, bumper cars and a little City Train, which snakes its way through the 'planet'), sand art and pinball stations, so you'll have a tough time tearing kids away. The easily accessible food court allows you to watch over your children in the large, soft play cage, but the place is generally unsupervised, so don't expect any babysitting service. There's also a ten-pin bowling centre.

Toby's

Level 3 Food Court, BurJuman Centre, Trade Centre Road, Bur Dubai (355 2868). **Open** 10.30am-10pm Sat-Tue; 10.30am-11pm Wed, Thur; 2-10.30pm Fri. **Admission** Dhs15-Dhs25/2hrs. **No credit cards**. **Map** p279 J5.

At Toby's tots under the age of four get to romp in their own colourful ball pit and soft play area, while bigger kids can frolic in a larger zone of slides, punch bags, space hoppers and swinging inflatables. There's a cafeteria, where parents and minders can sit and keep an eye on the tinies themselves, or the mall and food court just outside if they would prefer to leave over-fours in the capable hands of Toby's staff – the play pit is gate-controlled so there's no chance of any escapees.

Arts & crafts centres

Café Céramique

Town Centre mall, Beach Road, Jumeirah (344 7331). **Open** 8am-midnight daily. **Admission** *Studio fee* Dhs25; Dhs15 concessions. **Credit** AmEx, DC, MC, V. **Map** p282 C12.

This is indeed a café, but the name gives a hint as to its *raison d'être*: customers, both adult and children, are encouraged to select an unpainted item of ceramic crockery from the hundreds displayed (from Dhs10) and decorate it with their own designs. Staff then glaze and fire their handiwork, which is ready for collection a couple of days later. Whether or not you join in, you can enjoy a coffee or soft drink and delicious food (*see p108*). There is a great winter terrace with sea views, plus a programme of kids' workshops and activities. Note that the admission fee is reduced by 50 per cent on weekday mornings.

Crafters Home

Shop no.M-59, Mezzanine floor, Mazaya Centre mall, Sheikh Zayed Road (343 3045). **Open** 9am-9pm Sat-Thur; 4.30-9pm Fri. **Admission** *Studio fee* Dhs25; Dhs15 concessions. **Credit** MC, V. **Map** p283 E14.

An in-shop studio where you can create your own designs on ceramic, wood, plastic and more. Get crafty with all sorts of folk art including decorative painting, ceramic painting, sand art, jewellery making, foam flower art, vegetable carving, parchment craft and bead weaving. The cost of individual items is not included in the studio fee.

Dubai International Arts Centre

Beach Road (turn right towards the sea opposite Commercial Bank of Dubai), Jumeirah (344 4398). **Open** 8.30am-6.30pm Sat-Wed; 8.30am-3.30pm Thur. **Admission** *School holidays* Dhs75-Dhs150 per workshop. *Term-time* phone for membership details. **Credit** AmEx, DC, MC, V. **Map** p280 D9.

Dubai's only arts centre has a well deserved reputation for recruiting friendly, professional teachers. Hands-on classes include mixed media, ceramics, photography, mosaic, silk painting, dressmaking and calligraphy.

Do play with your food

Friday brunches are something of a tradition in Dubai, though cynics may fear it's one created by hotels keen to use up the week's leftovers in grand buffets. There are some great deals for adults involving limitless food and even champagne (*see p93*), and many outlets have followed suit for children, laying on all sorts of entertainments and tasty morsels. Here are five of the best child-friendly venues:

The Antigo restaurant at **Le Meridien Dubai** (*see p39*) has a Friday family brunch from 12.30pm to 3.30pm (Dhs98 for adults, six- to 12-year-olds half-price), with videos and games for restless little ones.

The Taj Palace Hotel (*see p39*) has a great Dhs88 Friday brunch deal (half price for six- to 12-year-olds, under-sixes free) with a clown, colouring pens and paper and special T-shirts. Look out too for occasional cooking lessons with the brunch chefs.

Nad Al Sheba (*see p71*) proves itself more than just a racetrack with the excellent value Family Friday Roast (noon-4pm; Dhs75 adults, Dhs25 four- to 17-year-olds, under-threes free): expect climbing toys, slides, puzzles, cartoons and a bouncy castle to keep kids occupied.

The InterContinental (*see p39*) and **JW Marriott** (*see p48*) both charge children according to their height, measured by a clown. The former features a magician, supervised games area, electronic games, ice-cream, candyfloss and popcorn machines.

Arts & Entertainment

Film & Theatre

Hollywood blockbusters, Bollywood's playground and the birth of home-grown film.

Film

Dubai's relationship with the big screen has always been slightly rocky. Film buffs question the dominance of multiplexes showing Hollywood blockbusters and straight-to-video-elsewhere action flicks; others salute recent efforts to generate home-grown talent and establish local festivals. However upbeat your analysis, the former does outweigh the latter and, for most visitors, a visit to the cinema here is nothing to write home about. The many multiplexes – there's pretty much one for every mall – are modern, with good sound systems and plenty of large screens showing the latest worldwide releases. Unfortunately, the fare is usually limited and mainstream, and few art-house or indie films make it to the emirate.

BOLLYWOOD AT HOME AND AWAY

In recent years, Dubai has become something of a playground for Bollywood and other Indian film stars, who can be spotted holidaying at the top-notch hotels, eating in the new Indian-fusion restaurants such as the One&Only Royal Mirage's Nina (*see p99*) and partying at some of the trendier clubs. Some even find time to actually shoot films.

Dubai is fast becoming flavour of the month for directors keen to include a backdrop of sand dunes, rolling waves and glamorous skyscrapers in their song and dance routines. The 2003 hit Boom, for example, starred Amitabh Bachchan, Bollywood's equivalent of Al Pacino, as a super-rich businessman with offices at the Burj Al Arab and a lifestyle to match. Western directors have also begun checking out the emirate as a location for desert-bound and futuristic flicks. The local government intends to exploit this trend fully, and has created plans for a dedicated site for film studios, dubbed, to date, 'film city'.

Besides Hollywood action fluff, Dubai's Indian and Emirati cinema-goers revel in popular Indian flicks, which arrive here a few weeks after opening in subcontinental

Dino Morea, the model-turned-Bollywood star, is one of Dubai's regular film-star visitors.

Fest behaviour

While the UAE is certainly slow out of the filmmaking traps, new initiatives are aiming to get the region's creative juices flowing. The Emirates Film Competition and proposed Dubai Film Festival are attempting to promote local filmmaking talent through backslapping and gong giving.

Established in 2002 and held in Abu Dhabi, the **Emirates Film Competition** (EFC) is a strictly regional affair and the rules stipulate that entries must include some local theme or element. The 2003 contest produced some unexpected gems, with the students of Abu Dhabi Women's College taking most plaudits. EFC's competitive element is accompanied by a showcase of features, documentaries and shorts from Europe and the Arab world, including a selection of winners from the Edinburgh Film Festival.

Launched at 2003's Cannes Film Festival, the inaugural **Dubai International Film Festival** (DIFF) is set to take place in December 2004 and promises to be an altogether glitzier affair. With an initial budget of Dhs5million, the organisers are aiming to beat the French at their own game: DIFF claims that more than

Flick chick: home-grown film talent.

100 film celebrities will put in an appearance, and it pledges to showcase the cream of world cinema. What remains to be seen is how the festival will deal with censorship issues and whether sexually explicit or politically sensitive films will be screened. And while the Cannes-massive may not be losing any sleep just yet, DIFF could still become an oasis of art-house in a world of mainstream monotony.

cities. Many of the smaller, older cinemas show Malayalam and Tamil films: like most of Dubai's Indian population, these films hail from the southern states. Even if you can't understand the language, it's an experience to take in the latest Bollywood release on a Thursday night (the first night of the Arabic weekend), preferably at the old-school open-air **Rex Drive-in** cinema in desert-bound Mirdif (it also has a seating area).

CENSORSHIP

The government censors don't usually face too many challenges with Indian cinema, but all films pass by them before hitting the big screen – and some more risqué Western offerings don't make it that far. The censors – currently two employees of the Ministry of Information and Culture – have gradually eased regulations over the years, but sex scenes are usually cut, as is any overtly religious content. In 2003 cinemas were forced to put up signs warning viewers that Morgan Freeman's part as God in the 2003 Jim Carrey film *Bruce Almighty* had been entirely cut, leaving a nonsensical storyline.

When it comes to politics, like in many other Arab countries, any recognition of Israel is a definite no-no – in fact the word itself can be

'beeped' out, as in the 2001 Robert Redford/Brad Pitt vehicle *Spy Game* – and censors have also been known to chop anything sensitive regarding the Arab world and its leaders. Violence and bad language, however, are rarely censored and nowadays many films pass without any cuts.

Censors claim that they are gradually adapting their rules to suit the times. Quizzed as to its motives, the Ministry maintains that it is merely following the wishes of the Emirati population at large and that, after all, Dubai's ruling sheikhs and their governments have a paternal duty to 'protect' the people and their traditions.

THE 'DVD' SOUK

Many frustrated cinephiles, whether they are anti-censorship or simply after a wider selection of movies, turn to Dubai's burgeoning cut-price DVD market. The souks are awash with illegal copies of DVDs and VCDs, and many offices and flats are served surreptitiously by hawkers carrying holdalls stuffed with films. Prices can be very low but beware, especially of recent releases: investing in a 'DVD' can be a hit-or-miss affair: the worst examples are taped shakily in cinemas and feature rows of Chinese cinema-goers' heads. Older films tend to be direct copies of existing DVDs and as such are of higher quality.

LOCAL TALENT

As for home-grown cinema, the UAE has been making strides recently – despite a widespread apathy towards cinema as an art form. Emirati students began making short videos about their lives and experiences in the late 1990s; they now compete for prizes in Abu Dhabi's **Emirates Film Competition** every March (*see p153* **Fest behaviour**), and some have shown at international film festivals.

These young filmmakers, particularly women, have produced some bold shorts about the massive changes that have taken place in Emirati society over the past 40 years. Some documentaries and fictional tales tackle taboo subjects, such as contact between young, unmarried men and women; *wasta*, the local system of using influence to gain favours; and incidences of poverty among Emiratis. Given their determination, and the influence of a few passionate local film buffs, the UAE could produce the first generation of filmmakers from the Gulf.

Dubai Cinema. *See p155.*

And there's some light at the end of the tunnel for art-house fans: the **Dubai International Film Festival**, scheduled for December 2004 (*see p153* **Fest behaviour**), looks set to attract quality film from around the Middle East, as well as Hollywood and other international premieres. Perhaps, over the years, Dubai will take on Cairo, Marrakesh and Beirut to become the key film festival of the Arab world. After all, this is the can-do, will-do city of the Middle East.

CINEMAS

Dubai's multiplexes are mostly located in malls; they are served by just a handful of distributors so they tend to show a similar selection of Hollywood and some other English-language films. The films are subtitled (none are dubbed) in Arabic and – if the reel is imported from Lebanon – in French as well. Most cinemas also screen one or two (unsubtitled) films from Egypt's commercial studios, plus a Hindi blockbuster; the latter usually has Arabic (but not English) subtitles. Smaller cinemas around town show a mix of Hindi, Malayalam and Tamil films.

Films open on a Wednesday, often with a midnight showing, with bankable, popular titles making it to Dubai at the same time or only a week or two after their openings in the USA. More unusual films and non-US English-language films can make it on to the distributor's schedule at any time, with some even appearing months after the DVD release. Late-night showings on Thursdays and Fridays are popular, especially with Emirati lads, but you'll rarely need to book a seat for daytime and weeknight screenings.

All cinemas are air-conditioned, sometimes to quite frosty temperatures, so take a long-sleeved shirt or cardigan. Besides censorship, be warned that some screenings suffer from rows of chatterers. Despite attempts to create mobile-free theatres, it's also not uncommon to be disturbed by a young man or woman with a penchant for text messages. However, most will desist or continue conversations outside the cinema if politely requested to do so.

Time Out Dubai magazine lists and reviews the month's screenings, but distributors and cinemas can change the programme with little warning so it's always best to phone to check in advance. If taking children with you, do also check with the cinema for the rating that has been assigned to the film – **G** (General), **PG** (Parental Guidance), **15** (aged 15 and above) and **18** (18 and over); while the UAE uses a similar certificate system to the USA and UK, it sometimes gives the film a different category or age bracket.

Arts & Entertainment

Streetwise Fringe Theatre.
See p157.

Multiplexes

These all show a similar programme of English-language (mainly Hollywood) films, with a smattering of Egyptian and Hindi blockbusters.

Century Cinema
Mercato Mall, Beach Road, Jumeirah (349 8765).
Tickets Dhs30. **Screens** 7. **Credit** AmEx, DC, MC, V. **Map** p282 C12.

CineStar
City Centre mall, Beach Road, Jumeirah (294 9000).
Tickets Dhs20 before 6pm; Dhs30 after 6pm.
Screens 11. **Credit** AmEx, DC, MC, V. **Map** p277 K2.

Grand CineCity
Above Spinneys supermarket in Al Ghurair City mall, Rigga Road, Deira (228 9898). **Tickets** Dhs25-Dhs35. **Screens** 8. **Credit** AmEx, DC, MC, V. **Map** p279 K3.

Grand Cineplex
Next to Wafi City mall, Garhoud (324 2000).
Tickets Dhs25-Dhs30. **Screens** 10. **Credit** AmEx, DC, MC, V. **Map** p277 J4.

Metroplex Metropolitan Hotel
At Interchange 2, Sheikh Zayed Road (343 8383).
Tickets Dhs25. **Screens** 8. **Credit** AmEx, DC, MC, V. **Map** p276 G5.

Local cinemas

The following independent cinemas show a mix of Malayalam, Tamil and Hindi films, usually with Arabic (but not English) subtitles.

Al Nasr Cinema
Near Al Nasr Leisureland, Oud Metha (337 4353).
Tickets Dhs15-20. **Screens** 1 (Malayalam & Tamil films). **No credit cards. Map** p277 J3.

Dubai Cinema
Near JW Marriott, Muraqqabat Street, Deira (266 0632). **Tickets** Dhs15-Dhs20. **Screens** 1 (Hindi films). **No credit cards. Map** p277 K1.

Galleria Cinema Hyatt Regency
Al Khaleej Road, Deira (273 7676). **Tickets** Dhs20.
Screens 2 (Malayalam & Tamil films). **No credit cards. Map** p279 J1.

Lamcy Cinema
Next to Lamcy Plaza mall, Oud Metha (336 8808).
Tickets Dhs20. **Screens** 2 (Hindi films). **No credit cards. Map** p277 J3.

Plaza Cinema
Opposite Bur Dubai taxi stand, Al Ghubaibi Road (393 9966). **Tickets** Dhs15-Dhs20. **Screens** 1 (Hindi, Malayalam & Tamil films). **No credit cards. Map** p278 G4.

Arts & Entertainment

You needn't go to the ends of the earth

for a better banking servi[

The deal

- Interest bearing current accounts in sterling, US dollar and euro
- All the facilities you would expect from a normal current account
- Visa debit cards giving you worldwide access to your funds
- Membership discounts on a range of products and services, a quarterly magazine, tax guide, repatriation guide, country reports

The reassurance

- Your savings will be with Lloyds TSB Offshore Limited in Jersey or with its Isle of Man branch. Lloyds TSB Offshore Limited is part of one of Britain's biggest banks
- Both islands are well-regulated, politically stable and enjoy excellent telecommunications links

The convenience

- Here, there and everywhere, you'll find it easy to keep in touch
- A personal account executive and team to answer y[questions and help you to make the most of your s[
- Telephone banking - 365 days a year
- Internet banking
- Selected country visits
- Local representatives in selected countries

To find out more please call: (+9714) 3422 550 for personal or business accoun[or e-mail: Ltsbob@emirates.net.ae

www.lloydstsb-offshore.com/club

Rex Drive-in

Mirdif turn-off on Airport Road, Garhoud (288 6447). **Tickets** Dhs15; free children. **Screens** 1 (Hindi films). **No credit cards. Map** p275 E2.
Dubai's only al fresco cinema; either park up and sit in your car or take a place in the open seating area.

Strand Khalid

Kahlid Bin Al Waleed Road (Bank Street), Karama (396 1644). **Tickets** Dhs15-Dhs20. **Screens** 1 (Hindi films). **No credit cards. Map** p279 K5.

Theatre

Dubai's visual artists are campaigning for museums and galleries to be built alongside commercial and residential towers, but the city's performers may have an even greater need: to date, there is no auditorium in the city dedicated to hosting (and nurturing) the performing arts. After years of fundraising, however, it looks as if a Dubai Community Theatre will be built in the next few years, and plans have even been put forward for an opera house. But for now, actors and musicians must strut their stuff in hotels, clubs and school theatres, converted to the cause.

While theatre has yet to truly flourish in Dubai, certain companies are enjoying success, both in English and Hindi. The **Streetwise Fringe Theatre** is a local company that imports English-language shows from the UK. The main Hindi theatre company, **Rangmanch**, recently set up an academy presided over by actor Kader Khan, and has continued its occasional mini theatre festivals, typically starring actors well known on the Indian theatre circuit. Performances and details for local amateur groups, such as the Chamber Orchestra, Big Band and Chorus, are listed in *Time Out Dubai* magazine.

OTHER PERFORMING ARTS

Public performances of Emirati poetry, song and dance are mainly limited to ceremonial occasions and traditional displays at the **Heritage & Diving Village** (*see p60*). While the strong tradition of poetry and storytelling, sometimes set to music, is handed down from nights around the camp fire, many of the songs derive from days on the pearling dhows, when team spirits would be buoyed through sea shantics based on each task, led by a *naha'an* (professional song leader).

At Eid and other celebrations, you're also likely to see *ayyalah* performances, which re-enact battles and hunting expeditions of (recently) bygone days, with groups of men beating sticks, and hurling swords or rifles high up into the air. Dressed in the bright *abayas* (cloaks) of the desert, groups of women engage in separate *na'ashat* dances, swinging their long hair and swaying to music. Local bands are made of players of *tubool* and *rahmani* (drums), *daf* (tambourine) and *nai* and *mizmar* (wind instruments) players. As for expat dance, there are some ballet schools and a lively salsa scene, but performances of Western classical dance are very rare.

As for the city's classical music scene, it is still in its infancy: local musicians recently formed an orchestra and there are some enthusiastic amateur choirs, but the really dedicated travel to **Abu Dhabi** for international concerts, often held at the new Cultural Foundation (*see p213*). Consult *Time Out Abu Dhabi* magazine for details. The UAE capital has two active classical music associations, one of which, the Abu Dhabi Concert Committee, stages the Al Ain Music Festival, a wonderful weekend of international concerts and recitals held every February. Occasionally, international performers invited by the Abu Dhabi Concert Committee or the various embassies make a visit to Dubai; these concerts take place at various venues and are listed in *Time Out Dubai* magazine.

Theatre companies

Dubai Drama Group

(333 1155/050 551 5407/www.dubaidramagroup.org)
Despite the city's lacklustre performing arts scene, this non-profit, amateur English-language theatrical group can lay claim to more than 100 members. From highbrow plays to thigh-slapping pantos, the well-supported group puts on a number of performances of varying quality a year, usually at the Dubai Country Club.

Rangmanch Theatre Company & Academy

Office 21, Block 13, Knowledge Village, near Interchange 4, Sheikh Zayd Road (391 3441/2/ 366 4523/mail@rangmanch.net). **Map** p274 A5.
Rangmanch runs mini theatre festivals throughout the year, featuring theatre companies from India (all plays are in Hindi), at various venues. Actor Kader Khan's academy – the first theatre school in the Gulf – also offers courses in all aspects of theatre, in English and Hindi .

Streetwise Fringe Theatre

331 1111/050 653 6930/www.streetwisefringe.com.
Streetwise imports plays, musicals and one-person-shows from the UK, including hits from the Edinburgh Fringe and pre-London runs. Often featuring young, upcoming actors, the monthly performances (October to May), which are usually held at the Crowne Plaza Hotel on Sheikh Zayed Road (*see p46*), are a treat for local luvvies and can be pretty much guaranteed to be of a high standard.

Arts & Entertainment

Galleries

More than just watercolours of camels.

Dubai – and the Gulf generally – is not exactly synonymous with contemporary art. Let's face it, most tourists are here for sun, sea and shopping, and the city's keenness for commerce over culture can seem all-consuming. But recently, perhaps since the restoration of wind tower houses and historical areas began in the late 1980s, the authorities have become increasingly aware of the need to both preserve traditions and create opportunities for contemporary art, theatre and music.

The **Majlis Gallery** was something of a pioneer, opening in the late 1970s, surviving demolition orders in the 1980s, and becoming a mainstay of the small commercial arts scene that emerged in the 1990s.

Besides Majlis, Dubai has two serious commercial galleries: **Total Arts at The Courtyard**, on a fascinating 'street' within a warehouse in the industrial area of Al Quoz, and the **Green Art Gallery** in Jumeirah. The latter tends to show quality work by artists, mainly painters, from the Arab world in a charming villa setting, and is a must for collectors. Total Arts is a large gallery set over two floors with a programme that mixes conservative calligraphers, innovative tribal and contemporary artists from Iran and the Arab world, and rare Iranian rugs, kilim and tribal weavings. Gallerist Dariush Zandi, a photographer, architect and off-road specialist, built the quirky Courtyard himself; the gallery and adjoining 'street' is an aesthetically pleasing mishmash of European, traditional local and north African architecture, and is home to a coffee shop, interiors gallery, photography studio and other arty outlets.

Other 'galleries' range from quality antiques, art and design outlets – such as **Hunar Gallery**, the **Creative Art Centre** and **Showcase Antiques** – to interiors shops (*see p133*). For a full list of art and interiors showrooms, see *Time Out Dubai* magazine; here we've listed the best contemporary galleries plus some art and antique showrooms. Local artists tend to congregate at the **Dubai International Arts Centre** in Jumeirah (344 4398; *see p151*) and there are other practical centres for budding artists, also listed in *Time Out Dubai* magazine.

Perhaps spurred on by Sharjah's success in the contemporary arts field – its Biennial is well respected in the contemporary art world

(*see p223*) – Dubai is showing signs of including public galleries, theatres, museums and opera houses in its grand development plans. But, for the moment, many local and international artists end up displaying their talents in hotel lobbies and shopping malls – no bad thing for the busy visitor.

Still, members of Dubai's first generation of expats born in the emirate, now in their 20s and 30s, show a commitment to fostering local art and importing cutting-edge talent from the Arab world, Iran and their diasporas. The **9714 Productions** crew (www.9714.com), for example, a mix of young Arab, Iranian and Emirati culturalists, stage excellent regular 'cultural club nights' where they feature exhibitions by local and international artists, photographers and architects, video screenings and live musicians, attended by enthusiastic audiences (*see p168* **Party politics**).

Contemporary galleries

Green Art Gallery
Street 51, villa 23, behind Dubai Zoo, Jumeirah (344 9888/www.gagallery.com). **Open** 9.30am-1.30pm, 4.30-8.30pm Sat-Thur. **Admission** free. **Map** p280 D10.

Housed in a typical Jumeirah villa, Green Art Gallery stocks a diverse selection of original paintings, limited edition prints, crafts and sculpture by established and upcoming contemporary artists from Lebanon, Syria, Iraq, Jordan and the rest of the Arab world. Regular solo and group exhibitions take place during the winter months.

Majlis Gallery
Al Fahidi roundabout, Bastakia, Bur Dubai (353 6233). **Open** 9.30am-1.30pm, 4.30-8pm Sat-Thur. **Admission** free. **Map** p278 H4.

This old wind tower house's delightful courtyard and series of exhibition rooms stock antique and new country-style furniture from India and the Gulf, plus Bedouin and contemporary jewellery and a range of ceramics and other interiors' accessories. In the winter months, there are regular shows by local and international artists – mainly watercolourists and designers.

Total Arts at The Courtyard
Off Sheikh Zayed Road, between Interchanges 3 & 4, just before Mercedes-Benz showroom, Al Quoz (228 2888/347 5050/www.courtyard-uae.com). **Open** 10am-1pm, 4-8pm Sat-Thur. **Admission** free. **Credit** AmEx, DC, MC, V. **Map** p274 B4.

Total Arts at The Courtyard. *See p158.*

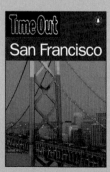

Majlis Gallery: soak up the atmosphere and take home an original. *See p158.*

At the end of a street of artsy shops and businesses is Dubai's biggest gallery. Through its atrium entrance are two floors of contemporary art, design and weavings. Like its owner and designer, Dariush Zandi, many of the artists hail from Iran – you're as likely to come across a huge show of rare, reasonably priced kilim and tribal weavings as you are calligraphy or contemporary photography. Exhibitions feature installations and contemporary work by local and international artists, and occasional shows of renowned Iranian masters.

Art & antique showrooms

Creative Art Centre

Behind Choithram supermarket, Beach Road, Jumeirah (344 4394/www.arabian-arts.com). **Open** 8am-6pm Sat-Thur. **Admission** free. **Credit** MC, V. **Map** p282 C12.

Two villas joined together to display fine art, antiques, gifts and souvenirs reflecting the heritage of the Gulf. Collector's items include chests, old Omani doors (made into coffee tables and console stands) and Bedouin silver, while gifts (from Dhs15) include freshwater pearls from Shanghai. Staff can assist with interior design and furniture restoration; there is also a good framing service.

Four Seasons Ramesh Gallery

Ground floor, Al Zomorrodah Building, Zabeel Road, Karama (334 9090/www.fourseasonsgallery.com). **Open** 9am-9pm Sat-Thur; 5-9pm Fri. **Admission** free. **Credit** MC, V. **Map** p277 J2.

The gallery holds a large collection of historical images of the UAE by renowned photographer Ramesh Shukla, as well as prints, paintings and interior design objects, from classical to contemporary.

Hunar Gallery

Street 49, Villa 6, Rashidiya (286 2224). **Open** 9am-1pm, 4-8pm Sat-Thur. **Admission** free. **Credit** MC, V. **Map** p275 E2.

Fine art from all corners of the world, including artistically decorated Japanese tiles and Belgian pewter and glass pieces, plus old Persian paintings and contemporary art.

Majlis Al Ghorfat Umm Al Sheif

Beach Road, past Dubai Zoo, Jumeirah 3 (394 6343). **Open** 8.30am-1.30pm, 3.30-8.30pm Sat-Thur; 3.30-8pm Fri. **Admission** Dhs1; free under-6s. **No credit cards**. **Map** p274 B4.

Built in 1955 as a summer residence for Sheikh Rashid Bin Saeed Al Maktoum, this atmospheric dwelling is now open to visitors. It's always very quiet here, giving you a chance to appreciate the peaceful, traditional *majlis* (meeting room), with its display of old coffee pots, carpets and other antique interior accessories. While you're here, also take the time to enjoy the traditional palm tree garden with *falaj* irrigation system, in which underground water is drawn to villages by manmade subterranean channels.

Showcase Antiques, Art & Frames

Beach Road, off Interchange 3, Sheikh Zayed Road, Umm Suqeim (348 8797/www.showcase antiques.net). **Open** 10am-1pm, 4-8pm Sat-Thur; 4-8pm Fri. **Admission** free. **Credit** AmEx, DC, MC, V. **Map** p274 B4.

Here you can count on a good display of antiques and art including dowry chests, silver Bedouin jewellery, silver *khanjar* knives, antique coffee pots and tables, plus furniture from Europe. Upstairs is a selection of British antiques. Staff are knowledgeable and well worth quizzing for ideas.

Nightlife

The city's denizens of the night have the world at their nicotine-stained fingertips, from funky Filipino bands to high-class vinyl pits.

Dubai's nightlife has come of age in recent times. Beer guts have given way to glamour, and where boozehounds were once torn between a smattering of British-style pubs, the city is now overflowing with upmarket wine bars, DJ joints and packed-out pleasure dens. Whether you're in the market for buckets of lager and cheesy disco or wallet-busting cocktails and roomfuls of wafer-thin Russians, there's a scene for every reveller.

The main reason for this upturn in fortunes is the hijacking of the mainstream scene by Dubai's forceful and fun-loving Lebanese population. Tired of slumming it in pedestrian taverns and nostalgic for the ostentatious revelry of Beirut, a number of promoters have set about bringing Dubai's club scene bang up to date. Cue glitter palaces with stunning light and sound systems, over-dressed, over-coiffed clientele, and more house music than you can shake a glow-stick at. Most clubs are open until 3am, but patrons push 'fashionably late' to the extreme – meaning places don't get going until 1am, leaving two hours of hardcore mayhem before bedtime.

Dubai's clubbers are a notoriously fickle crowd and one month's 'in' place is passé almost before the paint's dry. The result is a cynical club scene where nightspots desperately try to out-hip each other with big-name DJs, outrageously expensive drinks and escalating levels of exclusivity – often culminating in bars so elitist they have no customers. However, this one-upmanship has led to some truly stunning locations, from lavish clubs such as **Sho Cho's** (*see p177*) and **Kasbar** (*see p174*) to the trendy **M-Level** (*see p171*) at the Hilton Dubai Creek. Most of these upmarket joints will enforce a strict dress code, so you can't get away with trainers or scruffy garb, although jeans are usually permitted. In a blow for equality, this applies to both men and women.

Perhaps as a backlash against this cooler-than-thou ethos, a new generation of down-to-earth pubs are opening their doors to hordes of pint-hungry punters. Places like **Waxy O'Conner's** (*see p171*), the **Alamo** (*see p177*) and the **Lodge** (once a legendary crowd favourite, which reopened recently after a lengthy absence, *see p170*) pull in the punters with such delights as karaoke competitions, yards of ale and lightweight dance music, creating an almost Benidormian ambience. These venues will welcome you no matter what your get-up: trainers are pretty much the norm and shorts are fine during the daytime.

A Dubai weekend varies depending on which sector you work in – most local companies take Thursday and Friday off, while most Westerners opt for Fridays and Saturdays. This means that Thursday is always the big night of the week and Fridays are usually spent nursing hangovers over the town's variety of brunch spots (*see p93* **Brunching out**). However, unlike the weekend-obsessed Europeans, Dubai drinkers will celebrate on pretty much any day ending in 'y' and there is something going on every night of the week. Tuesday night, for example, is ladies' night, where a woman can crawl her way to inebriation courtesy of free drinks promotions at most bars. The schedule of touring DJs also encourages big-league beat merchants to play midweek.

Despite the stiff competition, drinking in Dubai is still an expensive business. By law, every alcohol outlet has to be housed in a hotel or hold a special licence, usually only awarded to social clubs or large sporting grounds. This means paying top whack for pick-me-ups; you'll struggle to find a tipple below Dhs15, and in classier joints you'll pay up to Dhs30 for a bottle of beer. On average, expect to pay Dhs20 for beers, wine and spirits; and when you chuck in taxi rides, admission prices and post-club *shoarmas* (doner kebabs) you're unlikely to get much change from Dhs200 for your night out. Despite being based in hotels, most venues have a separate entrance to keep well-refreshed patrons away from guests. Entry is mostly free, except for the very top hotels such as the Burj, but drinkers are not entitled to use the leisure facilities (pools, health clubs and so on).

THE RHYTHM OF THE NIGHT

Due to the extreme heat in summer and the lack of pedestrian-friendly areas, it's almost impossible to orchestrate a decent pub-crawl in the city. Complexes such as Wafi City and Dubai Marine Beach Resort do house a number of outlets, but most revellers opt for taxis to commute between pints. Cabs are cheap and plentiful, although the rather erratic driving can prove troublesome if you're feeling a little the worse for wear. Should the inevitable happen, there is no clean-up charge, but Dubai's cabbies work long hours for little pay, and a decent tip goes a long way.

The Achilles' heel of Dubai's nightlife is its live music scene. In far too many places, bland, synth-heavy cover bands churn out facsimile

The best Venues

For a quiet one
The vast terrace at **The Irish Village** (*see p173*) is great for a tranquil pint in the early evening.

For cheesy thrills
Groove to the dance classics of days gone by at **The Lodge** (*see p170*), **Rock Bottom Café** (*see p165*) and **Zinc** (*see p165*).

For serious dancing
The monolithic **MIX** (*see p165*) and the relatively tiny **Tangerine** (*see p165*) both offer a weekly roster of international DJs and home-spun talent, while **M-Level** (*see p171*) is the place to go for one-off shenanigans.

For outdoor schmoozing
The stunning **Rooftop** (*see p174*) will have you dancing on the ceiling; **Barasti** (*see p177*) boasts cracking views, a casual dress code and potent pick-me-ups; **QD's** (*see p171*) has the best al fresco panorama on the Creek.

copies of international soft-rock hits, while fading pop stars make occasional visits to cash in on Dubai's desperation – Simply Red, Deacon Blue and Paul Young have all trodden water here in recent times. However, there is light at the end of the musical tunnel. Two annual festivals made their debut in 2003: October's Gig on the Green – a one-day event that featured some top-drawer bands including Suede and the Fun Lovin' Criminals, and the **Dubai International Jazz Festival** (*see p142*), which brings some of the best horn-blowers in the world to town every January.

For regular live music there are two separate circuits, both dominated by imported bands playing other people's music. In both cases, groups tend to be hired on a six-month contract, meaning a quick turnover of talent. The mainstream scene centres on a trio of hotel-based melody huts: **Jimmy Dix**, **Rock Bottom Café** and **Zinc** (for all three, *see p165*). All three venues have versatile Western resident bands that will turn their hand to contemporary chart-toppers, pop anthems and what seems to be Dubai's adopted anthem – *Love Shack* by the B-52s.

The alternative clubs in Bur Dubai and Deira have developed their own scene, with a host of cracking Indian, African and Filipino bands

Arts & Entertainment

Beats working: DJ Lucas at **M-Level**. *See p171.*

banging out the hits. Although covers still rule, the delivery and reception is far more passionate than at most of the five-star bars.

Dubai's 'birds of a feather' mentality means that clubbing is almost entirely segregated in the city, with few hedonists venturing outside of their cultural clique. At its worst this 'stick to your own' policy can translate to pure racism disguised as a members-only policy.

Certain bars, predominantly old-school pubs patronised by Western expats, will block the admittance of anyone they feel is 'unsuitable', claiming you have to be a member to enter. While many bars' licences do depend on operating such a system, if you are white you are likely to breeze through unhampered. Maddeningly, there is little that can be done short of boycotting such establishments, and arguing with the bouncer is liable to yield nothing more than laryngitis.

Regardless of your particular brand of hedonism, you're bound to find a scene that suits. The only thing missing in the city is authenticity: confining bars to hotels means they lack the personal touch found in other parts of the world. On the other hand, when the fantasy consists of luxurious locations, open-air beach parties and superstar DJs, reality soon starts to look a tad overrated.

Bur Dubai

DJ bars/clubs

Cyclone
Al Nasr Leisureland, opposite the American Hospital (336 9991). **Open** 9pm-3am daily. **Admission** free. **Credit** AmEx, DC, MC, V. **Map** p277 J3.
This is without doubt the most depressing drinking establishment in the city. The Cyclone used to be a normal nightclub, but these days it draws an implausibly friendly female clientele who clamour for the attention of a number of men on the look-out for short-term company; and they get it. The music tends to be along commercial hip hop and chart-friendly R&B lines.

Ginseng
Wafi Pyramids at Wafi City mall, Oud Metha Road (324 8200). **Open** 7pm-2am daily. **Admission** free. **Credit** AmEx, DC, MC, V. **Map** p277 J3.
An intimate Asian-themed lounge bar, Ginseng has a formidable array of fierce cocktails, and while it's stylish, it's not as pretentious as other similar bars in the city. Entry is very much dependent on your look and the company you keep (an all-male posse will be politely moved along) but once inside you'll be privy to one of the most eclectic record boxes in town, with masterful chill-out mixes being weaved throughout the week. *See also p83.*

Arts & Entertainment

Jimmy Dix

Mövenpick Hotel Bur Dubai, 19th Street (336 8800).
Open noon-3am daily. **Admission** free. **Credit** MC,
V. **Map** p277 J3.

A grog-pusher and meat market cast from the same
no-frills mould as the Rock Bottom Café (*see below*),
Jimmy Dix attracts an up-for-it throng out to drink
themselves into oblivion. Although the poorly ven-
tilated scarlet interior gives the impression that
one is trapped in the lung of a chain smoker, the
decent cover band and resident DJ can whip up
an (admittedly subdued) storm with their airings
of old school pop, rock and lightweight dance, while
the cheap booze and unpretentious atmosphere are
both welcome.

MIX

Grand Hyatt Hotel, Oud Metha Road (317 1234).
Open 9pm-3am Sun-Fri. **Admission** free. **Credit**
AmEx, MC, V. **Map** p277 K3.

A musical monolith, MIX is a three-tier clubbing
complex containing what is reputed to be the Middle
East's largest dancefloor – and who's to doubt it?
Music varies from night to night, but the main room
tends to err on the side of house while the smart
upstairs area specialises in R&B and commercial hip
hop. The sheer vastness of the place makes it hard
to generate much of an atmosphere on weekdays,
but come the weekend (Thur, Fri) the revellers are
all but swinging from the rafters.

Rock Bottom Café

*Regent Palace Hotel, World Trade Centre Road (396
3888).* **Open** 7pm-3am daily. **Admission** free.
Credit AmEx, DC, MC, V. **Map** p279 J5.

Although it's officially a bar and restaurant rather
than a club, Rock Bottom only really comes alive as
other bars kick out and its own sound system cranks
up. Little more than a lowbrow cattle market, RB's
still pulls in an impressive crowd with its proven
blend of Bullfrogs (a highly potent cocktail that
utilises all the white spirits) combined with a resident DJ and live band, who pump out the pleasers
till closing time. There's even an in-house *shoarma*
joint for dancers with the munchies.

Tangerine

Fairmont Hotel, Sheikh Zayed Road (332 5555).
Open 8pm-3am daily. **Admission** free. **Credit**
AmEx, DC, MC, V. **Map** p281 G9.

After a slow start, Tangerine is beginning to curry
favour with Dubai's notoriously fickle clubbing fra-
ternity by lowering its stringent entry requirements a
notch (though a dress code is still in force) and hosting
some red-hot house nights. The interior is as lavishly
decorated as the patrons, and a hallowed VIP area lies
behind the red rope stage left. The 'Rine is the only club
in town to stock Skyy vodka, which claims to give a
hangover-free morning after. *Time Out* begs to differ.

Zinc

*Crowne Plaza Dubai Hotel, Sheikh Zayed Road (331
1111).* **Open** 7pm-3am daily. **Admission** free.
Credit AmEx, DC, MC, V. **Map** p281 G10.

An ever-popular Sheikh Zayed Road venue with a
large central bar, separate dining area and one of the
city's busiest dancefloors. The decor is metallic chic
and the mix of live music and tunes from the bar's
resident DJ attracts a lively crowd that is among the
most diverse in Dubai. It's packed almost every
night of the week, so has seen the development of
one element of international clubbing unheard of in
the city – queues at the door. *See also p106.*

Live music venues

Club Africana

*Rush Inn Hotel, Kahlid Bin Al Waleed Road (Bank
Street) (352 2235).* **Open** 9pm-3am daily. **Admission**
free. **Credit** AmEx, DC, MC, V. **Map** p278 H4.

Housed deep within the intestinal confines of the
Rush Inn Hotel, Club Africana is undoubtedly one
of Dubai's best-kept secrets. The house band is a 12-
strong Congolese collective who lay on free-form
African rapping, harmonising and soliloquising to
heart-stopping effect. Visit at 1am and the bar is
invariably packed, a throbbing sinew of electrified
energy; or pop along earlier in the evening, at around
11pm, for a couple of hours of laid-back ethnic tunes.
It's like the Buena Vista Social Club, only African
and in Dubai.

Pot head at **Aussie Legends**. *See p169.*

FIDEL

fidelclothing.co

Band substances: have a song and dance to live music at **Rock Bottom Café**. *See p165.*

Garden Rooftop

Wafi City mall, Oud Metha Road (324 7300). **Open** winter only, noon-1am Fri. **Admission** free. **Credit** AmEx, DC, MC, V. **Map** p277 J3.

Situated between two other bars (Seville's and Carter's, both perfectly fine drinkeries in their own right) lies the Garden, a combination of fake rocks and real grass, with a sunken volleyball court in amphitheatre style that doubles as a music venue. On Fridays throughout the winter, this al fresco venue hosts Peanut Butter Jam, where a variety of bands peddle their wares to a crowd lounging on luminous beanbags. The atmosphere is terrific, even if the bands vary in quality. Our advice? Arrive early for the fabulous flamenco guitarists and take your time at the bar as the bald bloke in the sleeveless top murders Radiohead.

Maharlika's

President Hotel, Trade Centre Road, Karama (334 6565). **Open** 6pm-3am daily. **Admission** free. **Credit** AmEx, DC, MC, V. **Map** p281 J6.

Maharlika's is one of Dubai's best live music venues – presuming, that is, that your favourite tunes come from Filipino cover bands. While lots of venues here offer this kind of thing, Maharlika's does it with unashamed style and draws a huge crowd pretty much every night of the week. The bands change occasionally, but the theme remains the same: six-or seven-piece Filipino cover bands heavy on guitars and thin young women with lots of flailing hair – it sounds awful but redemption is at hand by virtue of some of the singers and musicians actually being

extremely accomplished. Expect to hear Led Zep's *Stairway to Heaven*, the Cranberries' *Zombie*, some choice Guns N' Roses and anything else that you can shake your big hair to. A cracking little venue that always guarantees a top night out.

Manzil Indian

Rush Inn Hotel, Kahlid Bin Al Waleed Road (Bank Street) (352 2235). **Open** 9pm-3am daily. **Admission** free. **Credit** MC, V. **Map** p278 H4.

Manzil's is a popular venue where spotlights skid through whorls of dry ice and young clubbers vibrate to upbeat bhangra. A silk-covered crooner belts out show tunes as disaffected ladies try their hardest to look alluring while waiting to take to the stage and dance.

Marine's Club

Seaview Hotel, Al Mina Road (355 7734). **Open** 6pm-3am daily. **Admission** free. **Credit** AmEx, DC, MC, V. **Map** p278 F5.

A Filipino rock joint, Marine's is home to just enough denim-clad moshers to give the atmosphere a steely edge, yet not enough to provoke fear. The superb cover band charges the bar with a barrage of '70s, '80s and '90s power chord madness, never less than note perfect and delivered with the confident swagger of the truly bombastic. Strap on your air guitar and sing along with gusto.

Pancho Villas

Astoria Hotel, Al Nahda Street (353 2146). **Open** 7pm-3am daily. **Admission** free. **Credit** AmEx, DC, MC, V. **Map** p278 G4.

Arts & Entertainment

Pancho's is a venerable old man of the Dubai night scene, even if its halcyon days are but a fading memory. Once upon a time, no night out would have been complete without a visit to this rather lamely themed corner of Mexico, but no more. That said, PV is no bad place. It's a decent size, and usually fairly busy with a mixed crowd of old disco veterans and younger revellers lured in by the hallowed name and tales of yore. You'll find a rambunctious atmosphere and a decent band, and there's never less than a no-frills, old-fashioned good time to be had.

Savage Garden

Capitol Hotel, Mankhool Road, Satwa (346 0111). **Open** 7pm-3am daily. **Admission** free. **Credit** AmEx, DC, MC, V. **Map** p280 E7.
A Latino-styled tequila club and restaurant with an uninspiring Amazonian rainforest-style interior. In keeping with the theme, Savage Garden always has a strong South American band. As this guide went to press, the all-female band Caliente was in residence – a collection of Colombian Shakira lookalikes fronted by a sultry Cuban songstress. The dance-floor becomes packed in the early hours with South American expats and enthusiastic, if not effective, salsa aficionados shaking their stuff.

Pubs/bars

The Agency

Emirates Towers Hotel, Sheikh Zayed Road (330 0000). **Open** 12.30pm-1am Sat-Thur; 3pm-1am Fri. **Admission** free. **Credit** AmEx, DC, MC, V. **Map** p276 H4.
An upmarket London or New York-style wine bar, the Agency attracts affluent, well-dressed, well-behaved thirtysomethings. The bar's chilled-out

Party politics

The rise of DJ culture in Dubai has seen the emergence of a number of promoters who vye for the hedonists' dollar on a weekly basis. Competition is cut-throat and the rivalry between party throwers is fierce. At the time of writing, **Motion** was the cream of the clubbing crop. Backed by a number of sponsors, the promoters have the financial clout to fly in some of the biggest DJs in the

world and have developed a number of different brands including Motion Nights, Motion Beach and Motion VIP. DJs who have played under the Motion banner include Sander Klidenberg and Danny Rampling, with the names getting bigger by the week. Venues change depending on the event, but most nights tend to be held in exclusive outdoor venues such as the Mirage's Arabian Court or the Jumeirah Beach Club. But be it beachside or bar-bound, expect bongo bashers, podium dancers and some of the funkiest house music this side of Ibiza.

On the flip side of the clubbing coin is **9714 Productions** (*pictured*). Arty alternatives to Motion's mainstreamism, 9714 parties are more of a multimedia arts movement than a full-on dance affair. Expect anything from the latest Lebanese pop art and brain-melting lomography to screenings of cult flicks. In a similar, though slightly harder, vein look out for the **Global Funk** crew who lay down some of the dirtiest bass lines and best MCing in the Gulf. Both 9714 and Global Funk affairs are generally free and tend to be held in one of the Sheikh Zayed Road's trendier venues, such as the Novotel's Blue Bar (*see p169*) or the Fairmont's Tangerine (*see p165*).

Dubai's Lebanese contingent is well catered for by a number of promoters such as **Fluid**, **Chic Alors!** and **Primex**. All three tend to emphasise style over substance and err on the side of exclusivity, culminating in parties such as Beauty and the Beat, which tours from club to club shaking imported models' booties with lightweight house.

Big fun at **MIX**. *See p165.*

interior, a blend of dark wood and crimson velvet furniture, is made for conversation. It's a crying shame then that the exterior is so uninspiring – sat on ideas-above-its-station patio furniture and flanked by potted plants, you gaze out to a pair of escalators. Still, it does have one of the best wine lists in the city. *See also p105.*

Aussie Legends

Rydges Plaza Hotel, Satwa roundabout, Satwa (398 2222). **Open** 3pm-3am Sat-Wed, Fri; 1pm-3am Thur. **Admission** free. **Credit** AmEx, DC, MC, V. **Map** p280 F8.
Set on the ground floor of Rydges Plaza, the ever-popular Aussie Legends is, as the name implies, a 'down under' theme bar and grill with a small dancefloor and a well-used pool table. Antipodean tipples abound, including bottles of Crown lager and, when supplies allow, the joy that is Victoria Bitter. Big-screen sporting action draws in an impressively large crowd.

Blue Bar

Novotel, Sheikh Zayed Road, behind World Trade Centre (332 0000). **Open** noon-1am daily. **Admission** free. **Credit** AmEx, DC, MC, V. **Map** p281 H9.
One of the newest bars on the block, Blue combines fashionable decor, chilled-out vibes and an unusually good selection of draught Belgian beers to

potent effect. On regular nights, a bevy of TV screens blast out MOR pop and rock but the venue is often hijacked by roving parties whose sound-track is altogether more palatable.

Clapham Junction

Rush Inn Hotel, Kahlid Bin Al Waleed Road (Bank Street) (352 2235). **Open** 6pm-2am daily. **Admission** free. **Credit** AmEx, DC, MC, V. **Map** p278 H4.
The kick-off spot for many a Bur Dubai pub crawl, CJ's cranks out the mid '90s Britpop and indie while patrons perch on leopardprint stools surveying the action. By the early hours the bar is usually packed with tight clusters of expats and white-stilletoed women, all illuminated by constellations of Christmas lights and the kitsch, day-glo dancefloor.

Harry Ghatto's

Tokyo @ the Towers, Emirates Towers Hotel, Sheikh Zayed Road (330 0000). **Open** 7.30pm-3am daily. **Admission** free. **Credit** AmEx, DC, MC, V. **Map** p276 H4.
Nestled in the back room of a sushi restaurant, this karaoke venue is about as good it gets. The can't-swing-a-cat cosiness and twin microphone set-up inspire a brothers-in-song ambience. Dutch courage comes courtesy of imported Japanese brews and sake. At some point in the night, the staff are sure to show you how it's done.

The Lodge

Al Nasr Leisureland, near the American Hospital (336 9774). **Open** noon-3am daily. **Admission** free. **Credit** AmEx, DC, MC, V. **Map** p277 J3.

A cross between a British working men's club and a Costa del Sol slosh-pit, the Lodge is a legend among long-term expats. It's home to nine bars, two dancefloors and a massive outdoor arena, which sees up to 1,000 clubbers going for it in the winter months – despite its size, it's packed to the gills on Thursdays. Drinkers range from tottering trolley dollies to hard-nosed alcoholics. The atmosphere is invariably 'up' in the main area, lifted by the cheap drink offers and crowd-friendly music.

Long's Bar

Towers Rotana Hotel, Sheikh Zayed Road (312 2202). **Open** noon-3am daily. **Admission** free. **Credit** AmEx, DC, MC, V. **Map** p276 H4.

The main claim to fame of this hotel basement bar is that it has, well, the Middle East's longest bar. Unfortunately this also means that there's hardly any space for the punter to relax in, although there is a separate restaurant area and small dancefloor for the terminally footloose. During daylight hours, the bar tends to be littered with elderly sun-shunners drawn to the big-screen televisions. In the evening, the average age drops to the early 30s as Sheikh Zayed Road's business types stop by to chew the fat while knocking back monkey nuts. The later hours see the arrival of far too many older Brits with their young Filipino girlfriends.

Scarlett's

Emirates Towers Hotel, Sheikh Zayed Road (330 0000). **Open** 12.30pm-3am daily. **Admission** free. **Credit** AmEx, DC, MC, V. **Map** p276 H4.

Another three-in-one special, Scarlett's is a popular bar/restaurant/nightclub with a Dixieland theme looser than Miss O'Hara herself. The crowd is fairly young, mostly affluent and invariably dressed to the nines, spending their time drinking or frantically bashing the buttons on a pair of PlayStations. There are salsa lessons on Saturdays (Dhs35).

Trader Vic's

Crowne Plaza Hotel, Sheikh Zayed Road (331 1111). **Open** 7-11.30pm. **Admission** free. **Credit** AmEx, DC, MC, V. **Map** p281 G10.

A frankly bonkers Mai Tai lounge where the Polynesian band and the most potent cocktails in the UAE combine to create a magnificently carefree atmosphere. Seating is fairly limited and the bar is often crowded, so arrive early to take the weight off your feet and make the most of the happy hours (prices drop from astronomical to expensive). *See also p87.*

Vu's Bar

51st floor, Emirates Towers Hotel, Sheikh Zayed Road (330 0000). **Open** 7.30pm-1am daily. **Admission** free. **Credit** AmEx, DC, MC, V. **Map** p276 H4.

Laid-back elegance at premium prices has well-heeled conversationalists heading up to this swanky 51st-floor bar, where high-vaulted ceilings and

Waxy O'Conner's – only here for the beer. *See p171.*

impeccable good looks open on to one of the finest views in Dubai. Head up early on and watch the sun go down and the lights go up across the city. Stunning. *See also p82.*

Waxy O'Conner's

Ascot Hotel, Kahlid Bin Al Waleed Road (Bank Street) (352 0900). **Open** noon-2am daily. **Admission** free. **Credit** AmEx, MC, V. **Map** p278 H5.

In no way affiliated to the popular UK chain, Waxy's is an über-popular Irish theme bar. The pub's proprietors have lined up a deluge of deals to entice people along. The biggest bargain is the Friday funky brunch, where Dhs50 will get you a full Irish breakfast, five drink tokens and a buffet carvery. However, connoisseurs of quality nourishment be warned: the food element plays second fiddle to the drinking, which itself attracts the city's less salubrious old-school soaks. This lends itself to a rather charged atmosphere as the day wears on, but the craic is good early on. *See also p93.*

Deira

DJ bars/clubs

Ku-Bu

InterContinental Dubai Hotel, Baniyas Road (205 7333). **Open** 7pm-3am daily. **Admission** free. **Credit** AmEx, DC, MC, V. **Map** p279 J3.

When you consider that it's named after a tattoo on one's posterior, it's only fitting that the urinals are the highlight of this downtown drinking cranny. Not that this is a slur upon this fine DJ-driven sipping station, just that the joys of two-way mirrors have allowed the full of bladder to take in all the action bar-side while relieving themselves. The rest of the decor is a combination of comfy sofas and intimate booths loosely linked by the tattoo theme. Music varies from chilled house to lazy hip hop, encouraging head-nodding rather than full-on rug-cutting.

M-Level

Hilton Dubai Creek, Baniyas Road (227 1111). **Open** varies. **Admission** varies. **Credit** AmEx, DC, MC, V. **Map** p279 L4.

One of the hottest venues in town at the time of writing, the M-Level regularly hosts a number of one-off events by the big promoters. Luxurious and with more mirrors than a diva's dressing room, this is the venue to be seen pouting at. A mid-sized dancefloor, outdoor chill-out area and tongue in cheek glitter ball complete the effect.

Mystizo

InterContinental Dubai Hotel, Baniyas Road (205 7333). **Open** 6.30pm-3am daily. **Admission** free. **Credit** AmEx, DC, MC, V. **Map** p279 J3.

Mystizo is a rather schizophrenic affair: a restaurant-cum-bar-cum-nightclub. The multi-faceted venue is largely centred on a civilised eating area with a large satin-draped DJ bar out front. The invariably empty

club area is separated by a pair of steel doors and houses a rather sad Filipino duo playing their combination of Cher and Celine Dion covers to little more than the solitary barman.

Oxygen

Al Bustan Rotana Hotel, Casablanca Road, Garhoud (282 0000). **Open** 6pm-3am daily. **Admission** free. **Credit** AmEx, MC, V. **Map** p277 K2.

The only regular dance club on the city's east side, Oxygen hands over its sound system to both touring DJs and local talent. The club's original novelty factor – an air bar dishing out blasts of O_2 to dioxide-heavy clubbers – appears to have fallen by the wayside and the management now bank on drinks promotions and top DJs to pull in the punters. Despite being a relatively small venue, Oxygen has managed to attract some of the biggest names in dance – Danny Rampling and DJ Beki have both manned the decks in recent times. *See also p92.*

QD's

Dubai Creek Golf & Yacht Club, Garhoud Road (295 6000). **Open** 6pm-2am daily. **Admission** free. **Credit** AmEx, DC, MC, V. **Map** p277 K3.

Nestled in the grounds of the Dubai Creek Golf & Yacht Club, QD's is a must-visit during the winter months. A classy open-air affair, this wood-decked bar offers superb views across the creek, a clay pizza oven and all the shisha you can smoke. A regular DJ dishes out the chill-out vibe while patrons partake of a sundowner or two on the waterfront bar stools or crashed out on a beanbag.

Live music venues

Jules Bar

Le Meridien Dubai Hotel, Airport Road, Garhoud (282 4040). **Open** 11am-3am daily. **Admission** free. **Credit** AmEx, DC, MC, V. **Map** p277 L2.

A lively Garhoud venue with a truly eclectic crowd, where leopard print-wearing ladies rub up against clearly disinterested moustachioed men to the amusement of onlookers. A Filipino live band plays Sunday to Friday, with the emphasis on entertainment rather than musical endeavour, and the constant crowd participation, elaborate dance routines and flashy costumes gives the bar a well-deserved camp cabaret feel. A resident DJ fills in on Saturdays but can't really compete with the exuberance of a regular night.

Up on the Tenth

InterContinental Dubai Hotel, Baniyas Road (205 7333). **Open** 6pm-3am daily. **Admission** free. **Credit** AmEx, DC, MC, V. **Map** p279 J3.

A heart-warming (if wallet-straining) jazz bar, Up on the Tenth is the perfect spot for a pre-dinner pick-me-up or a solitary nightcap, even though the Manhattan-style decor is looking increasingly dated. The excellent in-house band lays down lashings of smooth tunes with a refreshing lack of self-indulgence, and the bar's location offers superlative views

across the Creek. As you might imagine, the ambience here is more cocktails and cashews than pints and pork scratchings.

Pubs/bars

Biggles

Millennium Airport Hotel, Casablanca Road, Garhoud (282 3464). **Open** noon-2am daily. **Admission** free. **Credit** AmEx, DC, MC, V. **Map** p277 K2.

The name takes you back to World War I, and this large aviation-themed pub is popular with older expats. The truly terrible decor comes complete with a mannequin parachuting through the ceiling, but the jovial atmosphere, big-screen sport and resident band-cum-entertainers keep the locals happy.

Champions

Hamarain Centre mall, JW Marriott Hotel, Muraqqabat Street (607 7977). **Open** 6pm-1am Sat, Fri; noon-1am Sun-Thur. **Admission** free. **Credit** AmEx, DC, MC, V. **Map** p277 K1.

This American sports bar and restaurant is one of the best places to watch sport in Dubai, with a multitude of TVs ensuring that you'll see the game no matter where you're standing or how busy the bar is. English Premier League matches are shown on Saturdays and Sundays and there is a pair of busy pool tables in the corner. A DJ plays a combination of chart pop and cheesy classics most nights.

Dubliners

Le Meridien Dubai Hotel, Airport Road, Garhoud (282 4040). **Open** noon-3am daily. **Admission** free. **Credit** AmEx, DC, MC, V. **Map** p277 L2.

An intimate Irish bar serving some of the best pub grub (and biggest pies) in town. The decor encompasses dark wood, Guinness posters and the back end of a truck to charming effect, and the drinkers are a friendly mix of locals and tourists. While the pub gets packed during televised sporting events, there is an outdoor courtyard to cope with overspill. The immediate area outside is not so attractive, comprising a solitary tree which appears to have died from loneliness. But there's a jovial atmosphere just around the corner, where diners at nearby restaurants finish their meal and step outside for *shisha*.

The Irish Village

Dubai Tennis Stadium, Garhoud Road (282 4750). **Open** 11am-1.30am daily. **Admission** free. **Credit** AmEx, DC, MC, V. **Map** p277 L3.

Situated along the exterior of Dubai Tennis Stadium, the Irish Village is a Dubai institution that is frequently packed with residents and tourists alike. An assortment of draught beers is available, including old country favourites, Guinness and Kilkenny, and a one-man-band churns out a combination of Irish folk and contemporary hits every day except Saturdays. Winter sees the 'IV' come into its own as crowds flock to take advantage of the expansive terrace. An absolute must. *See also p107.*

Lazing around at **The Irish Village**.

Arts & Entertainment

DJ bars/clubs

Boudoir
Dubai Marine Beach Resort & Spa, Beach Road (345 5995). **Open** 7.30pm-3am daily. **Admission** free. **Credit** AmEx, DC, MC, V. **Map** p280 D8.
This swanky, Parisian-style club ranks as one of the most exclusive venues in the city. Boudoir attracts a predominantly Lebanese crowd – if you want to get past the door staff you should be dressed to impress and preferably in a couple. Different theme nights range from R&B on Wednesdays to Eastern dance fusion on Fridays. Free champagne for women on Tuesdays all night long. *See also p97.*

Kasbar
The One&Only Royal Mirage Hotel, Al Sufouh Road (399 9999). **Open** 7pm-3am Mon-Sat. **Admission** Dhs50. **Credit** AmEx, DC, MC, V. **Map** p274 A5.
A *très chic* (not to mention *très* sheikh) nightclub within the Mirage's Palace section. Arranged on three huge levels, each decked out in authentic Moroccan decor, the Kasbar has private booths, a large dancefloor and a pool table in the basement. Opulence rules here, and its prosperous patrons are unlikely to be troubled by the staggering booze bills.

El Malecon
Dubai Marine Beach Resort & Spa, Beach Road (346 1111). **Open** 7pm-3am daily. **Admission** free. **Credit** AmEx, DC, MC, V. **Map** p280 D8.
The salsa scene is booming in Dubai, and one of the most original places to strut your stuff is the Malecon. This Latino hall houses a well-trodden dancefloor, blue message board walls – already graffitied to the max – a cosy leather cigar lounge and a bongo area, plus a great menu of spicy soups, fish and salad dishes. El Malecon is a genuinely different place to get your fandango fix, where a regular collective of merengue maniacs come down and give lessons to other Latino dance lovers, usually to the beat of the resident band, which plays every night except Saturday. In between the loud, zesty nights, it's the perfect venue to kick back, sip on a sangria and chill with friends.

The Rooftop
Arabian Court, The One&Only Royal Mirage Hotel, Al Sufouh Road (399 9999). **Open** 5.30pm-1am Mon-Sat. **Admission** free. **Credit** AmEx, DC, MC, V. **Map** p274 A5.
Possibly the finest drinking venue in the city, the Arabian Court Rooftop is a luxurious open-air sipping station with magnificent views out across the Gulf and the madness that is Palm Island. The soundtrack tends to be blissful chill-out tunes and,

Liquor and the law

Despite its liberal veneer, Dubai is still very much a Muslim state and as such alcohol is tolerated rather than celebrated. Here's the lowdown on legal tippling...

Bringing it in
It is perfectly legal to bring alcohol into the UAE – in fact, once you're through passport control the first thing you'll see is a duty-free shop. At present you're limited to four items per person, so whether it be mother's ruin or a drop of firewater, choose wisely. *See also p249* **Customs.**

Buying it there
Dubai Residents can buy alcohol from one of the city's booze shops providing they have a valid licence. Only one licence is awarded per household and the limit is dependent on salary.
The law demands that all bars be housed within hotels or private clubs, but often these links are tenuous to say the least, and most establishments will have their own entrances far from the hotel lobby. Although it is illegal for drinking establishments to encourage Muslims to break their faith by serving them

alcohol, don't be surprised to chance upon a local in national dress happily supping a pint; this is one law quite openly flouted.

Under the influence
Public displays of drunkenness are frowned upon so try to keep your behaviour restrained when in residential areas.
There is zero tolerance when it comes to the city's harsh under-age drinking and drink-driving countermeasures. You must be 21 to purchase or consume alcohol, and many bars will require photo ID before they serve baby-faced boozers. Drive with the faintest whiff of alcohol on your breath and you can expect to do some time in one of Dubai's far-from-friendly prisons as well as pay a small fortune in punitive fines. (It is worth bearing this in mind the morning after a heavy night – stay off the road until the last traces are out of your system.)
Dubai isn't really geared up for walking from pub to pub so opt instead for one of the city's inexpensive and omnipresent taxis, who will ferry you between as many cocktail lounges and gin joints as you wish.

Arts & Entertainment

Get a view at **The Rooftop**. *See p174.*

CENTURY CINEMAS

THE ULTIMATE CINEMA EXPERIENCE

believe.

DMC Amphitheatre, Dubai's open air arena.

while dancing does occasionally break out, it's more likely the crowd will be ogling the star-filled skyline from the comfort of the Arabian-themed seating. Highly recommended.

Sho Cho's

Dubai Marine Beach Resort & Spa, Beach Road (346 1111). **Open** 7pm-3am daily. **Admission** free. **Credit** AmEx, DC, MC, V. **Map** p280 D8.

The pioneer of Dubai's new wave of bars, Sho Cho's remains one of the very best. Sophisticated, classy and dead trendy, this is where the beautiful people go to play, pose and look pretty: you will not see an ounce of body fat in the place. Elegant, sleek young bodies drape themselves over painfully hip white sofas and seductively sip expensive drinks. Clothing is tight and minimal for both men and women. The crowd is mainly Lebanese and the vibe is ultra cool decadence. The new outdoor terrace overlooking the beach is a wonderful place to chill out Café del Mar-style.

Live music venues

DIMC

Le Meridien Mina Seyahi Hotel, Al Sufouh Road (399 3333). **Open** varies. **Admission** varies. **Credit** AmEx, DC, MC, V. **Map** p274 A5.

A brace of fantastic shore-side venues that host international DJs and the odd one-off concert, set in their own purpose-built grounds in the Dubai International Marine Club. The beachside *bayou* that is the Lagoon features a huge central bar and chilled swimming pool while Kemistry boasts a hundred square metres of green, green grass. Opening times vary so phone for details.

DMC Amphitheatre

Dubai Media City, off Interchange 5, Sheikh Zayed Road (391 4555). **Open** varies. **Admission** varies. **No credit cards. Map** p274 A5.

An expansive outdoor area set in the middle of the city's separate media enclosure, the Amphitheatre comes complete with real grass and its own lake. It hosts a number of one-off events, including the annual Dubai International Jazz Festival (*see p142*).

Pubs/bars

The Alamo

Dubai Marine Beach Resort & Spa, Beach Road (346 1111). **Open** noon-3am daily. **Admission** free. **Credit** AmEx, DC, MC, V. **Map** p280 D8.

The Alamo is everything Dubai used to be – and, evidently for some, still is. Popular for many years with middle-aged British male expats who still think they are in their local at home, the Alamo has a genuine old-world charm – Dubai style. The doorman is a vertically challenged Thai dressed in American civil war fatigues (the Alamo and all that). And, once through the swing doors, things are only marginally less surreal. In spite of the time-warp Tex-Mex feel, it's still possible to have a good night here. Pass by on a Friday and you'll find one of the best brunches in Dubai. *See also p93.*

Barasti

Le Meridien Mina Seyahi Hotel, Al Sufouh Road (399 3333). **Open** 8pm-1.30am daily. **Admission** free. **Credit** AmEx, DC, MC, V. **Map** p274 A5.

A cracking outdoor venue that sits on its own elevated platform above the Mina's private beach and expands around the hotel pool. As you'd expect from a Dubaian pool bar, dress is reasonably casual, and the place has a Caribbean-style feel. Alongside the usual alcoholic treats, the bar does a nice sideline in *shisha* pipes and offers the perfect setting to have a puff, looking out to sea. *See also p96.*

Boston Bar

Jumeirah Rotana Hotel, Al Diyafah Street (345 5888). **Open** noon-2am Tue-Sat, Fri; noon-3am Wed, Thur. **Admission** free. **Credit** AmEx, DC, MC, V. **Map** p280 F8.

Based on the bar in *Cheers*, the Boston is a gem of a boozer; unpretentious, lively, and great for big-screen sport and serious elbow bending. It can get very lively at the weekends, and dancing on the bar, while heavily discouraged, does occasionally break out. It's typically full of Brits, but occasionally attracts other nationalities. *See also p105.*

Sky View Bar

Burj Al Arab Hotel, Beach Road (301 7438). **Open** 11am-2am daily. **Admission** Dhs200 (redeemable at all bars & restaurants in hotel). **Credit** AmEx, DC, MC, V. **Map** p274 A4.

Despite being housed in the world's most exclusive hotel, the Sky View bar is a haven of tack – the interior resembles a gaudy '80s discotheque or a *Dr Who* set. The panoramic vista, however, cannot be bettered and the large windows allow you to gaze out across the Arabian Gulf, the neon-lit city or the expansive Palm Island. One word of warning – the drinks are as expensive as you'd expect.

Arts & Entertainment

Where would we be without technology? Technology that can take us to the mo
remote areas, and guarantee our return? Electronic Traction Control, Dynamic Stabil
Control, Electronic Air Suspension, Hill Descent Control, advanced GPS/TV navigati
system. All part and parcel of one of the most beautiful vehicles ever seen. You have
all with Range Rover. **Above it all.**

RANGE ROVER

Active Dubai

Spectator Sports

An energetic feast for fans of balls and bunkers, woods and whips.

For a relative lightweight in terms of size and population, Dubai packs a heavyweight punch when it comes to hosting major sporting events. The planet's highest-stakes horse-race, the $6 million Dubai World Cup (*see p139*), is just the icing on a particularly impressive cake which also includes golf, men's and women's tennis tournaments, rugby sevens, motor sports and water sports, making the emirate a sporting destination of major importance.

The oppressive summer heat forces anyone with any sense to retreat into air-conditioned comfort from May to August, so the calendar of sporting events is squeezed into an eight-month period: from September to April there is plenty of high-quality action for spectators to watch, with stars from Tiger Woods and Ernie Els to Venus Williams and Anna Kournikova among those who have visited Dubai in recent years.

They and many others like them have been drawn by the warm weather, Dubai's reputation for rolling out the red carpet and, of course, the prospect of particularly generous prize money. Some stars simply want a break from the harsh Northern European winter, including a growing number of British soccer teams who choose to hold training camps or practice matches here. Several England players liked what they saw so much during a stopover en route to the 2002 World Cup in Japan and South Korea that they have even bought houses on Palm Island (*see p27* **Size matters**), to great media interest.

However, if Dubai has been good for sport, then sport has also been extremely kind to the emirate, primarily as a highly effective marketing tool for the tourism sector. Pictures of Woods on the fairways at the Emirates Golf Club or Kournikova trying on jewellery in the Dubai gold souk have bounced around the world, securing TV pictures and publicity that cash simply could not buy. If appearance cheques have changed hands (rumour has it that Woods was paid $1 million just to turn up for the Dubai Desert Classic), then there have been no complaints about value for money.

The sole disappointing aspect is that the local sporting public has not always taken full advantage of these chances to observe the big names at close range. Attendances at the men's and women's tennis tournaments have been consistently disappointing, while they have been non-existent at others, such as a beach football tournament that featured the likes of Eric Cantona.

Anna Kournikova gets out of tennis whites.

Golf

The golfing calendar is dominated by one glorious event, the **Dubai Desert Golf Classic** (*see p139*). This tournament has grown rapidly into a world-class event and is now a respected fixture on the European PGA Tour, luring star players such as Tiger Woods, Darren Clarke, Mark O'Meara and Ernie Els to the wealthy emirate, with prize money totalling more than $1.2 million. Lucrative appearance fees alone have proved sufficient to entice the world's top players to UAE shores.

In the past the tournament has been staged at both the Emirates Golf Club and the Dubai Creek Golf & Yacht Club (*for both, see p190*), though various courses in the city enjoy the attention of stars in need of a practice session before the main event. The Jebel Ali Golf Resort

Bridled ambition

Few success stories in the world of sport can rival that of **Godolphin** (www.godolphin.com), the racing stable established by the Maktoum Royal Family. From humble beginnings in 1994, Godolphin – named after one of the three founding stallions of modern thoroughbreds – has grown to become a revolutionary force in racing around the world, with Dubai at its very epicentre.

The Maktoum family realised that the emirate, with its comfortable winter climate, was the perfect base to train and prepare horses for the European flat season, as well as for sending runners to other racing strongholds such as the United States, Australia, Japan, Singapore and Hong Kong.

The rest, as they say, is history. Godolphin racked up its 100th Group One (Classic and other races of international importance) winner in August 2003 and has the ambition, vision and financial clout to continue going from strength to strength.

Those victories came in 11 different countries on four continents, raising the profile of the sport and forcing rival stables to follow in Godolphin's footsteps. Sheikh Mohammed himself has proved to be the driving force behind the establishment of the World Series, an unofficial global championship for horses, jockeys, owners and trainers, which includes the Dubai World Cup (*see p139*) on its schedule.

Active Dubai

& Spa (*see p190*) hosts a curtain-raiser in the guise of a nine-hole challenge match. The Classic itself is well attended, drawing many amateur residents who play the same world-beating courses all year round. Some are most interested in the mass of corporate hospitality, but the tournament also enjoys its fair share of die-hard fans, happy to chase around after the pros. Security is very low-key; it's perfectly possible to come away with treasured autographs and photos.

Horse & camel racing

In sporting circles, Dubai is probably best known these days as the new international centre for horse-racing, thanks to the astonishing growth and indomitable strength of the Godolphin operation (*see p181* **Bridled ambition**). Yet while the Maktoums' private stable has proved itself on tracks around the world, it's still a special experience to watch some of the best horses on the planet strut their stuff on home turf.

The **Nad Al Sheba** horse-racing track (*see p71*), a short drive from the downtown area of the city, is the focal point and flagship facility for racing in the UAE, boasting a 2,000-metre turf course sitting inside a 2,200-metre dirt track, which can be configured to three different lengths. Each year this prestigious stretch of turf hosts the world's highest-stakes race, the $6 million **Dubai World Cup** (*see p139*), as well as the $21 million Dubai Racing Carnival,

The rudder band

Victory by name, victory by nature. That's been the story behind the emergence of the Dubai-based powerboat outfit **The Victory Team**, which has become a dominant force in the aquatic equivalent of Formula One. The similarities are striking: glamour, wealth and the occasional crash all contribute to this high-octane spectacle on water. A string of world titles, records and championship trophies have been secured by the Victory Team (www.victoryteam.org.ae) since it was formed in 1989, with throttleman Saeed Al-Tayer earning a place in the record books as the first Arab to win a hat-trick of Class One championship trophies in 2001. Each winter, Dubai hosts the last leg of the annual UIM Championship Class One World Offshore season (*see p142*; events are also held in Portugal, Germany, Britain, Norway, Australia, Qatar and Fujairah).

new for 2004. The World Cup meeting is regularly attended by some 50,000 people and in 2004 offered the single wealthiest card in history – a total of $15,250,000 up for grabs over seven races. The World Cup is the place to rub shoulders with the great and the good of Dubai, and there's as much action off the track as on it, not least at the Fillies & Fashion event, which has generous prizes for the best-dressed ladies. However, racing in Dubai is about far more than one big day in the sun. The Dubai Racing Carnival features 55 races (20 on turf, the rest on dirt) over a ten-meeting, nine-week period, leading up to the World Cup at the end of March.

Admission to racing at Nad Al Sheba is free, apart from the World Cup meeting, but the bad news for visitors who like to indulge in a flutter is that betting in the UAE is strictly illegal. Instead, prizes are on offer for correct predictions of race results.

As well as the Nad Al Sheba track, there is also a sand and oil surface racing track at **Jebel Ali** (phone 347 4914 for details) and a fibreturf track at **Ghantoot** (02 562 9050); both are a 30- to 40-minute drive south from downtown Dubai and 45 minutes from Abu Dhabi.

No visit to Dubai, though, is complete without a trip to another type of racing – the nearby **camel track**, also in Nad Al Sheba (see p73). The days of local residents climbing aboard one of these 'ships of the desert' for a gruelling trip across the sands to Abu Dhabi or Al Ain may be long gone, but camels remain revered in many Middle Eastern societies for their unique abilities. Racing camels are a breed apart, and the strongest and fastest specimens change hands for millions of dirhams. The camel-racing season in Dubai starts in November and runs through to April. Admission is free to the races at Nad Al Sheba, which usually begin on Thursdays and Fridays at 7am and are over by 8.30am (timings are later in Ramadan). For more information, see p142.

There had been criticisms from overseas that young children were illegally press-ganged into becoming jockeys, their light frames ensuring the speeding camels can run faster. UAE authorities have been sensitive to these concerns, and have taken steps to regulate the sport. Camel owners were threatened in 2003 with fines and jail sentences for breaking existing laws, which state that jockeys must be aged at least 15, weigh a minimum of 35kg (just over 77lb), be certified medically fit and have a valid UAE residence. Jockeys were issued with identity cards and are now subject to spot checks. Camel owners flouting the regulations have been told to expect a fine of

When in drome

Bahrain may have beaten Dubai in the race to attract Formula One Grand Prix racing to the Middle East, but the emirate could well have the last laugh with the opening of the first fully integrated automotive and motor sports facility in the region.

Due to be launched in 2004, the **Dubai Autodrome** will feature a world-class 5.3km (3 mile) motor racing track, an international-standard pit lane complex and a grandstand able to accommodate more than 5,000 spectators, including hospitality boxes for corporate customers.

The aim is to host all types of racing, from motorbikes to Formula One. Located next to the Arabian Ranches housing development, the autodrome will command a premium spot between Sheikh Zayed Road and the Emirates Road. Its remarkable facilities will also be made available to manufacturers and teams for winter testing, development work, vehicle demonstrations, product launches and driver training. An air-conditioned indoor karting facility, driving schools and a world-class off-road centre complete the concept, along with a multi-purpose business and leisure park for the burgeoning automotive industry.

Dhs20,000 for a first offence, a year-long ban from racing for a second infringement, and jail for a third transgression.

Motor sports

The Emirates Motor Sport Federation is responsible for organising a range of high-octane events including the Emirates Rally Championship, the 1,000 Dunes Rally and Autocross Championship. Dubai traditionally stages the final leg of the Middle East Rally Championship, usually in December, and also hosts the **Desert Challenge** (see p140), a rally-driving event held over five days in October which consistently attracts many of the world's leading drivers. The prologue to the 2003 event took place on the Palm Jumeirah, one of two man-made islands built to accommodate luxury housing off the coast of Dubai. The Desert Challenge is also the final round of the FIA Marathon World Cup for Cross-Country Rallies and the FIM Cross Country Rallies World Cup. See also above **When in drome**.

Active Dubai

Tiger Woods at the **Dubai Desert Golf Classic**. *See p180.*

Tennis

Many of the sport's biggest names, from Venus Williams and Anna Kournikova to Boris Becker and Tim Henman, have taken part in the annual back-to-back WTA and ATP tournaments under the umbrella of the **Dubai Duty Free Tennis Open** (*see p139*). The action unfolds at the purpose-built stadium in Garhoud. Many spectators take pub grub and liquid refreshment at the Irish Village (*see p107*) between games; the restaurants of the Century Village on the other side of the stadium also lay on lunch deals.

While players flock to Dubai to take full advantage of the city's magnificent hospitality and attractions, the general public has been a bit slower to show its enthusiasm, with early rounds routinely being played out in front of thin crowds. However, the finals normally attract a packed house and, while it's no Wimbledon, the well-designed stadium does offer a perfect chance for tennis fans to get that little bit closer to their idols. Home-grown players are treated to an encouraging reception, even if expats tend to save the most rousing cheers for stars hailing from their respective home countries.

Water sports

Dubai traditionally plays host to the finale of the **World Offshore Powerboat** racing season (*see p142*). The emirate is the base of the appropriately named Victory Team (*see p182* **The rudder band**), one of the most successful Class One outfits in the sport and boasting a string of world titles. February sees Dubai host an International Sailing Week Regatta; the only event of its kind, this growing spectacle pits ten to 17-year-olds racing in optimist and laser categories, and pulls in over 100 competitors from 14 nations each year. Dubai also hosts the biggest boat show in the region in March.

The Dubai International Marine Club, based at the Meridien Mina Seyahi hotel (*see p40*), is the body responsible for the growth of water sports in the UAE. It organises various meets each year to promote jet skiing, traditional rowing sports, wooden powerboat racing and traditional dhow sailing, as well as races for catamarans and lasers. Venues include the Mina Seyahi, Dubai Creek, Abu Dhabi, Ras Al Khaimah and Fujairah. Because many of these races take place some distance from the coast, spectator numbers are generally low.

Local legends

Although Dubai is best known for hosting international stars, it has a few of its own to boast about, including members of the Royal Family. When he's not busy with his duties as the Crown Prince of Dubai and Minister of Defence, **Sheikh Mohammed** devotes time to another of his passions, endurance horse-racing, even leading the UAE to success over a 160km (100-mile) course in the 2003 European Championships. **Mohammed bin Sulayem** has also put the UAE on the map, but thanks to his exploits behind the wheel. The Dubaian speedster has captured the Middle East championship 14 times since 1986 thanks to no fewer than 60 rally wins.

Mohammed Al-Qubaisi has a special place in the record books as the first UAE national to become a world champion. He defeated Australian Ian Bradford to win the 1988 AMF Bowling World Cup in Guadalajara, Mexico, and came within two points of repeating the feat in Hermosillo, Mexico, six years later.

Thomas Bjorn (*pictured*) may be Denmark's most famous golfer, but he's still claimed as a local hero thanks to the fact that he lives in Dubai and is affiliated to Dubai Creek Golf &

Yacht Club. The Great Dane's finest moment to date was overcoming Tiger Woods by two shots on home territory in the 2001 Desert Classic, but he has twice represented Europe in the Ryder Cup, including the stirring 2002 victory over the United States at The Belfry. He has the talent to claim a major one day, but must first overcome the trauma of letting a three-shot lead slip away in the 2003 Open at Sandwich, with only four holes left to play.

Participation Sports

Myriad activities in the land where rain never interrupts play.

For those who would rather take part than watch, Dubai offers just about every sport imaginable thanks to its cosmopolitan population and pleasant climate. The presence of thousands of workers from the subcontinent means that cricket is played widely and with great enthusiasm, both at an organised level and with impromptu games staged on patches of waste ground around the city every Friday. Football, which boasts a multicultural amateur expat league as well as a domestic professional league, is popular, while the city's beach culture ensures that all water sports have a healthy following, including the relatively new activity of kitesurfing, which has really taken off in the past couple of years.

The city now has several world-class golf courses that already attract top players to its Desert Classic (*see p180*), and there are an increasing number planned in the next few years, primarily because of the benefits of being perceived as a tourist golfing destination rather than because of any huge local demand.

This is the land where anything is possible, so after a morning's fishing trip you can brush up on your ice-skating or ice hockey; plans for

an indoor ski slope are also at an advanced stage as part of the ambitious Dubailand project (*see p193* **Sports City**).

Badminton

Intersportz
Next to Modern Bakery, behind Spinneys warehouse, off Sheikh Zayed Road, Interchange 3 (347 5833). **Open** 9am-10pm daily. **Price** Dhs25 per person. **Credit** (min Dhs200) MC, V. **Map** p277 B4.
Low prices make this (ageing) indoor sports centre popular. The air-conditioning system just about allows you to play in the summer, but be prepared to sweat. Bring your own racquets and shuttlecocks.

Basketball

Intersportz
Next to Modern Bakery, behind Spinneys warehouse, off Sheikh Zayed Road, Interchange 3 (347 5833). **Open** 9am-10pm daily. **Price** Dhs25 per person (includes basketball). **Credit** (min Dhs200) MC, V. **Map** p277 B4.
Five-a-side football pitches can easily accommodate fans of indoor hoops. *See above* **Badminton** for further information on the facilities.

Knocking 'em down at **Al Nasr Leisureland**. *See p187.*

Bowling

Al Nasr Leisureland
Oud Metha (337 1234). **Open** 9am-midnight daily.
Price Entrance fee Dhs10; Dhs5 under-10s; Dhs7 per
game. **Credit** MC, V. **Map** p277 J3.
Shoes are included in the admission charge at this
popular bowling centre. Group bookings are taken
but you must make a reservation in plenty of time;
fax details through to 337 6832.

Thunderbowl
*Near Defence roundabout, off Sheikh Zayed Road,
Interchange 1 (343 1000).* **Open** 9pm-midnight
daily. **Price** *Sat-Wed* Dhs10 per game. *Thur, Fri*
Dhs15 per game. *Shoe hire* Dhs2. **Credit** DC, MC, V.
Map p283 E13.
Bookings are recommended at this 20-lane centre
as it is always busy, particularly at weekends.

Cricket

Dubai Cricket Council Pitches
*Behind Dubai Police Officers' Club, Sharjah Road,
Jaddaf (information: Emirates Cricket Board,
Sharjah, 06 542 2991).*
The Dubai Cricket Council has 17 pitches, including
two grass wickets (one floodlit) on a huge expanse
of land behind the Dubai Police Officers' Club. The
pitches are the venue for any number of leagues,
including social, corporate and inter-hotel competitions, and matches are played virtually all year
round, even in summer. A stadium capable of stag-
ing international matches is on the drawing board
at Dubailand (*see p193* **Sports City**).

Intersportz
*Next to Modern Bakery, behind Spinneys warehouse,
off Sheikh Zayed Road, Interchange 3 (347 5833).*
Open 9am-10pm daily. **Price** Dhs25 per person.
Credit (min Dhs200) MC, V. **Map** p277 B4.
Indoor five-a-side football courts easily convert into
cricket nets. Although the ancient air-conditioning
system just about makes it possible to play in the
summer, you should be prepared to sweat it out a
bit. The price includes 'indoor' cricket bats and balls.

Fencing

Metropolitan Hotel
Sheikh Zayed Road, Interchange 2 (343 0000).
Open 6.30-8pm Sat, Mon, Wed. **Price** Dhs35 per
class; Dhs300 for 12 classes. **Credit** AmEx, MC, V.
Map p276 G5.
Learn fencing (épée, foil and sabre) or brush up your
expertise at the International Fencing Club of Dubai
with Master Zahi El Khoury, a former world championship finalist and Arabic champion.

Quay Health Club
*Mina A' Salam Hotel, Al Sufouh Road, Jumeirah
(366 8888/www.dubaifencingclub.com).* **Open**
Advanced 7.30pm Sat, Wed; 6.30pm Mon.

Where to...

Fire arrows
Meet the **Dubai Archery Group** (221 5839)
every Thursday at 3pm.

Go ballooning
Get up early with **Voyagers Xtreme** (345
4504) for aerial views of the emirate.

Go underground
Pot-hole with the experts from **Adventure
Unlimited** (03 768 7458) at Jebel Hafeet.

Jump out of a plane
Take tandem jumps at Umm Al Quwain
Aeroclub with the **Emirates Parachutes
Sports Association** (06 768 1447).

Ride mountain bikes
Get fit, then join **Biking Frontiers** (050
552 7300) for serious cycling adventures.

Shoot guns
Squeeze off a few rounds at the **Jebel Ali
Shooting Club** (883 6555).

Beginners 7.30pm Tue; 6.30pm Fri. **Price** Dhs35 per
session members; Dhs45 non-members. **Credit**
AmEx, DC, MC, V. **Map** p274 A4.
At time of writing, the head coach of this popular
club was Mihail Kouzev, who represented Bulgaria
in the pentathalon world championships. Fencers of
all ages and standards are welcome. Junior training
sessions are held every Friday at the Jumeirah Beach
Club (*see p40*) at 9.30am. Same prices apply.

Fishing

Bounty Charters
*Dubai International Marine Club, Le Meridien Mina
Seyahi Hotel, Al Sufouh Road, Jumeirah (050 552
6067).* **Open** by advance booking only. **Price**
Dhs1,700 4hrs; Dhs1,900 6hrs; Dhs2,400 8hrs;
Dhs2,600 10hrs. **No credit cards**. **Map** p276 G5.
South African Richard Forrester is at the helm of
Bounty Charters, an 11m (36ft) Yamaha Sea Spirit
game fishing boat. It can be booked for tailor-made
fishing trips, all year round (maximum six people).

Club Joumana
*Jebel Ali Hotel, Sheikh Zayed Road, Exit 13 (past
Interchange 7) (883 6000/www.jebelali-international.
com).* **Open** 8am-noon, 2-6pm daily. **Price** Dhs1,400
4hrs; Dhs2,600 8hrs. **Credit** AmEx, DC, MC, V.
Map p274 A5.
Club Joumana has one boat, the *Kingfish* (maximum
seven people per fishing trip). Full and half-day
excursions are available, with experienced crew on

Active Dubai

Karting is a popular pastime with petrol heads. *See p192.*

hand to steer you to the good spots; prices for both include soft drinks, tea and coffee, Danish pastries and croissants, plus the use of tackle.

Dubai Creek Golf & Yacht Club

Opposite Deira City Centre mall, Garhoud (295 6000/www.dubaigolf.com). **Open** for trips 7am-6pm daily. **Price** Dhs1,875 4hrs; Dhs2,125 5hrs; Dhs2,600 8hrs; Dhs250 extra hr. **Credit** AmEx, DC, MC, V. **Map** p277 K3.

The club's own 10m (32ft) single cabin boat is available for trips for up to a maximum of six people. The price includes tackle, bait and fuel, as well as a good supply of soft drinks (food and other drinks extra).

Le Meridien Mina Seyahi Beach Resort & Marina

Le Meridien Mina Seyahi Hotel, Al Sufouh Road, Jumeirah (399 3333/www.lemeridien-mina seyahi.com). **Open** departures 7am, 1pm daily. **Price** Dhs1,725 4hrs. **Credit** AmEx, DC, MC, V. **Map** p274 A5.

Tackle, bait, soft drinks and water are included in the price of these regular trips to some of the best fishing grounds in the Gulf (maximum six people). Good fish can be found throughout the year, but the prime months are considered to be January through March. Advance bookings are recommended (you'll be asked for a 50 per cent credit card deposit).

Yacht Solutions

Jumeirah Beach Hotel Pavilion Marina, Beach Road, Jumeirah (348 6838/www.yacht-solutions.com). **Open** for trips 7am-6pm daily. **Price** from Dhs1,600 for 4hrs to Dhs2,500 for 8hrs. **Credit** AmEx, DC, MC, V. **Map** p274 B4.

Yacht Solutions run one of the biggest operations in Dubai and offer a friendly, flexible service. There are three boats available for hire (maximum six per fishing trip for all).

Football

Dubai Expat League

For information, contact chairman Ray Nickson (050 423 4564).

The Expat League is an expanding 11-a-side league of like-minded footie fans (12 teams participate currently), sponsored by Umbro, who meet weekly to do battle on parks and pitches. Points-scoring games, invariably held at the Dubai Exiles Rugby Club (*see p193* **Rugby**), are friendly but competitive. There's also a seven-a-side tournament that runs in the summer. Keep an eye out for the comedic but well-intentioned *Time Out* team, sponsored by EA Sports. Chairman Ray Nickson will introduce ringers and new Dubaian residents to local team captains looking to make up numbers. There are also five-a-side indoor pitches at Intersportz, *see p186* **Badminton**.

Golf

Jokes about Dubai being the best place in the world for golfers to work on bunker shots are way out of date. Facilities here are first class, although costs can be on the steep side. This is largely because there's an extra expense built into a green fee here – millions of gallons of desalinated water are needed daily to prevent

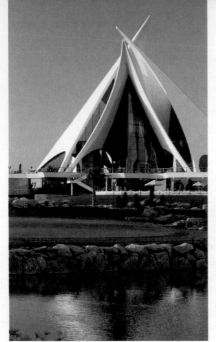

Dubai Creek Golf & Yacht Club.

the desert reclaiming these modern oases. Golfers should note that bookings for tee times for all clubs listed below (except Dubai Country Club) can be made through a central reservations office on 390 3931 or online at www.dubaigolf.com. The **UAE Golf Association** (www.ugagolf.com) is the governing body for the sport in this country. Yearly membership is Dhs200 and entitles players to reductions on green fees, lessons and merchandise at all UAE clubs.

Dubai Country Club

Al Awir, off the Ras Al Khor road south of Dubai (333 1155/www.dubai countryclub.com). **Open** 8am-6pm daily. *Driving range* 8am-8.30pm daily. **Price** Dhs65 per game, plus Dhs30 for piece of artificial turf. **Credit** AmEx, DC, MC, V. **Map** p277 K5.

Dubai's first golf club opened in 1971 and is still going strong. The club boasts 18- and nine-hole courses on sand; players buy and then carry a piece of artificial turf to play off, except for on the 'browns' (sand equivalents of greens), which are brushed regularly to ensure a smooth roll. Players must wear flat-soled shoes.

Dubai Creek Golf & Yacht Club

Opposite Deira City Centre mall, Garhoud (295 6000).

This landmark course closed in December 2003 for a year to allow for the complete redesign of the front nine holes. Luxury villas and a 240-room hotel are planned, with a view to transforming the club into a

tourist resort in the heart of the city within two years. The back nine holes will be virtually unchanged, and plans have been hatched for a new par-five 18th signature hole along the Creek's shoreline.

Emirates Golf Club

Sheikh Zayed Road, off Interchange 5 (380 2222/ www.dubaigolf.com). **Open** 6am-dusk daily (last tee-off 3.30pm). **Price** Dhs265-Dhs475. **Credit** AmEx, DC, MC, V. **Map** p274 A5.

Home to two fine courses and a Bedouin tent-inspired clubhouse, this is arguably the most eye-catching golfing facility in the region. The 7,101-yard Majlis course – the first grass facility in the Middle East – was the original home of the Dubai Desert Classic (*see p139 and p180*). Since 1996 it has been complemented by the 7,127-yard Wadi course, which features 14 lakes and numerous bunkers. Both are par-72 courses and make good use of the natural rolling desert terrain to ensure a serious test for players of all abilities. Many experts consider this to be the premier club in Dubai.

Jebel Ali Golf Resort & Spa

Jebel Ali Hotel, Sheikh Zayed Road, Exit 13 (past Interchange 7) (883 6000/www.jebelali-international. com). **Open** 7am-3.30pm (last tee-off) daily. **Price** Dhs140 members; Dhs150 non-members. **Credit** AmEx, DC, MC, V. **Map** p274 A5.

A nine-hole, par-36 course. Add in superb views of the Arabian Gulf, a salt-water lake and the colourful presence of preening peacocks, and a memorable round is guaranteed. The facilities include a driving range, 27-hole putting green and indoor swing room.

The Montgomerie

Emirates Hills, Sheikh Zayed Road, off Interchange 5 (390 5600/www.themontgomerie.com). **Open** 7am-1.50pm (last tee-off) Sat, Thur, Fri; 7am-4pm (last tee-off) Sun-Wed. **Price** Dhs550 Sat, Thur, Fri; Dhs425 Sun-Wed. **Credit** AmEx, MC, V. **Map** p274 A5.

The Montgomerie, designed by golfing star Colin Montgomerie, covers more than 200 acres of undulating links-style fairways. With 14 lakes and the small matter of 72 bunkers to avoid, drive placement is key here. Look out for the 13th hole and what is claimed to be the largest single green in the world, covering a staggering 5,394sq m (58,000sq ft).

Less competitive golfers who simply want to practise should consider the Academy by Troon Golf, which boasts a state-of-the-art swing studio, a nine-hole, par-three Academy course, short game area, putting greens and 'dummy' fairway – all floodlit.

Nad Al Sheba

Off the Dubai–Al Ain Road (336 3666/www.nadal shebaclub.com). **Open** 7.30am-8pm (last tee-off for 18 holes) daily; till 10pm for 9 holes. **Price** Dhs110-Dhs295. **Credit** AmEx, DC, MC, V. **Map** p274 C4.

The only floodlit 18-hole course in the Emirates has recently had a facelift, focusing on the back nine, all of which are inside the track of the world-famous Nad Al Sheba racecourse (*see p71, p142 and p182*).

A Scottish-style links course, it boasts a huge number of pot bunkers and its greens now feature a new variety of dwarf grass, ensuring a more consistent putting surface. One popular option here is the 'learn golf in a week' course. Facilities also include a rebuilt short game area and new grass practice tees.

Hashing

The world's largest jogging organisation is alive and well in Dubai, where several groups of 'drinkers with a running problem' meet. As with its international counterparts, the hashing movement here is primarily a fun way to stay fit and hopefully to make some new friends in the process. *See also p194* **Running**.

Barbie Hash House Harriers

348 4210. **Price** Dhs10 per hash (incl food). **No credit cards.**
This women-only hash meets on the first Tuesday of each month (apart from July and August). Bring a pink T-shirt, tiara and, yes, champagne, for post-run celebrations.

Creek Hash House Harriers

050 451 5847/www.creekhash.net. **Price** Dhs50 per hash. **No credit cards.**
The Creek Harriers meet each Tuesday, an hour before sunset. For venues and map, see the website.

Desert Hash House Harriers

050 454 2635/www.deserthash.net. **Price** Dhs50 per hash. **No credit cards.**

Enjoy runs (or walks) in the desert surrounding the city every Sunday, with men, women, children and even dogs joining in. Meets at a different location each week, phone or visit the website for details.

Moonshine Hash House Harriers

050 774 1580/www.deserthash.net/moonshine. **Price** Dhs10 per hash. **No credit cards.**
This once-a-month aerobic affair celebrates the night of the full moon. It is open to all, but novices take note: it's a more demanding run than the majority of local hashes.

Ice hockey

Al Nasr Leisureland

Oud Metha (337 1234/www.dubaimightycamels.com/ www.dubaisandstorms.com). **Price** *Mighty Camels* Dhs1,000 membership; *Sandstorms* Dhs700 membership. **No credit cards. Map** p277 J3.
Ice hockey in the desert? You'd better believe it. There are two thriving clubs based at Al Nasr's ice rink. The Mighty Camels boasts around a dozen nationalities among its current membership of 80, who practise twice a week (Sundays and Tuesdays, 8.30-11pm) and take part in regular tournaments and events overseas, besides hosting their own competition in Dubai at the end of the season, which runs from September to April. The Sandstorms, meanwhile, have four teams: novice (ages 5-8), junior (9-10), intermediate (11-13) and senior (14-18). They practise Saturdays (4.30-9pm), Mondays (7-9pm) and Wednesdays (5.30-7.30pm).

Hashers power walking the Jumeirah strip.

Kitesurfing at the **Arabian Gulf Kite Club**.

Ice-skating

Galleria Ice Rink

Hyatt Regency Hotel, Deira Corniche (209 6550).
Open 10am-1.30pm, 2-5.30pm, 6-9pm Sat-Thur;
10am-1.30pm, 2-5.30pm, 6-8pm Fri. **Price** Dhs25 incl
skate hire. **Credit** AmEx, MC, V. **Map** p279 J1.
This rink is somewhat surreally set in the centre of
a small shopping mall attached to the Hyatt Regency
Hotel, so expect bemused onlookers. Lessons are
available (from Dhs80 for a half hour).

Al Nasr Leisureland

Oud Metha (337 1234). **Open** 10am-noon, 1-3pm,
4-6.30pm daily. **Price** Dhs5 plus Dhs5 skate hire.
Credit MC, V. **Map** p277 J3.
Leisureland is a popular venue for ice-skaters of all
ages, particularly during the summer when the outdoor temperature soars off the scale. It is advisable
to call before you go to check the rink is open to the
public, as ice hockey is played every day and may
interfere with timings.

Karting

Dubai Formula 1

*Dubai Exiles Rugby & Football Club, Al Awir,
off the Ras Al Khor road south of Dubai (338
8828/f1dubai@emirates.net.ae).* **Open** 2-10pm
daily (flexible for corporate bookings). **Price**
Arrive and Drive (10mins) Dhs50. **No credit cards.**
Map p277 K5.

Activities include the Arrive and Drive ten-minute
taster, group racing, Grand Prix, plus corporate and
endurance events. The Middle East 24-hour pro-kart
Endurance Race Series, a yearly event that draws
race lovers from the world over, are held here.

Kitesurfing

Arabian Gulf Kite Club

*Jumeirah Beach, near University of Wollongong,
Beach Road, Jumeirah (050 455 5216/www.fatima
sport.com).* **Open** varies. **Price** varies. **No credit
cards. Map** p274 B4.
This spectacular and fast-growing hybrid sport has
become the coolest activity in Dubai over the past
couple of years. Head down to the Jumeirah coastline and you'll see some serious aquatic aerobatics
on show. The Arabian Gulf Kite Club can get you
started with its power kiting, display kiting and kite
buggy equipment.

Mountain biking

Desert Rangers

*Dubai Garden Centre Building, Sheikh Zayed Road
(340 2408/www.desertrangers.com).* **Open** 9am-6pm
Sat-Thur. **Price** from Dhs300 per person (min 4
people per trip). **Credit** MC, V. **Map** p274 B4.
Desert Rangers organises and designs tailor-made
treks for riders of all ages, abilities and strengths.
Guides, bikes, pick-ups and drop-offs are included
in the price.

Paintballing

Wonderland Theme & Water Park

Creekside Park, near Garhoud Bridge, Garhoud (050 651 4583). **Open** by booking. **Price** Dhs50 per 100 paintballs; Dhs120 rental of mask, clothing & paintgun. **No credit cards. Map** p277 K5.

Create your own Desert Storm at Dubai's only paintballing centre. The 'zone' is desert scrubland, but there are strategically placed barricades to spice up the action with choke- and vantage-points. Groups are divided into opposing teams before being given protective overalls, face masks, 'guns' and paint balls, followed by a safety demonstration. The organisers claim they will open any time of the day or night to accommodate visitors.

Pool

See also p197 **Snooker**.

Billiard Golden Hall

Al Habtor Building, near Ramada Continental Hotel, off Al Ittihad Road, Deira (262 9290). **Open** 9am-3am Sat-Thur; 2pm-3am Fri. **Price** Dhs15 per hr before 5pm; Dhs22 per hr after 5pm. **No credit cards. Map** p275 D2.

This smallish Deira pool hall lacks the dank mustiness that characterises so many others, boasting lava lamps in place of the trademark pink tasseled lampshades. Game play is fast, furious but friendly eight- and nine-ball.

Dubai Snooker Club

Just off Maktoum Bridge, behind the Dubai Printing Building, Bur Dubai (337 5338). **Open** 10am-2am Sat-Thur; 3pm-1am Fri. **Price** Dhs20 per hr. **No credit cards. Map** p277 J2.

Eight pool tables are available at this popular venue. It's a well-run club, though it takes care of its equipment rather better than its customers. The club is divided into three parts: one part for pool, one part for snooker (*see p197*), and one part housing a rather noisy network computer games centre.

Emirates Billiards Centre

Behind Ramada Continental Hotel, off Al Ittihad Road, Deira (262 6494). **Open** 10am-2am Sat-Thur; 2pm-2am Fri. **Price** Dhs25 per hr; amateurs Dhs5 per game. **No credit cards. Map** p275 D2.

This dark but spacious pool hall offers 11 tables and is a firm favourite with local players. There's a 'winner stays, loser pays' policy, but if you want to avoid playing with strangers you can book a table in advance. Internet, arcade and other table games are also available.

Millenium Avenue

Off Abu Hail Road, near Galadari roundabout, Deira (266 6595). **Open** 10am-2am Sat-Thur; 2pm-2am Fri. **Price** *Members* Dhs5 per hr mornings; Dhs10 afternoons and evenings. *Non-members* Dhs15 mornings; Dhs20 afternoons & evenings. **No credit cards. Map** p275 D2.

Sports City

Plans were unveiled in late 2003 for **Dubailand**, a Dhs18 billion theme park and tourist attraction set to feature six major projects, including what is being called Sports & Outdoor World. Covering an area of more than 19 million square metres (206 million square feet), this will cater to a range of sports with five designated centres, each built to internationally competitive standards. The Extreme Sports World will be home to a centre for such radical sports as motocross, rollerblading and skateboarding. Facilities will also be provided for the arts of dune buggying and indoor rock climbing.

Officials claim that Sports City will prove to be the region's premier sporting venue thanks to its three international-standard stadia comfortably equipped to stage top-level rugby, cricket and hockey matches. A sporting academy will also be established. Racing World will accommodate the Dubai Autodrome project (see *p183*), while Polo World will feature grounds hosting international teams and tournaments. Finally, Golf World will be a self-contained community with several 18-hole courses and a world-class golf academy.

The only pool joint in town with round tables. The balls are snooker size (smaller than pool balls), you win 25 points every time you sink a ball but lose it and give up 25 points to your opponent if you foul. There is no triangle. The game makes the oblong tables seem boring, but they are just as popular and you're likely to find yourself queuing for both.

Rugby

If you're in town for a while and fancy watching a game, or even kicking a conversion or two, the following clubs welcome spectators and might just take on a gifted ringer.

Dubai Dragons

Dubai Exiles Rugby Football Club, next to Dubai Country Club, Al Awir, off the Ras Al Khor road south of Dubai (050 457 0919/050 466 9337/ www.eteamz.com/dubai_dragons_rugby). **Map** p277 K5.

The Dragons are tenants of the Dubai Exiles (*see p194*) at their club and their biggest rivals, winning the Arabian Gulf Cup in 2003 and finishing second in the league. They also have a second XV that plays in the Emirates League, and are always on the look-out for new members.

Dubai Exiles

Dubai Exiles Rugby & Football Club, next to Dubai Country Club, Al Awir, off the Ras Al Khor road south of Dubai (333 1198/www.dubaiexiles.com). **Map** p277 K5.

The oldest rugby club in Dubai and still one of the biggest and most successful outfits in the region. The Exiles also has the best facilities, including four grass pitches. The 2003 Arabian Gulf league champions run second XV, veterans', women's, mini and junior sides.

Dubai Hurricanes

Dubai Country Club, Al Awir, off the Ras Al Khor road south of Dubai (333 1155/www.eteamz.com/dubaihurricanes). **Map** p277 K5.

Traditionally the Hurricanes have been a social team, but these days are also a force to be reckoned with in the Arabian Gulf League.

Running

Dubai Road Runners

050 624 3213/www.dubai-road-runners.com. **Price** Dhs5 per meet; free children, students. **No credit cards**.

Dubai Road Runners meet every Saturday at 6.30pm in the car park of the north entrance to Al Safa Park in Jumeirah (map p274 B3). Runners of all ages and abilities can choose to complete either one or two laps of the park (3.4km/2¼ miles per lap). The club organises five events each winter (with categories for juniors, vets and super vets).

Dubai Creek Striders

321 1999/www.dubaicreekstriders.com. **Price** Dhs5 per meet. **No credit cards**.

This club focuses on medium to long distance running. It meets Fridays at 6am, usually at the Trade Centre exhibition hall car park on Sheikh Zayed Road (map p281 G9); see the website for details. The multinational membership includes runners of all ages and abilities.

Sailing

Club Joumana

Jebel Ali Hotel, Sheikh Zayed Road, Exit 13 (past Interchange 7) (883 6000/www.jebelali-international. com). **Open** 10am-4pm daily. **Price** Dhs80 entrance fee (non-hotel guests); Dhs80 per hr Catamaran; Dhs60 per hr Laser. **Credit** AmEx, DC, MC, V. **Map** p274 A5.

At the time of going to press, the club had one catamaran and one laser boat available.

Dubai Offshore Sailing Club

Beach Road, by Wollongong University, Jumeirah (394 1669/www.dosc.org). **Open** *Sailing lessons* 9am-5pm daily. *Clubhouse* 8am-12.30am daily. **Price** Dhs25 entrance fee (non-members); Dhs180 2hr private lesson; Dhs100 group lesson. **Credit** DC, MC, V. **Map** p274 B4.

A busy and friendly non-profit-making club. Recognised by the Royal Yachting Association, the DOSC offers courses all year round (the Thursday and Friday Cadet Club is popular with younger sailors), and there are races every Friday. Mooring, storage, launch facilities and sail training are provided, and there is also a full social calendar. Private lessons in optimists, lasers and toppers are available.

Jebel Ali Sailing Club

Near Dubai International Marine Club (Le Meridien Mina Seyahi Hotel), Al Sufouh Road, Jumeirah (399 5444/www.jebelalisailingclub.com). **Open** 9am-8pm Sat-Wed; 9am-10pm Thur, Fri. **Price** lessons from Dhs450 (members), Dhs650 (non-members). **Credit** AmEx, MC, V. **Map** p274 A5.

Weekly races for adults and children are held here in a variety of vessels, from toppers and catamarans to lasers and cruisers. For children, there are three-hour Cadet Club sessions every Thursday (10am-noon, Dhs40), while experienced adult sailors can take advantage of free Laser 4.7 training.

Scuba diving & snorkelling

It's possible to dive and snorkel all year round in the Arabian Gulf off Dubai, but it should be noted that the dive sites off the east coast of the UAE, particularly Fujairah (*see p234*), are widely regarded as superior in terms of

Laser treatment: **Dubai Offshore Sailing Club.**

To dive for – snorkelling in the Gulf is an absolute must.

visibility and marine life. Most Dubai-based diving outfits organise trips to the east coast (about two hours' drive away). They will also accommodate mixed groups of divers and snorkellers. Quality snorkels, masks and fins are on sale at each of the dive centres listed below. Alternatively, ask for less expensive flippers and a facemask in the tourist shop of any Jumeirah beachside hotel.

Al Boom Diving

Opposite the Iranian Hospital, Al Wasl Road (342 2993/www.alboommarine.com). **Open** 10am-8pm Sat-Thur. **Price** Dhs1,700 PADI Open water course; Dhs1,000 Advanced open water course. **Credit** MC, V. **Map** p280 E9.

This one-stop dive shop is arguably the most comprehensive in the city, and is good for both casual visitors who just want to test the waters with a sample dive, and more experienced divers looking for a specific course. Dive trips can be arranged; the shop also rents equipment and handles maintenance and servicing. A complete range of Suunto diving computers, Tusa, Aqua-Lung, US Divers and Sea Quest equipment is available along with clothing and accessories.

Pavilion Dive Centre

Jumeirah Beach Hotel, Beach Road, Jumeirah (406 8827/www.jumeirahinternational.com). **Open** 9am-6pm daily. **Price** Dhs320 Discover scuba course; Dhs1,750 Open water course. **Credit** AmEx, DC, MC, V. **Map** p274 B4.

The luxury hotel-based centre claims to be the first and only Golden Palm five-star training institute to be established in Dubai. Pavilion offers a comprehensive range of dive courses, from beginner through to instructor development (twice a year, usually in May and October). Daily dive trips leave the marina at 10am, weather permitting, and return sometime between 1pm and 3pm.

Scubatec

Sana Building, Trade Centre Road, Karama (334 8988/scubatec@emirates net.ae). **Open** 9am-1.30pm, 4-8.30pm Sat-Thur. **Price** varies. **Credit** MC, V. **Map** p281 H7.

Scubatec's qualified instructors are licensed by the PADI and TDI (Technical Diving Instructor) organisations and provide a full range of courses. They can build a great deal of flexibility into timings to accommodate the schedules of visitors or residents. Services and repair facilities are available.

Active Dubai

Snooker

See also p193 **Pool**.

Dubai Snooker Club

Just off Maktoum Bridge, behind the Dubai Printing Building, Bur Dubai (337 5338). **Open** 9pm-2am Sat-Thur; 3pm-1am Fri. **Price** Dhs15 per hr. **No credit cards. Map** p277 J2.
A total of 15 full-size tables are available at this popular venue (very busy in the evenings), which also offers pool tables and PC games.

The Snooker Club

Metropolitan Hotel, Sheikh Zayed Road, Interchange 2 (343 0000). **Open** 6pm-1am daily. **Price** free. **Credit** (for drinks) MC, V. **Map** p276 G5.
The only place in Dubai where you can enjoy a free game of snooker, on the proviso you buy drinks at the (licensed) bar. Set behind the hotel by the softball courts, the club is a hidden gem. Hardly visited, comfortable and well air-conditioned, it's a perfect chill-out area. Darts are also available.

Snooker Point

Near Al Nasr Cinema, Oud Metha (337 7997). **Open** 10am-2am Sat-Thur; 2pm-3am Fri. **Price** Dhs16 per hr. **No credit cards. Map** p277 J2.
This rather seedy-looking joint boasts blue baize tables and an Arabic majority, though all are welcome. There is a local tournament at the beginning of each month. The club offers a juice bar and an internet café (Dhs20 per hr).

Snooker World

Opposite Dubai police headquarters, next to new labour office, Hor Al Anz East, Deira (268 5566). **Open** 10am-3am Sat-Thur; 2pm-3am Fri. **Price** Dhs22 per hr. **No credit cards. Map** p275 E1.
A club with a fresh interior, a winner-stays-on policy and a multinational crowd, Snooker World also offers internet use (Dhs10 per hr), *shisha* pipes and a screen in the coffee shop that plays two of the latest films every night for free. Tournaments are for locals only, but otherwise everyone is welcome to play.

Wakeboarding

Dubai Water Sports Association

Jadaf (324 1031/www.thewakeboardschool.com). **Open** 8am-6pm daily. **Price** *Facilities* Dhs30, plus Dhs15 entrance for non-members. *Lessons* Dhs50 members; Dhs75 non-members. **Credit** AmEx, MC, V. **Map** p277 K3.
Set on Dubai Creek, the WSA has two tournament ski boats, a slalom course and a full-sized jump. The clubhouse's faded charm makes a refreshing change from the city's sanitised beach clubs. Facilities include a lawn, swimming pool, Jacuzzi, children's playground and barbecue area. To get there, take the exit to Jadaf from Sheikh Zayed Road near Garhoud Bridge. Take the second right to a dirt track and follow signs marked 'TWS'.

Water-skiing

Club Joumana

Jebel Ali Hotel, Sheikh Zayed Road, Exit 13 (past Interchange 7) (883 6000/www.jebelali-international. com). **Open** 8am-noon daily. **Price** Dhs80 per 30 mins. **Credit** AmEx, DC, MC, V. **Map** p274 A5.
Non-hotel guests must pay an entrance fee of Dhs80. *See p194* **Sailing** for more information on facilities.

Dubai Water Sports Association

Jadaf (324 1031/www.thewakeboardschool.com). **Open** 8am-6pm daily. **Price** *Facilities* Dhs30, plus Dhs15 entrance for non-members. *Lessons* Dhs50 members; Dhs75 non-members. **Credit** AmEx, MC, V. **Map** p277 K3.
The versatile team will happily instruct you on two boards as well as one. *See above* **Wakeboarding** for more information on facilities and getting there.

Windsurfing

Club Joumana

Jebel Ali Hotel, Sheikh Zayed Road, Exit 13 (past Interchange 7) (883 6000/www.jebelali-international. com). **Open** 6.30am-10pm daily. **Price** Dhs50 per hr. **Credit** AmEx, DC, MC, V. **Map** p274 A5.
Non-hotel guests must pay an entrance fee of Dhs80. *See p194* **Sailing** for more information on facilities.

Surfdom: Getting away from it all.

Active Dubai

Health & Fitness

Work out, bronze up and get rubbed down in the city's clubs, gyms and spas.

Beach clubs

If your idea of paradise on earth is lazing in the sun by the sea with your every need catered for, then a visit to a beach club is a must. Most of the hotels located on Dubai's coast operate beach clubs and almost all are open to the public – the exceptions being the One&Only Royal Mirage, Dubai Marine Beach Resort & Spa and the Jumeirah Beach Club, which can be used only by hotel guests, club members and members' guests.

Beach clubs are massively popular with more affluent Dubai residents and tourists, and at weekends (Friday and Saturday) a large number of the Jumeirah crowd head down to hang out at venues like the Meridien Mina Seyahi's **Club Mina** and the **Ritz-Carlton Beach Club**, which charge anything from Dhs5,000 to Dhs10,000 a year for the privilege.

For a daily fee, visitors get access to the hotel grounds, private beach and swimming pool, and the attentive service you'd expect from a five-star property. However, if you want to use the hotel's other facilities such as a spa, health club,

tennis courts or water sports – virtually all beach clubs offer a complete range of marine activities – you are almost certain to incur an extra cost. The experience doesn't come cheap, but as a special treat it's hard to beat.

Caracalla Spa & Health Club
Le Royal Meridien Hotel, Al Sufouh Road, Jumeirah (399 5555/www.leroyalmeridien-dubai.com). **Open** 8am-8pm daily. **Price** (non-members) *Sat-Thur* Dhs100; Dhs40 concessions. *Fri* Dhs150; Dhs60 concessions. **Credit** AmEx, MC, V. **Map** p274 A5.
Annual membership had been frozen at the time of going to press, an indication of the popularity of this club. The admission fee gives free access to the beach and swimming pool; there are additional charges for the gym, sauna, steam room, Jacuzzi and hammam pools (five pools with different water temperatures), tennis and squash courts. A full range of water sports is available, and guests can also indulge themselves with various massage and aromatherapy 'treatments' (*see p204*).

Club Joumana
Jebel Ali Hotel, Sheikh Zayed Road, Exit 13 (past Interchange 7) (883 6000/www.jebelali-international. com). **Open** 7am-7pm daily. **Price** (non-members)

Beach-club heaven at Le Royal Meridien's **Caracalla Spa & Health Club.**

Sat-Thur Dhs80; Dhs40 concessions. *Fri* Dhs180; Dhs90 concessions. **Credit** AmEx, DC, MC, V. **Map** p274 A5.

Located about 40km (25 miles) south of town, the Club Joumana is known for its extremely friendly staff and luxurious facilities. For active types, the wide range of water sports available from its beautiful private beach includes water-skiing, windsurfing, banana boating and sailing (catamaran and laser); boat and fishing trips can also be organised. Back on dry land, Club Joumana boasts four floodlit tennis courts, two glass-backed squash courts and a badminton court, plus a gym, Jacuzzi and sauna. There are also two fresh-water pools with swim-up bars, a sea-water pool and a children's pool. Nearby is a par-36 nine-hole golf course (*see p190* **Jebel Ali Golf Resort & Spa**) and practice facilities.

Club Mina

Le Meridien Mina Seyahi Hotel, Al Sufouh Road, Jumeirah (399 3333/www.lemeridien-mina seyahi.com). **Open** 6am-9pm daily. **Price** (non-members) *Sat-Thur* Dhs100; Dhs200 incl lunch. *Fri* members only. **Credit** AmEx, DC, MC, V. **Map** p274 A5.

One of the trendier beach clubs, Club Mina's already luxurious facilities have recently been further improved. To the three large swimming pools and two smaller shaded pools for children, have been added a grass football pitch and an expanded gym with aerobic studio. The private beach stretches about a half a kilometre, and plays host to a wide range of sports (extra charge for motorised water sports and diving). The Barasti bar (*see p96*) is a great place to chill out.

Hiltonia Health & Beach Club

Hilton Dubai Jumeirah Hotel, Al Sufouh Road, Jumeirah (318 2227/www.hilton.com). **Open** *Beach & pool* 7am-7pm daily. *Health club* 7am-10pm daily. **Price** (non-members) Dhs75; Dhs30 concessions. **Credit** AmEx, DC, MC, V. **Map** p274 A5.

There's no shortage of things to do here: water sports include parasailing, kayaking, jet-skiing, knee-boarding and fishing trips. The health club has a well-equipped gym, sauna and steam room. For those on an extended stay, monthly memberships are available (Dhs550; Dhs650 couple).

Jumeirah Health & Beach Club

Sheraton Jumeirah Beach Resort, Al Sufouh Road, Jumeirah (399 5533/www.starwood.com). **Open** 7am-10pm daily (no pool lifeguards after 7pm). **Price** (non-members) free under-6s. **Credit** AmEx, DC, MC, V. **Map** p274 A5.

As well as two swimming pools, two floodlit tennis courts and two squash courts, the club also has a gym packed with the usual array of bikes, steppers, rowing machines and treadmills. Add in volleyball, a range of water sports, a sauna and steam room, and you won't run out of things to do in a hurry. Or you could just treat yourself to the Aqua Centre Spa, offering facials and a range of different massages and aromatherapy.

Club Mina's infinity pool and beach front.

Metropolitan Resort & Beach Club

Metropolitan Hotel, Al Sufouh Road, Jumeirah (399 5000/www.methotels.com). **Open** 8.30am-7.30pm daily. **Price** (non-members) Dhs75; Dhs25 concessions. **Credit** AmEx, DC, MC, V. **Map** p274 A5.

The Metropolitan Resort is undergoing a massive facelift, due to be completed by May 2005. A new state-of-the-art gymnasium, an additional spa, squash and tennis facilities are promised on completion. In the meantime, tennis courts are still available, as is a temporary gym. Until works are completed, however, the sauna, steam rooms and squash courts are closed. Fortunately, the beach is unaffected, with a range of water sports, from water-skiing to scuba diving (24 hours' notice needed).

Oasis Beach Club

Oasis Beach Hotel, Al Sufouh Road, Jumeirah (315 4034/www.jebelali-international.com). **Open** 9am-9pm daily. **Price** (non-members) *Sat-Thur* Dhs70; Dhs35 concessions. *Fri* Dhs88; Dhs44 concessions. **Credit** AmEx, DC, MC, V. **Map** p274 A5.

Archery and pétanque are just two of the many sports on offer at this lively four-star club, which tends to attract a young crowd thanks to its low prices. There is also a floodlit tennis court, beach volleyball and a soccer pitch, and water sports include windsurfing, wakeboarding, water-skiing, banana boat rides and snorkelling. What with a

Tan of the people: Catching rays in Dubai's parks and public beaches. *See p201.*

large pool with swim-up bar, an outdoor heated Jacuzzi, and the Coco Cabana beach bar and restaurant, the Oasis Beach Club probably represents the best value for money on the beach front. Non-guests at the hotel can apply for a 'Neighbourhood Privilege Club' membership. This is free and entitles holders to half-price admission during the week (Dhs15 discount at weekends), as well as a 25 per cent discount on food and drink.

Ritz-Carlton Beach Club

Ritz-Carlton Dubai Hotel, Al Sufouh Road, Jumeirah (399 4000/www.ritzcarlton.com). **Open** 6am-10pm daily. **Price** (non-members) *Sat-Thur* Dhs150; Dhs80 concessions; free under-4s. *Fri* members only. **Credit** AmEx, DC, MC, V. **Map** p274 A5.
The Ritz-Carlton Beach Club enjoys a spectacular setting, with a 350m (120ft) stretch of private beach as well as vast landscaped gardens. Facilities include four floodlit tennis courts, a grass soccer pitch, two squash courts, pitch and putt golf, and a comprehensively equipped gym. Personal trainers are on hand to answer any fitness questions, and classes available include power yoga and women-only 'aerotennis', a cross between aerobics and the racket sport. The spa now features two women-only treatment rooms, taking the overall total to ten, with a range of seductive options stretching from Balinese-style massage to Scentao hot stone therapy (for more details on the spa, *see p204*). Water sports are organised on request at an additional cost, and there's both an adults-only and a children-only pool. Activities are arranged every day for children aged from four to 12.

Health clubs

Given Dubai's climate and beach culture, there's a strong emphasis on health and fitness and achieving the body beautiful. However, there is tremendous diversity in the standards of health clubs, in terms of quality of instruction, facilities and value for money. Annual memberships can be anything from Dhs2,000 to Dhs6,000, but most clubs have short-term membership options as well. Listings for health-club facilities at the beach clubs start on p198.

The Aviation Club

Off Sharjah Road, Garhoud (282 4122/www.aviation clubonline.com). **Open** 6am-11pm daily. **Price** Yearly membership only: Dhs5,000 men, Dhs3,750 women. **Credit** AmEx, MC, V. **Map** p277 L3.
The Aviation Club is one of Dubai's most popular health clubs, and it was undergoing a four-phase upgrade at the time of going to press, to ensure it remains at the forefront of the fitness scene. A state-of-the-art gym and new ladies' changing rooms have already been unveiled; still being worked on but due for completion in May 2004 were a facelift for the men's changing rooms, construction of separate spas for ladies and gents, and additional group exercise studios.

The new additions will complement an already impressive list of club facilities, which include a fully equipped gym, six floodlit tennis courts, a swimming pool with 25m lap lanes, two squash courts, a dedicated spinning studio, a sauna, a steam room, plunge pools and a nine-hole par-three golf course.

City suntraps: beaches and parks

Those in search of sandy or grassy spots to bronze themselves are spoilt for choice in Dubai. Public beaches are free and easy to get to, and while they're not half as luxurious as the city's hotel beach clubs (*see pp198-200*), they're ideal if you're looking for some low-key ray-soaking. Bear in mind, however, that in rough weather the Dubai coast is plagued by strong offshore undertows and can be dangerous for swimming. It's not unheard of to see red flags warning against taking a dip in the water – nor lifeguards becoming increasingly annoyed by young males ignoring the sensible advice. You're also not allowed to take dogs on the beach, a rule which is increasingly being enforced by the police.

For sun lovers who prefer flora and fauna to sand and surf, the city is well endowed with lush green parks, maintained at phenomenal expense and tended with care. The three main kid-centric parks are Al Mamzar, Al Safa and Umm Suqeim parks (for full descriptions, *see pp147-148*): these all have excellent facilities for keeping children amused. For a more grown-up approach to your parklife, try basking in the sun in the verdant hotspots listed here. Do bear in mind, however, that the only public place where flesh can be shown is the beach; in the parks your shorts and T-shirts must remain firmly on.

Creekside Park

Umm Hurair, near Wonderland (336 7633). **Open** 8am-11pm Sat-Wed; 8am-midnight Thur, Fri. **Admission** *Park* free. *Cable car* Dhs25; Dhs10 concessions. *Children's City* Dhs15, Dhs10 concessions. **Map** p277 K3.
An enormous stretch of greenery that runs along 2.5km (1½ miles) of prime Creek frontage, Creekside Park has acres of pristine lawns and gardens where you can roll out a rug and get tanning. Those who wish to fish can do so from dedicated piers that jut out into the Creek. Joggers are well catered for with purpose-built tracks, rollerblade skating is permitted, and bikes can be hired from Gate 2. A cable car (the emirate's first when it opened in 2000) gives an aerial view over the water.

Jumeirah Beach Park

Jumeirah 2, next to Jumeirah Beach Club (349 2555). **Open** 8am-10.30pm Sat-Wed; 8am-11pm Thur, Fri; women & children only

Sat, Sun. **Admission** Dhs5; Dhs20 per car including occupants. **Map** p282 A15.
A popular hangout thanks to its ample, well-manicured gardens, which tumble down to a narrow but well-maintained strip of beach, Jumeirah Beach Park is a pleasant place to start working on your tan. The park is particularly busy on Friday afternoons, when people gather around barbecue pits for all-day burger-eating and socialising.

Kite Beach

Umm Suqeim 4, behind Wollongong University. **Map** p274 B4.
Kitesurfing and parasailing have taken off in a big way in Dubai and the long stretches of undeveloped sand at the most southerly end of Jumeirah are collectively named after the activity that takes place on them practically every day of the week. For surfers these beaches offer unbroken expanses of ocean, free from breakwaters. For those who have less strenuous pursuits in mind, fear not – there's plenty of space to stretch out and sunbathe.

Mushrif Park

Near Mirdif (288 3624). **Open** 8am-11.30pm daily. **Admission** Dhs3; Dhs10 per car. *Swimming pool* Dhs10; Dhs5 concessions. *Train* Dhs2. **Map** p275 F3.
Drive past Dubai airport and continue out of town: ten minutes later, and just past the residential area of Mirdif, you'll arrive at Mushrif Park, a surprisingly huge swathe of green filled with wildlife and crossed by a dinky train service. Assert your tourist credentials by leaping aboard a camel before soaking up the rays in your very own landscaped plot.

Russian Beach

Jumeirah 1, next to Dubai Marine Beach Resort & Spa. **Map** p280 D9.
One of the city's best-known public beaches and the closest one to the centre of town, Russian Beach (also known as Open Beach) is popular with an eclectic mix of residents because it offers easy access and – during calm weather – safe bathing. The shoreline is made up of several beaches that nestle within manmade breakwaters. When you've had enough sand and water fun, it's just a stone's throw from the many cafés and stores lining the northern end of Beach Road.

Active Dubai

Burning calories the cycling way at **The Aviation Club**. *See p200.*

The club's aerobics studio must be the biggest and busiest in Dubai, hosting several classes a day including BodyPump, BodyCombat, boxercise, yoga and circuit training.

The Big Apple

Emirates Towers Boulevard mall, Sheikh Zayed Road (319 8661/www.jumeirahinternational.com). **Open** 6am-10pm daily. **Price** *Gym* Dhs35 per day. *Classes* Dhs25. **Credit** AmEx, DC, MC, V. **Map** p276 H4.

The Big Apple features an array of Nautilus, Startrak, Stairmaster and Concept II equipment. There are no swimming, sauna or steam room facilities, but aerobic classes cover everything from BodyPump to spinning. Membership packages are available, and considering the swanky location, they're excellent value.

Club Olympus

Hyatt Regency Hotel, Deira Corniche (209 6802/www.dubai.regency.hyatt.com). **Open** 7am-11.45pm daily (swimming pool till 11pm). **Price** free to hotel guests. *Non-guests* (ID required) Dhs50 per day Sat-Wed; Dhs60 Thur, Fri. **Credit** AmEx, DC, MC, V. **Map** p279 J1.

Salsa and karate classes are available at this city centre club. Also on offer is a Nautilus gym and running track, which circles the two floodlit tennis courts. A pair of squash courts, an outdoor swimming pool, spa, sauna, steam room, Jacuzzi and splash pool complete the line-up of facilities; the outside deck is particularly popular in the cooler winter months.

Dimension Health & Fitness Club

Metropolitan Hotel, Sheikh Zayed Road, Interchange 2 (407 6704). **Open** 6am-midnight daily. **Price** *Facilities* Dhs40 per day. *Classes* Dhs20-Dhs30. **Credit** AmEx, DC, MC, V. **Map** p276 G5.

A 25m outdoor swimming pool is one of the main attractions at this club, although there is also a well-equipped gym packed with an assortment of free weights and Nautilus equipment, a Jacuzzi, steam room and sauna. The studio offers various classes, including fencing (*see p187*) and kickboxing. To wrap it up, try a Chinese-style massage (Dhs150 for an hour); Indian massage is also available.

Fitness Planet

Al Hana Centre, Dhiyafah Street, Satwa (398 9030/www.bgroupme.com). **Open** *Mixed gym* 6am-11pm Sat-Thur; 4-10pm Fri. *Women's gym* 7am-9pm Sat-Thur. **Price** (non-members) *Facilities* Dhs30 per day. **Credit** AmEx, MC, V. **Map** p281 F8.

FP is a busy gym where the emphasis on is free weights and resistance machines, which means it attracts serious bodybuilders and weightlifters. For women who might find the main gym a bit intimidating, there's a separate women's area, Fitness Planet Hers, on the mezzanine level. Other facilities include a Jacuzzi, steam room and sauna. Membership packages start at three months.

Lifestyle Health Club

Sofitel City Centre Hotel, Port Saeed (603 8825/www.accorhotels.com). **Open** 6.30am-11pm Sat-Thur; 8am-8pm Fri. **Price** *Facilities* Dhs50 per day. *Aerobics classes* Dhs30. **Credit** MC, V. **Map** p277 K2.

The best Treatments

Ayurvedic

Take life-affirming Indian massage at **Cleopatra's Spa** (*see p204*) and **Indian Ayurveda** (*see p204*).

Balinese

Calm the mind with traditional palm pressure techniques at the **Ritz-Carlton Spa** (*see p204*).

Chinese

The oriental touch is on offer at **Dimension Health & Fitness Club** (*see p202*).

Moroccan

For a light massage after a trip to the beach park, see **Spa Thira** (*see p206*).

Swedish

Go Nordic at **Caracalla Spa & Health Club** (*see p198 and p204*) and **Ayoma Spa** (*see below*).

This hotel-based club stretches over three floors: the reception, two squash courts, sauna and steam room are on one level; the gym and aerobics studio on the next; and an outdoor swimming pool and floodlit tennis court are on the roof. The gym is packed with resistance and cardiovascular machines; different aerobic classes are held each day in the studio.

Nautilus Academy

Al Mussalla Towers, Kahlid Bin Al Waleed Road (Bank Street), Bur Dubai (397 4117). **Open** 6am-11pm daily. **Price** *Facilities* Dhs40 per day; Dhs350 per month. *Classes* (members only) Dhs30. **Credit** AmEx, DC, MC, V. **Map** p278 H4.

One of the best-equipped gyms in the city, with a vast array of Nautilus machines and cardiovascular equipment. There are separate studios here for spinning and aerobics, and two squash courts. There is also a small outdoor pool, a steam room, sauna, Jacuzzi and café.

Nautilus Fitness Centre

Crowne Plaza Hotel, Sheikh Zayed Road (331 4055). **Open** 6am-10pm Sat-Wed; 8.30am-8.30pm Thur, Fri. **Price** *Facilities* Dhs50 per day. *Classes* Dhs15 members; Dhs25 non-members. **Credit** MC, V. **Map** p281 G10.

The focus at this centre is on Nautilus fitness training techniques, but there are also free weights and an array of cardiovascular machines. The long list of aerobic classes stretches from powerpump to Tae-Bo and yoga, and even belly-dancing for those who want something a bit more exotic. Other facilities include a squash court, table tennis, sauna, steam room and outdoor swimming pool.

Pharaohs Club

Wafi Pyramids at Wafi City mall, off Oud Metha Road (324 0000/www.waficity.com). **Open** 7am-10pm Sat-Thur; 9am-9pm Fri. **Price** Dhs5,500 annual membership; swimming pool (non-members) Dhs100. **Credit** AmEx, DC, MC, V. **Map** p277 J3.

One of the most prestigious clubs in Dubai, Pharaohs offers members luxurious surroundings and an impressive array of facilities. There are well-equipped gyms for men and women, the latter benefiting from exclusive use of the main gym on Wednesdays and Sundays, in the mornings until 1pm. Steam rooms, plunge pools and Jacuzzis are provided as well as a large swimming pool and a separate pool in which, with a flick of a switch, you can attempt to swim against the tide. The club also boasts a climbing wall, three floodlit tennis courts, two squash courts and a comprehensive range of fitness classes. Members qualify for a 25 per cent discount on treatments at Cleopatra's Spa (*see p204*).

Spas

The past few years have witnessed a veritable explosion in spa culture in Dubai, and now there are dozens of places where you can be pampered to your heart's (and your body's) content. Because of the quality of the competition, these spas tend to be at the very top end of the market in terms of surroundings and the quality of treatments on offer.

Assawan Spa & Health Club

Burj Al Arab Hotel, Beach Road, Jumeirah (301 7338/www.jumeirahinternational.com). **Open** 6.30am-10pm daily. **Price** Dhs300 1hr basic massage. **Credit** AmEx, DC, MC, V. **Map** p274 A4.

This lavishly decorated club is located on the 18th floor of Dubai's iconic landmark, providing spectacular views of the Arabian Gulf. There are separate male and female areas boasting a total of eight spa treatment rooms, a sauna, steam bath, plunge pool, Jacuzzi and solarium. Espa and La Prairie facials are offered, as well as wraps, massages and hot stone treatments. Don't expect all this to come cheap; however, if you're seeking a once-in-a-lifetime experience then this is the place to check out. Non-guests can also book treatments here, subject to availability.

Ayoma Spa

Taj Palace Hotel, Al Maktoum Street, Deira (211 3101/www.tajhotels.com). **Open** 10am-10pm daily (last booking 8pm). **Price** Dhs250 1hr basic massage. **Credit** AmEx, MC, V. **Map** p279 A3.

Three different styles of massage are available at this atmospheric and relaxing spa, progressing from Ayurvedic to Balinese and Swedish. Friendly staff will happily recommend appropriate treatments according to the desired effect. Facials and various acts of delightful pampering are also available. As well as separate saunas and steam rooms, the spa also features a swimming pool and Jacuzzi.

Active Dubai

Caracalla Spa

Le Royal Meridien Hotel, Al Sufouh Road, Jumeirah (399 5555/www.leroyalmeridien-dubai.com). **Open** 9.30am-8pm daily. **Price** Dhs240 1hr basic massage. **Credit** AmEx, DC, MC, V. **Map** p274 A5.

This spa is normally open only to hotel guests and members of the Caracalla club (*see p198*) – treatments can be booked by other visitors and residents if there are any free times, but such is the popularity of this venue that this is rare. Dedicated steam and sauna rooms plus a Jacuzzi serve both men and women. Treatments available include 50-minute aromatherapy massages, one-hour 'wellbeing' (face and body) massages and exotic facials.

Cleopatra's Spa

Wafi Pyramids at Wafi City mall, off Oud Metha Road, Bur Dubai (324 7700/www.waficity.com). **Open** *Women only* 9am-8pm Sat-Thur; 10am-8pm Fri. *Men* 10am-10pm Sat, Mon-Fri; 10am-7pm Sun. **Price** Dhs230 1hr basic massage. **Credit** AmEx, DC, MC, V. **Map** p277 J3.

For the ultimate in spa treatments check out the luxurious and exotic Cleopatra's. As the name implies, the whole facility has an Egyptian theme and is visually stunning. The usual facials and wraps are available as well as some very different treatments, including the gorgeous aroma stone massage, in which the body is massaged with hot energy-filled 'batu' stones from Indonesia and exotic oils.

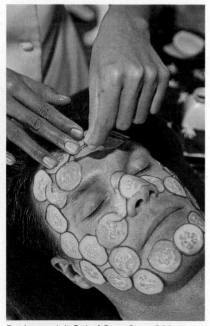

Real men visit **Satori Spa**. *See p206.*

Ayurvedic treatments are also offered, as is Ionithermie, a detox and slimming treatment to tone muscles and smooth the skin. A sports therapist is available for specialised and remedial massage.

Dubai Marine Beach Resort & Spa

Beach Road, Jumeirah (304 8081/www.dxbmarine.com). **Open** 10am-7pm daily. **Price** Dhs250 1hr basic massage. **Credit** AmEx, DC, MC, V. **Map** p280 D8.

This spa boasts six qualified therapists who use Guinot and Espa beauty products. There are three treatment rooms where visitors can enjoy relaxing massages, facials and body treatments.

Indian Ayurveda

Shop B201, Al Attar Centre, Kuwait Street, Karama (396 0469). **Open** 9am-1pm, 4.30-9.30pm Sat-Thur; 9am-6pm Fri. **Price** Dhs100 1hr massage. **No credit cards.** **Map** p279 J5.

For a no-frills full body, face and head massage, this is the place to go. The masseurs are all trained professionals from Kerala in southern India. Shower facilities are available.

One&Only Royal Mirage Spa

One&Only Royal Mirage Hotel, Al Sufouh Road, Jumeirah (399 9999/www.royalmiragedubai.com). **Open** *Women only* 9.30am-1pm daily. *Mixed* 2.30-7pm daily. **Price** Dhs275 1hr basic massage. **Credit** AmEx, DC, MC, V. **Map** p274 A5.

The magnificent Health & Beauty Institute at the Royal Mirage Spa covers an area of 2,000sq m (21,500sq ft), divided over two levels. On the upper floor, the Givenchy Spa has separate areas and opening times for women; the rest of the time, it's mixed. It features 12 treatment rooms including an exclusive suite for private consultations, a resting area, an organic juice bar and a Givenchy boutique. The lower floor boasts an authentic oriental hammam with a traditional heated marble massage table, plus two steam rooms and two private massage rooms. The institute also offers two Jacuzzis, a whirlpool and a plunge shower.

Ritz-Carlton Spa

Ritz-Carlton Dubai Hotel, Al Sufouh Road, Jumeirah (399 4000). **Open** 6am-10pm daily (massages 9am-6pm daily). **Price** Dhs265 1hr basic massage. **Credit** AmEx, DC, MC, V. **Map** p274 A5.

The heady Balinese theme at the Ritz-Carlton Spa is a well-executed concept, running thoughout the decor and artwork and extending to an all-Balinese staff. Available treatments include a Balinese Boreh massage and Nirvana herbal body wrap. There is a total of eight treatment rooms and a salon dedicated to hair and beauty treatments, as well as a Jacuzzi, sauna and steam room.

European and marine spa treatments are also available, using minerals, salts from the Dead Sea and natural sponges. Additional treatments include waxing, electrolysis, vibromassage and reflexology. Individual treatment times vary, ranging from a half-hour or one-hour session up to the two top

One&Only Royal Mirage Spa. *See p204.*

Bed of heaven: The women's treatment room at the **Ritz-Carlton Spa**. *See p204.*

treatments that last six hours: guests with time to spare can choose the marine-based Calming Sea package or the Eastern Delight Oriental treatment.

Royal Waters Health Spa

Al Mamzar Centre, Sharjah Road, Deira (297 2053). **Open** *Women only* 9am-5pm daily. *Mixed* 5pm-midnight daily. **Price** Dhs225 1hr basic massage. **Credit** AmEx, MC, V. **Map** p275 E1.

The Royal Waters is a high-tech spa, but less intensely posh than the hotel-based establishments, and offers a more intimate, less intimidating experience. Treatments available include a full hydrotherapy circuit, Eastern and Western massage and slimming treatments. The premises also contain a swimming pool, sauna and steam rooms.

Satori Spa

Jumeirah Beach Club Hotel, Beach Road, Jumeirah (310 2754/www.jumeirahinternational.com). **Open** 9am-9pm daily. **Price** Dhs250 1hr basic massage. **Credit** AmEx, DC, MC, V. **Map** p282 A15.

The list of treatments at this exclusive club is seemingly endless, from eye lifts and facials to sessions in Thai massage and reflexology. Although this is technically a members' and hotel-guests' club, it was possible at time of going to press for non-members to book a fully self-indulgent day of pampering for Dhs499 (make sure to book at least 24 hours in advance). This covers two spa treatments, lunch and access to the gym and beach.

Spa Thira

Opposite Jumeirah Beach Park, Beach Road, Jumeirah (344 2055). **Open** 9am-8pm Sat-Wed; 9am-2pm Thur. **Price** Dhs300 90min facial treatment. **Credit** DC, MC, V. **Map** p282 A15.

A women-only one-stop beauty shop in the heart of Jumeirah, Spa Thira offers a range of treatments, from facials and manicures to soft-laser hair removal and light Moroccan-style massages. Once you've had the full treatment, you can go and show off your new, ultra-relaxed look while topping up your tan in neighbouring Jumeirah Beach Park.

Willow Stream Spa

Fairmont Hotel, Sheikh Zayed Road (332 5555/ www.fairmont.com). **Open** 6am-midnight daily. **Price** Dhs250 1hr basic massage. **Credit** AmEx, DC, MC, V. **Map** p281 G9.

High-quality treatments are the name of the pampering game at the sublime, high-design Willow Stream Spa, which covers just under 4,000sq m (40,000 sq ft) at the Fairmont hotel. As well as separate whirlpools, saunas and steam rooms for men and women, it also boasts two large outdoor swimming pools, positioned to catch the morning and afternoon sun respectively. There is a wading pool for children and a lounge open to all. As for treatments, guests can enjoy a vast range of seductive options, including everything from a sea-scrub body polish to a detox hydrobath treament, as well as facials, skin treatments and waxing.

Active Dubai

The UAE

Getting Started

Break from Dubai's creature comforts – there's a federation of fun out there.

The UAE is not so much a country as a federal affiliation of seven power bases, called emirates, originally brokered by the British years ago under the flag of the Trucial States. Today, each of the emirates – **Abu Dhabi**, **Ajman**, **Dubai**, **Fujairah**, **Ras Al Khaimah**, **Sharjah** and **Umm Al Quwain** – has sworn fealty to the president Sheikh Zayed Al Nahayan, adored leader of Abu Dhabi. He is seen as the father of the modern UAE federation, formed in 1971, and each emirate has enjoyed the federation's collective strength ever since – not to mention the generosity of Abu Dhabi's rulers and their vast oil reserves.

The UAE lies along the south-eastern tip of the Arabian peninsula. Qatar is to the north-west; Saudi Arabia to the west and south; Oman to the south-east and north-east (*see map pp270-71*). No other emirate can match Dubai for its commercial vitality and levels of customer service, and yet the enlightened tourist will find time to explore the wider UAE's tapestry of sun-drenched beaches, cool mountain escapes and bustling cities rich with cultural experiences. Drive south along the coast from Dubai for a little under two hours to reach the capital, **Abu Dhabi** (*see p209*), or head briefly north into the chaos of **Sharjah** (*see p222*) to discover unexpected pockets of quiet reflection. Adventure awaits you further north still, in the wild reaches of **Ras Al Khaimah** (*see p229*), while superb snorkelling abounds along **Fujairah** and the east coast (*see p234*).

A challenge posed by old Arabia to would-be explorers is its continuing lack of public transport. Buses are as cramped as they are economical. There are no trains whatsoever. Nonetheless, the government's determination to build smooth efficient highways is paying off. Our advice if heading out of Dubai is to hire a 4x4 for the short-term (for further information, *see p244; see also p221* **Four by four play**) and enjoy your new-found freedom.

Coast to coast UAE: from **Abu Dhabi** on the Arabian Gulf, to the tip of the Indian Ocean.

The UAE

Abu Dhabi

From island-hopping to Iranian souks to intimate dining, Abu Dhabi boasts seductive weekend escapes.

Few regions can claim to have undergone such fundamental change over the past 50 years as the emirate of Abu Dhabi. Even well into the 1950s the largest of the UAE's seven emirates (roughly twice the size of Belgium) was little more than a barely populated stretch of desert, home to a clutch of nomadic Bedouin tribes and several sparse villages. The emirate's island capital, also called Abu Dhabi, then boasted little more than small-scale agricultural systems and a collection of traditional *barasti* (palm-frond) huts, synonymous with the austere Bedouin lifestyle. Only 30 years ago the city still lacked proper roads and a reliable supply of electricity. Today it's a powerhouse of the Arab world, perched atop vast oil reserves.

FROM PEARLS TO BLACK GOLD

The Ban Yas Bedouin tribe settled Abu Dhabi in the 1760s, recognising that the island offered good fishing and stood as a natural stronghold. They dubbed the region Abu Dhabi ('Father of the Gazelle') and would thereafter lead a largely unchanged existence for nearly 200 years. Legend tells that the city owes its unorthodox name to gazelle tracks found by a wandering party of Bedouin hunters. The nomads followed the tracks into a shallow inlet of the sea to discover they emerged again on the shore of the facing island and ended at a spring of fresh water. They quickly returned to their base in the Liwa oasis and reported this to their leader, Sheikh Dhiyab Bin Isa, who decreed that the island should thereafter be known as Abu Dhabi in honour of the auspicious find.

The discovery of a fresh-water well encouraged the ruling Al Nahyan family to relocate from their home in Liwa to Abu Dhabi, securing the city's first steps on its rise to prominence. And the good times continued through the 1800s, as residents grew prosperous from a seemingly endless supply of pearls found off Abu Dhabi's lengthy coastline. But if pearl cultivation was to propel Abu Dhabi into pole position as the richest and most important emirate at the beginning of the 1900s, it would also serve as the city's (temporary) downfall. When a worldwide recession decimated the pearl market in the 1930s, the city fell into a period of steady decline. By the end of the decade it had fallen far enough to be considered the poorest of the emirates, forcing potentate Sheik Shakhbut bin Sultan to investigate other potential sources of revenue. Somewhat fortuitously, he granted drilling rights to the British – who had been present in the region since 1892 in the role of protectorate – and the search for oil began. In 1958 huge offshore oil reserves were found; Abu Dhabi became the first of the Gulf States to export oil in 1962, earning an estimated $70 million per year that decade from black gold alone. Today, roughly two million barrels of oil are exported around the globe every 24 hours. Current estimates suggest this will continue for the foreseeable future.

The British left the Gulf region in 1971 and the seven factional emirates united to form the UAE, declaring Abu Dhabi to be the provisional capital. Sheikh Zayed Al Nahayan was welcomed as the new state's first president and has been elected every five years since. In 1996 the word 'provisional' was dropped from Abu Dhabi's title, making it the official, permanent capital city.

THE CITY TODAY

The modern city of Abu Dhabi is essentially unhurried, a proud, reserved place set by the clear waters of the Arabian Gulf. Wide boulevards are lined with trees that belie its desert origins, running through a 20th-century grid-based traffic system amid clusters of high-rise blocks. A beautiful corniche runs the length of the city, curled between the coast and the less-than-picturesque highway that stretches on to Dubai. There is an oddly engaging range of finely manicured – and often statue-bedecked – roundabouts, a liberal scattering of fountains, and more green than you'll find anywhere in the UAE bar the Garden City of Al Ain (*see p220*).

And yet there's a feeling of constant flux that underpins this conservative capital. Roadworks and building sites surround most junctions and city blocks. Even the corniche sits in the shadow of the new highway project, well underway at the time of writing. Such signs of change are hardly surprising, given the entire city has risen from nothing in just 30 years.

Although it's the capital, the city of Abu Dhabi is a lot smaller – and far more parochial – than its famous neighbour Dubai. Whereas

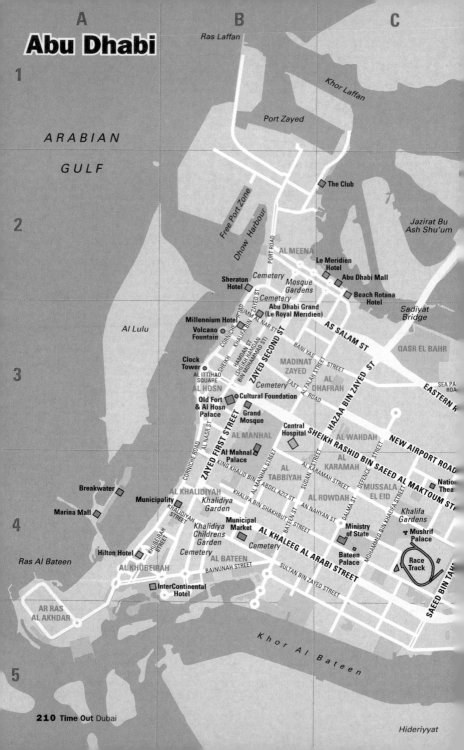

Abu Dhabi

A
B
C

1

Ras Laffan

Khor Laffan

ARABIAN

Port Zayed

GULF

Jazirat Bu
Ash Shu'um

2

The Club

Free Port Zone

Dhow Harbour

Port Road

AL MEENA

Le Meridien
Hotel

Cemetery

Abu Dhabi Mall

Sheraton
Hotel

Mosque
Gardens

Beach Rotana
Hotel

Cemetery

Sadiyat
Bridge

Abu Dhabi Grand
(Le Royal Meridien)

AS SALAM ST

QASR EL BAHR

Al Lulu

Millennium Hotel

Volcano
Fountain

BANI YAS

MADINAT
ZAYED

3

Clock
Tower

AL
DHAFRAH

SEA PA

EASTERN R

Cemetery

AL ITTIHAD
SQUARE

East

AL HOSN

ROAD

Cultural Foundation

Old Fort
& Al Hosn
Palace

Grand
Mosque

Central
Hospital

SHEIKH RASHID BIN SAEED AL MAKTOUM ST

AL WAHDAH

NEW AIRPORT ROAD

Corniche Road

AL MANHAL

Al Mahnal
Palace

King Khalid Bin

AL
TABBIYAH

AL
KARAMAH

National
Thea

Breakwater

AL KHALIDIYAH

Municipality

Khalidiya
Garden

AL ROWDAH

MUSSALA
EL EID

Marina Mall

Khalidiya
Market

AL KHALEEG AL ARABI STREET

Khalifa
Gardens

4

Hilton Hotel

Khalidiya
Childrens
Garden

Municipal
Market

Cemetery

Ministry
of State

Mushrif
Palace

Ras Al Bateen

AL KHUBEIRAH

AL BATEEN

Bainunah Street

Bateen
Palace

Race
Track

SAEED BIN TA

InterContinental
Hotel

AR RAS
AL AKHDAR

Khor Al Bateen

5

210 Time Out Dubai

Hideriyyat

the oil has all but run dry in Dubai, which has opened its doors in a bid to boost its coffers with tourist dollars, Abu Dhabi's vast reserves have allowed it to remain unashamedly Arabic. The past few years have seen a noticeable effort to attract tourists, with international-standard hotels and facilities, but at its heart this remains a traditional Middle Eastern city. And, while Abu Dhabi is liberal by Arabic standards, it is advisable to watch your behaviour even when passing through. Overt drunkenness and lasciviousness should be confined to private places, and revealing outfits are best avoided. Gone are the days when such things would result in jail time, but too much skin on show will still attract slack-mouthed stares from pretty much everyone you meet.

Sightseeing

Unable to dazzle tourists with the glitz of neighbouring Dubai, Abu Dhabi offers a quiet charm all of its own. Whether lazing on a private beach, stretching your legs in an oasis of greenery or exploring the unique arrangement of islands off the emirate's northern coast, the capital boasts inspirational sights aplenty – if you know where to look.

Just east of Abu Dhabi you'll find **Al Maqtaa Fort**, next to Al Maqtaa Bridge on the Airport Road. Now some 200 years old, the fort was originally built to keep bandits away from the city's riches. Another fortification to have witnessed great change is **Qasr Al Husn**, or the White Fort, which stands on the corner of Khalid Bin Waleed and Al Nasr Streets (map p210 B3). Built at the end of the 1700s, it once served as the official residence of the rulers of Abu Dhabi but is now open to the public.

Residents will tell you that Abu Dhabi is the cultural heart of the UAE, and the **Cultural Foundation** takes pride of place. The only facility of its kind in the region, it hosts temporary art exhibitions and local performances between visits from international artistes; expect dinner theatre, amateur dramatics and the occasional touring ballet group. For other live entertainment, try the **Al Raha Theatre** (02 556 0176). Opened in 2003, it's one of the most sophisticated – and, at Dhs81 million, most expensive – auditoriums in the Middle East.

For further insights into the rapid transformation of the UAE, culture-junkies can sneak a glimpse of the past at the **Dhow Harbour**, still worked by doughty craftsmen, and the **Heritage Village**, a faithful representation of a small nomadic camp. A less interactive but fairly comprehensive account of Abu Dhabi's oil-based boon can be had at the **Petroleum Exhibition**. But arguably the most accurate portrayal of modern Abu Dhabi's ambitions can be told by the new Kempinski Hotel, known to locals as the **Conference Palace Hotel** (map p210 A4). The entire left side of the breakwater has been taken up for the past few years with the construction of this enormous complex. Scheduled to be completed by the end of 2004, the Conference Palace Hotel will become the region's (nay world's) second seven-star hotel. Built to accommodate heads of state and high-level international conferences, its first major event will be the 2004 meeting of the Gulf Cooperation Council. Rumour abounds that it will match the magnificence of Dubai's Burj Al Arab, with a more authentic Arabian flavour. Stop by to decide for yourself.

Arabia is famous worldwide for its racing thoroughbreds, its ancient bloodlines and the passion with which the Emirati people hold the equestrian arts. The breeding of winning horses is a serious business and the **Golf & Equestrian Club** (02 445 5500, map p210 C4) holds races every Sunday from November to April. In a surprisingly efficient use of space, there is a par-70 golf course located within the racetrack, which closes two hours before the racing begins. Green fees for 18 holes are Dhs230. Less prestigious but far more accommodating is the **Airport Golf Club** (02 575 8040), an 18-hole sand course chiselled into the land alongside the airport and open to anyone – even transit passengers with a few hours to kill.

While it's no Paris, the city also boasts a surprisingly decent network of parks. Slap bang in the centre of the city is **Capital Gardens** (map p210 B3), a delightful assortment of manicured lawns gathered around a central pond – known to erupt into aquatic action whenever the mood takes it. Refreshments come courtesy of vending machines and a small cafeteria. Be prepared to pay a dirham to get in, should you be able to get the little man's attention.

The **New Corniche** park (map p211 D4), found on the east side of the island, is a haven for birdwatchers and anglers. Picnic tables are popular on warm winter evenings, while it's always well lit and clean. **Khalidiya Garden** (map p210 B4) doesn't have a cafeteria but does offer vending machines and billiard-table-like lawns. For a quiet stretch, the **Old Airport Garden** (map p211 F4), next to the ice-skating rink, is far from the madding crowd, has swings for the kids and is beautifully ornamental.

Trainspotter types might even fancy a gander at the largest flagpole in the world (map p210 A4), which currently resides at the end of Abu Dhabi's breakwater.

Abu Dhabi's **Airport Road**.

Cultural Foundation

Opposite Etisalat building, Airport Road (02 619 5223). **Open** 8am-2pm, 5-9.30pm Sat-Thur; 5-8pm Fri. **Admission** varies. **Map** p210 B3.

This vast centre for the arts is proof of a very real desire to stimulate artistry in a land where so much energy is put into making cold hard cash. As you might expect from a building with such a noble purpose, there's a hushed atmosphere throughout the network of corridors and arched courtyards. The summer months excluded, the Foundation fills its lecture halls with residents drawn to international acts, primarily musicians but speakers and actors too. The Foundation publishes a wealth of Islamic texts and is home to the National Archives.

Dhow Harbour

Al Bateen. **Admission** free. **Map** p210 B4.

A step back into the ancient Arabic world of ship-building, the famous dhow harbour offers an intriguing look at the maritime skills all but lost to the modern gulf region. It's a hive of activity, and when not too busy the craftsmen are (in the most part…) happy to talk about their work and allow photographs of the crafts they are working on.

Heritage Village

Behind the Abu Dhabi Exhibition Centre, Mussafah Road (off Airport Road) (no phone). **Open** 8.30am-5pm daily. **Admission** free. **Map** p211 E4.

A faithful representation of the small nomadic camps typical of the Bedouins who roamed the land before the oil boom, the village is a hands-on attempt to show what life was like a century ago. Make rope

from date-palm husks, drink the terribly pungent Arabic coffee, and even ride on a camel. On odd occasions there are demonstrations of ancient crafts and farming, while on Fridays you can watch falcons swoop to their waiting handlers. A traditional (in all but price) souk sells a range of tourist mementos.

Petroleum Exhibition

Corniche Road East, near Volcano Fountain (02 626 9715). **Open** 7am-2pm Sat-Wed. **Admission** free. **Map** p210 B3.

Although it's a rather dry account of the region's rise from a pearl- to oil-rich region, the Petroleum Exhibition is nevertheless the most comprehensive account in the city of how Abu Dhabi transformed itself from a small desert hamlet into one of the world's largest oil producers.

Beaches & islands

If you crave an escape from urban Abu Dhabi, almost every hotel in the city has its own private stretch of shoreline. Abu Dhabi boasts several public beaches too and, unlike in other emirates, they're off limits to vehicles so you won't have to dodge Pajeroo every few minutes or suffer overly loud car stereos. There are countless scenic if rugged stretches around the peninsular (near the Khalidiya Palace Hotel and up past the InterContinental Hotel) without facilities like changing rooms and shops. Otherwise, the best beach in town is **Al Raha**, easily the most convenient in terms of amenities and refreshments. For a little more exclusivity,

The UAE

Take up Gulfing: get out on the water.

women can avoid the male of the species altogether at **Al Dana Ladies' Beach**.

There is no need for the more adventurous tourist to stop at the shore, however. Abu Dhabi is unique among the UAE in its wealth of islands. Over 200 of them lie just off the coast, in varying sizes and levels of inhabitation. Small wonder that hopping from island to island is one of the emirate's more popular pastimes. If you don't own a boat you'll need to hire one – with driver – from a hotel beach club. This is the safer option in any case, as the water is dangerously shallow in areas and any would-be captain must be able to navigate the treacherous dredged channels.

The rather large island opposite the Corniche is **Lulu Island** (map p210 A3), a manmade lump that's famous to date for having been built with no real purpose in mind. Depending on what you read, it is destined to become a Fun Island theme park, a private residential island for Sheikh Zayed himself, or an entertainment complex. It is also due to be linked to Abu Dhabi by way of bridges and tunnels, but nothing of substance had arisen at the time of writing. To enjoy this unfathomable island in the meantime, make use of the private beach owned by the Abu Dhabi Grand Hotel (*see p219*) for Dhs50 per day (Dhs75 at weekends).

Slightly further out is **Sa'diyat Island** (map p211 D1), a popular destination for overnight and weekend trips. The island is home to basic facilities in the form of boat moorings, chalets

and an entertainment hall. It's commonly used as a base for various water sports, including jet-biking and water-skiing.

Motor about 5 kilometres (3 miles, or some ten minutes) south of Abu Dhabi and you'll come to **Futaisi Island**, an inhabited but private island some 40 square kilometres (15 square miles), owned by Sheikh Hamad Bin Hamdan Al Nayan. Home to old quarries from where stone for Abu Dhabi's forts was once dug, the island is now being developed as a tourist retreat and nature reserve.

West of Abu Dhabi is **Sir Bani Yas Island**, home to a nature reserve and conservation programmes dedicated to preserving indigenous animals. Security is enforced and visits can only be made on organised tours.

There are many other small, uninhabited bits of green dotted out to sea but within easy reach of the city. Popular outcrops include Bahraini, Cut and Horseshoe, but all are good for a day's exploring and secluded sun-soaking. You'll often find a cluster of windsurfers taking brief respite on Surf Reef, gathering themselves amid the swirling offshore breezes.

Al Dana Ladies' Beach

Just past the Hilton Hotel, Corniche Road (02 665 0129). **Open** noon-6pm Sat-Wed; 10am-6pm Thur, Fri. **Admission** Dhs10; parking Dhs5. **Map** p210 A4. Besides boasting a man-free environment, Al Dana beach offers a cafeteria and swimming pool. It is typically open to dusk (around 6pm).

Al Raha Beach

Past Umm Al Nar roundabout. **Admission** free.
A clean and relatively recent beach development,
Al Raha is one of the city's favourite sun traps. A
small section is cordoned off for women only, while
the rest is free to all. A small cafeteria sells snacks
and soft drinks.

Where to eat & drink

The finer bars and restaurants of Abu Dhabi
are to be found almost exclusively within the
city's premier hotels. While this causes several
eateries to suffer from a lack of character, it
does guarantee a certain quality of food and
service, and means that alcohol is available.

Art Cauldron

Al Falah Street, opposite Navy Gate (02 644 4309).
Open noon-4pm, 6pm-midnight daily. **Main courses**
Dhs30-Dhs45. **No credit cards. Map** p210 C3.
Not located in a hotel – and therefore not able to
serve alcohol – this bohemian basement hideaway
has a lot of atmosphere, great decor and an inventive international menu. Portions are huge, and
ingredients and service top-notch. We particularly
recommend the penne contadina, served in a delicious sun-dried tomato sauce.

Al Fanar

*Abu Dhabi Grand Hotel (Le Royal Meridien), Khalifa
Bin Zayed Street (02 674 2020).* **Open** 6-11am,
12.30-3pm, 7.30-11pm daily. **Main courses** Dhs40-
Dhs60. **Credit** AmEx, DC, MC, V. **Map** p210 B3.
Abu Dhabi's only revolving restaurant is a fine dining emporium which offers stunning views over the
city. The regularly-changing gourmet menus are
well planned and executed, making the Al Fanar the
ideal place for a multi-course formal meal. It's also
famous for lavish, laid-back Friday brunches with
unlimited champagne.

The Fishmarket

*InterContinental Hotel, Bainunah Street (02 666
6888).* **Open** 12.30-3pm, 7.30-11pm daily. **Main
courses** Dhs50-Dhs100. **Credit** AmEx, MC, V.
Map p210 A4.
One of our favourite restaurants in Abu Dhabi, the
Fishmarket has perfected the art of pick-your-own-
ingredients dining. Choose your fish, your sauce and
your style of cooking and get ready for fun.

Jazz Bar

Hilton Hotel, Corniche Road (02 681 1900). **Open**
7.30pm-1am daily. **Main courses** Dhs50-Dhs65.
Credit AmEx, DC, MC, V. **Map** p210 A4.
The venue is stylish, the service super-friendly, the
food classy contemporary and the entertainment
upbeat. The Jazz Bar is also conveniently positioned
next to a club, so if you fancy a little post-dinner
dancing and schmoozing you're in business. Tables
cannot be pre-booked, so unless you arrive early
expect to be sipping cocktails by the bar while you
wait (highly recommended).

Maharaja

*Le Meridien Hotel, north end of Sheikh Zayed Second
Street (02 644 6666).* **Open** 12.30-3.30pm, 7pm-
midnight Sun-Fri. **Main courses** Dhs40-Dhs90.
Credit AmEx, DC, MC, V. **Map** p210 C2.
An evening trip to Maharaja is a massive pleasure
from start to finish, the near-ultimate in spicy dining. The menu is not vast, but the dishes are so alluring and exotic that you will either feel frustrated or
order too much. The leg of lamb is beautifully tender, and the saag apki pasand is the most exciting
thing to happen to spinach since Popeye.

Al Mawal

Hilton Hotel, Corniche Road (02 681 2773).
Open 12.30-3.30pm, 7.30pm-2.30am daily. **Main
courses** Dhs40-Dhs70. **Credit** AmEx, DC, MC, V.
Map p210 A4.
Pay an evening visit to Al Mawal and take an
exhaustive culinary journey through Lebanese cuisine. A superb and enormous spread of hot and cold
mezze is on hand for starters, and should be followed
up by lamb chops and kebabs grilled to perfection,
making sure that you always leave this place with
a smile on your face.

Prego's

*Beach Rotana Hotel, next to Abu Dhabi Mall, north
end of 9th Street (02 644 3000).* **Open** noon-3pm,
7-11pm daily. **Main courses** Dhs50-Dhs80. **Credit**
AmEx, DC, MC, V. **Map** p210 C2.
Prego's is more trattoria than stuffy Italian eaterie,
and offers a variety of different areas to sit and eat,
including an elegant outdoor terrace. The food is
happily unpretentious, unfussy and damn tasty to
boot and the wine list is excellent. Pizza dough is
flamboyantly thrown into rounds in front of you,
topped with goodies and cooked fresh in the special
wood-burning oven.

Rodeo Grill

*Beach Rotana Hotel, next to Abu Dhabi Mall, north
end of 9th Street (02 644 3000).* **Open** 12.30-
3.30pm, 7-11pm daily. **Main courses** Dhs60-Dhs80.
Credit AmEx, MC, V. **Map** p210 C2.
Rodeo Grill is an upmarket restaurant with all the
trimmings. It offers American-style food with a large
serving of class, and if it's meat you're after, RG
delivers some of the finest in town. Start with beef
tartare with a dollop of Iranian caviar, take in a
dreamily tender fillet and finish off with chocolate
mud pie with bourbon – enough to fell even the
toughest of tough cowboys.

El Sombrero

Sheraton Hotel, Corniche Road (02 677 3333).
Open noon-3.30pm, 7pm-midnight daily. **Main
courses** Dhs40-Dhs65. **Credit** AmEx, DC, MC, V.
Map p210 B2.
This classy modern take on the traditional cactus-
and-sombrero-draped Mexican diner serves excellent, smartly assembled food. It's a warm, intimate,
pastel-coloured space, low-lit by pretty star lamps
and filled with elegant Latino strumming from the

The UAE

Vasco's: Med chefs at the Hilton.

in-house band. The salt-rimmed Margaritas and punchy spiced prawns sautéed with tequila are particularly worthy of mention.

Vasco's

Hilton Hotel, Corniche Road (02 681 1900). **Open** noon-3pm, 7-11pm daily. **Main courses** Dhs40-Dhs60. **Credit** AmEx, DC, MC, V. **Map** p210 A4.
Vasco's is a revelation: it is without question one of Abu Dhabi's finest restaurants. The decor is nautical, with lots of portholes and Navy trappings on show. The cooking is a blend of European cooking styles and produce with Asian herbs, spices and additions, and the service is easily among the best in the city.

The Wok

Crowne Plaza, Hamdan Street (5th Street) (02 621 0000). **Open** noon-4pm, 7-11pm daily. **Main courses** buffet Dhs95. **Credit** AmEx, DC, MC, V. **Map** p210 B3.
The Wok runs different buffet themes every night but the format remains the same – Dhs95 for as much food and drink as you can safely consume in one go. Unlike a number of other eat-and-drink offers the staff are only too keen for you to take advantage, suggesting extra dishes and leaving uncorked bottles close at hand. Not the finest eaterie in Abu Dhabi but for a well-lubricated evening with food to fill the space between drinks it's ideal.

Nightlife

Though the population in Abu Dhabi is predominantly Arabic, there is a fairly lively Western expat scene centred on a number of

bars that seem to take it in turns to be this week's must-be-seen-in venue. These are found in the plethora of world-class hotels to which the city is home; as is the case in Dubai, Islamic law forbids the sale of alcohol outside of these establishments, with the exception of certain clubs and off-licences – where you need a licence to shop.

Although this would seem to be a fairly restrictive set-up, the city has enough good bars and clubs to keep the nightlife scene varied, if not especially exciting. After a few months in town you'll know everyone, and even the short-stay visitor will be made to feel more than welcome.

a.m.p.m.

InterContinental Hotel, Bainumah Street (02 692 5214). **Open** 5pm-2am Sat-Tue; 5pm-4am Wed, Thur; 5pm-2am Fri. **Admission** free. **Credit** MC, V. **Map** p210 A4.
Chrome-wrapped and ultra-modern in design, this smart-looking DJ palace ultimately suffers from an abject lack of crowd activity. The music is as lively as it's loud, but there are often more people in the DJ booth than on the dancefloor. A good night is to be had if you can bring the atmosphere with you.

La Bodega

Zakher Hotel, Umm Al Nar Street (02 627 5300). **Open** 6pm-2.30am daily. **Admission** free. **Credit** AmEx, MC, V. **Map** p210 B3.
A really rather good Filipino bar, La Bodega is home to an enthusiastic band, even by Filipino standards, and an equally expressive Filipino crowd. Entertaining but dark and crowded, there's not

much room for conversation and no chance of a quiet beverage; you may find the regular clientele a little too welcoming.

Captain's Arms

Le Meridien Village, Le Meridien Hotel, north end of Sheikh Zayed Second Street (02 644 6666). **Open** noon-1am daily. **Admission** free. **Credit** AmEx, DC, MC, V. **Map** p210 C2.

A loosely themed English bar, with an even looser nautical side-theme, this slightly dual-personality pub sees maritime memorabilia hanging on the walls alongside the odd piece of sports equipment. Punters typically head outside to drink under the stars and join fellow revellers milling around Le Meridien Village (*see p218*). The guests are as eclectic as the decor, ranging from pipe-smoking jumper wearers to the younger alcopop crowd.

Harvesters

Sands Hotel, Sheikh Zayed Second Street (02 633 5335). **Open** noon-2am daily. **Admission** free. **Credit** MC, V. **Map** p210 B3.

As English as a joke about your mother-in-law and just as old-fashioned, this no-frills basement bar is famous for its live bands. It's a good option to kick off the weekend, but a general lack of atmosphere on weeknights means you are likely to end up listening to pony-tailed men in leather waistcoats talk about motorbikes.

Hemingway's

Hilton Hotel, Corniche Road (02 681 1900). **Open** noon-midnight Sat-Wed, Fri; noon-1am Thur. **Admission** free. **Credit** AmEx, DC, MC, V. **Map** p210 A4.

The best ladies' night in Abu Dhabi is held here every Tuesday, when women of all ages drink their fill for free and men of but one objective don't. The busy bar delivers a great atmosphere most nights of the week and many bar-hoppers will circulate between the Jazz Bar next door and Tequiliana, the Hilton's entertaining but cheerfully blasé cattle-market nightclub.

Heroes

Crowne Plaza Hotel, Hamdan Street (5th Street) (02 621 0000). **Open** noon-1.30am Sat-Mon, Wed, Thur; noon-2.30am Tue, Fri. **Admission** free. **Credit** AmEx, DC, MC, V. **Map** p210 B3.

That it's the unofficial HQ of the Abu Dhabi Rugby Club should give some insight into the ambience of this sports-themed American diner. With good pub grub and matches shown reliably on big TVs, even the occasional buffeting by a very large man with masking tape round his ears can be forgiven.

Rock Bottom Café

Al Diar Capitol Hotel, Meena Street (02 678 7700). **Open** 9pm-3am daily. **Admission** free. **Credit** MC, V. **Map** p210 B2.

Long gone are the days when people shoehorned themselves into this faux-American diner to drink cocktails until they fell over. Now it's an altogether

quieter affair in terms of clientele, if not live music, where volume is often used to fill the gap between talent and skill. Ever-popular with those who don't want to go home but have run out of options, RBC can give you a good night out — but only if by 'good' you mean 'wasted'.

Sagram

Emirates Plaza Hotel, between Hamdan & Meena streets (02 672 2000). **Open** 7.30pm-2.30am daily. **Admission** free. **Credit** AmEx, MC, V. **Map** p210 B3.

A lick of paint wouldn't go amiss in this Indian club. But if the venue is showing its age, the entertainment is nevertheless spot on. Traditional dancing and music, expertly performed and lapped up by an eager crowd, make for an eye-opening night out. Worth it for the social experience, if not the beer.

Shopping & souks

The twin colossi of the **Abu Dhabi** and **Marina Malls** dominate Abu Dhabi's modern shopping scene; the similar-sized American-style shopping centres offer quick and easy food courts, cinemas and a range of wares from domestic goods to designer labels.

But by far the most interesting (and hectic) shopping experience in the capital is at the **old central souk** and **new central souk** (map p210 B3). They are your prime source of more traditional Arabic knick-knacks and the usual (suspect) range of Celvin Kline and Adidos clothing. Expect to find cheap shoes, bags, clothes and toys. You name it, it's here – and it's not expensive if you haggle like a demon (never pay more than Dhs70 for a fake Rolex). A bridge links the two markets, running between Hamdan (5th) and Khalifa streets. Over 500 shops and stalls open at seemingly random times between 8am and 11pm, depending on the enthusiasm of the owners. Most shops will appear rather dingy and dirty on the outside, and also on the inside, but there are plenty of bargains to be found by the discerning shopper. Far more predictable is the afternoon siesta, ensuring that all trade stops between 1.30pm and 4pm. A fire in 2003 destroyed a significant part of the old souk and rumours abound that the area will soon be demolished to make way for a modern air-conditioned marketplace. Abu Dhabi will lose a treasured part of its past if the modernists have their way.

It's also worth visiting the **Iranian souk** (map p210 B2), found next to Port Zayed. Goods fresh off the boats from Iran arrive every three or four days: on sale are all manner of Iranian carpets, ornaments, terracotta trinkets and the like. Haggling is seen as a sport in these parts and you're likely to indulge in a round as much to pass the time as to procure bargains.

For a taste (and smell) of authentic Arabic life, you should pay a trip to the **fish**, **meat and produce souk**, also known as the **vegetable souk** (map p210 B3), nestling between Al Nasr and Istiqlal streets. It's a proper, stench-filled food market, and prices are lower than in a supermarket. Get there early (before 8am) if you want to buy decent produce – or simply enjoy the flurry of early-morning business conducted with typical Arabic volume and energy.

Abu Dhabi Mall

North end of 9th Street (02 645 4858). **Open** 10am-10pm Sat-Wed; 10am-11pm Thur. **Map** p210 C2.
Connected to the Beach Rotana Hotel, this shopping centre is not quite as large as its rival Marina Mall but home to a greater range of outlets. It features most designer brands such as Levi's and Guess, a cinema and a whole host of eateries.

Marina Mall

The Breakwater (02 681 2310). **Open** 10am-10pm Sat-Tue; 10am-11pm Wed, Thur; 2-10pm Fri. **Map** p210 A4.
The biggest mall in Abu Dhabi, Marina Mall boasts great views of both the sea and the city thanks to its commanding location on the breakwater. A favourite with young families, it offers a huge kid's playland, a cinema and economical one-stop shops like Ikea and Carrefour.

Where to stay

Because of the compactness of the city, Abu Dhabi's hotels are all conveniently placed near shops, restaurants and places of interest. There are no districts large enough to make a useful geographical distinction between one hotel and another, but tourists may opt to stay on the beach or in the city centre – and so listings are categorised as such below.

Room rates vary throughout the year, with the summer months (June to September) the best time to pick up a bargain because of the sudden hike in temperature. The rates shown here should be used only as a comparative guideline and all prices should be checked before booking. Hotel and government taxes of 16 per cent are added on top of these rates. Also note that these figures are rack rates; one call and a little bargaining can sometimes more than halve them.

Beach resorts

Beach Rotana

Next to Abu Dhabi Mall, north end of 9th Street (02 644 3000/fax 02 644 2111/www.rotana.com). **Rates** Dhs1,000-Dhs1,100 single/double; Dhs3,000-Dhs9,000 suite. **Credit** AmEx, DC, MC, V. **Map** p210 C2.

Perfectly placed adjacent to the expansive Abu Dhabi Mall, the Beach Rotana is up there with the best hotels Abu Dhabi has to offer. It's supremely elegant inside and out with its own beach, several quality restaurants and one of the capital's best bars in Polynesian franchise Trader Vic's. A recently opened beach club has enhanced the picturesque beach area of the hotel and is home to a fully equipped gym and health facilities.

Hilton

Corniche Road (02 681 1900/fax 02 681 1696/www.hilton.com). **Rates** Dhs600 single/double; Dhs1,100-Dhs3,200 suite. **Credit** AmEx, DC, MC, V. **Map** p210 A4.
A pretty hotel overlooking the Arabian Gulf, the Hilton positively demands that you relax. Guests can enjoy unlimited access to its beach club, which sports an outstanding private beach, spa and Jacuzzi. For the more active, superb leisure facilities include a split-level gym and cardio area. In the rooms, there is enough space to swing a cat, possibly two, should you be so inclined, and floor to ceiling mirrors make it feel very open.

InterContinental

Bainunah Street, Al Khalidya (02 666 6888/fax 02 665 6158/www.ichotelsgroup.com). **Rates** Dhs850-Dhs950 single/double; Dhs1,590-Dhs8,250 suite. **Credit** AmEx, DC, MC, V. **Map** p210 A4.
Best known for its beach marina and picturesque green surroundings, the InterContinental is one of the city's best hotels, with first-class facilities, sumptuous furnishings and an array of great outlets. Located slightly away from the main hustle and bustle of central Abu Dhabi, it is close enough to be convenient, but far enough away to ensure a relatively undisturbed beach lounging and great views.

Le Meridien

Tourist Club area, north end of Sheikh Zayed Second Street (02 644 6666/fax 02 645 5715/www.lemeridien.com). **Rates** Dhs1,200-Dhs1,300 single/double; Dhs2,500-Dhs6,000 suite. **Credit** AmEx, DC, MC, V. **Map** p210 C2.
On the other side of Abu Dhabi Mall from the Beach Rotana, Le Meridien is another international standard hotel, situated by the beach and centred on the tranquil Meridien Village, a stretch of greenery around which are congregated a variety of excellent al fresco food and beverage outlets. A recently opened spa centre is worth visiting for the traditional Turkish hammam treatment.

Sheraton

Corniche Road (02 677 3333/fax 02 672 5149/www.starwood.com/sheraton). **Rates** Dhs600-Dhs650 single/double; Dhs1,225-Dhs4,549 suite. **Credit** AmEx, DC, MC, V. **Map** p210 B2.
Despite its rather sandcastle-like appearance (rather reminiscent of Luke Skywalker's home in *Star Wars*), and dubious salmon colouring, the Sheraton is easily one of the capital's best hotels, with a great location and a number of world-class outlets. Alas,

the beach is closed until late 2004 while the government re-carves the Corniche, but after that it should have its own manmade lagoon.

City hotels

Abu Dhabi Grand (Le Royal Meridien)

Khalifa Bin Zayed Street (02 674 2020/fax 02 674 2552/www.lemeridien.com). **Rates** Dhs850-Dhs950 single/double; Dhs1,500-Dhs3,000 suite. **Credit** AmEx, DC, MC, V. **Map** p210 B3.

Soon to be re-branded as Le Royal Meridien, this plush 31-storey hotel resembles a city skyscraper in all but the revolving Al Fanar restaurant slowly sliding around the roof (*see p215*). It affords great views both over Abu Dhabi city centre and the islands dotted not far out to sea. As well as being close to everything worth doing, it's got a great Irish bar, PJ O'Reilly's, on the ground floor.

Al Ain Palace

Corniche Road (02 679 4777/fax 02 679 5713/ www.alainpalacehotel.com). **Rates** Dhs400-Dhs575 single/double; Dhs800 suite. **Credit** AmEx, DC, MC, V. **Map** p210 B3.

One of the oldest hotels in Abu Dhabi, and therefore one of the smallest, the inauspicious Ally Pally, as it is usually referred to, has a place in the heart of everyone who's lived in Abu Dhabi for a long period of time. This is due in no small part to its rambunctious bars and enjoyable no-frills eateries. Not grand or especially luxurious, it nonetheless offers inexpensive accommodation and a very good location in the shadow of the Abu Dhabi Grand (*see above*).

Crowne Plaza

Hamdan Street (5th Street) (02 621 0000/fax 02 621 7444/www.crowneplaza.com). **Rates** Dhs675-Dhs750 single/double; Dhs1400 suite. **Credit** AmEx, DC, MC, V. **Map** p210 B3.

Centrally located, the Crowne Plaza is in prime position to take advantage of both the shopping and beach-based activities that Abu Dhabi has to offer. The Roman-style rooftop pool is a must for all guests, as is the hugely popular basement bar Heroes (*see p217*).

Millennium Hotel

Khalifa Bin Zayed Street (02 626 2700/fax 02 626 0333/www.millenniumhotels.com). **Rates** Dhs890 single/double; Dhs1,990-Dhs12,000 suite. **Credit** AmEx, DC, MC, V. **Map** p210 B3.

From its chandelier dominated reception to the chunky brass doorknobs, the Millennium oozes quality. The luxury five-starrer overlooks both the Capital Gardens and the Corniche, with great views whichever side of the building you are situated on. Facilities include a functional – if not fantastic – lap pool, a fine sauna and gym and four classy bars and restaurants. The decor is a nice mix of dark woods and marble, while the staff carry out their business with competent but unobtrusive efficiency.

Millennium Hotel.

Novotel

Hamdan Street (5th Street) (02 633 3555/fax 02 634 3633/www.novotel.com). **Rates** Dhs500 single/double; Dhs800 suite. **Credit** AmEx, DC, MC, V. **Map** p210 B3.

Located on the busy Hamdan Street in between the rabble of shops and shopping centres that make up this part of Abu Dhabi, the Novotel is a pleasant, no-frills hotel within walking distance of the central souks and a world of shopping pleasures.

Sands

Sheikh Zayed Second Street (02 633 5335/fax 02 633 5766/www.sands-hotel.com). **Rates** Dhs850-Dhs950 single/double; Dhs1,500-Dhs5,000 suite. **Credit** AmEx, DC, MC, V. **Map** p210 B3.

Even though most hotels in Abu Dhabi are close to the main facilities, the Sands is perhaps the most centrally located, close to the two malls, the Corniche and the various souks. Landlocked, it doesn't have a beach, but there's an adequate pool on the roof and a small fitness centre. Not one of the most luxurious of the city's hotels, but easily one of the best value.

Resources

Hospitals

Al Noor *Khalifa Bin Zayed Street (02 626 5265).* **Map** p210 B3.
Central *Corner of Al Karamah & Bateen Streets (02 621 4666).* **Map** p210 B3.

The UAE

Internet

Street Net Café *Abu Dhabi Mall, north end of 9th Street (02 645 4141).* **Internet** Dhs15 per hr. No credit cards. **Map** p210 C2.

Police station

Police HQ *Sheikh Zayed First Street (02 446 1461).* **Map** p210 B4.

Post office

Central post office *East Road (02 621 5415).* **Open** 8am-8pm Sat-Wed; 8am-6pm Thur. **Map** p210 B2.

Tourist information

Ministry of Information & Culture *Near the police station, Airport Road (02 445 3000).* **Open** 7.30am-2pm Sat-Wed. **Map** p210 C4.

Getting there

By car

From Dubai, simply get onto Sheikh Zayed Road and keep on trucking in a straight line for 150km (95 miles); the closer you get the more roadsigns you'll see. The road turns into Airport Road as you enter Abu Dhabi.

By bus

Minibuses from Bur Dubai bus station cost Dhs20; there are no specific departure times, as the drivers will wait for the bus to fill before setting off (they are therefore usually rather cramped). They'll take you to the bus station in the heart of Abu Dhabi.

By taxi

Dubai to Abu Dhabi will cost you about Dhs220-Dhs250; pay the metered fare or agree a price beforehand. Contact Abu Dhabi taxis on 02 444 7787.

Al Ain

The second largest city in the emirate of Abu Dhabi, Al Ain is a great place for a short restorative break. Dubbed 'the garden city', it has flourished into an area of outstanding natural beauty thanks largely to Sheikh Zayed's personal commitment and massive forestation program. There is plenty to savour in this quiet retreat of tree-lined boulevards and low-rise buildings, including the UAE's **Natural History Museum** (Al Khubaisi, 03 761 2277); **Al Ain Museum** (Zayed Bin Sultan Street, 03 764 1595), the country's largest collection of historical artefacts; and the UAE's biggest zoo (**Al Ain Zoo and Aquarium**, near the traffic police HQ, Zoo roundabout, 03 782 8188).

Located about 160 kilometres (100 miles) east of Abu Dhabi and the same distance south-east of Dubai, Al Ain is a one and a half hour drive from both. There are also domestic and international flights to Al Ain International Airport (03 785 5555). The best time to visit is in the winter, when time can be spent exploring the ancient archaeological sites, the hot springs in the Jebel Hafeet mountains and the smelly but entertaining camel market.

Where to eat, drink & stay

Al Ain InterContinental

Near Al Ain Mall, Ernyadat Road (03 768 6686/ fax 03 768 6766/www.ichotelsgroup.com). **Rates** Dhs600 single/double; Dhs1,000-Dhs3,000 suite. **Credit** AmEx, DC, MC, V.

A sprawling complex that's a focal point of the Al Ain social scene in the evenings, the InterCon has a series of top-notch outlets and clean, functional rooms. Popular with families for its network of pools and laid-back attitude, this is a fine hotel indeed. For quality pick-your-own-ingredients dining, try the Fishmarket restaurant (open 12.30-3.30pm, 7.30-11pm Sun, Tue-Thur). Main courses range Dhs50-Dhs100; tuck into fresh seafood grilled with oyster, ginger and garlic sauces. Less fun but far classier is the Luce restaurant (open 12.30-3pm, 7.30-11pm daily), a sliver of Milanese chic reflected in the ultra-modern decor and discreet Luce branding. For a true gourmet pasta revelation, try the parpadelle bolognese made with duck mince.

Al Ain Rotana Hotel

Zayed Bin Sultan Street (03 754 5111/fax 03 754 5444/www.rotana.com). **Rates** Dhs700 single/ double; Dhs1,200-Dhs1,600 suite. **Credit** AmEx, DC, MC, V.

The low-rise Rotana boasts a stunning pool and modish, well turned-out rooms. Tennis courts, a well-stocked gym and fabulous massage facilities round off this, the poshest hotel in the city. Its popular eateries include Min Zaman (open 1-4pm, 8pm-12.30am daily). Main courses cost in the region of Dhs50; expect mountains of salad, a bakery's worth of bread, nutty houmous, salty vine leaves and moutabel, followed by fattoush and kibbeh. Also on hand is the popular Trader Vic's bar (open noon-1am daily, meals served 12.30-3pm, 7-11pm). Its winning French/Polynesian formula (main course average Dhs30-Dhs45) is delivered with gusto by the charming staff in a restaurant hung with South Sea paraphernalia. Get stuck into spicy nasi goreng, Singapore noodles, BBQ lamb ribs and the outstanding Trader Vic's Calcutta and coconut island curries.

Hilton Al Ain

Follow signs from city centre to Sarroj (03 768 6666/ fax 03 266 0000/www.hilton.com). **Rates** Dhs600-Dhs650 single/double; Dhs850 suite. **Credit** AmEx, DC, MC, V.

This good-value branch of the Hilton empire has large, comfy rooms equipped with balconies where you can take your time over a generous breakfast. Sink-in armchairs, bouncy beds, myriad satellite channels and speedy room service make it a good option if you'd rather spend a lazy weekend than go out on the town.

Four by four play

The Liwa area is famous – and rightly so – for being the region's ultimate off-road challenge. It is to desert driving what the Great Barrier Reef is to diving. It is a mecca, not just to UAE residents but also to adrenaline junkies the world over. Towering dunes and deep gullies combine with contoured peaks to create an unparalleled adventure playground. When your vehicle lifts you to the top of one of these peaks, the sheer size and magnitude of the Liwa region becomes apparent. The rippling dunes, still dark in the hazy morning light, take on the appearance of an enormous frozen sea stretching out before you.

Liwa sits at the very southern edge of the emirate of Abu Dhabi, about 40 kilometres (25 miles) from the Saudi border, and is effectively the edge of the infamous Rub Al Khali or Empty Quarter. This seemingly endless stretch of sand dunes on the rim of the Liwa oasis and extends east, south and west into Oman, Yemen and Saudi Arabia – with 974 square kilometres (370 square miles) of it in Saudi alone. The dune peaks can reach over 300 metres (1000 feet).

It used to take the Bedouin nine days to get from Liwa to Abu Dhabi – it now takes about three hours to drive. But you can still get a sense of the unbelievable hardships that life in the desert must have held when you stand at the top of a dune and see nothing but sand in every direction.

The secret to successful and safe desert driving is to know your vehicle and its limitations. An understanding of the signs of the desert is also key, but harder to come by – it's a treasure possessed only by the most experienced drivers. You will get stuck, you will get frustrated and, unless you are very careful, you will get lost. But you will also experience proper off-road desert driving. Exhilarating, scary and very challenging, this is not an area to be taken lightly – buried cars are occasionally unearthed by shifting sands.

Simple tips on sand driving

- Work on keeping up your momentum at all times – that's the secret.
- Reduce your tyre pressure by at least a third.
- Always park facing downhill – so that starting again is no problem.
- Stick to high-range 4-wheel drive, using low gears.
- Only shift into 4-wheel drive low-range when you expect particularly difficult driving or if you get stuck.
- Drive in convoy with at least one other vehicle; if one party gets into trouble, the other can tow or winch them out of it.
- Take a used track where possible – this minimises the destruction and disturbance of the desert.
- When descending a dune, keep in low gear and in a straight line.
- If you get stuck don't spin the wheels – get out your shovel and, after digging the wheels clear, put a mat or blanket under those wheels that have no traction. Rocking can also be used to ease you out of trouble.

Northern Emirates

From castle crags to drag-racing, the northern strip of the Arabian Gulf coast is the UAE's adventure playground.

The further north one goes, the more Dubai's glitz pales in the face of the stark, brutal beauty of old Arabia. The familiar cityscape merges with the urban sprawl of **Sharjah** and **Ajman**, until the desert asserts its authority once more and you arrive at the outer reaches of **Umm Al Quwain** and **Ras Al Khaimah**. It's not just the mountains and plains that appeal here. The northern emirates are wild: wild beaches, wild sports, wild people. Though small in area, this is great road-trip country.

Sharjah

The Dubai–Sharjah road boasts one of the most off-putting sights in the Emirates. Deeply unimaginative high-rise apartment blocks, surrounded by blowing sand in summer and flood water in winter, hardly constitute a welcome mat. Sharjah's insane traffic, confusing road system and bad signposting do little to stimulate the visitor either.

But hidden in the crowded city are some of the best museums and markets in the country. Consider **Al Hosn Fort**, the **Art Museum** and the **Arabian Wildlife Centre** at **Desert Park**: all are of an extremely high standard and suitable for all ages and nationalities. Ignore the naysayers, take a day away from Dubai's sparkle, and get stuck into some of the finest centres of Arab, Islamic and wildlife research in the world.

HISTORY

Sharjah's roots lie to the north of its modern geography, in and around what is now the emirate of **Ras Al Khaimah** (*see p229*), which replaced the ancient capital of Julphar as a local trading hub some time in the 17th century. Sharjah grew as a competing power to Ras Al Khaimah and things came to a head in 1814, when Sultan Ibn Saqr, a former Ras Al Khaimah ruler, seized Sharjah and declared it a separate sheikhdom. He then annexed Ras Al Khaimah to his new base following the sacking of the city by a British expedition in 1819.

Thus began a game of chess, in which Ras Al Khaimah would move in and out of Sharjah's fold several times. Sharjah became signatory to the 1820 General Treaty of Peace between the British and nine local Arab sheikhdoms. But while the British installed a garrison in the region and a political agent in Sharjah, different factions continued to feud. The British became more active, signing a treaty to create a six-month truce during the pearling season with the principal Sheikhs in 1835. This was renewed for ten years in 1843. In 1853, a 'perpetual maritime truce' was signed, giving the area the name 'Trucial Coast'. By 1893, the British had effectively turned the Trucial Coast into a protectorate, even though the British flag did not fly anywhere other than from its military bases and agents' buildings.

However, the back-and-forth swings of family politics did not end under British dominance; coups in Sharjah took place in 1951 and 1965 and there was an assassination only months after the British withdrawal in 1971. An attempted coup in 1987 was ended by consultation between the ruling families of all the emirates. Despite the intrigue, Sharjah grew rapidly from the 1960s onwards. It has become today a major trading hub and manufacturing base despite, or perhaps because of, the oil that has helped Abu Dhabi and Dubai to prosper. Sharjah's trading history still stands it in good stead today, though it has also been aided by investment from Saudi Arabia.

Sightseeing

Sharjah was crowned UNESCO cultural capital of the Arab world in 1998, and the area's reputation as a centre of artistic excellence goes beyond the United Arab Emirates, or even the Gulf area. Uninformed arty cynics might dispute the difficulty of earning such a title, but the emirate boasts no less than 15 museums (out of a current total of 21 throughout the UAE) and has grand plans for further contemporary galleries and workspaces. Several face onto **Arabic Calligraphy Square**, a haven of artistry that seems miles away from industrial Sharjah. It's also worth an educational stroll around the **Heritage Area**, a complex of old buildings and renovated structures clustered just a minute's walk from the Rolla Street taxi stand.

Archaeological Museum

Halwan District, off Cultural Square (06 566 5466). **Open** 9am-1pm, 5-8pm Sat, Mon-Thur; 5-8pm Fri. **Admission** free.

Sharjah's **Quran roundabout**, where giant scholars come to study.

This large museum presents local archaeology beautifully. Stretched across several halls full of audiovisual wonder, man's first and subsequent steps across the Arabian Peninsula are documented chronologically. Clear displays of finds from Sharjah's many Stone Age, Iron Age and Bronze Age sites sit alongside lovingly wrought models of the emirate's first houses. Touch-screen computers provide images from museum archives and educational games for children.

Art Museum

Al Shuwaiheyn, behind the bazaar, close to the waterfront (06 568 8222). **Open** 9am-1pm, 5-8pm Sat, Sun, Tue-Thur (Wed afternoon women & children only); 5-8pm Fri. **Admission** free.

Eighteenth-century paintings, documents and maps from the personal collection of the ruler of Sharjah sit here alongside occasionally awful abstract art. The permanent collection is brightened by an active programme of exhibition-exchange with international museums, and the museum is home to the Sharjah International Art Biennial, held in spring (usually April) every odd-numbered year. There is a handy coffee bar in the museum, and basement parking is available.

Desert Park & Arabian Wildlife Centre

Sharjah Airport Road (direction Al Dhaid), Interchange 9 (06 531 1999). **Open** 9am-6.15pm Sat-Wed, public holidays; 2-6.15pm Fri. Last tickets 5.30pm. **Admission** Dhs15; under-15s free. **No credit cards.**

This world-class educational and research facility houses Arabia's most important captive breeding centre for endangered species. There's an incredibly advanced public zoo in the Arabian Wildlife Centre, besides an innovative natural history museum (06 531 1411) and an excellent children's education park. More than 100 species of animal roam around the varied habitat re-creations, while in the vast indoor aviary thousands of birds swoop mere inches above your head.

Heritage Museum

Al Shuwaiheyn, between the waterfront & Al Hosn Avenue (Bank Street) (06 569 3999). **Open** 9am-1pm, 5-8pm Sat-Sun, Tue-Thur; 5-8pm Fri. **Admission** free.

Housed in the old courtyard home of the Al Naboodah family, the buildings are a fascinating example of traditional UAE architecture and include displays of old clothing and heritage items. For the modern-day equivalent, take in the nearby Al Arsah Souq, an alley packed with antiques and jewellery.

Al Hosn Fort

Al Hosn Avenue (Bank Street), Heritage Area (06 512 9999). **Open** 9am-1pm, 5-8pm Sat, Sun, Tue-Thur (Wed afternoon women & children only); 5-8.30pm Fri. **Admission** free.

Al Hosn Fort was built in 1820 by Sultan Ibn Saqr, the first of the Qawasim sheikhs (*see p227 and p230*) to make Sharjah his capital. The fort was the political centre of the emirate until it was demolished in 1969 to make way for the modern buildings that now typify the city; only two walls and a 12m (40ft)

The UAE

The past survives at **Al Hosn Fort**. *See p223*.

Walk west to the large defensive tower visible from Al Hosn Fort, turn north into Arabic Calligraphy Square and you'll find this intriguing museum. The galleries are filled with beautiful works by Arab, Persian and Turkish artists, while the calligraphy and ceramics studios host students developing their ideas in the cool of winter.

Shopping & souks

While a handful of large, pristine malls have emerged in recent years, Sharjah's traditional souks continue to thrive at the Ar-Ruba flyover end of the Corniche Road (and vice versa). Next to the Oil Supply Post sits the **fish souk** (open 5-11am), where dhows berth and offload their catch direct to around 50 fresh fish shops facing the quay on Khaled Lagoon.

On the opposite side of the road is the single-storey **vegetable souk**, with fruit and veg from around the world crammed up against more than 100 shopfronts. It's very popular with Sharjah's diverse community of residents but not as cheap as one might imagine, with six tangerines, for example, costing Dhs5. This is because, given the local climate, most of the produce is imported. Check the date stalls for superb produce from Iran, Iraq, Saudi Arabia and the UAE itself – a kilo (just over two pounds) of deliciously sticky Saudi dates will set you back just Dhs10.

On the same side of the corniche, taking up a large swathe of the road, is the fantastically comprehensive **plant souk**, and behind this flea market of flora lies the livestock souk (follow signs for 'Bird And Animal Market' on the Corniche Road), offering cows, sheep and goats from Somalia and Pakistan, as well as young bulls that will be fattened in Fujairah for fighting (or, more accurately, butting – *see p234*). With chickens running around and Bedouin boys driving pick-ups with goats in the back, this is a more accurate example of modern UAE country ways than any number of heritage museums.

From here, walk through to the poultry pushers of the **bird souk**. Another long, slim building, this souk is lined with shops selling every kind of bird imaginable – including pheasants, peacocks, baby ostriches, song birds and parrots. Be warned though: many birds are in the sort of cramped conditions that you may find unpleasant to witness.

tower were left standing. The original 19th-century structures were renovated in 1996, and the rest of the complex was rebuilt to its original design; the fort now houses a museum, with a series of exhibition rooms surrounding the central courtyard. Inside are weapons, coins, jewellery and information about the pearl trade of old.

Islamic Museum

Al Gharb, off Al Hosn Avenue (Bank Street), Heritage Area (06 568 3334). **Open** 9am-1pm, 5-8pm Sat, Sun, Tue-Thur; 5-8pm Fri. **Admission** free.
Along a narrow lane behind Arabic Calligraphy Square you'll find the old wooden door of Sharjah's single-storey Islamic Museum. This houses an important collection of rare Arabic manuscripts, a major Islamic mint exhibition featuring silver dinars and dirhams from the Abbasid and Umayyad periods (from the sixth century AD), plus archaeological artefacts from the Islamic era. Particularly fascinating are navigational instruments used by ancient Arabic seafarers and an extraordinary 'upside down' map of the world that was drawn 1,000 years ago by Sharif Al Idrisi.

Museum for Arabic Calligraphy & Ornamentation

Al Gharb, off Al Hosn Avenue (Bank Street), Heritage Area (06 568 3334). **Open** 9am-1pm, 5-8pm Sat, Sun, Tue-Thur; 5.30-8.30pm Fri. **Admission** free.

Blue Souk

Al Majaz, Corniche Road, close to Khaled Lagoon. **Open** 9am-1pm, 4-11pm Sat-Thur; 9am-noon, 4-11pm Fri. **No credit cards**.
Also known as Souk Al Markazi, the Blue Souk is set in a huge green space dotted with fountains, looking much like a cross between a European central

train station and a mosque – a perfectly atrocious example of Sharjah's modern, wedding cake-style architecture. The crème brûlée colours of the interior and fiddly wrought iron don't help to dispel the image, but you should be here to shop, not critique, especially as the souk is fully air-conditioned, allowing proper browsing even in the height of summer.

There are around 600 shops in the Blue Souk, making it the largest single wholesale and retail market for handicrafts and textiles in Arabia. It is not an Arab market in the true sense; the vast majority of goods sold are Indian in origin. And do not expect to find genuine antiques. If you are told that what you are looking at is over five years old, be very careful. But if you find a shopkeeper you are comfortable with sit down, drink tea, and bargain away to your heart's content.

There are, in effect, two identical souk buildings, connected by bridges. The ground floor of the building nearest the lagoon is mostly taken up with gold, textile, perfume and camera shops; the one furthest away sells ready-made clothes and electronics. Look out for wooden furniture from Jaipur in Rajasthan, Iranian and Pakistani carpets, and handmade textiles. Highest quality pure silk Nepalese pashminas should cost less than Dhs250 and you can get Indian pure wool pashminas for around Dhs90. One of the best bargains is a 1.5m-long (5ft) chain-stitched rug from Kashmir, which you should be able to pick up for less than Dhs150.

Sahara Centre
Al Nahda Street (06 531 6611). **Open** 10am-10pm Sat-Wed; 10am-11pm Thur; 2-11pm Fri. **Credit** MC, V.

Sharjah's contribution to the UAE's love of all things mall, the Sahara Centre is huge and snakelike: it curls along with hundreds of shops clinging to the first-floor insides. It has many of the shops one might find in Dubai, and, perhaps surprisingly, several Dubai doesn't (the excellent Shuh Shoes for example). But the real winner must be Adventureland on the second floor. This indoor fun park boasts Wacky Racer mini-dodgems (Dhs6), a Log Jam water ride (Dhs7.50), and even two indoor roller-coasters: one for teens (Dhs7.50) and one for children (Dhs6). Afterwards, stuff yourself silly at the food court.

Sharjah City Centre
Al Wahda Street (06 533 2626). **Open** 10am-10pm Sat-Thur (Carrefour 9am-midnight); 2-10pm Fri (Carrefour 9-11am, 1.30pm-midnight). **Credit** MC, V.

This mall has the same Lego-like colour and feel as Dubai City Centre (it's owned by the same company), without the variety of shops. Its Carrefour is similar to its counterparts in Dubai, and so huge it sells absolutely everything.

Souq Al Majarrah
Corniche Road, next to Masjid Jamila Mosque. **Open** 9am-1.30pm, 4-10.30pm daily. **No credit cards**.

Souk Al Majarrah is a gorgeous structure, with vaulted ceiling and Corinthian columns styled, in part, on the most beautiful souks of Damascus and Aleppo in Syria. The shops cater exclusively to Arab women's and men's fashions, notably *abayas* (cloaks), handbags, shoes and perfume. The only shop not selling some form of fashion item is Mujezat Al Shifa Honey (06 565 8707), where you

Blue Souk, Sharjah's shopping mecca. *See p224.*

The UAE

can pick up 500g of Afghani-Pakistani lotus honey for Dhs50. For those who don't subscribe to Viagra, royal jelly is Dhs30 for a 15g pot and ginseng is Dhs25 for 20g.

Where to eat, drink & stay

Coral Beach Hotel

Coral Beach roundabout, Beach Road (06 522 9999). **Rates** Dhs400 single/double. **Credit** MC, V.

With its coastline dominated by massive ports, it often feels like Sharjah isn't by the sea at all. The Coral Beach Hotel puts paid to that. A small and slightly cranky four-star, it has an excellent private beach that is actually a manmade cove. There's a large raised swimming pool overlooking the beach, a 'rockery' for children, slides and a circular 'bar' area (remember this is Sharjah, so no alcohol is served). A second pool is set right outside the hotel in reasonably extensive gardens.

Radisson SAS

Ahmed bin Dareish Square, Corniche Road (06 565 7777). **Rates** *Sept-Mar* Dhs350 single; Dhs450 double. *Apr-Aug* Dhs250 single/double. **Credit** MC, V.

The Radisson SAS may be getting on a bit, but its pyramidal blue glass and cream cladding hide what is still one of the loveliest (and largest) atriums in the world. The lobby has a gift shop that is, for some inexplicable reason, filled with Dubai tat, and an exorbitantly priced Cappuccino coffee shop (tea and coffee Dhs11.50; average meal Dhs38). But the whole atrium is filled with the calming noise of what lies inside – an indoor arbor, or as the hotel likes to call it, a 'tropical rain forest'. With that famous forest animal, the duck, waddling happily in its streams, a meal on the decking downstairs in the Calypso Café is charming, even if the food is standard hotel fare (fish and chips Dhs45; meze Dhs35). There's a very 1970s-looking beach, with wooden parasols dotted along a little curved bay.

Sharjah Rotana Hotel

Al Khaleej Square, Ar-Ruba flyover (06 563 7777). **Rates** Dhs500 single; Dhs600 double; Dhs700-Dhs800 suites; Dhs2,000 suite. **Credit** AmEx, MC, V.

A clean and functional four-star, the Sharjah Rotana is a proven respite from the maelstrom of Sharjah outside. The Al Dar Restaurant on the first floor serves decent Western cuisine such as sandwiches, salads and steaks, though the piped jazz music befits its plastic feel.

Resources

Hospitals

Kuwaiti Hospital *Kuwait Road (06 5242 111).*
Al Dhaid Hospital *Al Dhaid, 50km (30 miles) inland from Sharjah (06 882 2221).*
Al Zahra Private Hospital *Opposite the clock tower, Al Zahra Square (06 561 9999).*

Internet

Radisson SAS Hotel *Corniche Road (06 565 7777).* **Internet** Dhs30 per hr.

Police station

Traffic Police HQ *Abu Tina (06 554 1111).*

Post office

Central post office *By Municipality roundabout, Al Soor (06 572 2219).* **Open** 8am-8pm Sat-Wed; 8am-6pm Thur.

Tourist information

Sharjah Commerce & Tourism Development Authority *Off Arouba Road, towards the Corniche (06 556 6777/www.sharjah-welcome.com).* **Open** 7.30am-2pm Sat-Wed.

Essentials

It is illegal for women to wear clothes showing upper arms or too much leg, and to be in a car with someone who is not related, though this is mainly aimed at stopping prostitution. Alcohol is strictly illegal anywhere in Sharjah, including its enclaves on the east coast. Unlike Dubai, you cannot expect English to be spoken everywhere. It's clichéd but true: a few words in Arabic go a long way; *see p260.*

Getting around

Taxis in Sharjah are generally cheaper than in Dubai. Note, however, that they are unmetered, and we've had complaints of travellers being ripped off. No ride within Sharjah city should cost more than Dhs10. Note also that many drivers won't take you if they don't understand you. Delta Taxis (06 559 8598) does pick-ups.

Getting there

By car

Sharjah is clearly signposted on Dubai's major roads. The easiest option is to cross Garhoud Bridge and continue north straight along the freeway to Sharjah.

By bus

Transport buses leave from the Deira taxi stand near Al Nasr Square, whenever the bus is full (normally every 20-30 minutes; cost Dhs5. They'll stop anywhere en route to Rolla Square in Sharjah.

By taxi

From Dubai you can take any of the usual metered cabs at roughly Dhs20 from Deira, Dhs40 from Bur Dubai and Dhs60 from Jumeirah. However, if you get an unlicensed cab you can haggle for a cheaper price. Unfortunately, when returning you must use a Sharjah taxi; these tend to be older than their Dubai equivalents, unmetered, and driven by men who haven't learnt what indicators or brakes are for. Expect to pay around Dhs30 to travel back as far as Bur Dubai.

Ajman

The length of sand called Ajman Corniche is no major tourist pull unless you're sunning yourself in one of the resort hotels that line it, but if you're parched after a hard day's museum-hopping in Sharjah, Ajman has perfected the plastic-table-and-bottled-beer-only art of the eastern Arabian boozer. However, first it's time for a bit of a history lesson.

When the seafaring Qawasim tribe took control of the lower Gulf coast in the mid 18th century, the tiny coastal strip of Ajman fell under their sway. But soon after the British destruction of the Qawasim fleet at Ras Al Khaimah in 1819, the British declared Ajman independent, leaving power firmly entrenched in the hands of the Al Abu Khurayban clan of the An-Naim tribe. Ajman was signatory to British Trucial treaties of 1820, 1835, 1843 and 1853, and became subject to the Residency of the Persian Gulf in 1892.

Vestiges of this era are the several locally built *burj* (defensive towers) that dot the coast, and the large and well renovated 18th-century fort, now inland at the centre of the city – ask for **Dowar Al Hosn** or Al Hosn roundabout. Alternatively, at the roundabout before the Ajman Kempinski hotel, look for the Ajman Chamber of Commerce building on your right-hand side. Turn right here and continue straight over the next roundabout. The fort is on the left and the **Ajman Museum** it now houses has some fascinating material you won't find anywhere else in the emirates.

Fishing has always been the main industry in this 259 kilometre square (100 square miles) emirate; traditional fishing vessels can still be seen all along Ajman's coast. Ajman port has been transformed into a major dhow-building centre and an important dockyard, located on the northern side of the creek, only a few kilometres from the centre of town. But the truth is that, being without oil, Ajman has been largely dependent on federal money for its development since it joined the United Arab Emirates in 1971.

With the incorporation of hundreds of companies at Ajman Free Zone and Ajman Industrial Area, the population of the emirate has grown from around 80,000 in 1992 to around 125,000 in 2003. Indeed the expansion of Dubai, Sharjah and Ajman now means that the emirate is part of a coastal conurbation that starts at Jebel Ali in Dubai and ends at Ajman's northernmost border with Umm Al Quwain, a distance of around 100 kilometres (60 miles).

Many people now live in Ajman, but work in Sharjah or Dubai, as rents in Ajman are so cheap. Ajman has two inland enclaves in the Hajjar mountains, Masfut and Manama, on the Sharjah road that runs to the east coast, though they are little more than hamlets with nothing to tempt the tourist.

Ajman Museum

Al Hosn roundabout, Aziz Street, by Central Square (06 742 3824). **Open** times vary, phone to check. **Admission** Dhs4; Dhs2 under-7s. **No credit cards.** Displays depicting weird and wonderful medical and religious practices give a fantastic if eerie insight into life as it must have been led for centuries among the coastal Bedouin. It isn't a large collection, but it certainly delves deeper than most displays of so-called heritage. There is also a working wind tower (*see p25* **The world's first air-con**) in one corner of the fort, where one can sit beneath to feel the breeze it creates.

Where to eat, drink & stay

The latest addition to Ajman's resort culture is the five-star **Ajman Kempinski** (06 745 1555). Far from cheap (minimum around Dhs800), it still manages to get regular block bookings from German and Russian tour operators. Guests tend to stay within the hotel confines (there's little else to do in Ajman), but that does mean the hotel has some good restaurants, namely **Sabella's Trattoria & Pizzeria** and **Bukhara**, which has some great North Indian food. There is also a lovely veranda café, the 24-hour **Café Kranzler**, where you can sit out just metres from the sea.

Hai Tao is the Kempinski's Chinese outlet, but for an equally good yet cheaper meal (if in the considerably more basic surroundings of an old villa), try the **Blue Beach Restaurant** halfway down Ajman Corniche, on the opposite side of the road to the sea. The charming family running the place are from Shanghai, and specialise in food from that area (superb braised duck, Shanghai style, is Dhs45, but you can eat a lot cheaper if you want).

Close by is the four-star **Safir Dana Resort** (06 742 9999). The name is a slight misnomer because it doesn't actually have a private beach. Staff will, however, bring parasols and service to you on the public beach opposite from the Al Seef Café inside the hotel. Rooms in the Safir Dana Resort go for as low as Dhs100 a day, over three days, in low season. Call ahead and you can haggle on rates.

Ajman's first resort hotel was the **Ajman Beach Hotel** (06 742 3333; not to be confused with the Ajman Beach Resort, which is a restaurant and bar complex full of Russian and Chinese 'entertainers'). The Ajman Beach Hotel is expensive in high season and at weekends, because guests normally stay no longer than a few hours. A full night's sleep costs Dhs250 single and Dhs350 double including tax. The beach is uninspiring, but is otherwise fine if everywhere else is fully booked.

Resources

Tourist information

Ministry of Information & Culture *Near Kempinski Hotel, the Creek end of Arabian Gulf Street (06 744 4000/www.uaeinteract.com).* **Open** 7.30am-2pm Sat-Wed.

Getting there

By car

From Dubai, get on to Sharjah's Ar-Ruba Street by turning left underneath Sharjah Gate Square, cross Khaled Lagoon, and then at Khaleej Square roundabout turn left to the coast. The Ajman–Sharjah border is at the Coral Beach Hotel roundabout by the sea.

By bus

Dubai Transport buses leave for Ajman from the Deira taxi stand (near Al Nasr Square), cost Dhs7; buses leave when they are full.

By taxi

A metered taxi from Dubai to Ajman Corniche costs around Dhs40 from Deira, Dhs60 from Bur Dubai and Dhs80 from Jumeirah.

Umm Al Quwain

What Dubai has turned into five-star resorts and beach clubs, Umm Al Quwain has left relatively untouched. Aerial maps show great swirls of mangrove, and sandbars dot its coastline. But this image of rustic tranquillity is only half a reason to visit. The other half involves the smell of burning rubber, the sight of people screaming as they fall from planes and the blam-blam of shotguns. Umm Al Quwain is the UAE's fastest growing extreme sports spot. And does it very well.

Take **Emirates Car & Motorcycle Racing Club** (06 768 1166) for example, where a rather clever bid by the ruler of Umm Al Quwain to keep local lads from killing each other in high-octane motorway death-duels has spawned a fast-growing racing scene. The Racing Club now has full drag, motocross, auto-cross – even supercross tracks. Every Thursday and Friday night, upwards of 15,000 people come to watch local teams compete in some of the world's fastest cars. If you want to watch Nissan Skyline GTs charging round a circuit like a scene from *The Fast and the Furious*, head 15 kilometres (9½ miles) north of the Umm Al Quwain roundabout – opposite the beached

Ilyushin-76 cargo plane that marks the territory of the Aeroclub. The action tends to run from 8pm till midnight and entrance is free.

Across the road, the **Umm Al Quwain Aeroclub** (06 768 1447) is another adrenalin-junkies' dream. Here you can sky-dive from 9am to sunset. Tandem jumps go for Dhs750, while qualified jumpers can have a go from as little as Dhs80; a parachute student's 'accelerated free fall package' is Dhs4,900. Opposite the Aeroclub is the **Umm Al Quwain Shooting Club** (06 768 1900). You used to be able to shoot everything from Uzis to AK-47s here, but the federal ministry in charge withdrew licences for this across the UAE in 2003; you are now limited to single- and double-barrelled shotguns. You can shoot these Saturday, Thursday and Friday, from 2pm to 9pm, with 25 cartridges costing Dhs65.

If all this fills you with horror, head a bit further up the road to **Dreamland Aqua Park**, a haven of family-friendly sanity – almost. More calming still is **Umm Al Quwain Fort**, very similar to other forts in the region, but with better access to rooms and walkways than any of them.

Dreamland Aqua Park

Umm Al Quwain–Ras Al Khaimah road (06 768 1888). **Open** 10am-6pm Sat-Wed; 10am-8pm Thur, Fri. **Admission** Dhs40; Dhs20 5-11s; free under-5s. **Credit** AmEx, MC, V.
The place might be bang in the middle of nowhere, but the water rides and food stalls easily match the fun of Jumeirah's Wild Wadi (*see p148*), even if it's not as swanky.

Umm Al Quwain Fort

Al Lubna Road, Old town (06 765 0888). **Open** 9am-1pm, 5-8pm Sat, Sun, Tue-Thur; 5-8pm Fri. **Admission** Dhs4; free children. **No credit cards**. The fort has a well displayed jewellery collection, in-depth weapons collection and two rooms showing material from the emirate's Ad-Dur archaeological site. Most interesting of all, however, is the extraordinary story pinned to a wall of one of the towers. It relates (if you can decipher the slightly obscure English) the story of the murder of Ruler Ahmed Bin Ibrahim Al Mualla by his cousin-servant in 1929, and how the people of Umm Al Quwain burnt the murderer alive inside the tower.

Where to eat, drink & stay

The **Flamingo Beach Resort** (06 765 0000) is one of those strange, desolate coastal resorts on the lower Gulf that reminds one of the Eagles' song, 'Hotel California'. Still, it has good service and is reasonable value for money. For Dhs300 you get a double room and the opportunity to lounge around a large open grassy space with pool, bar, and incredibly cheap booze – food stops at 10pm, but as the concierge says, 'liquor is 24 hours'. The hotel offers an unusual pastime: crab hunting. For Dhs85, you get taken out to the creek by motor launch for a couple of hours of night diving along the shores of **Al Siniyyah Island**. The trip includes snacks and dinner; staff cook your catch on the beach.

We can't advise staying at the **Barracuda Hotel** (06 768 1555), because firstly, it is expensive (Dhs350-Dhs550 depending on whether you choose old or new accommodation) and secondly, the smell of sewage on the tide is unbearable. However, you can always stock up at the **Barracuda Liquor Shop** (06 768 1124; open 8am-12.30am; back window counter 12.30am-8am). You don't need a licence to buy alcohol here. This famed booze souk has a massive selection of wine from around the world and Australian and South African 'vintages' can go for as low as Dhs15 on special offer. It also has Smirnoff at Dhs50 per litre or 24 cans of Heineken for Dhs90 – massively cheaper than the equivalent stores in Dubai.

The bottom line is that you shouldn't feel obliged to stay in Umm Al Quwain. If you've got this far you have probably come by car, and it is only a few more kilometres north to the more attractive surroundings of Ras Al Khaimah's Bin Majid Resort (*see p231*) or Al Hamra Fort Hotel (*see p232*).

RAK and ruin: welcome to **Ras Al Khaimah**.

Resources

Tourist information

Ministry of Information & Culture *Off Abu Bakr Al Siddiq Road (06 765 6663/www.uaeinter act.com).* **Open** 7.30am-2pm Sat-Wed.

Getting there

By car

Take the Dubai–Sharjah Road and keep going north until you hit UFO roundabout (so named because of its concrete, UFO-shaped building on one side), then take the second exit towards Cultural roundabout. From Cultural roundabout take the second exit. Filter right at the next major junction, take the third exit left, and head straight for about 20km (12½ miles) until you hit Umm Al Quwain roundabout. Turn left to go into town, or head 15km (9½ miles) straight on to the Aeroclub.

By bus

Dubai Transport buses leave for Umm Al Quwain from the Deira taxi stand near Al Nasr Square (buses depart once they are full); cost Dhs10. To return, take a taxi (around Dhs60).

By taxi

A metered taxi from Dubai to Umm Al Quwain town centre costs around Dhs180 from Deira, Dhs200 from Bur Dubai and Dhs240 from Jumeirah. Ras Al Khaimah taxis waiting behind Deira bus station will be cheaper. Haggle.

Ras Al Khaimah

Ras Al Khaimah is the wild west of the United Arab Emirates. Fiercely independent and entrenched in tradition, its people are hardy and direct in manner. Their homes are set in some of the harshest yet most beautiful scenery in the country – among huge mountains, dry plains, desert and sea. Ras Al Khaimah town may not be much to look at, but its surrounds are well worth a visit.

Ras Al Khaimah's trading history reaches deep into the Bronze Age, when Mesopotamian texts name the area the 'Land of Magan'. Pottery finds show that its inhabitants had contact with the advancing civilisations around the Arabian Gulf as early as the Ubaid Period (5000-3800 BC). When most of Europe continued to be in the grips of the Stone Age, local people here buried their dead accompanied by painted beakers, spouted jars, incised stone bowls and personal ornaments, suggesting highly sophisticated societies.

Named Julfar by the 12th-century Arab explorer, Al Idrisi, the region today known as Al Khaimah then fell under the sway of the Kingdom of Hormuz, the growing island-empire based in the sea-straits separating the

The UAE

Wadi Bih

This spectacular drive not only has breathtaking mountain views, but also fascinating medieval stone dwellings and terraced fields to boot. The drive described here in fact passes through two wadis: **Wadi Bih** from the Ras Al Khaimah side, taking you over the top of the mountain at almost 1,000 metres (3,500 feet), and **Wadi Khab Al Shamis**, the descent to the UAE's east coast. The terrain is not strictly 4x4 territory, as the road is a well graded gravel track. But this does depend on whether there has been heavy rain in the mountains, which can bring down huge boulders and really chew up the surface, preventing you from driving all the way through the wadi to Dibba.

The route from Dubai passes through four emirates in the 100 kilometres (60 miles) up the coast to Ras Al Khaimah. On reaching the Clock Tower roundabout on the outskirts of the city, take a right. Then continue straight on through the next roundabout and intersection, eventually turning right about 4.5 kilometres (2¾ miles) further on, just opposite some small shops. A few kilometres further, on the right-hand side, is the clearly marked entrance to Wadi Bih. There are two police checkpoints, the first of which will require some identification, so make sure that you have your driver's licence or passport with you. Insurance cover for Oman is also a good idea. At the second checkpoint, follow the road to the right, in front of the fence, and then up the hill. Though this is a dry wadi with no running water, there are fantastic views and many opportunities for mountain biking and hiking. There is also an avid group of rock climbers who meet up here most weekends for a solid work-out on the rock; if you are passing through on a Thursday or a Friday keep your eyes open for human specks working their way up the towering faces.

The history of this area is gripping, with many of the stone houses and fields you see having been in use since the 13th and 14th centuries. It is great to explore on foot, but take care to respect the heritage and leave everything untouched. One of the most common inhabitants of these mountains is the Brandt's hedgehog, distinguished by its long ears and legs. You will often see them scuttling over the road at dusk.

Musandam (in modern-day Oman, *see p233*) from Persia. Its flourishing wealth did not go unnoticed, and the Portuguese invaded the Empire of Hormuz in 1507, sacking tributary cities along the east coast of Oman and taking Hormuz itself in 1514. But constantly harried by local tribes, the Ottomans and their Omani vassals, not to mention the Dutch, British and Persians, the Portuguese were finally ousted in 1622, leaving a turmoil of competing powers and navies. Julfar increasingly lost importance as first Safavid Persia, then the Al Yaruba Omani Empire took loose control of the area. Julfar was abandoned and the centre of trade moved four kilometres (two and a half miles) to the south. The new town was called Ras Al Khaimah, which literally translates as 'the Head of the Tent'.

Ras Al Khaimah became the home base for a local tribal confederation known as the Qawasim. The decline in Omani power in the area allowed Qawasim sailors to take control of the trade along the Gulf, Musandam and northern Omani coasts – as well as commerce in the Indian Ocean. The Qawasim declared the independence of Ras Al Khaimah and the growing town of Sharjah from the Omani empire in 1749.

The collapse of the world pearl market in the early 20th century harmed Ras Al Khaimah immeasurably. As with all of the towns of the lower Gulf, it fell into abject poverty. Limited oil production from 1969 onwards helped matters, and while Ras Al Khaimah sought to remain independent from the Federation of United Arab Emirates (lasting out for 44 days after its signing on December 2, 1971), in the end, joining a federation backed by Abu Dhabi's oil reserves was the only option. The emirate received a boost with the 1980s discovery of the offshore Saleh oil field and has since worked hard to develop its cement and ceramic industries for export. However, it remains far poorer than Abu Dhabi or even Dubai, and consequently has a reputation for being Arabia's equivalent of the 'Wild West'.

Sightseeing

The city of Ras Al Khaimah is cut into two sections by the creek, the Khor Ras Al Khaimah. The western section is the original **old town**, known as such, housing Ras Al Khaimah's National Museum and a number of souks. The eastern part is the newer **Al Nakheel** district, largely a commercial and business zone with a few hotels and a new shopping complex called Manar Mall. The two sections are connected by a single large bridge across the creek.

National Museum of Ras Al Khaimah

Old town (07 233 3411). **Open** *June-Aug* 8am-noon, 4-7pm Sat, Sun, Tue-Fri. *Sept-May* 10am-5pm Sat, Sun, Tue-Fri. **Admission** Dhs2; Dhs1 children; photo permission Dhs5.
No credit cards.

From the Umm Al Quwain highway, head straight towards old Ras Al Khaimah at the first (clock tower) roundabout. Go left at the second roundabout and the fort is 200 metres on your right. Once past the rather sullen guards, you'll find a lovely tree-lined courtyard with a selection of pearling, fishing and pottery-making exhibits – with the most detailed labelling in Arabic and English of any of the northern Emirati forts. Most interesting are the reproduction paintings of the first British naval expedition in 1809. They depict the attack on Ras Al Khaimah, and are accompanied by text promoting the thesis of the current ruler of Sharjah, Sheikh Dr Sultan bin Mohammed Al Qasimi, that the Qawasim weren't responsible for piracy in the area (read the references he cites and make up your own mind). There are also excellent pieces of silver tribal jewellery and a Baker Rifle, the first standard issue rifle given to the British Army in the 1800s.

Ras Al Khaimah Shooting Club

Khuzam Road, first right after walled Ruler's Palace (07 236 3622). **Open** 3-8pm daily.
No credit cards.

Marksmen used to come to this club from far and wide – the RAK Shooting Club is best public facility in the UAE. They once shot 'big boys' toys' such as M-16s, AK-47s and 9mm Brownings, but these were spirited away shortly before the palace coup of June 2003. This leaves shotguns available for skeet and trap shooting at Dhs50 for 25 cartridges – a whole Dhs10 cheaper than at the Umm Al Quwain Shooting Club.

Tower Links Golf Course

Khuzam Road, opposite walled Ruler's Palace (07 227 9939). **Open** 8am-10.30pm daily. **Rates** To be confirmed upon opening.

This latest addition to the United Arab Emirate's remarkable golfing boom will open fully in mid 2004 when it unveils a 9-hole floodlit facility; this will be followed later in the year by a further nine holes, a clubhouse and an academy. Designed by Gerald S Williams of the USA and built by Hydroturf, Tower Links is unusual in that it abuts a huge mangrove reserve at the base of Ras Al Khaimah's creek. Consequently, the course grass is not the usual Bermuda, but an entirely new, saline tolerant species, called paspallum.

Where to eat, drink & stay

Bin Majid Beach Resort

Umm Al Quwain–Ras Al Khaimah coast road, just before RAK Ceramics (07 244 6644). **Rates** *Oct-June* Dhs390 single/double; Dhs525 suite. *July-Sept* Dhs250 single/double; Dhs425 suite. **Credit** AmEx, MC, V.

Plunging cliffs in the **Musandam.** *See p233.*

The UAE

This four-star beach chalet hotel is peaceful, with the ramshackle air of the Costa del Sol circa 1975. You'll find several bars, coffee shops, an 'Indian' nightclub and what must be one of the smallest hotel gift shops in the world (around 2.5m/9ft wide).

Al Hamra Fort Hotel
Umm Al Quwain–Ras Al Khaimah coast road, 25km (15 miles) from Dreamland, 20km (12½ miles) from Ras Al Khaimah centre (07 244 6666/www.alhamra fort.com). **Rates** Dhs600 single; Dhs700 double. **Credit** AmEx, MC, V.
With distinctive wind towers on top of its villas and a unique two kilometre-long (1¼ miles) private beach, this hotel is a hidden gem. Enjoy some water sports before having a drink at the delightful covered bar outside, or at the Italian and Arabic restaurants inside. It's well worth dropping in for afternoon tea in the lobby café (Dhs12 for two), even if you're heading further north. Ask about villa rates.

Al Nakheel Hotel
Al Muntasir Street, opposite Dubai Islamic Bank, Nakheel District (07 228 2822). **Rates** (incl taxes) Dhs100 single; Dhs150 double. **Credit** MC, V.
Not the most salubrious establishment in town, but definitely the quirkiest, Al Nakheel has the northernmost bar in the Emirates; called Churchills, it is a hangout for expat Brits, Omani oilmen and Filipino workers – perfectly bizarre. Rooms are grubby and bare, but the hotel is friendly and cheap.

Hilton Ras Al Khaimah
New Ras Al Khaimah, by the bridge (07 228 8888). **Rates** (incl breakfast & tax) Dhs380-Dhs480 single; Dhs410-Dhs510 double. **Credit** AmEx, MC, V.
The Hilton's five stars hang by a thread – but if decor is cheap and cheerful, the service is efficient and friendly; the food is pretty good and there is a great wood-panelled bar called Havana for unwinding after a hard day's wander. Try the Hoof 'n' Fin Steakhouse for a full meal. Besides a fairly uninspiring pool and tennis courts, there is access to a fitness centre and water sports at the Hilton Beach Club, a five-minute shuttle bus ride away.

Resources

Tourist information
Ministry of Information & Culture *Off King Faisal Road (06 765 6663/www.uaeinteract.com).* **Open** 7.30am-2pm Sat-Wed.

Getting there

By car
Take the Dubai–Sharjah Road and keep going north until you hit UFO roundabout (so named for its concrete UFO-shaped building). Take the second exit to Cultural roundabout, and there, take the second exit again. Filter right at the next major junction,

Tomb raiders

The UAE may not give the impression of having much in the way of history or heritage, but if you have the time and interest, there are fascinating details to discover. In the mountains around Ras Al Khaimah you will find signs of man's passing in the petroglyphs (etched rock carvings) and the numerous headstones from old burial grounds. In fact, Ras Al Khaimah is home to some of the most well documented and restored archaeological sites in the country.

The first site can be found at **Falayah**. From the Lantern roundabout in Ras Al Khaimah go 3km towards the airport, take the U-turn and come back 300m and turn right. You will see the recently renovated buildings just down on the right. These buildings, consisting of three complexes, were built by the Qawasim family, the ruling family of Ras Al Khaimah. They date from the 18th century and are of great historical importance, as this is where the major Peace Treaty of 1820 was signed, the foundation from which the future UAE would spring. Another extensive archaeological area is at **Shimal**. Continue on the main road

through Nakheel, heading towards Rams. Just 5.2km from the last set of traffic lights in Nakheel and going towards Rams, turn right at the signpost for Sheba's Palace. There are tombs on the left of the road just 500m after you've turned in. You will also see the impressive round tomb from the Umm An Nar period (about 3,000BC), fenced off on the right hand side of the road. Continuing along the road, head towards the mountains until you reach a large flat-topped hill that is also fenced off. Park the car and you can walk up the recently constructed stone steps that will take you all the way to the top, where the ruins of an ancient palace await. Myth would have it that this was the palace of the Queen of Sheba, but it is likely to have been the home of the ruler of Julfar. The view over the palm plantations to the sea is impressive.

To learn more, enquire at **National Museum of Ras Al Khaimah** (*see p231*). During the winter months there are regular teams of expat archaeologists who delight in telling tourists about their finds and even organise visits to their respective digs.

and take the third exit left. Head straight past Umm Al Quwain (about 20km/12½ miles) to the first roundabout (a further 46km/just under 30 miles). Continue straight for Ras Al Khaimah old town or, for the newer side of town, turn right two roundabouts later and cross the bridge.

By bus
Dubai Transport buses to Ras Al Khaimah leave from the Deira taxi stand near Nasr Square when they are full; cost Dhs20. To return, take a Ras Al Khaimah taxi, about Dhs80.

By taxi
A metered taxi from Dubai to Ras Al Khaimah town centre costs about Dhs180 from Deira and Dhs220 from Jumeirah. Ras Al Khaimah taxis waiting behind the Deira station cost around Dhs80. Haggle.

Musandam

The peninsula north of Ras Al Khaimah, the Musandam, actually belongs to Oman. Until about ten years ago, there was no tourist access to this area because of tight security due to its strategic military importance, situated right on the Strait of Hormuz. It is a magnificent, unspoilt area of rugged beauty, nicknamed the 'Fjords of Arabia' because of the mountains that plunge directly into the sea, creating countless inlets and coves.

On reaching the town of **Khasab**, the smart move is to hire a boat from the port, saying you want to head for **Telegraph Island** (be prepared to haggle). This will take you round into the first fjord, which is about a half an hour ride. Even in the height of summer a trip here is idyllic and you can always slip over the side for a quick swim. Secluded azure bays, leaping dolphins, excellent snorkelling and quaint local villages at the feet of rugged mountains are just some of the sights that await. You can also plan a longer trip and camp out on a beach.

It is not possible to rent diving gear in Khasab, so come fully equipped or book a diving trip through **Khasab Travel & Tours** (266 9950). A half-day dhow trip (9am to noon) costs Dhs150 per person; a full-day trip (9am to 4pm) is Dhs200, or Dhs300 with diving; and a camping trip (requiring six people minimum) will cost you Dhs73 each. You can also rent a 4x4 from the same company at Dhs800 for a full day and Dhs450 for half a day. A word of warning: tours need to be organised before going to Khasab as availability is far from guaranteed.

Once back in port, drive to the top of **Jebel Harim** mountain for stunning views and temperatures that become some eight degrees cooler as you approach 2,000 metres (7,000 feet) in altitude. You can continue past the military dome on the summit for a little way, but must

return on the same path (there is no access allowed through the checkpoint at the bottom of Wadi Bih).

Where to eat, drink & stay

Golden Tulip Hotel
Khasab coast road (00 968 830777). **Rates** Dhs350 single/double. **Credit** AmEx, MC, V.
A relatively new addition to the Musandam area, the Golden Tulip Hotel is nestled on the coast as you make your way into Khasab. There are 60 compact but clean rooms, a pool, restaurant and bar – and all with terrific sea views.

Khasab Hotel
Khasab coast road (00 968 830271). **Rates** single Dhs200; double Dhs300; apartments (sleeping 6 people) Dhs500. **Credit** AmEx, MC, V.
For many years the only hotel to greet you in the Musandam was the Khasab. It has 15 rooms and the service is genuine and friendly. There are also four apartments that sleep 6 people each. The restaurant is refreshingly olde-worlde, with basic but tasty food. The hotel can also sometimes arrange a rental car – for example a 4x4 for around Dhs250 per day. It's best to check when making your reservation.

Resources

Tourist Information
Omani Consulate *Off Khalid bin Al Waleed Road, Bur Dubai, Dubai (397 1000).* **Open** 7.30am-2.30pm Sat-Wed.

Essentials

Visa regulations
Gaining a visit visa to enter Oman is seldom the problem. Obtaining one takes ten minutes (depending on your nationality) at the Omani border post or Khasab Airport – don't forget your Omani car insurance as you will need to show proof of coverage. The major issue is actually being allowed to re-enter the UAE, as any single entry visit visa is cancelled when you leave the border. This trip is only possible if you come from one of the 33 countries eligible for a visit visa on arrival in the UAE; check with Dubai Tourism & Commerce Marketing (223 0000).

Getting there

By car
It takes just over 2hrs to reach Khasab from Dubai, depending on how quickly you get through the border. The trip is just 70km (45 miles) from Ras Al Khaimah and amazingly picturesque.

By plane
Oman Air (Dubai office 395 8080) flies Dubai–Khasab (45-minute flight) Monday, Wednesday and Friday at 2.15pm.

The UAE

East Coast

Great diving, beautiful mountain scenery and quirky hotels are what these Indian Ocean getaways are all about.

Enjoy the quiet life at **Fujairah**.

The east coast is beautiful – and quite different from the rest of the UAE. It is the Hajjar mountain barrier that gives it its unique character, cascading a short distance down to the Indian Ocean from the interior, bisected by wadis and scattered with hamlets and towns. A more humid climate than the Gulf coast means that farms and fields cover the narrow coastal strip, and centuries of battles and invasions have littered this landscape with forts and archaeological sites.

The main power may be the emirate of **Fujairah**, but Fujairah's land mass is dotted with villages that owe allegiance to Ras Al Khaimah or Sharjah on the UAE's north coast. Lovely beaches, staggering scenery and a gentle pace of life make the east coast a fabulous place to explore, both above and below the water.

Despite their unique scenery and wildlife, the areas to the south and west of Fujairah remain some of the most unexplored territory in the UAE. From the mangroves of **Khor Khalba** and hot springs of **Ain Al Gamour**, to the ruined houses of **Wadi Hayl** and the

tomb of **Al Bithnah**, charming and secretive treasures await the curious tourist (*for all, see p236*). The coast north from Fujairah to **Dibba** (*see p240*) and the border to the Musandam peninsula (*see p233*) boasts the most relaxed hotels and the finest remote beaches in the Emirates – not to mention the dive sites off **Khor Fakkan** (*see p238*) and **Al Aqah** (*see p239*), which rank among the world's best.

Fujairah

The drive from Dubai to Fujairah via Al Dhaid is a treat in itself, taking you through deep desert and mountain villages. Spectacular new mountain roads are being built (already passable in two-wheel drive vehicles) from Ras Al Khaimah on the Arabian Gulf coast (*see p229*) to Dibba and Fujairah, and from Sharjah to Kalba, but at the time of writing the Al Dhaid route is the simplest.

From Dubai, jump onto the E44 Emirates link road west (direction Al Awir/Hatta/Oman). From the Bu Kidra Interchange at the end of Dubai Creek, travel 18 kilometres (11 miles) to the third interchange and go left (north) onto the E611, heading for Sharjah/Al Dhaid. After 19 kilometres (12 miles) go west towards Al Dhaid on the E88.

This takes you through rolling dunes, and finally you come over the crest of a hill to find the oasis of **Al Dhaid** stretched before you. Go left at the first roundabout in the town, then right at the next roundabout towards Manama. Keep going straight on. After 20 kilometres (12½ miles) or so you'll dip down into a bowl of gravel lined with stalls, known as **Friday Market**. With carpets, plants, pottery and fresh fruit for sale, the market presents the perfect opportunity to put your haggling skills to the test. You can buy pretty pottery candle covers for Dhs15 or less; kitsch Pakistani carpets are also a favourite (those featuring Sheikh Zayed's face are top of our shopping list). Don't get fleeced, as none of the items are old and few are worth much.

The most expensive goods are the attractive Iranian patterned silk carpets, which you should be able to pick up for less than Dhs450. You can also stop for snacks such as fresh corn-on-the-cob for less than Dhs4, and grab a *chai* (thick sweet Indian tea) for 50 fils at the New Restaurant.

Further on through the mountains lies the nondescript town of **Masafi** (Ras Al Khaimah's mountain enclave), best known for its mineral water production. The first junction you come to takes you left (north) to **Dibba** at the northern tip of the UAE's east coast before the Musandam Peninsula, or right (south) to **Fujairah** town and **Kalba** at the Oman border, passing via the small townships of Diftah, Blaydah and Bithnah.

Fujairah was a part of the Qawasim sheikhdom based in Sharjah until the local Al Sharqi branch of the Qawasim gained some autonomy in 1903. The British then recognised Fujairah as independent from Sharjah in 1952. But it is not local politics that gives Fujairah its distinct atmosphere. With the Hajjar mountain range running parallel to the east coast from Al Ain to Ras Al Khaimah, Fujairah has always been cut off from the rest of the UAE and the first all-weather road through the mountains only opened in 1975.

Despite new high-rise buildings along the main drag, much of Fujairah is a one-storey sprawl that can appear to be operating in a different time zone to the rest of the UAE. The rustic look extends to Fujairah Museum. Outside the summer months, one can watch an unusual test of wills – bullfighting, Fujairah style. This bloodless sport pits two bulls against each other in a fit of head-butting, while their owners hold them by rope.

For a similarly surreal spectacle, head down to Al Gurfa Street off the Plaza Cinema roundabout. Left, just after the roundabout, there is a multi-coloured pitch oiled for 'slippery football', essentially a game of soccer where keeping your balance is half the challenge. The origins of this are shrouded in mystery but if there are teams playing while you're passing it makes an entertaining diversion.

Fujairah Museum

Head inland & follow signs from Coffee Pot roundabout, Al Gurfa Street (09 222 9085). **Open** 8.30am-1.30pm, 4-6pm Sun-Thur; 2-6pm Fri. **Admission** Dhs3; Dhs1 children. **No credit cards.** This bizarre building is close to collapse, with a ceiling that would be at home in an Edwardian parlour. Nonetheless, it houses a fabulous collection of archaeological remains taken from local sites, which easily rival those in the more prestigious Archaeological Museum in Sharjah (*see p222*). The building is supposed to be a temporary measure until restoration work at the 360-year-old fort behind it has been completed. However, at the time of going to press, the move looked to still be some time off.

Where to eat, drink & stay

At the Coffee Pot roundabout, just before the Hilton Hotel, is Al Owaid Street, which takes you towards the shoreline. Here, you'll find the teapot shape of the **Fujairah International Marine Club** (09 222 1166). It houses the Armada Bar, which has excellent pub grub, and an interesting mix of locals, expats, dive centre workers and the occasional crew from visiting boats. You can also replenish yourself at the **Fujairah Youth Hostel** (09 222 2347), on the left-hand side of Al Faseel Street, parallel to the Corniche; it is excellent value at Dhs15 for members and Dhs30 for non-members.

Hilton Fujairah

Just off Coffee Pot roundabout, Al Gurfa Street (09 222 2411). **Rates** Dhs650 single; Dhs700 double. **Credit** AmEx, MC, V.
The Hilton is a charming retreat, where delicate fountains surround a shady courtyard and spill into mosaic-lined swimming pools. Of course, it's got a private stretch of beach, and the bar and beach huts overlooking the beach give it even more of a Mediterranean feel. A refurbishment a couple of years ago also means the rooms are clean and attractive. The hotel can arrange jet-skiing, water-skiing and diving trips.

Resources

Tourist information

Ministry of Information & Culture
Off Jerusalem Road (09 222 4190/www.uaeinteract. com). **Open** 7.30am-2pm Sat-Wed.

The UAE

Getting there

By car

For full details of driving the 130km (80 miles) to Fujairah from Dubai, *see pp234-5.*

By bus

Buses to Fujairah go every half hour from Deira taxi stand near Al Nasr Square; cost Dhs35. You can't return by bus, but will have to take a taxi (*see above*).

By taxi

Dubai's metered cabs will cost Dhs170-210 depending on pick-up point and destination. In Fujairah, you can pick up taxis from the Karachi Durbar side of Plaza Cinema roundabout. A local taxi (taking up to six people) costs around Dhs80 for a journey back to Dubai.

Khor Kalba

As the most northerly mangrove forest in the world, Khor Kalba supports a unique eco-system that makes for a fascinating visit. From Fujairah, turn southwards down the coast towards Kalba, which is only about 10 kilometres (6 miles) away. Drive through the town and on reaching the beginning of the swamps on your left-hand side, take a left onto a well-used track that hugs the outer edge.

Glimpse traditional life on the east coast.

Follow this track round quite naturally and take the bridge onto the sandy area between the sea and the swamps.

The mangrove is inhabited by two of the planet's rarest birds: the white-collared kingfisher 'kalbaensis' (the 55 breeding pairs here are the only ones in the world) and the Sykes's warbler. Even if you are not an avid bird-watcher it is still worth the detour for the peace and natural beauty. There are tracks along the shore from the Kalba Corniche that are suitable for four-wheel drives, but do not under any circumstances drive over vegetation or close to the waterline. Contact Dubai-based **Desert Rangers** to arrange canoes to observe the wildlife (*see p75* **Tour operators**).

Just a few kilometres south of Kalba, and inland from the coast, the tiny Fujairan village of **Awalah** sits on the north side of a wadi that runs from east to west. Sitting atop a terrace overlooking the wadi is a 19th-century mud-brick fortified house. The building covers the western corner of an Iron Age fortified enclosure, which still boasts visible defensive walls more than 2.3 metres (7 feet) thick and up to 60 metres (200 feet) long, preserved in places to almost 1.5 metres (5 feet) above today's ground level.

Ain Al Gamour

The hot springs at Ain Al Gamour are surrounded by a gorgeous oasis of trees and vegetation. Scalding water bubbles up and feeds a small pool where you can take a dip, next to the parking area. To get there, drive south past Kalba looking for the Adnoc service station. Pass the roundabout for the main road up into the mountains and take the next turn right on to a graded track 1.3 kilometres (3/4 miles) later. After some 2.5 kilometres (1½ miles), take the next fork left and follow the signs for Ain Al Gamour.

Al Bithnah

Al Bithnah, situated 13 kilometres (8 miles) west of Fujairah town (signposted off the main Fujairah–Masafi road), holds two important archaeological sites. An impressive fort was built here in 1735 to guard the strategic route across the Hajjar mountains through Wadi Ham. There is also a much older tomb, which was once a communal burial site; it has been estimated that this was in use from 1350 BC to 300 BC. Discoveries have shown that the village was a stopover for trading caravans from the Far East. To find out more about this interesting site, visit the Fujairah Museum (*see p235*).

Good diving and snorkelling at
Snoopy Island. *See p240.*

Wadi Hayl

Wadi Hayl is situated in startlingly beautiful
scenery, and is home to an abandoned village
and the best-preserved mountain fort in the
UAE. This is a short off-road trip, and as such
is perfect to link with a visit to the east coast.

From the outskirts of Fujairah, jump on to
the Masafi–Fujairah road from the roundabout
and go less than a kilometre west, looking left
for signposts opposite the police station to
Hayl Castle or Palace (22 kilometres/13½ miles
from Masafi). Two-wheel drive cars can easily
reach the fort by turning left towards the quarry
(the signpost reads 'Al Hayl Palace 4km') after
turning off the main road. Four-wheel drives
can continue straight on through the abandoned
village of Hayl.

Hayl village's ruined houses and terraces
follow the water course and its tributaries.
Keep an eye out for the hundreds of 4,000-
year-old petroglyphs depicting animals, horses
and riders that cover boulders on either side
of the wadi.

Bear right at the fork at the end of the track
after the village and you will find the **fort** (some
call it a fortified house) perched on an isolated
outcrop. The fort has been dated to between AD
1470 and 1700, though much of today's structure
is not thought to be more than about 100 years
old, when it doubled as the palace of Sheikh
Abdullah bin Hamdan Al Sharqi. It is built with
natural materials – stone and mud bricks mixed

with straw, and wooden floors. There is a
watchtower on the hill behind, and numerous
ruins of smaller houses surrounding it. The
main track continues on past the fort and
although it doesn't lead to any other specific
areas of interest, it's an attractive drive. You
can leave the track at any point and explore
further up one of the side wadis.

Getting there

By car

The simplest way to get to explore the south and
west is to start at Fujairah itself (*see pp234-5*), but
as this guide went to press a road was being built
through the Hajjar Mountains to Kalba on the Oman
border, accessible from Dubai.

To pass through breathtaking mountains and
incredible tunnels, head east from Dubai to Hatta
(*see pp69-70*). Pass Hatta's main roundabout (with
Hatta Fort Hotel on your left) and 2.8km (2 miles)
further on take the next tarmac left towards
Huwaylat and Munay. The twisting road from here
on in is a lovely drive. After 11km (7 miles), take the
second exit left at the Huwaylat roundabout towards
Munay. In 9km (5½ miles) at Munay, turn right,
down onto the motorway heading east. This takes
you past mountain strongholds and through an
amazing feat of engineering in the shape of the
1.2km-long (just over half a mile) Gillay tunnel.
The road then snakes down through Wadi Moudiq
on the other side of the Hajjar to Kalba's first
roundabout – just follow the coast north (left)
past the swamps to Kalba and on to Fujairah.

If you get lost anywhere along the coast don't be afraid to ask the (older) locals. A smattering of Arabic is useful (*see p260*), a map even more so.

Khor Fakkan

The second largest town on the east coast after Fujairah, Khor Fakkan is certainly its cleanest. Wide streets and well-tended gardens make it a pleasant place to wander, even if there are few specific attractions worth visiting. If you're low on vitals and need to hit the shops, the covered souk by the container terminal at the far south of the port is perfect for fresh produce.

Known as Chorf to Venetian jeweller Gasparo Balbi in 1580, Khor Fakkan has the remains of a Portuguese fort, which was most likely destroyed during hostilities when the Persian navy invaded the east coast in 1623 under the command of the Omani, Sheikh Muhammad Suhari. According to the German traveller Carsten Niebuhr, Khor Fakkan belonged to a sheikh of the Qawasim by 1765, and today the town is another east coast enclave belonging to the Qawasim emirate of Sharjah.

Khor Fakkan attracts a steady stream of divers, but also offers a few attractive inland sights, most notably **Wadi Wurrayah**. Guaranteed to provide cool, shady, watery relief from baking temperatures and blazing sun, the wadi's highlight is its waterfall, an area of natural beauty spoilt only by graffiti and litter left by misguided visitors.

The entrance to Wadi Wurrayah is off the main road that runs north between Khor Fakkan and Dibba. There are therefore two sides from which you can approach the entrance to the wadi. If you are travelling north up from Fujairah, then from the roundabout at the Oceanic Hotel in Khor Fakkan, continue for almost 5 kilometres (3 miles) and make a U-turn just beyond the third roundabout. Double back on yourself for 700 metres (slightly more than a quarter of a mile) before taking the tarred road off to your right. If you are coming at it from the opposite direction, from Dibba, then the turning will be on your right, around 2.4 kilometres (1½ miles) from the Badiyah roundabout.

This tarred road continues straight, forking after roughly 5 kilometres (3 miles). At the fork you can take either road as they join up just over a kilometre further on. The turning not to miss is in the second major dip in the wadi, 1 kilometre (half a mile) after the forked roads join up again. If you are in a 4x4, you can turn right into the wide wadi bed at this point, but if you are in a normal car, then keep to the left and follow the tarred road for just under 3 kilometres (2 miles), where you will have a

great view from above the waterfall. You can park and climb down from here, being careful as the gravel can be very loose.

If you are following the 4x4 track, the wadi gets quite narrow and twists and turns between high stony walls. The surface is quite rough and stony and the going will be pretty slow for the next few kilometres. There is a fair amount of vegetation along the edges that adds to the atmosphere and when the wadi opens out, you'll find the deep, all-year-round pool, fed by the waterfall. Inevitably, the size of the waterfall depends on the season, with it becoming little more than a trickle in the hot summer months.

Where to eat, drink & stay

Note that no alcohol is served in Khor Fakkan, as it is part of the Emirate of Sharjah.

Khor Fakkan Youth Hostel

Opposite Oceanic Hotel, follow signs from northern roundabout, Coast Road (09 237 0886). **Rates** Dhs25 YHA members; Dhs40 non-members. **Credit** AmEx, MC, V.
A charming and cheap alternative to the Oceanic Hotel – many visitors use this 24-bed hostel as their base for the dive centre at the Oceanic. The hostel is squeaky clean, has kitchen facilities, and is run by a charmingly efficient Filipino called Rudy. If you are a single woman then Rudy will give you a separate room if appropriate.

Oceanic Hotel

Near Khor Fakkan dam, follow signs from northern roundabout, Coast Road (09 238 5111). **Rates** Oct-mid May Dhs400 single; Dhs500 double. *Mid May-Sept* Dhs300 single/double. **Credit** AmEx, MC, V.
At the top end of the scale, the Oceanic tucks into a knoll of rock on the Indian Ocean. It has a rather funky, if musty, 1970s kitsch feel, mature gardens, a great swathe of white-sand beach and a good diving centre. Rates are reasonably high, though you can negotiate outside of the high season.

Badiyah

North of Khor Fakkan and 38 kilometres from Fujairah, the tiny village of Badiyah has little to offer the visitor except a gentle stroll by the sea, but at the side of the main Khor Fakkan-Dibba road sits **Badiyah Mosque** – the oldest in the UAE. Dated as early as 1446 (predating the Portuguese invasion of the area by more than 50 years), the mosque (also known as Al Masjid Al Othmani) represents a unique feat of engineering for its time, with four small domes supported by a central pillar, stone carvings and special shelves for the holy Koran. The mosque has been prettified in recent years, replete with fake well and a lick of off-cream paint. Unusually for mosques in the UAE,

Five-star comfort and blessed isolation at **Le Meridien Al Aqah Beach Resort**.

visitors can enter outside of prayer times when accompanied by a guide (who lives next door). The imam (leader of prayers) is in fact a very friendly man who will engage you in conversation given half a chance. It's worth a short hike up the mountain to look at the two watchtowers perched behind the mosque and to take in the view.

Al Aqah

There are two very good reasons to head for Al Aqah (16 kilometres/10 miles from Khor Fakkan and 18 kilometres/11 miles from Dibba): the contrasting attractions of the swish surroundings of **Le Meridien Al Aqah Beach Resort**, and the faded charms of the relaxed and intimate **Sandy Beach Motel**.

Where to eat, drink & stay

Le Meridien Al Aqah Beach Resort
From Dubai, head east towards Sharjah, through Al Dhaid to Masafi, then take the Dibba Road and follow the signs for 35km/22 miles (09 244 9000).

Rates Dhs500-Dhs800 single; Dhs800-Dhs1,000 double; suites Dhs1,500-Dhs9,000. **Credit** AmEx, MC, V.

You can't miss Le Meridien. Its glass and concrete modernism would sit quite happily on Dubai's shoreline. Critics say it is incongruous in the beautiful though remote setting between the mountains and the Indian Ocean that it inhabits, and it is certainly a surprise to see the uncompromising structure loom from nowhere as you round the corner of the coast. But the spacious rooms have good views of the Hajjar mountains and ocean, and it has all the facilities one associates with a five-star hotel in the UAE, such as a beautiful beach, good restaurants and a health club. It also has a surreal nightclub that at the time of going to press had a bizarre act called 'The Golden Girls' performing – don't be fooled by the name, rather than American pensioners, this group consists of Russian dancing girls.

Sandy Beach Motel
Head east from Dubai towards Sharjah, through Al Dhaid to Masafi, then take the Dibba Road and follow the signs for 35km/22 miles (09 244 5555).
Rates (incl tax) Dhs303 single; Dhs385 double; Dhs418-Dhs605 chalet. **Credit** AmEx, MC, V.

The UAE

Squatting in the shadow of Le Meridien, the simpler Sandy Beach Motel is nonetheless a favourite among divers and expatriates who want to get away from everything Al Aqah stands for. With mature gardens, a lovely beach and one of the best dive centres in the area, the motel is a haven of tranquillity. You'll love or loathe the faded decor, but you'll really feel as if you're getting away from Dubai's big hotel chains. Arguably, Sandy Beach's greatest attraction is the fact that is it located directly opposite **Snoopy Island**, an outcrop in the ocean so called because its shape vaguely resembles the shape of the cartoon dog reclining on top of his kennel. The area around the rock is great for snorkelling and diving, though the dive centre at the motel also offers more technical dives in the Omani waters of the Musandam. The restaurant is basic (average meal Dhs50), with the best dishes tending to be those that include meat and grilled fish bought in the local markets.

Dibba

Prior to the coming of Islam, no state had ever been able to control the tribes of Arabia. The Persian Sassanids tried it, Byzantium tried it, even Southern Arabian states gave it a good shot – all failed. This tradition of complete independence from external powers ended in AD 633, with the final battle in the Ridda Wars (Wars of Apostasy).

According to custom, many Arabian Bedouin tribes swore personal allegiance to the prophet Mohammed, so when he died in around AD 632, their allegiance was over. By refusing to accept the leadership of his successor, his father-in-law Abu Bakr, they were challenging outside control – as they had done for hundreds of years. But now they were also challenging Islam. And Abu Bakr was having none of it. He amassed a Muslim army to crush their resistance, just as he had done elsewhere on the peninsula. The huge battles at Dibba (there are 10,000 gravestones in a cemetery here) marked the end of the Muslim re-conquest of Arabia. It was also the beginning of state control from Mecca (in modern-day Saudi Arabia), and the beginning of Islamic expansion beyond it.

Thankfully the Dibba of today is a much calmer setting for the visitor. There are actually three Dibbas: **Dibba Muhallab** (also called Dibba Al Fujairah – belonging to Fujairah), **Hosn Dibba** (belonging to Sharjah) and **Dibba Bayah** (Oman). There are no border posts here and it is possible to cross into any part of the conurbation without hindrance – just make sure you don't have a car crash in Dibba Bayah without Omani insurance. The three Dibbas share an attractive bay, fishing communities, Portuguese fortresses, wadi waterfalls and excellent diving locations.

To get to a lovely beach, first follow the coastline until you reach the tiny **Dibba port** ('Mina Bayah' in Arabic) on the far northern edge of the town. It's just a few hundred metres from the Globe roundabout. It's a very active fishing harbour where you can see the day's catch spread out on the ground and the air is loud with locals bartering, and, if you're so inclined, you can charter a fishing boat or dhow from here for a short trip. Once past the port, continue along the main road away from town and then take the sandy track that forks right after about 1.5 kilometres (just under a mile). This will take you towards a stretch of beach by the mountains in the very corner of the bay. The beach is a well-known spot for camping, picnics and excellent snorkelling.

Where to eat, drink & stay

Holiday Beach Motel

Head east from Dibba towards Khor Fakkan, for 5km/3 miles along the coast road (09 244 5840). **Rates** *Oct-June* Dhs385 studio chalets; Dhs485 single chalets; Dhs685 double chalets. *July-Sept* Dhs325 studio chalets; Dhs400 single chalets; Dhs585 double chalets. **Credit** AmEx, MC, V.
A superb place to dive from, this hotel is however at the ramshackle end of the quality spectrum, and its chalets overlook a distinctly underwhelming expanse of grass and a basic pool. However, Maku Dive Centre (09 244 5747) is run by superb instructors and comes highly recommended. The motel has an Arabic nightclub with a Moroccan band and a Pakistani nightclub complete with Bangladeshi singers. But, as with all the nightlife spots on the east coast, neither are 'happening' places and they border on the tacky.

Getting there

By car

If you don't want to get to the north via the Masafi–Dibba–Fujairah loop (*see p235*), there is a road being built to connect Ras Al Khaimah (*see p229*) with Dibba through the startlingly harsh and beautiful Ruus Al Jibal, part of the Hajjar mountains. At the time of writing the road was only half complete, making it an interesting off-road experience. With graded tracks leading on and off perfect tarmac, it is passable even in a two-wheel drive vehicle – just beware rock transporters along the way.

By taxi

To travel directly to Dibba and the north by taxi, Dubai's metered cabs will cost Dhs200-Dhs240 depending on pick-up point and destination. On the way back, in the unlikely event that a local cab driver won't take you back to Dubai, have him drop you off in Fujairah, and get a cab from there.

Directory

Directory

Getting Around

Arriving & leaving

By air

Dubai International Airport

switchboard 224 5555/
flight information 216 6666/
www.dubaiairport.com.
One of the most highly acclaimed airports in the world, DIA is currently undergoing an elaborate and extravagant expansion programme (scheduled for completion in 2006). This includes a new terminal (the airport's third) exclusively for Emirates airline flights.

Almost all major airlines arrive at the main **Sheikh Rashid Terminal 1**. Here the Dubai Duty Free (224 5004) is the last port of call for the purchase of alcohol before entering Dubai's 'hotel-only' licensing restrictions (*see p249* **Customs**). The airport's facilities include shops, internet and banking services, restaurants, business facilities, a bar, a hotel and a regular raffle that gives you the chance to win a luxury car. Tickets cost Dhs500, but odds are favourable as there is a draw every time 1,000 are sold.

The smaller **Terminal 2** caters largely for cargo, charter flights and commercial airlines from Iran and the CIS countries. There is also a VIP terminal known as Al Majalis.

There is a card-operated E-Gate, which enables those who carry the relevant 'smart card' to check in and travel unhindered, using only their fingerprints for identification. For more information see the airport website.

TO AND FROM THE AIRPORT

DIA is in Garhoud, about five kilometres (three miles) south-east of the city centre. If you're staying at one of the big international hotels, you'll get a complimentary **limousine** or **shuttle bus** transfer to and from the airport.

Otherwise, **taxis** are the most convenient and practical form of transport. There is Dhs20 surcharge on pick-up from the terminal (instead of the usual Dhs3). This means that the journey from the airport to the city centre costs around Dhs30, while the return journey is Dhs13 or so. It takes about ten minutes to get to Bur Dubai, and Jumeirah and the hotel beach resorts are about half an hour away.

There are **bus** links to and from both terminals every 20-30 minutes for around Dhs2, although timings are somewhat erratic and routes can be lengthy. Route 401 goes from the airport to Al Sabkha bus station and the 402 goes to Al Ghubaiba, running through the centre of the city. From Deira station, located opposite the Al Ghurair Centre on Al Rigga Road, the numbers 4, 11 and 15 will take you straight to Terminal 1, as will the 33 and 44 from Bur Dubai. All buses are air-conditioned. Call 227 3840/800 4848 or visit www.dubaipublictransport.ae for more details.

AIRPORT PARKING

There are short- and long-term parking facilities at the airport. Tariffs range from Dhs5 per hour in the short-stay car park to Dhs30 per day for up to ten days in the long-stay.

Airlines

Flight information 216 6666.
All airlines operating regular flights into DIA are listed on the airport website; some of the most popular are listed below. Note that some airlines ask you to reconfirm your flight 72 hours before departure, and that cheaper tickets will often incur a penalty fee for alteration or cancellation.

Air France *information 294 0049/ reservations 294 5899/ticket sales 294 5991/www.airfrance.com.*
British Airways *reservations & ticket sales 307 5777/ www.britishairways.com.*
Emirates *214 4444/ www.emirates.com.*
Gulf Air *271 3111/3222/ www.gulfairco.com.*
KLM *335 5777/www.klm.com.*
Lufthansa *343 2121/ www.lufthansa.com.*
Qatar Air *229 2229/221 4210/ www.qatarair.com.*
Royal Brunei (no alcohol served on board) *information 351 4111/ticket sales 316 6562/www.bruneiair.com.*

By road

The UAE is bordered to the north and east by Oman, and to the south and west by Saudi Arabia. Road access to Dubai is via the Abu Dhabi emirate to the south, Sharjah to the north, and Oman to the east.

There is no charge for driving between emirates, but if you are travelling to or from Oman or Saudi Arabia you need to show your passport, driving licence, insurance and visa. To cross the border with Oman costs Dhs20 per person, plus the price of a visa (Dhs13 for those UAE residency, Dhs60 for those on a visit visa). Your car will be searched: carrying alcohol is prohibited and may mean being turned away.

Getting on track

Dubai has no existing train system, but there are plans in the pipeline for the city's first urban railway, with costs estimated at Dhs2.8 billion. The proposed 37-station metro monorail is due to open in 2008 with two lines: one connecting the airport to Jebel Ali via Deira, running along Sheikh Zayed Road to the Defence roundabout at Interchange 1; the other beginning at Al Nahda Road on the north side of the airport and meeting in Deira at what will be the main station at Al-Ittihad Square.

All the highways linking Dubai to other emirates and Oman are in good condition. Ensure your vehicle and the air-conditioning are in good working order, as it is inevitably hot and the drive through the Hajar Mountains to Muscat, the capital of Oman, takes around five hours.

Check with **Immigration** (398 0000) before you leave for any changes in travel policy. Traffic enquiries: **Emergency Offices** (223 2323/www.dubai publictransport.ae).

See also below **Navigation**, *p244* **Driving** *and p245* **The fast and the furious**.

By sea

The only passenger sea access is from Iraq or Iran; journey time more than two days, around Dhs630 return. For schedules and details contact the **Dubai Ports Authority** (881 5000/www.dpa.co.ae). Alternatively, you can call **Rashid Port** (345 1545), which operates sea routes to Port Bandar Abbas and Port Bandar Lankah in Iran, and Port Umm Qasr in Iraq.

Navigation

Thanks to its modern highway system, most of Dubai is fairly easy to get around. However, in some places the existing infrastructure has struggled to cope with the growth of the city, most notably the Garhoud and Maktoum bridges spanning the Creek and the Shindagha tunnel underneath it. During rush hours (7-9am, 1-2pm, 5-7pm), serious tailbacks can develop. However, plans have now been announced for a third bridge over the Creek, which should ease congestion when it opens in 2006.

Other blackspots include the old part of Deira and the Dubai-Sharjah Road. Even modern Sheikh Zayed Road is showing signs of strain, with slow-moving traffic heading towards the Jebel Ali Free Zone, the Media and Internet Cities and Abu Dhabi in the morning and coming into Dubai in the early evening.

Despite the relatively good road system, Dubai can be a dangerous place to drive in. There are high numbers of road accidents and deaths, caused largely by speeding and poor lane discipline. Many drivers tailgate, chat away on their mobiles, and do not use their indicators or mirrors (*see p245* **The fast and the furious**).

The easiest way to get around is by taxi (*see below*). **Water taxis**, or abras (*see p244*), are also available on the Creek, but while they're an interesting tourist experience, they're not practical for covering the whole city.

Public buses (*see below*) are not tourist friendly, and are primarily used by workers unable to afford cars or taxis.

The biggest problem you are likely to face getting around Dubai is the lack of an accurate system of street names. Some of the larger roads and streets are known by their name, but most are just numbered. This means that in almost all cases your destination is identified by a nearby landmark, usually a hotel or building.

See also p246 **Addresses**.

Public transport

Buses

The public bus system is rarely used by tourists, owing to the convenience of taxis. The service is extremely cheap but routes can be convoluted and timings erratic.

Timetables, prices and route maps are available from the main bus stations of **Al Ghubaiba** in Bur Dubai (342 11130) and by the **Gold Souk** in Deira (227 3840). Or call the main information line on 800 4848 (6am-10pm daily) or visit www.dubaipublictransport.ae.

Should you decide to brave a bus trip, try to have the correct money since change for larger notes is rarely available. All bus stops are request stops. Eating, drinking and smoking are not allowed on board; the front three rows of seats are reserved for women. Passengers without tickets are liable for prosecution.

Monthly bus passes (Dhs95, good value if you use the bus more than three times a day) are available from the depots at **Al Ramoul** and **Al Qusais**.

Taxis

Official taxis are well maintained, air-conditioned and metered. Fares are Dhs1.5 per kilometre (0.3 mile); there is also a Dhs3-Dhs3.50 cover charge depending on the time of day. The two biggest companies are Dubai Transport Company (208 0202)

Directory

and National Taxis (336 6611). Unofficial (unmetred) taxis are best avoided, as they tend to be older cars with poor air-con. If it's the only option available, be sure to agree a price before entering the car. Taxi drivers usually have a reasonable grasp of English, so you shouldn't find it too difficult to explain where you want to go.

If you're in an outlying area of the city you should consider booking a taxi, online from www.dubaipublic transport.ae or by calling 208 0808. Fares for longer journeys outside Dubai should be agreed in advance (there is also a 12-hour service available, with petrol and driver included).

Drivers have a reputation for being honest, so if you should lose something in a taxi, in many cases your driver will find a way to return it to you. Failing this, call the company you used and give the time, destinations (to and from) and taxi number and they will do their best to help.

Water taxis

Abras are water taxis that ferry both Dubai workers and tourists across the creek for about 50 fils (100 fils = Dhs1). The boats run between 5am and midnight, carry about 20 people and take just a few minutes to make the crossing from Bur Dubai on the south bank of the Creek to Deira on the north, or vice versa.

See also p63 **Abra rides**.

Driving

People drive on the right in Dubai, and seatbelts are compulsory in the front seats. In residential areas, the speed limit is normally between 60 kilometres/hour (35 miles/ hour) and 80 kilometres/ hour (50 miles/hour). On the highways within the city it is 100kmh (60mph); outside the city limits, 120kmh (75mph).

Although in theory there are fines and bans for a whole series of offences, in reality it's rare to see these enforced. Consequently, don't expect much in the way of road rules or driving etiquette if you venture out by car.

See also p243 **Navigation** *and p245* **The fast and the furious**.

Traffic fines & offences

The official traffic police website (www.dxbtraffic. gov.ae) is comprehensive and gives a list of fines for offences, details on licence requirements, contact numbers and so on. All offences are listed under Kiosk Locations and Violations.

If caught driving or parking illegally by the police, you can be issued with a *mukhalifaa* (fine). If caught by a speed camera you'll normally be fined Dhs200. When hiring a car, it's routine to sign an agreement of responsibility for any fines you may incur.

Check if you've racked up any traffic offences on www.dubai police.gov.ae or call 268 5555. Fines can be paid online, or at the Muroor (Traffic Police Headquarters), near Galadari Roundabout on the Dubai-Sharjah road.

Traffic accidents

If you are involved in a serious traffic accident, call 999; if it's a minor collision, call 345 0111 (Bur Dubai) or 266 0555 (Deira). If you do not report any scratch or bump to the traffic police, insurers will almost certainly reject your claim.

If the accident was a minor one and no one was hurt, move the car to the side of the road and wait for the police to arrive. If there is any doubt who is at fault, or if there is any injury (however slight), do not move the car, even if you are blocking traffic. If you help

or move anyone injured in an accident, the police may hold you responsible if anything happens to that person.

Breakdown services

There are two 24-hour breakdown services, the **AAA (Arabian Automobile Association)** (800 4900/ non-members 285 8989/ www.aaauae.com) and **IATC Recovery (International Automobile Touring Club)** (800 5200/www.iatcuae.com). If you are driving when the car breaks down, try to pull over on to the hard shoulder. The police are likely to stop and will give assistance. If you're in the middle of high-speed traffic, it will be unsafe to get out of the car. Instead, use a mobile to call the police from the relative safety of your vehicle. Other breakdown services (not 24-hour) include:

Ahmed Mohammed Garage
050 650 4739.
Dubai Auto Towing Service
359 4424.

Vehicle hire

Most major hire companies have offices at the airport (12 companies have 24-hour outlets there; *see p245*) and hotels. Before renting a car, check the smallprint, especially the clause relating to insurance cover in the event of an accident, as this can vary considerably from company to company.

Drivers must be aged over 21 to hire a small car, or 25 for a medium (two-litre) or larger 4x4 vehicle. You'll need your national driving licence (an International Driving Permit is recommended, although it is not legally required). You'll also need your passport and one of the major credit cards. Prices range from Dhs77 per day for a small manual car, to Dhs1,000 for something like a Lexus LS430. Motorbikes are not available for hire in Dubai.

The fast and the furious

The UAE has one of the world's highest death tolls from road accidents per capita, and when you drive along one of the main highways, it's not hard to see why. Few people adhere to traffic regulations, and speeding, undertaking and use of the hard shoulder are all frequent occurrences. All cars sold into the UAE have an audio warning when speeds exceed the 120km/h (75mph) speed limit – not that this deters the country's fast-living roadhogs; some even go so far as to have the devices illegally removed.

Don't be surprised to see other bizarre and dangerous manoeuvres, like drivers reversing around roundabouts because they've missed their turn, or indicating right and then turning left. The government seems to be taking some steps to curb the problem, with the installation of speed cameras on most main roads and regular road-safety awareness campaigns. However, this is all undermined by the fact that the police seldom seem to enforce the law.

If you decide to take to the wheel yourself, the bottom line is that you require eyes in the back of your head and should be prepared for the unexpected. One of the most unpleasant things you're likely to experience is extreme tailgating, as many drivers think it acceptable to drive up behind you until they're virtually touching your bumper in a bid to get you to move over and let them pass. If you're unable to move because the lane next to you is occupied, it's not unheard of for the driver behind to try and squeeze into the gap between your car and the central reservation in a bid to overtake.

Many resident expats pay that little bit more and opt for a large, sturdy vehicle – often a 4x4 – purely on the grounds of increased safety. It's something you should consider if you're hiring a car.

Autolease *224 4900.*
Avis *224 5219.*
Budget *224 5192.*
Cars *224 5524.*
Diamond Lease *220 0325.*
Europe *224 5240.*
Fast rent a car *224 5040.*
Hertz *224 5222.*
Patriot *224 4244.*
Sapo *224 4511.*
Thrifty *224 5404.*
United Car Rentals *224 4666.*

Fuel stations

At the time of writing, the cost of petrol was Dhs4 a gallon; so you should expect to pay less than Dhs40 to fill your tank. There are 24-hour petrol stations on all major highways. Most petrol stations also have convenience stores selling snacks and drinks.

Parking

Many areas in the city centre have introduced paid parking in a bid to reduce congestion. Prices are reasonable (Dhs1 or Dhs2 for a one-hour stay, depending on location), but sadly it doesn't seem much easier to get a parking space. Normally the paid parking areas are operational only at peak times (generally from 8am to noon and 4pm to 9pm), and it will be free to park there outside of these hours, or on a Friday or public holiday. If you park illegally or go over your time limit, the penalty charge is Dhs150, increasing to Dhs165 if you don't pay within 14 days. Generally your car hire company will pay them for you and charge them to you at the end of your lease.

Particular black spots include the warren of streets in 'old' Bur Dubai, the stretch of Sheikh Zayed Road between the Crowne Plaza and Shangri La hotels, and most of Deira.

Parking in shopping malls is free, but if you visit any of them on a Thursday or Friday evening expect huge queues and delays, particularly at the City Centre mall.

Most hotels have extensive parking facilities for visitors, including valet services.

Road signs

Road signs are in both English and Arabic, which makes matters easier for the Western visitor, but the sheer scale of the American-style highway system (up to five lanes on either side at some points) means you have to stay alert, especially at the junctions on Sheikh Zayed Road that have multiple exits.

Walking

This is only a realistic option at certain times of year – it's pretty much out of the question to go for an outdoor stroll between May and September due to the intense heat and humidity – and in certain areas of the city.

The best places to take a stroll include the Creek-side areas of Bur Dubai and Deira, and the stretches of beach in Jumeirah and Umm Suqeim. The rest of the city simply isn't designed with pedestrians in mind. In some areas, there aren't even pavements. The size of some of the highways means that crossing the road is impossible unless you're prepared to gamble with your life. This can sometimes mean having to take a taxi journey just to get to the other side of the street.

Directory

Resources A-Z

Addresses

Dubai is not divided into postcodes. While street addresses are slowly being introduced, at present all official addresses are postbox numbers and the majority of roads are numbered, but not identifiable by anything other than nearby landmarks. Any resident here will happily point you in the direction of the Ritz-Carlton or the Jumeirah Beach Hotel, but few of them will know an actual address. Taxi drivers know most of the significant landmarks, but it's worth carrying a map with you just in case.

Common reference points used as landmarks in Dubai are hotels, shopping malls and some of the bigger supermarkets.

Alternatively, while you're here, try to get hold of the comprehensive Dubai Municipality Map from **Book Corner** (*see p119*), or from any Emarat Petrol station. It costs Dhs30.

The comprehensive map section in this guide starts on p270.

Age restrictions

You must be aged 18 to drive in Dubai (21 to rent a small car, 25 to rent a large one) and buy cigarettes, although the latter does not appear to be vigorously enforced. In restaurants and bars you must be 21 to drink.

Purchase of alcohol from an off-licence shop is not possible without a licence, which can only be obtained on your behalf through your employer.

Attitude & etiquette

Dubai is a cosmopolitan city, with hundreds of different nationalities, and it has a well deserved reputation for being tolerant and relaxed. However, it is a Muslim state and must be respected as one. Most 'rules' concerning cultural dos and don'ts are basic common sense and courtesy, with particular respect needing to be shown for Islam and for the royal family. The following are general guidelines.

In formal situations, it is polite to stand when someone enters the room and to extend a handshake to all the men in the room when you enter, only offering your hand to Arab women if they do so first. It is courteous to ask Muslim men about their family, but not about their wives.

You may find yourself addressed by a title followed by your first name – for instance, Mr Tom – and it's not unusual for a woman to be referred to by her husband's name – Mrs Tom.

Avoid offending locals with public displays of affection (and flesh) and remember that loose, conservative clothing is both sensitive and sensible. This is particularly true during Ramadan, when everyone is expected to dress more conservatively. If you go to a nightclub in Dubai you won't find dress codes to be any different to those in the West, but if you're at the Heritage Village you should show discretion. Even at the private beaches belonging to hotels, topless bathing is not allowed, and some also ask women not to wear thongs.

Be respectful about taking photographs, and always ask for consent. Communication can at times be frustrating, but patience is crucial in a nation where time holds a different significance and civility is paramount.

For further information contact the **Ministry of Information & Culture** on 261 5500 or the **Sheikh Mohammed Centre for Cultural Understanding** on 344 7755.

See also pp29-33 and p255 **Religion**.

In terms of getting by on a day-to-day basis, information,

Travel advice

For up-to-date information on travel to a specific country – including the latest news on safety and security, health issues, local laws and customs – contact your home country government's department of foreign affairs. Most have websites packed with useful advice for would-be travellers.

Australia
www.dfat.gov.au/travel

Canada
www.voyage.gc.ca

New Zealand
www.mft.govt.nz/travel

Republic of Ireland
www.irlgov.ie/iveagh

UK
www.fco.gov.uk/travel

USA
http://www.state.gov/travel

expansion and efficiency are buzzwords in Dubai, but while the personal services can sometimes astound, the all-too-common collapse in communication can astonish. There is a tendency to be more keen to help than capable of carrying it through, and often telephone conversations will leave you more confused than when you started.

Far less harrowing is using the internet (*see p252* **Internet**), with countless sites offering straightforward facts and advice for the tourist. Throughout this guide, both websites and telephone numbers are given wherever possible.

Business

Dubai has been incredibly proactive in its bid to establish itself as the business hub of the region, and consequently every effort is made to welcome new business and corporate care in the city is the envy of the rest of the world. Dubai's booming economy is aided by low labour costs, minimal taxes, free zones, a secure convertible currency and a liberal community.

A safe, secure environment has attracted international interest on a scale unrivalled anywhere. The city's main economic activities are non-oil trade, oil production and export, and more recently, tourism.

Airport business centres

All passengers using Dubai International Airport can use these 24-hour facilities:

Airport International Hotel Business Centre

216 4278/www.dubaiairport.com. **Map** p277 L2.
Comprises five meeting rooms (capacity from six to 18 people), one conference room (capacity 60

people), eight workstations, state-of-the-art communication systems, as well as full secretarial and office services support facilities.

Global Link

Departures level, near Gate 16, Terminal 1, Dubai International Airport (266 8855/www.dubai airport.com). **Map** p277 L2.
This business centre provides passengers with six ISD booths, workstations, internet connection, fax and secretarial services.

Business publications & directories

There are two monthly business magazines based in Dubai, *Arabian Business* and *Gulf Business*, while the *Gulf News* and *Khaleej Times* newspapers have comprehensive daily business sections.

For a list of all the registered companies in the UAE, visit www.ameinfo.com. Alternatively, visit the Dubai E-Government portal at www.dubai-e.gov.ae to view business links and to get news or find out more about setting up shop in Dubai.

See also p253 **Media** *and p261* **Further Reference**.

Conference & exhibition organisers/ office hire

Dubai is able to handle any seminar, conference or trade exhibition, whatever its size, since large halls and spacious showrooms are readily available in all major hotels. Several public institutes have also been developed to host significant events, such as the recent **Dubai International Convention Centre** (332 1000/www. dwtc.com), which staged the annual IMF convention in October 2003.

Dubai offers a comprehensive range of facilities catering for small meetings through to major

international conventions. Most of the city's hotels provide business facilities/ venues with all the necessary support services. Otherwise, the **Dubai World Trade Centre** or DWTC and **Dubai Chamber of Commerce & Industry** or DCCI (for both, *see below*), are two useful points of contact for services and recommendations. Call for further details.

Dubai Chamber of Commerce & Industry

Baniyas Road, on the Creek, Rigga, Deira (228 0000/www.dcci.gov.ae). **Open** 8am-4pm Sat-Wed. **Map** p279 K4.
The DCCI exhibition halls and auditoriums have been developed to accommodate exhibitions, trade and social fairs, new product launches and any other exhibition that requires a large, open, flexible space.

Dubai World Trade Centre

Sheikh Zayed Road, near Za'abeel roundabout, Satwa (332 1000/ www.dwtc.com). **Open** 8am-4pm Sat-Wed. **Map** p281 G9.
The DWTC incorporates the Dubai International Convention Centre. It comprises nine interconnected, air-conditioned exhibition halls covering 37,000sq m (14,285sq ft), and is available for lease either on an individual basis or in any combination of more than one hall.

Courier companies

The companies listed here provide freight-forwarding services, domestic services, logistics services, catalogue services, packing and moving services . They also offer other source and delivery services (meaning that they will find what you want and deliver it). They are open 24 hours a day and, usefully, can be contacted both by telephone and internet. All of them accept major credit cards. The UAE postal service, **EMPOST**, offers an express delivery

Directory

service known as Mumtaz Express (*see p255* **Postal services**).

DHL
800 4004/www.dhl.com.

FedEx
331 4216/www.fedex.com.

TNT
285 3939/www.tnt.com.

Free zones

These vast designated business districts, housing around 2,500 companies, offer huge incentives like 100 per cent ownership for foreign businesses, no import duty or corporate tax, and leasehold land ownership.

Dubai Airport Free Zone Authority
202 7000/www.dafza.gov.ae.

Dubai Internet City (DIC)
391 1111/www.dubaiinternet city.com.

Dubai Media City (DMC)
391 4555/www.dubaimediacity.com.

Jebel Ali Free Zone Authority
881 5000/www.jafza.co.ae.

Hours

Working days vary hugely owing to religious and cultural differences. Almost everyone outside the hospitality and retail sectors has Friday off, but some have a Thursday/Friday weekend, others have a Friday/Saturday weekend, and still others work a six-day week with only Friday off. Government offices have the Thursday/Friday weekend.

Working hours during the day can also vary, with some firms still operating a split-shift system (normally 8am-noon and 4-8pm), though this is becoming increasingly rare.

Licences

The basic requirement for all business activity in Dubai is a licence (commercial/professional/industrial) issued by the Dubai Department of Economic Development. For more information about applying for a business licence, contact the **Ministry of Economy and Commerce** on 295 4000/www.uae.gov.ae.

Sponsors

The regulation of branches and representatives of foreign companies in the UAE is covered in the Commercial Companies Law. This stipulates that the companies may be 100 per cent foreign-owned providing a local agent (UAE national) is appointed. These agents (also known as sponsors) will assist in obtaining visas in exchange for a lump sum or a profit-related percentage. The exceptions to this rule are the free zones (*see above*), where no local sponsor is required.

Translation services

There are dozens of different communities in Dubai, covering many languages and dialects, but English is widely spoken, particularly in a business context. However, if you need something translated into Arabic you can try one of the following. (Note that none of them accepts credit cards).

Eman Legal Translation Services
Room 104, 1st Floor, above Golden Fork Restaurant, Nasr Square, Deira (224 7066/ets@emirates.net.ae). **Open** 9am-6pm Sat-Wed; 9am-2pm Thur. **Map** p279 L3.

Ideal Legal Translation & Secretarial
Room 17, 4th Floor, above Al Ajami Restaurant, Al Ghurair Centre, Al Riwqa Street, Deira (222 3699/ideal@emirates.net.ae). **Open** 8am-1pm, 4-8pm Sat-Thur. **Map** p279 K3.

Lotus Translation Services
Room 411, 4th Floor, Oud Metha Office Building, Oud Metha Street, near Wafi Centre, Bur Dubai (324 4492/lotrnsrv@emirates.net.ae). **Open** 9am-5.30pm Sat-Wed; 9am-2pm Thur. **Map** p277 J3.

Useful organisations

American Business Council
16th Floor, Dubai World Trade Centre, Sheikh Zayed Road (331 4735/www.abcdubai.com). **Open** 8am-5pm Sat-Thur. **Map** p281 G9.

British Business Group
BBG Office, Conference Centre, British Embassy, Al Seef Road (397 0303/www.britbiz-uae.com). **Open** 8.30am-5.30pm Sat-Wed. **Map** p279 J4.

Department of Economic Development
DCCI Building, Baniyas Road, Deira (222 9922/www.dubaided.gov.ae). **Open** 7.30am-2.30pm Sat-Wed. **Map** p279 K4.

Dubai Chamber of Commerce & Industry
DCCI Building, next to Sheraton Hotel, Baniyas Road, Deira (228 0000/www.dcci.gov.ae). **Open** 7.30am-2.30pm Sat-Thur. **Map** p279 K4.

Consumer

While people flock to Dubai to shop, there are no statutory rights to protect consumers, except the right to recover the paid price on faulty goods. But even here, unless you are prepared to take it to court, exchange is as far as many stores will go.

Tourists with consumer-related problems, enquiries and complaints can contact the **Department of Tourism and Commerce Marketing** (223 0000). For complaints about purchased items, the **Emirates Society for Consumer Protection** in Sharjah (06 556 7333) may also be able to assist, while the **Dubai Economic Development Office**

(222 9922) will try to help people who have problems with expiry dates and warranties.

Customs

There is a duty-free shop in the airport arrivals hall. Each person is permitted to bring into the UAE two litres (3.5pints) of spirits, two litres (3.5pints) of wine, ten cartons of cigarettes, 400 cigars, two kilograms (4.5lb) of tobacco, and a 'reasonable amount' of perfume.

No customs duty is levied on personal effects entering Dubai. For more extensive explanations on any duty levied on particular products, see the Dubai Airport website with links to the Municipality site at www.dubaiairport.com (224 5555).

The following are prohibited in the UAE and import of these goods will carry a heavy penalty: controlled substances (drugs), firearms and ammunition, pornography, unstrung pearls, pork, raw seafood and fruit and vegetables from cholera-infected areas.

For further information call the **Dubai Customs** hotline on 800 4410 or check out www.dxbcustoms.gov.ae. *See also p255* **Prohibitions**.

Disabled

Generally speaking, Dubai is not disabled-friendly While things are starting to improve, many places are still not equipped for wheelchair access. Most hotels have made at least token efforts, but functionality still plays second fiddle to design, meaning that facilities for the disabled have largely been swept under the carpet. Those that do have some specially adapted rooms for the disabled include the Burj

Al Arab, City Centre Hotel, Crowne Plaza, Emirates Towers, Hilton Dubai Creek, Hilton Dubai Jumeirah, Hyatt Regency, Jumeirah Beach Hotel, JW Marriott, Oasis Beach Hotel, Madinat Jumeirah, Ritz-Carlton Dubai, Renaissance, One&Only Royal Mirage and Sheraton Jumeirah. Most of these are reviewed on pages 36-54.

The airport and major shopping malls have good access and facilities, and some of the **Dubai Transport taxis** (208 0808) are fitted to accommodate wheelchairs. While there are designated disabled parking spaces in nearly all car parks, many able-bodied drivers fail to respect these and park there themselves, although a disabled window badge is required unless they wish to incur a fine.

Drugs

Dubai adheres to a strict policy of zero drugs tolerance. There are lengthy sentences and harsh penalties for possession of a non-legal substance, and there have been several high-profile cases of expatriates serving time for such offences. Drug importation carries the death penalty, although no executions have been carried out in recent years. However, even association with users or importers carries a stiff penalty. For more information see the police website at www.dubaipolice.gov.ae.

Electricity

Domestic supply is 220/240 volts AC, 50Hz. Sockets are suitable for three-pin 13 amp plugs of British standard design; however, it is a good idea to bring an adaptor with you just in case. Adaptors can also be

purchased very cheaply in local supermarkets. Appliances purchased in the UAE will generally have two-pin plugs attached. If you have any queries you can get in touch with the **Ministry of Electricity** by calling 262 6262.

Embassies & consulates

For enquiries about commercial services, visa services, passport services, consular services and press and public affairs, contact your country's embassy or consulate. In Dubai, they are usually open 8.45am-1.30pm Sunday-Thursday. If you need to contact an official urgently, don't despair, as there is usually another number on its answer service for help outside working hours.

Your embassy provides emergency legal services (the stress being on 'emergency', since it has no authority over the UAE legal system if you are caught breaking the law), consular and visa services, and educational information and advice.

For a list of all embassies in Dubai log on to www.dwtc.com/directory/governme.htm. For a list of embassies abroad, see www.embassyworld.com. *See also p246* **Travel advice.**

Australia
1st Floor, Emirates Atrium Building, Sheikh Zayed Road, between Interchange 1 & 2 (321 2444/ www.austrade.gov.au). **Open** 8am-3.30pm Sun-Wed; 8am-2.45pm Thur. **Map** p276 G5.

Canada
7th Floor, Juma Al Bhaji Building, Bank Street, Bur Dubai (314 5555/ www.canada.org.ae). **Open** 8am-3.30pm Sat-Wed. **Map** p279 J5.

New Zealand
15th Floor, ABI Tower, Sheikh Zayed Road (331 7500/www.nzte.govt.nz). **Open** 8.30am-5pm Sun-Thur. **Map** p281 G9.

Directory

South Africa

3rd Floor, Dubai Islamic Bank Building, Bank Street, Bur Dubai (397 5222). **Open** 8am-4pm Sat-Wed. **Map** p279 J5.

United Kingdom

British Embassy Building, Al Seef Road, Bur Dubai (309 4444/ www.britain-uae.org). **Open** 7.30am-2.30pm Sat-Wed. **Map** p279 J4.

USA

21st Floor, Dubai World Trade Centre, Sheikh Zayed Road (311 6000/www.usembabu.gov.ae). **Open** 8.30am-5pm Sat-Wed. **Map** p281 G9.

Emergencies

For **police** call 999, for **ambulance** call 998 or 999 and for the **fire brigade** call 997. The **coastguard** can be contacted on 345 0520 and there is also a **helicopter service**. If you dial 999 or 282 1111, in an emergency Dubai Police will send a police helicopter, which they guarantee will be with you within eight minutes.

See also p255 **Police**, *below* **Health** for a list of hospitals *and p251* **Helplines** for general support and advice groups.

Gay & lesbian

Homosexuality is prohibited in the UAE.

Health

Dubai has well-equipped public and private hospitals (*see below*). Emergency care is free for all UAE nationals, visitors and expatriates from the Al Wasl, New Dubai and Rashid hospitals below. All other treatments are charged to tourists, so it's advisable to have medical insurance as well as travel insurance.

For further information contact the **Ministry of Health** (MOH) on 306 6200 or the **Department of Health & Medical Services** (DOHMS) on 337 1160. Both are open

during normal government hours, from Saturday to Wednesday. For those people whose countries have a reciprocal medical agreement with the UAE, further treatments are available.

The city has high standards of hygiene and cleanliness so the likelihood of picking up an infection or virus is low.

Accident & emergency

Only emergency cases at the public hospitals are seen free of charge in A&E. All of the hospitals above have 24-hour A&E departments.

Contraception & abortion

Most pharmacies prescribe contraception over the counter and only some require prescriptions. It is widely known (although not officially condoned) that this includes the 'morning after' pill. The **American Hospital** (*see above* **Health**) has a Family Planning clinic (309 6877).

Dentists

Good dentists are readily available, including orthodontists and cosmetic dentists, though prices can be hefty. For a 24-hour emergency dental service, phone 332 1444.

Doctors

Most of the big hotels have in-house doctors, or you can ring your local embassy for their recommendations (*see p249* **Embassies & consulates**).

Hospitals

The three main **Department of Health** hospitals in Dubai are listed below. For

information on the services available, visit www.dohms.gov.ae.

Al Wasl Hospital

Oud Metha Road, south of Al Qataiyat Road, Za'abeel (324 1111/www.dohms.gov.ae). **Map** p277 J3.

New Dubai Hospital

Opposite Hamria Vegetable Market, after Hyatt Regency Hotel, Deira (271 4444/www.dohms.gov.ae). **Map** p278 H2.

Rashid Hospital

Oud Metha Road, near Al Maktoum Bridge, Bur Dubai (337 4000/ A&E 337 1323/www.dohms.gov.ae). **Map** p277 J2.

Below are four private hospitals in Dubai that have Accident & Emergency departments. Note that all private health care must be paid for, including emergency care. Hospitals are required to display price lists for all treatments at reception.

American Hospital Dubai

Off Oud Metha Road between Lamcy Plaza & Wafi Centre, Al Nasr, Bur Dubai (336 7777/www.ahdubai.com). **Map** p277 J3.

Emirates Hospital

Opposite Jumeirah Beach Park, next to Chili's restaurant, Beach Road, Jumeirah (349 6666/www.emirates hospital.ae). **Map** p282 A15.
As well as an A&E facility, the Emirates Hospital has a 24-hour walk-in clinic (though you're required to pay Dhs150 for the first consultation).

Iranian Hospital

Corner of Al Hudeiba Road & Al Wasl Road, Satwa (344 0250/ www.irhosp.co.ae). **Map** p280 E9.

Welcare Hospital

Next to Lifco supermarket in Garhoud, Deira (282 7788/ www.welcarehospital.com). **Map** p277 L3.

Insurance

Public hospitals in Dubai (*see above*) will deal with emergencies free of charge. They have good facilities and their procedures (including the use of sterilised needles and the provision of blood transfusions) are reliable and hygienic.

Medical insurance is often included in travel insurance packages, and it is important to have it unless your country has a reciprocal medical treatment arrangement with the UAE.

While travel insurance typically covers health, it is wise to make sure you have a package that covers all eventualities, especially as for serious but non-emergency care you would need to attend a private hospital or clinic, where treatment can be quite expensive.

Opticians

See p136.

Pharmacies

There is no shortage of extremely well stocked and serviceable pharmacies in Dubai, with no formal policy of prescription: all you need to know is the name of the drug you need.

Normal opening hours are 8.30am-1.30pm, 4.30-10.30pm Saturday-Thursday and 4.30-10.30pm Friday, but some open on Friday mornings as well. A system of rotation exists for 24-hour opening, with four chemists holding the fort at any one time for a week each. For a list of the 24-hour pharmacies on duty, check the back of the local newspapers or log on to www.dm.gov.ae. Alternatively, you can call the **DM Emergency Offices** on 223 2323, who can point you in the direction of the nearest pharmacy.

Prescriptions

Most drugs are available at the pharmacies without prescription. Otherwise

pharmacists will dispense medicines on receipt of a prescription from a GP.

STDs, HIV & AIDS

To secure residency in Dubai, you have to undergo a blood test and anyone identified as HIV positive is not allowed to stay in the country.

Despite there being no official figures, it is widely accepted that there is a genuine problem with sexually transmitted diseases, due in part to the large numbers prostitutes in the city.

Sunburn/ dehydration

The sun in the UAE can be fierce throughout the year, so heatstroke and heat exhaustion are always a risk. Adequate sunglasses, hats and high factor sun creams are essential, particularly for children. The importance of drinking large quantities of water to stave off dehydration cannot be emphasised enough.

Vaccinations

No specific immunisations are required for entry to Dubai, however it would be wise to check beforehand if you are travelling from a health-risk area – a certificate is sometimes required to prove you are clear of cholera and yellow fever if you are arriving from a high-risk area. Tetanus inoculations are usually recommended if you are considering a long trip.

There are very few mosquitoes in the towns and cities, and since it is not considered to be a real risk, malaria tablets are rarely prescribed for travel in the UAE. If you are planning on camping near the mountains or exploring wadis in the evening, cover up and use

a suitable insect repellent. If you are in any doubt, consult your doctor before your trip.

Polio has been virtually eradicated in the UAE and hepatitis is very rare.

Helplines

For a comprehensive list of contacts for the various government departments, log on to www.dm.gov.ae. Alternatively. you can call the customer services line on 800 4567 for all information relating to the Municipality Services. The 24-hour **Emergency Office** (223 2323) can direct you to the various offices outside hours, or if you have the name of the organisation you want, you can get the number from directory enquiries on 181.

Listed below are two of the most popular support groups. For a full list of support groups see the *Yellow Pages* at www.yellow pages.net.ae. The free magazine, *Connector*, has a directory of smaller help and support groups. For support and services specific to female travellers, *see p259* **Women**.

Alcoholics Anonymous

394 9198.
This 24-hour information line tells you where and when meetings are being held at different locations in Dubai.

Stop Smoking Programme

343 4090.
The organisers of the Stop Smoking Programme can arrange free appointments with a doctor for a one-on-one session. Services are available to visitors as well as local residents.

Special Families Support Group

393 1985.
A voluntary group for families with special needs children from all over the Gulf, with monthly meetings and social events.

ID

Bars and clubs will check ID if they don't think you look over 21, and it's also necessary for car hire. The most requested form of ID for tourists is passports, so it's worth having some photocopies made in advance.

Although no national ID card exists at the moment, plans are afoot to issue all residents of the UAE with 'smart cards', which will replace all other forms of identification (driving licence/labour and health cards etc) by the end of 2004. The cards will link to all government departments and carry personal information like the individual's blood group, fingerprints and other biological characteristics. This is primarily being introduced to increase the speed and efficiency of services and provide a population census.

See also p246 **Age restrictions**.

Insurance

While the crime rate in Dubai is exceptionally low, it is still worth insuring yourself before you travel. Travel insurance policies usually cover loss and theft of belongings and medical treatment, but be careful to check what is included, and any clause that might be disputed, especially if you're intending to take part in activities like desert off-roading and scuba diving.

Car insurance will be covered by any creditable, authorised car hire company and anyone holding a valid licence should be able to get insurance. However, do check if you are covered for insurance for the Sultanate of Oman, since many parts of the UAE have a 'porous' border. You may find yourself driving within Oman without warning –

the road to Hatta, for example, will take you through Oman in several places.

Medical insurance is often included in travel insurance packages and it is vital to have it, since health care in private hospitals can be very expensive. Emergency care is available free of charge at the government hospitals (*see p250* **Health**). Be careful to keep all documents and receipts of any medical payments you make, as you will have to claim them back later.

For a list of insurance companies check out www.yellowpages.net.ae.

Internet

Dubai is leading the way in the global movement towards electronic government. You can now do seemingly everything online, from paying a traffic fine to booking a taxi . Given the language barriers you can encounter with phone calls, websites are often the most efficient way to gain information.

The government organisation, **Etisalat**, controls the server and is the regulator of content. Consequently there is an element of censorship, with pornography and gambling sites blocked. If the network fails there can be no service at all for hours at a time, although thankfully this is uncommon. The only exceptions to censorship are the free zones in and around the city, which connect independently to the international web. You can contact Etisalat by dialling 101, or log on to www.etisalat.com.

The **EIM** (Emirates Internet and Multimedia) kiosks provide public access to email, news and business information, enabling users to access the net from anywhere irrespective of their email provider. The kiosks can be found in airport

waiting areas, shopping centres and hotel lobbies, and take various methods of payment.

Otherwise, almost every hotel has some form of internet access and there are net cafés dotted around the city.

Language

English is widely spoken and understood in Dubai.

See also p260 **Language**.

Left luggage

There is a left-luggage storage facility at the airport, costing Dhs20 per bag per half day (12 hours). Call 213 3233 if you are an Emirates passenger; passengers of all other airlines, call 216 1734.

Legal help

There is no equivalent of the Citizens Advice Bureau in Dubai, so if you get into a situation where you require legal help or advice, you should contact your country's embassy (*see p249* **Embassies & consulates**). Be aware that they foreign embassies cannot override any law in the UAE and will not sympathise if you claim ignorance of those laws. They can, however, offer advice and support and give details of your legal status and options. Otherwise, contact the **Ministry of Justice** for advice or information on proceedings, on 282 5999.

There is no free legal aid in Dubai, and with such strict laws and severe sentencing it is best to avoid getting this far. The government has also established a Department for Tourist Security, whose purpose is to guide visitors through the labyrinth of the law and to liaise between the tourists and the Dubai police; it can be contacted on 800 4438.

For a full list of law firms, see www.yellowpages.net.ae.

Libraries

You must be a resident to borrow from Dubai's libraries, but most will be happy for you to browse or use the reading room, where there is a broad selection of English-language books. The **Dubai Municipality Central Library** allows the public to view its collections online, offering title search, browsing and reservation from home. You can also contact them by calling 226 2788.

British Council (BC)

BC Building, Maktoum Bridge, Bur Dubai (337 0109/www.britishcouncil. com). **Open** 8am-8pm Sat-Thur. **Map** p277 K2.

DM Library

Al Ras Street, opposite St George Hotel, near Gold Souk, Al Ras (226 2788/www.dpl.dm.gov.ae). **Open** 7.30am-9.30pm Sat-Wed; 7.30am-2.30pm Thur. **Map** p278 G3.

Dubai Lending Library

International Arts Centre, opposite the Mosque, Beach Road, Jumeirah (337 6480). **Open** 10am-noon, 4-6pm Sat-Thur. **Map** p280 D9.

Lost property

Theft in Dubai is an extremely rare occurrence but if you are a victim of crime, you should contact the nearest police station or report it to the special **Tourist Police** unit (800 4438). This will be necessary for validation of your travel insurance claims.

If you lose something, most unclaimed items are taken to a general holding unit known as **Police Lost & Found**, which can be contacted on 216 2542. If you have lost something on a bus or abra, call the **public transport information line** on 800 4848 and ask for Lost & Found. If you think you've left something in a taxi, get in touch with the relevant company (*see p243*).

The **airport** has a 24-hour lost property line (216 2542). To minimise the aggravation of losing important documents, always make a copy. If you should lose your passport, report it immediately to the police and contact your embassy (*see p249* for details of embassies).

Media

Despite the creation of **Dubai Media City** (complete with the slogan 'freedom to create'), the media in the UAE is still subject to government censorship, though direct clashes are rare as most organisations operate a policy of self-censorship. This means you'll never see anything that criticises the UAE royal families or the government, and that there are no film scenes involving nudity. However, in the past couple of years, censorship has definitely become more relaxed, with references to alcohol and images of bikini-clad babes now allowed. Most international publications are available here, though the black marker pen of the censors ensures that overtly sexual images are covered up.

Newspapers & magazines

There are three English daily newspapers in Dubai: *Gulf News*, *Khaleej Times* and *Gulf Today* (Dhs2-Dhs3). All three publish local and international news, though *Gulf News* is generally perceived as the strongest of the trio. It has a weekly magazine, *Friday*, and also publishes an entertainment guide on Wednesdays.

The city's magazine sector has become increasingly competitive in recent years and there are a wealth of magazines now published

in Dubai. Monthly entertainment and listings magazines include *Time Out Dubai*, *What's On* and *Connector*. Lifestyle magazines include *Emirates Home* and *Identity* (interior decoration), *Ahlan!* (Dubai's answer to *Hello!*), and *Jumeirah Beach* (coffee-table glossy). There are also free tourist magazines available in some hotels, though most of them are of dubious quality.

Radio

Dubai has five English-language stations, featuring a mixture of British, Canadian and Australian DJs, though unfortunately the quality of programming and presenting is generally pretty low. They are:

Channel 4 FM, 104.8FM. Modern chart, dance and R&B music.
Dubai FM, 92.0FM. Government-run station that plays a mixture of older hits and contemporary chart music.
Emirates 1 FM, 100.5FM. Modern chart, dance and R&B music.
Emirates 2 FM, 98.5FM. Easy listening.
Free FM, 96.7FM. Mostly modern chart, but Free FM also has a number of specialist shows.

Television

The Dubai government runs two English-language channels: **Channel 33**, which shows dated programmes like *The Bold & The Beautiful*, and the **Dubai Business Channel**. Most residents and hotels have a satellite package of some form, with **Showtime** and **Star** among the most popular, thanks to offerings like The Movie Channel, BBC Prime and the Paramount Comedy Channel. In the past year, MBC's **Channel 2** has been making big waves as a free service that screens a mixture of Hollywood films, the latest TV series and even UK Premiership football.

Directory

Money

The national currency is the dirham. At the time of going to press, UK£1 was equal to Dhs6.75, but this is unusually high and the rate tends to fluctuate between Dhs5-Dhs6. The US$ has been pegged to the dirham at a fixed rate of Dhs3.6725 since 1980.

Notes come in denominations of Dhs1,000 (silver), Dhs500 (red), Dhs200 (blue), Dhs100 (red), Dhs50 (purple), Dhs20 (blue), Dhs10 (green) and Dhs5 (brown). There are Dhs1 coins and then 50, 25 and 10 fils, though in practice you will rarely use these lower denominations.

ATMs

The majority of UAE banks and many hotels have ATM machines, which offer a convenient way of withdrawing UAE dirhams. Most credit cards and Cirrus- and Plus- enabled cash cards are accepted. Check with your personal bank for charges for withdrawing cash overseas.

Banks

There are a number of international banks in the city such as HSBC, Citibank, Standard Chartered and Lloyds TSB, as well as locally based operations such as the National Bank of Dubai and Dubai Islamic Bank. Opening hours are normally 8am-1pm Sat-Wed, and 8am-noon Thur. All are shut on Fridays. The banks offer comprehensive commercial and personal services and transfers, and exchanges are simple.

Bureaux de change

Rates vary and it is worth noting that the airport is the first place you can, but the last place you should, change your money. There are several money changers in the city centre (Bur Dubai and Deira) who tend to deal only in cash but whose rates (sometimes without commission) can challenge the banks', particularly with larger sums of money. Travellers' cheques are accepted with ID in banks and hotels and other licensed exchange offices that affiliate with the issuing bank. There is no separate commission structure but exchange houses make their money on the difference between the rates at which they buy and sell. At time of press, they were buying UK£1 at Dhs6.734, and selling at Dhs6.777. Below are the main bureaux de change:

Al Fardan
Al Fardan Headquarters, Nasr Square, Maktoum Street, next to Citibank, Deira (228 0004/ www.alfardangroup.com). **Open** 8.30am-1pm Sat-Thur; 4.30-8.30pm Fri. **Map** p279 L3.

Al Ghurair
Burjuman, Halid Bin Walid Road, Bur Dubai (351 8895). **Open** 10am-10pm Sat-Thur; 4-10pm Fri. **Map** p279 J5.

Thomas Cook Al Rostamani
Next to Al Khajeel Hotel, Road 14, Al Nasr Square, behind HSBC bank, Deira (222 3564/www.alrostamani exchange.com). **Open** 9am-1pm, 6-9pm Sat-Thur; 5-9pm Fri. **Map** p279 L4.
Phone this branch for details of other locations.

Wall St Exchange Centre
Near Naif Police Station, Naif Road, Deira (800 4871). **Open** 8.30am-10pm Sat-Thur; 8.30-11.30am, 4.30-10pm Fri. **Map** p279 J2.

Credit cards/cheques

All major credit cards are accepted in the larger hotels, restaurants, stores and supermarkets. Acceptance of cheques is less widespread and some places will ask for another method of payment.

Bouncing cheques is a criminal offence and can result in heavy fines and, in some cases, a jail sentence.

The UAE was slow to jump on the debit card bandwagon but a handful of the bigger chain stores accept Visa Electron and Switch cards; check with individual retailers.

Tax

Dubai has made its name through the absence of direct taxation, with thousands of expat workers enjoying tax-free salaries. However, there are some 'hidden' taxes, such as the ten per cent municipality tax included in food and hospitality costs, and, for those with a licence, a sales tax on alcohol from off-licences (often a steep 30 per cent). There is no corporate tax except for oil-producing companies and foreign banks.

Natural hazards

The sun is Dubai's biggest natural hazard, particularly in summer, and the best way to survive it is by using a high-factor sun cream and covering up appropriately.
See also p251
Sunburn/dehydration.
Sandstorms can occur in the winter months and these make driving hazardous. There are also rainstorms during the same period and if you are camping or driving in or near wadis, you should leave immediately as torrents of water can gush down, sweeping away anything in their path.

If you drive outside Dubai, you should also watch out for camels – several accidents in recent years have involved camels running onto the road and colliding with cars. Aside from any injury you may suffer, you will also be expected to pay for the camel, which can be extremely costly.

Opening hours

The concept of the Saturday/ Sunday weekend doesn't apply in the Middle East, since Friday is the Muslim holy day. With so many different cultures living, working and praying under the same parasol, as it were, the weekends vary enormously, with Europeans tending to take Friday and Saturday off, while government departments have Thursday and Friday off.

Unfortunately, there are also no clear-cut rules when it comes to retail outlets either. The most common shopping hours are 10am-1pm and 4-9pm for stand-alone stores, but shops in malls are open 10am-10pm. The exception is Friday, when most don't open until 2pm or 4pm.

Police

In an emergency call 999. If you just want information, www.dubaipolice.gov.ae is a good place to start. If you want to report something confidentially or think you have witnessed something illegal, there is a hotline (Al Ameen Service) on 800 4888.

Postal services

The Emirates postal system is run solely by Empost and works on a PO Box system, although a postal delivery service is planned for the future. All mail in the UAE is delivered to centrally located post boxes via the Central Post Office. With Dhs160 and an email address you can apply for a personal PO Box, and you will receive notification by email when you receive registered mail or parcels. There is also a service that delivers parcels to your door for Dhs9.

Hotels will handle mail for guests and you can buy stamps at post offices, Emarat

petrol stations and card shops. Shopping malls such as City Centre and Lamcy Plaza have postal facilities. Delivery takes between two and three days within the UAE but up to ten days or longer for deliveries to Europe and the USA. Be aware that the service can be erratic so don't be too surprised if sending something to your home country takes longer than planned. All postal enquiries can be directed to the **Empost** call centre on 334 0033, 8am-8pm Saturday-Thursday. Alternatively, call the **Emirates Post Head Office** on 262 2222, 7.30am-2.30pm Saturday-Wednesday.

Central Post Office
Za'abeel Road, Karama (337 1500/ www.empostuae.com). **Open** 8am-11.30pm Sat-Wed; 8am-10pm Thur; 8am-noon Fri. **Map** p277 J3.

Prohibitions

The law is very strict with regards to the consumption of alcohol (other than in a licensed venue or a private residence), illegal drugs and gambling. Pornography is also prohibited. Israeli travellers are not allowed into the UAE and there can even be complications if you have recently visited Israel and have a visa stamp in your passport.

Religion

Islam is the official religion in the UAE. Around 16 per cent of the local population is Shi'a Muslim and the remainder Sunni Muslims. While Dubai is the most multicultural and therefore most tolerant of the emirates and other religions (except Judaism) are respected, it is still a Muslim state. The faithful congregate five times a day to pray and you will hear the call to prayer being sung from local mosques all over Dubai.

Tourists need to be extra sensitive if they are visiting during Ramadan, the ninth month of the Muslim calendar, when Muslims fast during daylight hours to fulfil the fourth pillar of Islam. Ramadan lasts for approximately one month but the time of year varies as it is determined by the lunar calendar (the dates move forward by approximately 11 days each year). During this period, bars will not serve alcohol before 7pm and clubs are shut as no loud music or dancing is allowed. You must not be seen eating, drinking or smoking in a public place during daylight hours, although some restaurants erect screens to allow people to eat and drink in private. In 2004, Ramadan is expected to commence on October 15 (*see also p31* **Ramadan dos and don'ts**).

Owing to its relative tolerance, Dubai has a variety of Christian churches and Hindu temples. For details of places of worship, see www.yellowpages.net.ae.

See also pp29-33, p246 **Attitude & etiquette** *and p258* **When to go**.

Safety & security

Contrary to some perceptions of the Middle East, Dubai is one of the safest places in the world to visit. Indeed, the UAE has in recent years twice been designated the world's safest holiday destination by the international travel industry. Crime in Dubai is minimal, with the problem issues restricted to areas such as money laundering that don't tend to impact directly on the tourist or resident. Security is high and places like accommodation blocks and malls are well manned by private guards. Nevertheless, it is always a good idea for the visitor to take

Directory

out travel insurance, and to follow the normal precautions to safeguard yourself and your valuables.

Study

Dubai has developed an extensive and respected education system in only 30 years. Locals enjoy extremely high standards of free education, while expats tend to send their offspring to private schools and colleges. There are more than 100 of these, catering for all nationalities.

If you wish to learn Arabic there are a number of language centres in the city, by far the most popular of which is the Arabic Language Centre.

Arabic Language Centre

Dubai World Trade Centre, Sheikh Zayed Road (308 6036/ info@dwtc.com). **Open** 8.30am-6.30pm Sat-Wed. **Map** p281 G9. Arabic courses for all levels are held on a termly basis throughout the year.

Telephones

The international dialling code for Dubai is 971, followed by the individual Emirates code: 04 for Dubai. Other area codes are Abu Dhabi 02, Ajman 06, Al Ain 03, Fujairah 09, Ras Al Khaimah 07 and Sharjah 06. For mobile phones the code is 050. Delete the initial '0' of these codes if dialling from abroad.

Operator services can be contacted on 100; directory enquiries are on 181. Alternatively, consult the *Yellow Pages* online at www.yellowpages.net.ae, which in many cases can be quicker and less frustrating. To report a fault call 170.

Making a call

Etisalat (www.etisalat.com) operates a monopoly on all telecommunications in the UAE, and on the whole the service is very good. Local calls are free and direct-dialling is available to 150 countries.

Cheap rates for international direct calls apply from 9pm to 7am and all day on Fridays and public holidays. Pay phones, both card- and coin-operated, are located throughout the UAE.

To make a call within Dubai, dial the seven-digit phone number; for calls to other areas within the UAE, dial the area code (*see above*) followed by the seven-digit phone number.

To make an international phone call, dial 00, then the country code (44 for UK; Australia 61; Canada 1; Republic of Ireland 353; New Zealand 64; South Africa 27 and USA 1), then the area code, omitting the initial 0, then the phone number.

Public telephones

There are plenty of public telephones which accept either cash or phone cards. Phone cards for local and international use are available in two denominations (Dhs30 or Dhs45) from most Etisalat offices, supermarkets, garages. and pharmacies. Coin-operated phones take Dh1 and 50 fils.

Mobile telephones

Dubai has one of the world's highest rates of mobile phone usage and practically everyone has at least one cellular phone. A reciprocal agreement exists with over 60 countries allowing GSM international roaming service for other networks in the UAE. There is also a service (Wasel) that enables temporary Etisalat SIM cards (and numbers) lasting 60 days (or until your Dhs300 credit runs out) for use during your trip if your network is not covered, or if you do not have a GSM phone. Calls are charged at local rates and the network has good coverage.

See p252 **Internet**.

Time

The UAE is GMT + 4 hours, and has no seasonal change of time. So, for instance, if it is noon in London (winter time), it is 4pm in Dubai; after British clocks move forwards for BST, noon = 3pm in Dubai.

Tipping

Hotels and restaurants usually include a 15 per cent service charge in their bills; if it is not included, adding ten per cent is normal if not obligatory. It is common to pay taxi drivers a small tip, just rounding up the fare to the nearest Dhs5 being the norm. For other services (supermarket baggers/ bag carriers/petrol pump attendants/hotel valets) it is common to give at least a couple of dirhams.

Toilets

There are well-kept free public toilets in malls and parks, and most hotels will let you use their facilities free of charge. Petrol stations have conveniences but conditions vary. Restrooms in souks and bus stations are usually for men only.

Tourist information

Department of Tourism & Commerce Marketing

10th-12th Floor, National Bank of Dubai Building, Baniyas Road, Deira (223 0000/www.dubai tourism.co.ae). **Open** 7.30am-2.30pm Sat-Wed. **Map** p279 K4. It may be a mouthful to say, but the DTCM exists as the government's sole regulating, planning and licensing body of the tourism industry in Dubai. It has information centres around the city, the most immediately useful being in the arrivals lounge at the airport (224 5252). Its one-stop information centres provide maps, tour guide information, business and conference advice, hotel information, and aim to answer any other query the visitor to Dubai may have.

Most of the larger shopping malls (*see pp112-16*) also have their own visitor information centres.

Visas & immigration

Visa regulations are liable to change, so it is always worth checking with your travel agent or the UAE Embassy in your home country before leaving. Overstaying on your visa can result in detention and fines (a penalty charge of Dhs100 per day that you're over). Nationals of Israel may not enter the UAE. Your passport must have at least two months (in some cases, six) before expiry left to be granted admission into the UAE, but it's best to check before booking your flight.

The following nationalities will not need to obtain a visa before travelling to Dubai/ the UAE; they will receive it upon arrival at the airport.

America
USA, Canada.

Asia
Japan, Brunei, Singapore, Malaysia, Hong Kong, South Korea.

GCC (Gulf Cooperation Council) countries
Saudi Arabia, Qatar, Bahrain, Oman, Kuwait, UAE.

Oceania
Australia, New Zealand.

UK
Citizens of the UK will be granted a free visit visa on arrival in the UAE: passports will be stamped with the visa as you pass through Immigration at any airport in the UAE. Although the visa may be stamped for 30 days, it entitles the holder to stay in the country for 60 days and may be renewed once for an additional period of 30 days for a fee of Dhs500.

Western Europe
France, Italy, Germany, The Netherlands, Belgium, Luxembourg, Switzerland, Austria, Sweden, Norway, Denmark, Portugal, Ireland, Greece, Finland, Spain, Monaco, Vatican City, Iceland, Andorra, San Marino, Liechtenstein.

To establish or confirm the permitted duration of stay, contact the UAE Embassy or Consulate in your country at the addresses below. Failing that, the contacts given in **Travel advice** (*see p246*) will keep you up to date on the latest visa requirements – which seem prone to regular, unannounced changes. The countries not listed above require a visa.

UAE embassies abroad

Australia
36 Gulgoa Circuit, O'Malley ACT 2606, Canberra, Australia (2-6286 8802/uae embassy@big pond.com/ www.users.bigpond.com/UAEEMBA SSY). **Open** 9am-3pm Mon-Fri.

Canada
45 O'Connor Street, Suite 1800, World Exchange Plaza, Ottawa, Ontario, K1P 1A4 (613 565 7272/ safara@uae-embassy.com/www. uae-embassy.com). **Open** 9am-4pm Mon-Fri.

South Africa
980 Park Street, Arcadia 0083, Pretoria, South Africa (342 7736-9). **Open** 9am 5pm Mon-Fri.

UK & Republic of Ireland
30 Prince's Gate, London SW7 1PT (020 7581 1281/embcommer@ cocoon.co.uk). **Open** 9am-3pm Mon-Fri. *Visa section* 9am-noon Mon-Fri.

USA
3522 International Court, NW Washington DC, 20008 (202 243 2400/New York office 212 371 0480/www.uae-embassy.org). **Open** 9am-4pm Mon-Fri.

Multiple-entry visas

Multiple-entry visas are available to business visitors who have a relationship with either a multinational company or other reputable local business, and who are frequent visitors to the UAE.

This type of visa is valid for six months from the date of issue and the duration of each stay is 30 days. The validity is non-renewable. The cost of this visa is Dhs1,000. The visitor must enter the UAE on a visit visa and obtain the multiple entry visa while in the country. The visa is stamped on the passport.

96-hour visa for transit passengers

As a way to promote Dubai's city tours, transit passengers stopping at Dubai International Airport for a minimum of five hours are eligible for a 96-hour transit visa which enables them to go into the city for that period of time. Passengers wanting to find out about this are advised to go to the City Tours desk in the airport arrivals lounge to make a booking for one of the several tours on offer. The visa is issued free but the tour service is not. This visa is only available to those travelling onwards from Dubai and not returning to the original country of departure.

Water & hygiene

The tap water in Dubai comes from desalination plants, and while technically it is drinkable, it doesn't taste great. As it costs only Dhs1 for a litre of bottled water, almost everyone here chooses to buy their drinking water, though be aware that some restaurants and hotels place ridiculous mark-ups on drinking water. Outside of Dubai you should avoid drinking water from the tap and you might even want to consider using bottled water for tasks like brushing your teeth.

Directory

Average monthly climate

Month	Temp °C/°F	Rainfall (mm)	Relative humidity (%)
Jan	23/32	11	71
Feb	25/77	38	72
Mar	29/84	34	68
Apr	33/89	10	65
May	38/100	3	62
June	39/102	1	65
July	40/104	2	85
Aug	40/104	3	85
Sept	39/102	1	69
Oct	35/95	2	70
Nov	30/86	4	69
Dec	26/79	10	72

For links to see the latest satellite images of the weather conditions in the Middle East and Europe, go to http://www.uaeinteract.com/uaeint_misc/weather/index.asp.

General standards of food hygiene are extremely high in Dubai, though caution should be shown if you decide to try some of the smaller roadside diners. If you are in any doubt, avoid raw salads and *shoarmas* (meat cooked on a spit and wrapped in pitta bread).

Outside the city limits, milk is often unpasteurised and should be boiled. Powdered or tinned milk is available and this is probably a safer bet, but make sure that it is reconstituted with pure water. You may also want to avoid dairy products, which are likely to have been made from unboiled milk.

Weights & measures

The UAE uses the metric system, although British and US standard weights and measures are widely understood. Road distances are given in kilometres.

What to take

Lightweight summer clothing is on the whole ideal in Dubai, with just a wrap, sweater, or jacket for cooler winter nights and venues that have fierce air-conditioning. Although the dress code in the UAE is generally casual, guests in the more prestigious hotels such as the Ritz-Carlton and the Royal Mirage do tend to dress more formally in the evening.

Since you are visiting a Muslim country, bikinis, swimming costumes, shorts and revealing tops should be confined to beach resorts. Women are usually advised not to wear short skirts and to keep their shoulders covered in public places like malls, but even this unwritten code is becoming increasingly relaxed, as you'll see when walking around. In bars and clubs it really is no different from in the West, with tans shown off to the max.

With such a wealth of shopping facilities, there is precious little you can't get hold of in Dubai. That said, visitors cannot buy alcohol from off-licences – so be sure to stock up when you arrive at the airport at Dubai Duty Free (*see p242*).

When to go

Climate

Straddling the Tropic of Cancer, the UAE is warm and sunny in winter, and hot and humid during the summer months. Winter daytime temperatures average a very pleasant 24°C, although nights can be relatively cool (12–15°C on the coast and less than 5°C in the heart of the desert or high in the mountains). Local north-westerly winds (*shamals*) frequently develop during the winter, bringing cooler windy conditions and occasionally sandstorms.

Summer temperatures are in the mid 40s, but can be higher inland. Humidity in coastal areas averages between 50 and 60 per cent, reaching over 90 per cent per cent in summer – even the sea offers no relief as the water temperature can reach 37°C.

Rainfall is sparse and intermittent. In most years it rains during the winter months, usually in February or March, but occasionally earlier.Winter rains take the form of short, sharp bursts, and the very occasional thunderstorm. Generally appearing over the mountains of the south and east of the country, these rumbling cloudbursts can give rise to flash floods, but the rainfall averages about five days in the year.

In terms of when to go, you really can't go wrong if you visit any time between November and March, as you're virtually guaranteed beautiful weather every day. June to September can be unbearably hot and humid during the day, although hotel bargain deals can still make it an attractive proposition. Also bear in mind when Ramadan is taking place (see p255 **Religion** and p31 **Ramadan dos and don'ts**).

Public holidays

There are two different kinds of public holidays, those that are fixed in the standard calendar, and those religious days that are determined by the lunar calendar and therefore vary from year to year. The precise dates are not announced until a day or so before they occur, based on local sightings of phases of the moon.

The **fixed dates** are: New Year's Day (1 January), Mount Arafat Day (11 January), Accession of HH Sheikh Zayed as Ruler of the UAE (6 August), and UAE National day (2 December).

The **variable dates** are: Eid Al Adha – a three-day feast to mark the end of the haj pilgrimage to Mecca (January/February/March); Ras al-Sana – the start of the Islamic New Year (February); Mawlid al-Nabi – the prophet Mohammed's birthday (May); Lailat al Mi'raj – the accession day of the prophet Mohammed (September); and Eid Al Fitr – the three days at the end of Ramadam (November).

Women

The cultural differences between locals and expats in Dubai are obvious, and the traditional advice for women in any big city – catch taxis if you're unsure about the area, don't walk alone at night and so on – should still be heeded, but all women here tend to enjoy a high standard of personal safety.

If you are wearing revealing clothing in a public place you will attract stares, some of simple condemnation and others of a more lascivious nature. That said, physical harassment is very rare, particularly as the local police are swift to act against any offenders.

The traditional *abaya* (long black robe) and *sheyla* (head scarves) worn by Emirati women is something you are less and less likely to see on the younger women of Dubai, who tend to wear Western-style clothes in the city. The metal face masks (burkha) are largely reserved for the more conservative women in rural areas.

This development in itself goes some way to illustrate the changing roles of women in the UAE, championed by its multicultural epicentre: Dubai. With the instigation of an education system available to women (female students now outnumber male) and the government's active encouragement of women in the workplace, attitudes have clearly evolved and statistics claim that women now fill up 40 per cent of the civil service jobs.

Dubai International Women's Club (DIWC)

Opposite Mercato Mall, Beach Road, Jumeirah (344 2389). **Open** 8am-5pm Sat-Thur. **Map** p282 C12. This social club has around 150 members who meet four times a month. They organise events for charities both in Dubai and overseas.

International Business Women's Group

345 2282/www.ibwgdubai.com. The IBWG is an organisation for women in the business world, and meets on a monthly basis to exchange ideas and offer advice. Call or check the website for further details of meetings.

Working in Dubai

Given its dramatic expansion plans, there are plenty of job prospects in the UAE for young professionals. In order to find work here, it is advisable to visit and do some networking. It's a relatively small community and consequently it's quite easy to make contacts. There are numerous recruitment service companies in the city (you can find a full list at www.yellowpages.ae).

In order to work here you must be sponsored by an employer (or a spouse with an employer who is their sponsor), who will help you to arrange a transfer of your visit visa to a residency visa. It can be a long drawn-out process, part of which requires you to submit to a blood test checking for HIV/AIDS.

The following are useful contacts for those considering working in Dubai. For more general information and advice on setting up a business, visit www.uaeinteract.com, or see the comprehensive business website and directory at www.ameinfo.com.

See also p247 **Business**.

Dubai Naturalisation & Residency Administration (DNRA)

Trade Centre Road, near Bur Dubai Police Station, Bur Dubai (398 0000/www.dnrd.gov.ae). **Open** 7.30am-2.30pm Sat-Wed. **Map** p281 H8. The DNRA presides over procedures and laws for all forms of transaction related to expatriate entry and residence in the United Arab Emirates (including tourist visas).

Directory

Language

Arabic is the official language of Dubai, and Urdu and Hindi are also widely spoken and understood, but English is the predominant language. However, while attempting them might be grammatically challenging, a few Arabic phrases are always appreciated. Some basic words and phrases are given below, listed in phonetics. Capitals are not used in Arabic, but are used below to indicate hard sounds.

With Arabic possessing so many different dialects and sounds from English, transliterating is never easy. We've opted to go for a predominantly classical option with a few of the more useful colloquial phrases thrown in.

Getting by

Hello *marhaba*
How are you? *kaif il haal?*
Good morning *sabaaH il khayr*
Good evening *masaa' il khayr*
Greetings *'as-salamu 'alaykum*
Welcome *'ahlan wa sahlan*
Goodbye *ma' 'is-salaama*
Excuse me *afwan*
Sorry *'aasif*
God willing *insha'allah*
Please (to a man) *min fadlak* (to a woman) *min fadlik*
Thank you (very much) *shukran (jazeelan)*
Yes/No *na'am/laa*
I don't know *lasto adree* or *laa 'a-arif*
Who?/What? *man?/matha?*
Where?/Why? *ayina/lematha?*
How much? (cost) *bekam?*
How many? *kam?*
The bill please *alfatourah min faDlak*

Advanced pleasantries

Do you speak English? *titkallam inglizi*
I don't speak Arabic *ma-atkallam arabi*
Nice to meet you *yusadni moqapalatak*

What's your name? *ma esmok?*
My name is … *esmei …*
How old are you? *kam amrk?*
What's your job?/ Where do you work? *ma heya wazefatuk?/ ayna tam'al?*
Where do you live? *ayna taskun?*
I live/I work in Dubai *askun/a'amal fi Dubai*
How is the family? *kayfa halou l'a ila*
Congratulations *mabrook*
Happy birthday *eid meelad sa'eed*
You are very kind *anta lateef jedan*
With pleasure *bikul siroor*
Good luck *ha'z'zan sa'eedan*
Have a good trip *atmna lak rehla muafaqa*
Thanks for coming *shukran limajee, ak*
Best wishes *atyab al-tamniyat*
When will I see you? *mata sa'araak?*
Wait a little *intazarni kaliln*
Calm down *hadia nafsak*
Can I help you? *hl astateea'i musaa'adatuk?*

Numbers & time

Zero *sifr*
One *waahid*
Two *itnain*
Three *talata*
Four *arba'a*
Five *khamsa*
Six *sitta*
Seven *sab'a*
Eight *tamanya*
Nine *tis'a*
Ten *'ashra*
Eleven *heda'ash*
Twelve *itna'ash*
Thirteen *talata'ash*
Fourteen *arba'atash*
Fifteen *khamista'ash*
Sixteen *sitta'ash*
Seventeen *sabi'ta'ash*
Eighteen *tamanta'ash*
Nineteen *tis'ta'ash*
Twenty *ishreen*
One hundred *me'ah*

Sunday *al-ahad*
Monday *al-itnayn*
Tuesday *al-talata*
Wednesday *al-arba'a*
Thursday *al-khamees*
Friday *al-jum'a*
Saturday *al-Sabt*
Day *yom*
Month *shahr*
Year *sanah*
Hour *sa'aa*
Minute *daqiqa*
Today *al yom*
Yesterday *ams/imbarah*
Tomorrow *bukra*

People

He/She *houwa/hiya*
I/Me *ana*
We *nahnou*
You (to one male) *anta* (one female) *anti* (to a group) *antom* (to several women) *antonna*
They (male and female) *hom* (female only) *honna*
Father *ab*
Mother *umm*
Son *ibn*
Daughter *ibnah*
Husband *zauj*
Wife *zaujah*
Brother *akh*
Sister *ukht*
Child *tifl*

Getting around

Airport *matar*
Post office *maktab al barid*
Bank *bank*
Passport *jawaz safar*
Luggage *'aghraad*
Ticket *tath karah*
Taxi *Taxi*
Car *say-yarra*
City *madina*
Street *share'h*
Road *tareeq*
Bridge *jisr*
Mosque *Jame'h* or *messjed*
Bazaar *souk*
Boat – *markab*
Beach – *il-shat'i*
Customs *jumrok*
Library *maktabeh*
Shop *mahall*
Museum *mathaf*

Further Reference

Books

For a full list of Arabic authors and bookshops, visit www.uaeinteract.com.

Frauke Heard-Bay
From Trucial States to United Arab Emirates
In 1971, the seven sheikdoms at the southern end of the Persian Gulf, the Trucial States, formed the state of the United Arab Emirates, which soon found its feet on the world stage as a member of the UN, OPEC and the Arab League. This academic volume examines the historical and social movements that have shaped the present-day UAE.

Alan Keohane
Bedouin: Nomads of the Desert
This photographic portrait pays tribute to the ancient tribal customs that survive among those who continue their annual journey across the desert plains. This collection is a timely reminder of the importance of preserving the UAE's traditions.

Martin Lings
Muhammad, His Life Based on the Earliest Sources
A fascinating account for those wishing to learn more about the origins of Islam.

Alistair MacKenzie, Pamela Grist, Christopher Brown
Images of Dubai and the United Arab Emirates (Explorer Series)
This coffee-table tome comes highly recommended. Stunning photographs are divided into four categories: landscapes, seascapes, cityscapes and escapes.

Edward Said
Reflections on Exile & Other Essays
With their powerful blend of political and aesthetic concerns, Said's writings have changed the field of literary studies.

Jeff Sampler
Sand to Silicon
This book is geared towards those with a more business-orientated interest in Dubai. Sampler examines how this tiny emirate has become a major player on the international stage through internal, bold decisions and its openness to outside influence.

Wilfred Thesiger
Crossing the Sands
This eccentric British travel writer was one of the last of his kind. He is best known for two books, *Arabian Sands*, which recounts his travels in the Empty Quarter of Arabia between 1945 and 1950, and *The Marsh Arabs*, an account of the people living in the marshlands of southern Iraq.

Jeremy Williams
Don't They Know It's Friday? Cross-Cultural Considerations for Business & Life in the Gulf
Another business handbook, this one addresses the cultural aspects of life in all GCC countries and deals with the realities of business practice, as well as the stresses and strains of operating in the Gulf as a Western visitor or expatriate.

Daniel Yergin
The Prize: The Epic Quest for Oil, Money & Power
These 800 pages on the historical role of oil are certainly not everybody's cup of tea, but for those with an interest in the greasy stuff and its role in power politics, business, diplomacy and world history, this is an exceptionally detailed, well-informed account.

Magazines

For a monthly preview of the top events, meal deals, hot tickets and local listings, pick up a copy of *Time Out Dubai*. Free magazines *Connector* and *Aquarius* carry listings and discount vouchers; they're distributed at various malls and public places around town.

Travel

As well as the following, check out the **Dubai Explorer** series of guides, which includes the Family Explorer, Off Road Explorer and Underwater Explorer.

Dubai City Guide
www.dubaicityguide.com.
Guide to Dubai shopping, events, hotels, restaurants and sightseeing information.

UAE Internet Yellow Pages
www.uae-ypages.com.
Invaluable resources full of local listings.

Maps
www.geocities.com/fayarus/dubailinks.
Useful maps of the city.

Websites

www.uaeinteract.com
General info on the United Arab Emirates.

www.uaeinteract.com
Website for the Ministry of Information & Culture.

www.dubaipolice.gov.ae
Local police website.

www.dubai-e.gov.ae
Official government website.

www.dubaitourism.co.ae
A handy website with general tourism information.

Transport

The following websites are useful:

www.dubaiairport.com
News from Dubai International Airport.

www.dpa.co.ae
Messages from the Dubai Ports Authority for water transport.

www.dubaipublic transport.co.ae
Bus timetables and schedules.

Directory

Index

Advertisers' Index

Please refer to the relevant pages for contact details

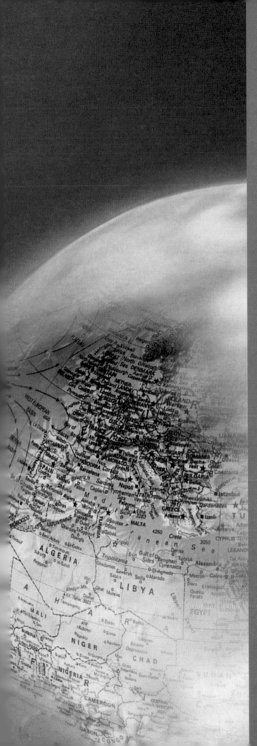

Place of interest and/or entertainment	■
Bus station	■
Park	■
Hospital	■
Hotel	■
Restaurant	●
Area name	**AL RAS**

Maps

IRAN

Jazireh ye Hormoz

Jazireh ye Qeshm

Jazireh ye Larak

Strait of Hormuz

Musandam
Peninsula

OMAN

Ash Sham

Khaymah Cape

Rams

Digdagga

Haffah Cape

Ras Al Khaimah

Dibba

Rul Dibba

Umm Al Quwain

Idhn

Badiyah

Fakkan Bay

Hamriya

Manama

Jabal Adham
1,128 m.

Khor Fakkan

Ajman

Sharjah

Gulf of
Oman

DUBAI

Al Dhaid

Gulf

Jazireh ye Kish

Jazireh ye Forur

Sir Abu Nu'ayr

See pp274-275

Al Awir

Al Haba

Mileiha

Fili

Fujairah

Al Liseli

Margham

Ghanadah Cape

Hatta

Coast

Al Samha

Al Faqa

Ash Shu'ayb

See pp2

Abjan

Al Haiyir

Sweihan

ABU DHABI

At Khatam

S a'diyyat

Mafraq

Bani Yas

Al Saad

Al Ain

bu al
rab

Al Khatam

Bu Samarah

arif

At Taff

Ayn Al Faidah

To Muscat

Al'Arad

Al'Qua'a

OMAN

Al Humrah

Sabkhah

Al Khis

Jarrah

Je'eisah

iwa

Hamim

At Rabbad

Umm a Zummul

TimeOut
Dubai

An intelligent guide to lif

Street Index

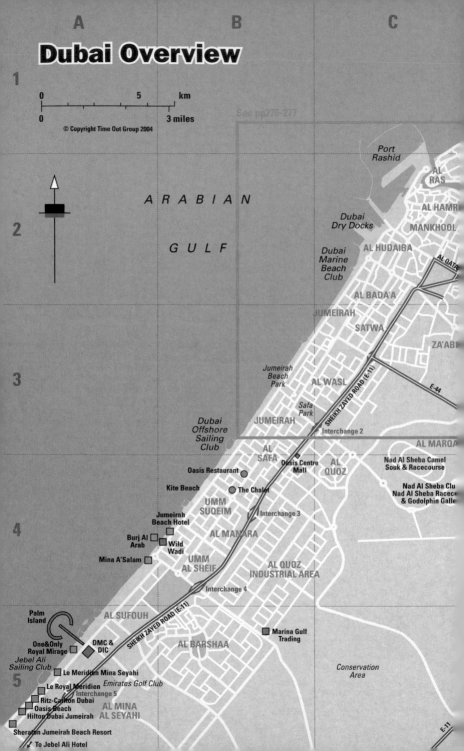

Dubai Overview

0 5 km
0 3 miles
© Copyright Time Out Group 2004

See pp276-277

A R A B I A N

G U L F

Port Rashid

AL RAS

Dubai Dry Docks

AL HAMRI

MANKHOOL

Dubai Marine Beach Club

AL HUDAIBA

AL QATA

AL BADA'A

JUMEIRAH

SATWA

ZA'ABI

Jumeirah Beach Park

AL WASL

SHEIKH ZAYED ROAD (E-11)

E-44

Safa Park

Dubai Offshore Sailing Club

JUMEIRAH

Interchange 2

AL MARQA

AL SAFA

Oasis Centre Mall

AL QUOZ

Nad Al Sheba Camel Souk & Racecourse

Oasis Restaurant

Kite Beach

The Chalet

Nad Al Sheba Clu
Nad Al Sheba Racec
& Godolphin Galle

UMM SUQEIM

Interchange 3

Jumeirah Beach Hotel

AL MANARA

Burj Al Arab

Wild Wadi

UMM AL SHEIF

AL QUOZ INDUSTRIAL AREA

Mina A'Salam

Interchange 4

Palm Island

AL SUFOUH

SHEIKH ZAYED ROAD (E-11)

One&Only Royal Mirage

DMC & DIC

AL BARSHAA

Marina Gulf Trading

Jebel Ali Sailing Club

Le Meridien Mina Seyahi

Emirates Golf Club

Conservation Area

Le Royal Meridien

Interchange 5

Ritz-Carlton Dubai

AL MINA AL SEYAHI

Oasis Beach

Hilton Dubai Jumeirah

Sheraton Jumeirah Beach Resort

To Jebel Ali Hotel

E-11

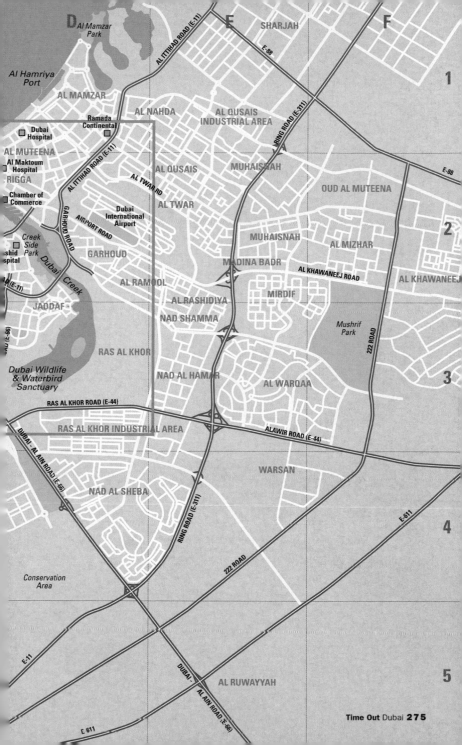

F G H

0 _____ 2 _____ km
0 _____ 1 mile
© Copyright Time Out Group 2004

1

Port
Rashid

AL DAGHAYA

AL SHINDAGHA

AL SOUQ
AL KABEER

AL MINA

AL RAFFA

2

ARABIAN

GULF

*Dubai
Dry Docks*

AL MANKHOOL ROAD

MANKHO

See pp280-281

AL HUDAIBA

AL MINA ROAD

AL ADHID ROAD

AL JAFILIYA

*Dubai
Marine
Beach
Club*

AL WASL ROAD

3

BEACH ROAD

AL BADA'A

AL SATWA ROAD

Dubai Zoo

2ND ZA'ABEEL

AL K

See pp282-283

JUMEIRAH

AL SATWA

Towers Rotana
Hotel

Emirates Towers

4

*Jumeirah
Beach
Park*

Dusit Dubai

AL WASL

RAS AL KHOR ROAD (E

SHEIKH ZAYED ROAD (E-11)

BEACH ROAD

5

JUMEIRAH

AL WASL ROAD

Safa Park

Al Safa Complex
(Park'n'Shop)

Metropolitan
Hotel

AL MARQ

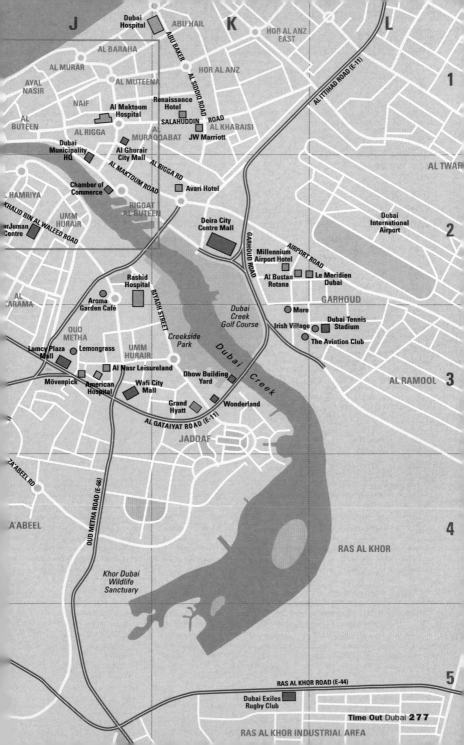

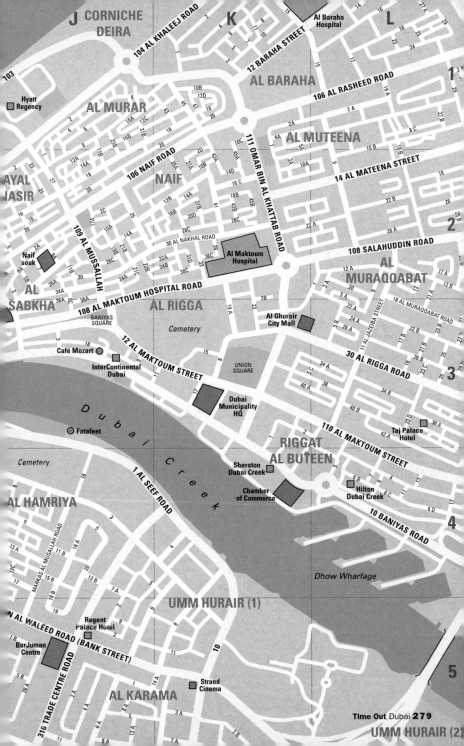

CORNICHE DEIRA

J

104 AL KHALEEJ ROAD

103

Hyatt Regency

AL MURAR

K

Al Baraha Hospital

12 BARAHA STREET

AL BARAHA

106 AL RASHEED ROAD

L

1

AL MUTEENA

14 AL MATEENA STREET

106 NAIF ROAD

NAIF

111 OMAR BIN AL KHATTAB ROAD

AYAL JASIR

109 AL MUSSALLAH

30 AL NAKHAL ROAD

Al Maktoum Hospital

108 SALAHUDDIN ROAD

AL MURAQQABAT

2

Naif souk

AL SABKHA

108 AL MAKTOUM HOSPITAL ROAD

AL RIGGA

BANIYAS SQUARE

Cemetery

Al Ghurair City Mall

11 AL JAZEIRA STREET

18 AL MURAQQABAT ROAD

30 AL RIGGA ROAD

3

Café Mozart

12 AL MAKTOUM STREET

InterContinental Dubai

UNION SQUARE

Dubai Municipality HQ

110 AL MAKTOUM STREET

Taj Palace Hotel

D u b a i   C r e e k

Fatafeet

RIGGAT AL BUTEEN

Cemetery

1 AL SEEF ROAD

Sheraton Dubai Creek

Chamber of Commerce

Hilton Dubai Creek

10 BANIYAS ROAD

4

AL HAMRIYA

MARKAS AL MUSSALLAH ROAD

Dhow Wharfage

UMM HURAIR (1)

N AL WALEED ROAD (BANK STREET)

Regent Palace Hotel

BurJuman Centre

310 TRADE CENTRE ROAD

Strand Cinema

AL KARAMA

UMM HURAIR (2)

5

F **G** **H** **J**

6

25

AL RAFFA

304 AL MINA ROAD

306 MANKHOOL ROAD

AL HUDAIBA

MANKHOOL

303 AL ADHID ROAD

President Hotel

AL KARAMA

7

310 TRADE CENTRE ROAD

AL QATAIYAT ROAD

AL JAFILIYA

AL KIFAF

8

Rydges Plaza

SATWA ROUNDABOUT

agen-zs Café

Ravi's

305 AL DHIYAFA STREET

310 TRADE CENTRE ROAD

ZA'ABEEL

9

306 SATWA RD

SATWA

Dubai World Trade Centre

Fairmont Hotel

Ibis

Novotel

305 2ND ZA'ABEEL ROAD

310 SHEIKH ZAYED ROAD

TRADE CENTRE

10

Crowne Plaza Dubai

Horse Racecourse

11

500 m
0
0   500 yds
© Copyright Time Out Group 2004

A R A B I A N

G U L F

12

13

14

Jumeirah Beach Park

Jumeirah
Beach Club

JUMEIRAH (2)

302 BEACH ROAD

304 AL WASL ROAD

302 BEACH ROAD

311 AL UROUBA STREET

Mercato
Mall

Creative Art
Centre

Town Centre
Mall

15

JUMEIRAH (3)

282 **Time Out** Dubai

Majlis Ghorfat
Um Al Sheef

313 ALATHAR
ST

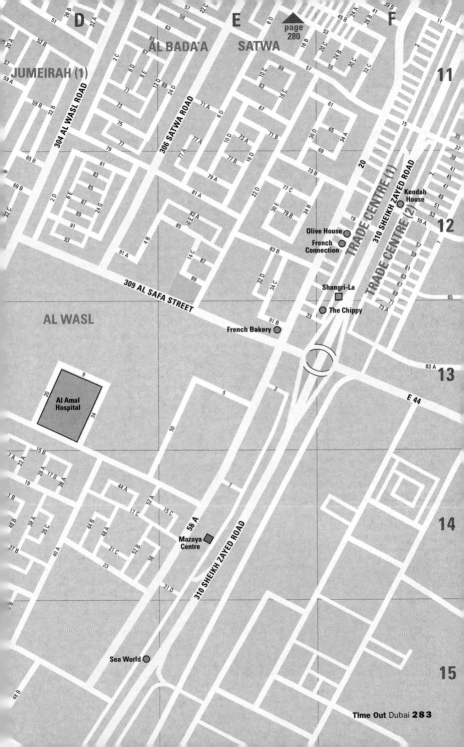

Highlights

Suggested itineraries...

FOR INDULGENCE

Check out the **Gold & Diamond Park** (*p67*) or **gold souk** (*p118*) for tailor-made jewellery, and the designer gear at **Villa Moda** (*p125*) or one of the city's malls (*p112-16*). Spend a blissful afternoon sinking into a treatment at **Cleopatra's Spa** (*p204*), then head to Gordon Ramsay's **Verre** (*p92*) for an ultra-romantic evening of fine dining. Enjoy the beachside views at **Majlis Al Bahar** (*p96*) and finish off with a lazy drink or two on the jazz-fuelled **Rooftop** bar at the One&Only Royal Mirage (*p174*). If you've won the lottery, catch a glimpse of the Arabian oryx and the finer things in life by staying at the **Al Maha** desert retreat (*p68*), a snip at $1,300 per night. If you haven't, console yourself at **Boudoir** (*p174*) – women get free champagne all night on a Tuesday.

FOR ENLIGHTENMENT

Kick things off by taking an educational tour around the **Jumeirah Mosque** (*p67*) and jumping aboard an **abra** (*p63*). Make time to taste Arabic cuisine at waterside café **Fatafeet** (*p80*) or clamber on the **Al Mansour Dhow** (*p88*) for a boat-bound supper tour of the Creek. For an insight into the city's history, a trip to **Dubai Museum** (*p60*) inside Al Fahidi Fort is mandatory. Wander through the quiet alleyways of **Bastakia** (*p59*), with its restored wind towers, then taste tobacco with real flavour in one of city's **shisha bars** (*p103*). If you've time to take a trip out of town, the museums of **Sharjah** (*p222*) are second to none, while the capital **Abu Dhabi** has a preserved **Dhow Harbour** and **Heritage Village** (*p212*).

FOR FAMILY FUN

Visit the imaginative educational zones of **Children's City** (*p148*) and the less instructional but equally entertaining rides of **Encounter Zone** (*p150*) – don't miss the chamber of horrors and 3-D cinema. Pick up the pace the next day on the thrilling waterslides of **Wild Wadi** (*p148*). For something more sedate, admire the bird's-eye perspective from the cable car at **Creekside Park** (*p201*), enjoy **Jumeirah Beach Park**'s natural beauty and clean coastline (*p201*), then in the afternoon take the kids to **Café Céramique** (*p151*) to decorate pots and mugs while you take a caffeine break.

FOR EXCITEMENT

Head off to **Big Red** (*p71*) for a day of dune bashing, or take a trip over to **Hatta Pools** (*p70*), where you can swim by the waterfalls. High-octane sports fans can jump out of a plane (*p228*), or drive north to **Ras Al Khaimah**, the UAE's answer to the Wild West (*p231*).

Back in the city, there's no better sight than thoroughbreds pounding the turf in winter at **Nad Al Sheba** (*p142*). For those who can't bear to stand on the sidelines, get involved in Dubai's new **kitesurfing** craze (*p192*), face off against your mates in a **paintballing** contest (*p193*) or learn how to **dive** (*p194*).

In the evening, strut your salsa stuff at **El Malecon** (*p174*) or go dirty dancing at the **Rock Bottom Café** (*p165*). A pulse-racing view of the city can be had at **Vu's** (*p82*) on the 50th floor of the Emirates Towers.

FOR RELAXATION

Tap into Dubai's rich café culture: sit next to the huge birdcage at **Shakespeare & Co** (*p104*) or eat your fill of hyper-indulgent cakes in the hidden courtyard at **Gerard's** (*p108*). If it's Friday, spend the whole day grazing over one of the city's bargain brunch deals (*p93*). To appreciate the glitzier side of Dubaian life – without upping the pace – take in 18 holes at the celebrity-designed **Montgomerie** golf course (*p190*).

To get away from the city, escape on a sun-kissed **fishing excursion** (*p187*) or to the pristine beaches of **Fujairah** (*p234*). Return to Dubai to tell your tales over a chilled beer at dusk – the **Barasti** bar (*p177*) is a perfect spot for a sundowner.

City of gold – be dazzled by Dubai's souks.

TimeOut Dubai Please let us know what you think

About this guide...

1. How useful did you find the following sections?

	Very	Fairly	Not very
In Context	☐	☐	☐
Where to Stay	☐	☐	☐
Sightseeing	☐	☐	☐
Eat, Drink, Shop	☐	☐	☐
Arts & Entertainment	☐	☐	☐
Active Dubai	☐	☐	☐
The UAE	☐	☐	☐
Directory	☐	☐	☐
Maps	☐	☐	☐

2. Did you travel to Dubai...?

Alone ☐   With children ☐
As part of a group ☐   On vacation ☐
On business ☐   To study ☐
With a partner ☐   I live here ☐

3. How long was your trip to Dubai? (write in)

_____ days

4. Where did you book your trip?

Time Out Classifieds ☐
On the Internet ☐
With a travel agent ☐
Other (write in) ☐
_____

5. Where did you first hear about this guide?

Advertising in Time Out magazine ☐
On the Internet ☐
From a travel agent ☐
Other (write in) ☐
_____

6. Is there anything you'd like us to cover in greater depth?

_____
_____
_____

7. Are there any places that should/ should not* be included in the guide? (*delete as necessary)

_____
_____
_____

9. What city or country would you like to visit next? (write in)

_____
_____

About other Time Out publications...

10. Have you ever bought/used Time Out magazine?

Yes ☐   No ☐

11. Do you subscribe to Time Out London?

Yes ☐   No ☐

12. Have you ever bought/used any other Time Out City Guides?

Yes ☐   No ☐

If yes, which ones?
_____

13. Have you ever bought/used other Time Out publications?

Yes ☐   No ☐

If yes, which ones?
_____

8. How many other people have used this guide?

none ☐ 1 ☐ 2 ☐ 3 ☐ 4 ☐ 5+ ☐

About you...

14. Title (Mr, Ms etc): ☐

First name:
Surname:
Address:

Postcode:
Email:
Nationality:

15. Date of birth: ☐☐/☐☐/☐☐
16. Sex: male ☐ female ☐
17. Are you...?
Single ☐
Married/Living with partner ☐

18. What is your occupation?

19. At the moment do you earn...?

Under £15,000 ☐
Between £15,000 and £19,999 ☐
Between £20,000 and £24,999 ☐
Between £25,000 and £39,999 ☐
Between £40,000 and £49,999 ☐
Over £50,000 ☐

☐ Please tick here if you'd like to hear about offers and discounts from Time Out and relevant companies.

Time Out Guides

FREEPOST 20 (WC3187)
LONDON
W1E 0DQ

2